eGODS

eGODS: FAITH VERSUS FANTASY IN COMPUTER GAMING

William Sims Bainbridge

OXFORD
UNIVERSITY PRESS

OXFORD

UNIVERSITY PRESS

Oxford University Press is a department of the University of Oxford.
It furthers the University's objective of excellence in research,
scholarship, and education by publishing worldwide.

Oxford   New York
Auckland   Cape Town   Dar es Salaam   Hong Kong   Karachi
Kuala Lumpur   Madrid   Melbourne   Mexico City   Nairobi
New Delhi   Shanghai   Taipei   Toronto

With offices in
Argentina   Austria   Brazil   Chile   Czech Republic   France   Greece
Guatemala   Hungary   Italy   Japan   Poland   Portugal   Singapore
South Korea   Switzerland   Thailand   Turkey   Ukraine   Vietnam

Oxford is a registered trade mark of Oxford University Press
in the UK and certain other countries.

Published in the United States of America by
Oxford University Press
198 Madison Avenue, New York, NY 10016

Library of Congress Cataloging-in-Publication Data
Bainbridge, William Sims.
eGods : faith versus fantasy in computer gaming / William Sims Bainbridge.
p.   cm.
Includes bibliographical references and index.
ISBN 978-0-19-993581-9 (alk. paper)—ISBN 978-0-19-993583-3 (pbk. : alk. paper)
1. Internet games—Social aspects. 2. Fantasy games—Social aspects. 3. Internet games—Religious aspects.
4. Fantasy games—Religious aspects. 5. Role playing. I. Title.
GV1469.17.S63B35   2013
794.81—dc23   2012026597

9 8 7 6 5 4 3 2 1

Printed in the United States of America
on acid-free paper

TABLE OF CONTENTS

LIST OF TABLES

eGODS

1 DISBELIEF

A priest strides rapidly along the road from Northridge Abbey through Goldshire to Stormwind City, excited that he has been sent for advanced training in the Cathedral of Light. In the Temple of the Moon at Darnassus, a priestess learns new supernatural healing techniques while bathed in moonbeams and standing beneath a colossal statue of the goddess Elune. At the top of a precipice in an archipelago of magic-shrouded islands, an anthropologist studying shamanism wonders if she can trust a totem to save her if she leaps toward the rocks far below. In a remote valley, a shaman prepares to attack archaeologists whose digging will desecrate his people's holy burial grounds, activating a protective totem before unleashing his pious rage. The first of these four religious professionals is a Human, but the others are a Night Elf, a Draenei, and a Tauren. Indeed, none of them are people, exactly, but the avatars of people in the dominant massively multiplayer online role-playing game, *World of Warcraft*.[1]

It is easy to dismiss such avatars as mere tokens in a game, yet through them the user experiences a marvelous world, often for many hundreds of hours, frequently encountering religious symbolism. Imagine that a devoutly religious person said to a *World of Warcraft* player, "I can't believe you take that stuff seriously!" The player could reply, "Same to you, buddy!" If games are not real, then neither is art, or music, or drama, or sports, or politics, or the stock market, yet all of these are real in their socioeconomic consequences. To a significant degree, they are also real in their psychological impact: belonging either to a smug religious sect or to a successful *World of Warcraft* guild can give pride to a person who lacks social status in the wider world. What about the psychology of faith?

Religion has always been deeply involved in the creative arts, but the relationships between them are changing.[2] Perhaps we shall come to see religion merely as an especially solemn art form. Suspension of disbelief is the essence of art, according to Samuel Taylor Coleridge, and electronic games are a new and powerful art form that often depicts religion.[3] Yet we may wonder whether suspension of disbelief is really very different from belief itself. Traditional religions took their faith very seriously, and pious believers today would be shocked if told their God was not very different from an elf's image on a computer monitor. Yet much may be gained by thinking from that admittedly radical perspective.

At his passing, King Arthur said, "The old order changeth, yielding place to new, and God fulfills Himself in many ways, lest one good custom should corrupt the world."[4] This famous quotation takes on new meaning if we consider that God was part of the old order, even undeniably a good custom. In Norse Ragnarok and German Götterdämmerung, the old Pagan gods were swept aside by the tide of history, yet they like Arthur still live in our imaginations. If humans are by nature lovers of fantasy, then little may be lost if they consider all their gods to be fantasies.

An interesting topic that some erudite anthropologist should explore—and much existing literature touches on—is the extent to which preliterate peoples really *believed* their myths about the supernatural. In the absence of written scriptures and enduring formal organizations, one would think that the myths of preliterate peoples were chaotic and ephemeral, although cultural consolidations might occur locally for brief periods of time. Many classic studies suggest that these cultural mythologies were indeed dynamic and varied over time and space from highly diffuse notions that have little coherent force to relatively well-defined ideologies that have some of the flavor of modern religions.[5] We cannot resolve these fascinating issues here, but it seems safe to say that firm conviction in a well-defined dogma is not the natural state of human religion, but one possible situation that arises within the context of particular social conditions, such as the emergence of strong states that demand loyalty from their citizens.[6] Indeed, the term *faithful* can mean *loyal*; a true patriot is a self-sacrificing rather than a fact-speaking one, and conviction may arise as much from social demands as from personal needs for emotional security.

We can speculate that when ancient people sat around the campfire in the evening, telling tales of heroes, gods, and demons, they knew that all of them were fantasies. But somewhere, across the centuries, the church and state required faith, and faith bred hope in a way that made it precious, which it never had been at the dawn of humankind. Perhaps the cruel necessity to hold rich farmland against enemies that gave rise to knights in armor also demanded uniformity of belief from dukes and peasants alike. But then, the Industrial Revolution and the subsequent Information Revolution deposed the landed aristocracy, sent the peasants to work in factories, and educated everybody to a new level of skepticism. I am proposing a *curvilinear model of religion*: faith was fluid and inseparable from fantasy early in human history, and it will be the same late in human history, but near the middle of human history the social conditions associated with agricultural empires favored the emergence of religious bureaucracies that demanded faith.

Here stand three disbelievers: an Atheist, an Agnostic, and an Aesthetic. The Atheist is certain that God does not exist: end of story. The Agnostic is not sure, or suggests it is impossible to decide, or is unwilling to express personal views about such a sensitive topic: The story never begins. The Aesthetic knows that tales about gods are fables, rather than facts, but some of those fables are quite beautiful: For sake of art, not truth, we can tell endless stories.

Not far away stand three believers: a Conservative, a Moderate, and a Liberal. The Conservative is convinced not only that the holy scriptures tell the literal truth but that any culture that contradicts the scriptures is evil and must be banned. The Moderate is a person of faith who makes a clear distinction between religious fact and artistic fiction, granting the latter some freedom to play with spiritual concepts, so long as nobody takes them seriously. The Liberal feels that religion and the arts both express deep human longings, and that both may contain some metaphoric truth, but is perplexed over what we should really believe.

Many modern fantasy media exist, from movies and television shows, to comic books and novels, to the latest videogames. The best of the solo-player computer games and massively multiplayer online gameworlds are the most effective media for fantasy, because they allow a person to experience magic directly and to act in the fantasy world as if it were real. They take us back to those dark nights of ancient days, when the lights and shadows flickered on the trees around the fire, and it was easy to imagine that the monster described by the storyteller stood nearby in the darkness. Thus, the newest secular technology returns us to the origins of religion so we "arrive where we started and know the place for the first time."[7]

Before we consider gods, priests, cults, and other major concepts in the domain of religion, it will be useful to learn a modest amount about each of several gameworlds, to get a sense of their variety. To do so, I shall briefly describe three real-time strategy games that have a religious dimension, then three massively multiplayer online gameworlds in which the player experiences everything through an avatar and religious implications abound. All of these can be described as virtual worlds, although they differ greatly in visual style and the degree to which the action is primarily social.

Playing God

There are many varieties of computer games, and many games are hybrids of different varieties, so any fully accurate description would need to be long and complex. But at a first approximation, the type usually called *real-time strategy* (RTS) games has two connections to religion. First of all, these are often called *god games* because the player takes the role of a god, existing outside the world and commanding the action from an Olympian height. The player of an RTS is not represented by an avatar and does not see the world from ground level but directs armies or nations, as a chess player does but usually in a much more complex and often realistic world. These may be solo-player games, in which the goal is to build the power of a simulated city or nation in competition with others operated by the computer. Or they may be multiplayer games in which a few opponents communicate online.

Second, religion is often one of the features of the simulated society commanded by the player, although usually a minor one. We will consider three examples that reveal interesting issues about religion: *GodStoria*, *Rome: Total War*, and *Spore*. *GodStoria* is one of the very few attempts to build a traditionally Christian religious gameworld, and with all due respect to its creators, for a game released in 2010 it is technologically very primitive. This probably reflects the very limited investment capital available for developing Christian games, as well as the fact that the game was still under development when it was released to the public.

It is best described as a real-time strategy game, and it is also a *browser game*, because it is played online through a web browser. Some browser-based gameworlds employ graphic software to produce a three-dimensional immersive environment, but *GodStoria*, like many others, presents a sequence of two-dimensional web pages, each one updated on the basis of decisions the user made on the previous page. Thus, technically it is a minimalist virtual world, representing the features of the real world in an extremely abstract manner. For example, when soldiers are sent into battle, they are not depicted on the computer screen, whereas in *Rome: Total War*, to be described shortly, every single soldier can be seen, even though they are commanded in groups rather than individually.

GodStoria is based on the biblical book of Genesis. The major first section of this evolving game, which was available to be explored when I did my research, is set in the time outlined near the end of Genesis 11. Ur is depicted as a wide desert territory in which each player has set up a village. The goal is to develop the economy, defend the village, and prepare for an ultimate move to Canaan. For example, *GodStoria*'s tutorial has the user click on a farm in the two-dimensional image on the screen, switches to a screen presenting data about the farm, and requires the user to click "Update" to invest resources to improve the farm. The same is then done for a timber camp, a mine, and a clay pit. All these investments begin to pay off in providing materials, first of all to build a warehouse on land selected by the user, to store the materials. The general principle of strategy games is to go through a period of building resources, training soldiers, and then perhaps engaging in military competition against other tribes. Of special interest here is that *GodStoria* allows the user to build some architecture that has religious implications, including these as described on its building list page:

- *Temple*: Temples allow you to receive God's blessing and enhance spiritual attack power. Temples with higher levels allow players to receive more blessings. In the temple you can read the word of God and increase your faith.
- *House of Prayer*: Houses of prayer enhance spiritual defense. Houses of prayer with higher levels further increase spiritual defense.
- *Altar*: Here you can offer sacrifices to God at the altar. Decreased faith is restored whenever you offer a sacrifice.
- *Sheep Pen*: Sheep are raised here. Sheep are given as offerings to God and are used as food during a feast. Sheep pens with higher levels can raise more sheep.

Spiritual attack power and spiritual defense are variables that interact with many others in determining the outcome of a battle. An early challenge for players is keeping up their faith, which starts at 100 percent but gradually drops as it is eroded by stone effigies representing competing faiths that are set up in the neighborhood. A player's first experience of battle will be sending a platoon of soldiers out to destroy such an effigy, but after a while the computer will rebuild it, so it must be destroyed repeatedly. In the early months of *GodStoria*'s existence, players complained on the forums that it was costly to sustain faith, yet faith did not offer much in the way of benefits. This can be seen either as a superficial remark about the unfinished nature of the game at that time or as a profound critique of real religion.

At the beginning, each player has one "hero," named Abram. He is not depicted through an animated character, but merely as a two-dimensional portrait on web pages where decisions are made about him. In building an army, one really just assigns numbers to the hero, representing his capabilities and the number of soldiers of various kinds assigned to him. His march to the site of a battle is depicted merely by the passage of time. When a player is constructing one building, no others can be built simultaneously, and the construction goes in stages that take set periods of time. That is the real-time part of the definition of RTS. The strategy part is deciding how to invest resources, including when and where to send the hero to battle. After a while, I was given a choice of two names for a second hero, and I chose Crescens, the name of one of the absolutely most obscure characters in the Bible. Crescens is mentioned only in 2 Timothy 4:10 as one of the first Christians.

Although set early in Jewish history, *GodStoria* is a Christian game, which even uses the symbol of the cross in its logo. Using the online resource Bible Gateway, it took only a few moments to determine that the translation of the Bible used by *GodStoria* is Today's New International Version (TNIV), which seeks to use modern language while preserving the poetic quality of earlier translations, but which has been criticized for replacing male-centered language with gender-neutral language.[8] This is an interesting illustration of the fact that any well-established religion needs to deal with cultural change and constantly renegotiate its relationship to its tradition. This is not new, as the relationship of Christianity to Judaism reminds us. Indeed, Today's New International Version is not merely a Christian translation but a Protestant one, and yet Genesis and the game are about the early legends of the Jews.

Rome: Total War is a splendid commercial real-time strategy game that depicts many actual battles from Roman history, but concerns religion only in a minor way, as one of the factors in building up one's resources between battles, of which I fought several dozen during my research. The prologue is a tutorial that explains how one builds towns with a growing economy and ruling family as the basis for recruiting an army. The first task is to gain proficiency with the user interface by commanding a very small force that tipped the balance in a major battle between Romans and Gauls in 329 BC. Rome had only just secured the Latins under its hegemony, when a Gaulish army advanced south into Italy. The Senate instructed Captain Decius to stop them, and he in turn sought aid from Gaius Julius, who commanded 42 spearmen, 40 archers, and 24 mounted warriors including himself. Gaius Julius is not an avatar through which the player experiences the world but a hero like Abram or Crescens in *GodStoria*, a key resource commanded in parallel with other resources.

In the game small groups of Gauls detached themselves from their army and crossed a bridge over a narrow river to attack Gaius Julius, but he annihilated them, crossed the bridge in the opposite direction, and struck at the rear of the rather ragged Gaulish army deployed against the forces of Decius. Using his own bodyguard, in one of the times I played this battle, Gaius Julius was able to kill the enemy commander, Dumnorix. He performed splendidly, losing only seven of his triarii spearmen, compared with losses of 185 of the 430 men commanded by Decius and 442 of the 452 commanded by Dumnorix. When he killed Dumnorix, he proclaimed, "This is a day for votive games as a true enemy has gone to join his ancestors. May he trouble them as much as he did us!" This exclamation, of course, was merely text built into the game, triggered by killing Dumnorix.

As a reward for his decisive contribution to the Roman victory, Gaius Julius was given a much larger retinue of soldiers and sent northward to seize the Etruscan town of Tarquinii. Of his 462 Romans, 400 survived, after having killed every last one of the 362 defenders, who were under the command of some mere Greek named Admetos. Gaius Julius then settled down to run the town, build its economy, and strengthen his Julian family, assisted by a bounty of 10,000 denarii awarded him by the Senate. He built a shrine to Jupiter, which symbolized the loyalty of his followers, and built roads to facilitate trade and rapid deployment of his army. His son Cnaeus Julius came of age, and another son, Secundus Julius, married a woman named Minervina. We should not quibble about the fact that Minervina is an Etruscan name, because clearly it was time in the course of history for Rome to absorb Etruria. Gaius Julius rejoiced: "Marriage and the home are the bedrocks of Roman greatness, and a strengthening of Rome is a blessing from the Gods."

After one conquers a town in *Rome: Total War*, the surviving inhabitants will be restless, and it is important to convert them to Roman values in order to exploit them economically. Thus, one of the first tasks for a conqueror is to tear down any existing shrines or temples, because they remind the populace of its former culture, and build a Roman shrine or temple. In many RTS games, religion is used either to pacify the population one controls or in some cases to increase the dissatisfaction of the enemy population. This is a completely cynical view of religion, as a tool used by the elite to control subordinate populations.

Many other RTS games use religion in this way, thereby offering an implicit criticism of this influential human institution. The most useful additional example is *Spore*, because it also reveals more about the god-game concept. Launched in 2008, *Spore* was presented by a National Geographic television documentary as a supposedly realistic depiction of biological evolution, following a lineage of fantasy creatures from the single-cell stage in the ocean, through animal, tribal, and civilizational stages, to colonization of distant planets in the fifth and final stage.

In the civilization stage of the game, as the official guidebook explains, there are primarily three different cultural modes that the player's strategy can follow: "A military nation seeks to expand its borders by conquering all other cities, while a religious society wins control of other cities by winning the hearts of its citizens. An economic culture creates vast wealth and uses it to expand its sphere of influence."[9] This is interesting, first of all, because it suggests that three major societal institutions are functional equivalents of each other, and a society can either be based on religion, or ignore it altogether.

Religious people may find this rather insulting, because it treats faith as a tool by which powerful people can control weak people. If the people of a city are unhappy, perhaps because they are paying high taxes to support the war effort, religion can be used in *Spore* either to make them happy or to exploit their misery by inspiring them to revolt. A player may intentionally block trade with a city he or she wishes to conquer, specifically to make the population unhappy, then bombard them with religious propaganda to make them easy prey for conquest. In *Spore*, players do not battle against each other, so the enemy is always operated by the computer, following its own inhuman algorithms.

As a god game, *Spore* could not be based upon the actual scientific theory of evolution by natural selection from random variation, because the god—that is, the player—needs to be in control of what happens.[10] However, evolutionary programming is a standard technique going back decades in computer science.[11] As a very minor example, I myself published a computer program (and a book chapter about that program) in 1987 in which fireflies having just four genes buzzed around, mated, reproduced, and competed in a small gene pool, illustrating how easy it was to model genetic mutation, heritability, and differential reproduction on a computer.[12] While it has no connections to the creationist movement in religion, for the purposes of giving the player the central role in the game, *Spore* constructed a world in which biological evolution followed creationist principles. At every point in the creatures' evolution, the player shapes them, giving them legs or wings or whatever, on the basis of a personal, godlike decision.

Playing an Avatar

The standard term for a character who represents the user in a computer environment is *avatar*, originally a Hindu religious term for the terrestrial manifestation of a god.[13] There is a growing literature on the myriad ways in which such virtual personas relate to their users, and when a good deal of unique identity is invested in one, we tend to call it a *character*. Except when debating this issue, this book will use the term *avatar* precisely because of its religious implications. In a massively multiplayer online role-playing game (MMORPG or just MMO), the user experiences a virtual world through a single primary avatar, interacting with other avatars and with nonplayer characters (NPCs) that behave like avatars but are operated by the computer. Religion plays central roles in three of the very highest-quality examples: *Lord of the Rings Online*, *Dark Age of Camelot*, and *World of Warcraft*.

Released in 2007, *Lord of the Rings Online* (LOTRO) is faithfully based on J. R. R. Tolkien's novel *The Hobbit* and the *Lord of the Rings* trilogy. Whereas RTS games are often called god games, MMOs are sometimes called *sandbox* games. This term suggest a wide territory in which a person may play with great freedom, in contrast with the more traditional solo-player videogames of earlier years that were linear and in which the player was forced to follow a narrow track, surmounting all the challenges in a set order. Gamer terminology is in constant flux, and a decade into the twenty-first century, sandbox MMOs are often contrasted with *themepark* MMOs, with the latter having supremacy in the market. The difference is the degree of freedom experienced by the player, higher in sandbox games than in themepark games. The themepark metaphor is very apt, suggesting an amusement park consisting of a number of separate rides and other attractions, organized around a particular theme. Once one gets on the roller coaster, one cannot get off until the ride ends, but one has a choice between the roller coaster and the merry-go-round. Similarly, themepark MMOs offer great freedom until one enters a well-defined portion of it, whether a separate part of the computer database, as in the case of a dungeon, or an action-defined sequence like a quest arc.

LOTRO is a themepark that offers many paths to choose from, for example selecting one of four avatar races, which begin their lives in different geographical locations facing different dramatized tutorials: Human, Hobbit, Dwarf, or Elf.[14] It allows the user to create multiple avatars, running them one at a time but having different characteristics and locations in Middle Earth, with which to explore huge, colorful, diverse landscapes while undertaking story-related quests and ascending a ladder of experience levels that confer social status. For my own research, I created two characters, an adventuresome Elf scholar who explored the entire world and achieved the top 65 level of experience, at the time I did this research, and a modest Hobbit who remained within the Shire and reached only level 20.

LOTRO emphasizes cooperation on many levels, including in large persistent social groups called *kinships*. Players also interact with thousands of NPCs, operated by simple artificial intelligence and database access program routines. These include enemies who must be killed, vendors with whom economic exchanges can be conducted, and quest givers who assign players the missions that form the heart of the action. It also offers complex economies for production and exchange of virtual goods, including sophisticated auction systems, and the opportunity to own a virtual house and fill it with virtual furniture and artifacts. One thing that LOTRO lacks is churches and temples, for the same reason that the Garden of Eden lacked them. The entire world is an allegory of Christian religion, in which every place is equally sacred.

Hobbit fiction became remarkably popular in the 1960s, among young people seeking the meaning of life.[15] Tolkien denied that his stories were topical allegories reflecting real-world events, but clearly they expressed abstract moral principles.[16] The claim he sought to deny was that his ring story was an antidote to Wagner's *Ring of the Nibelung*, and an English response to the two world wars against the Germans. The stories do focus on a war, but it is one in which good-hearted people belonging to the four races must unite in opposition to incarnate evil. Tolkien was a devout Roman Catholic, and thus an advocate for a

Universal Church to which all peoples would belong.[17] Writing in a Catholic nation and thus largely for a Catholic audience, French sociologist Émile Durkheim argued that religion represents the society, and that a unified religion like Catholicism did this more successfully than a fragmented tradition like Protestantism, incidentally considering Anglicanism not really to be a form of Protestantism but more like Catholicism.[18] Like his Anglican friend C. S. Lewis, Tolkien was concerned about the tension between temptation and renunciation, which entails avoiding the temptation to use science to fulfill our lusts, and thus renouncing many technologies.[19]

The central metaphor of the Hobbit books is a magical ring that must be destroyed before it falls under the control of evil, thereby giving evil the power to do infinite harm. Found by the hobbit Bilbo in the cave home of Gollum, who lived near the goblins he resembles, it must be carried by Bilbo's nephew Frodo on a long and perilous journey to be destroyed in a raging volcano. Evil manifests itself in two ways. First, the devil Sauron commands vast armies in an attempt to seize the ring for his own purposes. Second, evil lurks hidden in the inner self of an individual person—such as the otherwise noble character Boromir, who died shortly after giving in to the temptation to seize the ring for himself. The player's avatar in LOTRO never gets the opportunity to be tempted thus, but does meet Bilbo, Frodo, and other key characters, and visits many locations described in the first two novels in the series, *The Hobbit* and *The Fellowship of the Ring*. A player can briefly adopt the character of one of Sauron's evil minions, but only through a temporary change of identity, and in their normal state the avatars of different players cannot fight each other and are repeatedly encouraged to cooperate, for example in completing quests that cannot be accomplished alone.

Dark Age of Camelot (DAoC) depicts competition among three great realms in the Dark Ages of northwest Europe: Albion (England), Hibernia (Ireland), and Midgard (Scandinavia).[20] Thus it is a bridge between fantasy and reality, because it depicts with at least moderate fidelity the folklore of these three societies. Each of these three cultures offers innumerable environments and quests for the player, but they are also locked in intermittent warfare with each other, in what is called *realm-versus-realm* combat. Thus, avatars are encouraged to cooperate within their own realms, and to fight to the virtual death against avatars from the two other realms. There exists no overarching moral imperative, and the three realms have entirely separate religious cultures.

Although Albion possesses churches, they contain little specifically Christian symbolism. The tombstones that miraculously appear when avatars die differ in symbolism by realm, the Hibernian ones displaying the famous circled Celtic cross, the Albion one carrying a picture of the Holy Grail, and the Midgard ones decorated with a T-shaped representation of Thor's hammer, Mjöllnir, under two carved dragon heads. The symbol carved into the Round Table could be mistaken for a Celtic Cross, or, for that matter, a German Iron Cross or a cross pattée, but really its shape is designed merely to blend into the round table, and thus it has four equal arms that grow wider as they extend from the center.

Camelot, the capital of Albion, is depicted anachronistically as a formidable medieval city, complete with a cathedral and housing the Round Table in a high castle. Standing just outside Jordheim, the capital city of Midgard, is a nonplayer character named Snorri Sturluson, who gives the player's avatar a quest or two. Sturluson was an actual Icelandic historian who wrote the *Prose Edda* around the year 1200, a Christian who wrote sympathetically about Pagan traditions. Apparently he respected the people of pre-Christian times, and believed that gods are mythologized versions of actual historical figures, the theory of legends technically called *euhemerism*.[21] Of course, the folkloric connections were intended by the creators of the gameworld, who proclaimed:

> Camelot has an immediately identifiable background that will be familiar to anyone with even the most cursory knowledge of mythical history. The Arthurian legends, the Norse Sagas, and to a lesser extent, Celtic folklore, are all represented in the game. The gods in the game will come from the pages of well-known mythology—gods like Odin and Thor, heroes like Cuchulain, Lancelot, and Galahad will all be part of the game's background.[22]

The legends of Arthur are based in the assumptions of the medieval society in which the stories were written down, yet his period was the Dark Ages more than five hundred years earlier. In my brief textbook *Online Multiplayer Games*, I used DAoC to illustrate my concept of *vector history*. This concept belongs to historiography, our understanding of how the viewpoints of historians themselves are a product of history, and thus change over time. Here is my definition: "A *vector history* is one that looks at a particular point in past time from another, later point in past time, or from a different culture. Note that in doing a vector history we select a point of view (in time and cultural space) that is not our own, and then look at a third point in human history from that perspective."[23] When we distance ourselves from a historical account created by an earlier generation, we often label it a *legend*.

Dating from 2004, *World of Warcraft* (WoW) is the most popular full-featured virtual world, reaching twelve million long-term subscribers worldwide.[24] The setting is a distant planet, Azeroth, and the disintegrating fragment of a second planet, existing in a universe where the laws of nature are different from those in our world. There is a medieval quality to the worldview; for example, the planets are flat, and the key elements of nature are earth, air, fire, and water. Instead of having a coherent set of overarching socially constructed categories—the dualism of good versus evil or the trinity of three equal but different realms in competition with each other—WoW is based on the dynamics of inescapable chaos, in which categories are complex and constantly reforming. There does exist a dichotomy of two factions, the civilized Alliance and the barbarian Horde, and an avatar in one cannot talk with an avatar in the other. Different versions of WoW exist, with different rules for combat between players, but in principle even the two great factions are only temporary coalitions of races that could easily fragment.

In the original 1994 two-person strategy game *Warcraft: Orcs and Humans*, the tribal Orcs invaded the civilized lands of the humans. They battled each other in a manner similar to chess, but over complex terrain rather than a simple chessboard, and with evolving sets of game pieces depicted as active virtual characters. By the time WoW itself was released a decade later, the world had become vastly larger and more complex, and both Orcs and Humans had assembled large coalitions to compete with each other. Orcs were in the Horde, to which minotaur-like Tauren, voodoo-practicing Trolls, and zombie-like Undead also belonged. The Alliance included not only Humans but also Dwarves, Gnomes, and Night Elves. In 2007 two other races were added, the Blood Elves joining the Horde and the Draenei joining the Alliance. In 2010, after I completed my research, two more races were added, the technophiliac Goblins in the Horde and druidic Worgen in the Alliance.

I ran avatars in all of the races before Goblins and Worgen were added. Each of these ten races had a distinctive culture, history, and symbolic relationship to science and technology, but some were more noteworthy than others. Both the Tauren and the Night Elves preserve nature. They share some of the same religious assumptions, although otherwise their cultures are quite different. Both the Undead and the Blood Elves employ dangerous technologies that despoil the environment, biological warfare in the case of the Undead and technologies equivalent to nuclear energy in the case of the Blood Elves. The Dwarves and Gnomes share the same city and the same love of apparently more benign technologies, including civil and mechanical engineering in the case of the Dwarves and broken computers plus unsuccessful spaceflight technologies in the case of the Gnomes. The Draenei are a technologically advanced species that are exploring the options for returning to their ancient traditions. Most Horde races are barbarians, and so they possess shamans rather than priests, whereas elaborate priesthoods exist among some of the more civilized cultures.

World of Warcraft is remarkable for the great diversity of religious groups it depicts, many of which are populated entirely by nonplayer characters and to which a player's avatar cannot belong. In a few cases, it is possible to build a positive reputation with a group of NPCs, doing quests for them and receiving benefits in return. But often a nonplayer religion is a cult or sect that must be battled, holding its own virtual territory where quests must be completed. The landscape is dotted with shrines and other sacred places, and some of the major cities possess huge temples. WoW takes a postmodern approach to religion and morality, regarding them both as extremely problematic. For example, a central member of the team who created WoW, Chris Metzen, published a marvelous story based on the WoW mythos, "Of Blood and Honor," that debates two incompatible moral codes.[25] One defines morality as loyalty to one's own family and clan, and the other is based on an abstract code of behavior that treats strangers the same as family members. This suggests just one of the many ways in which the philosophies of the most complex games connect to social theory.

The New Paradigm

The theoretical tradition on which this book is based might be called *exchange theory*, *social cognition theory*, *rational choice theory*, or the *New Paradigm* of the sociology of religion.[26] Truth to tell, it has many variants and draws upon a breadth of prior work in other traditions, so there may not be any one term to describe it. The variant described here was developed by Rodney Stark and myself, and may be the most fully developed explanatory theory of religion, presented in seven axioms, 104 definitions, and 344 derived propositions, which we do not have the space to cover thoroughly here.[27] Given the importance of the strategic exchange of value and information to the theory, it could even have been described as a variant of game theory that emphasizes impression management through role playing and reality defining.[28] Aspects of this theory have been simulated using game-like computerized multiagent systems.[29] Its key principle is that the human mind evolved to solve practical problems following cognitive explanations, and when it proves impossible to achieve a strongly desired goal, people are open to religious explanations that promise to satisfy desires by some supernatural means. Religion thus serves as a socially supported *compensator* that compensates people psychologically for the lack of desired rewards.

Central to the theory is the cognitive-emotional concept of compensators: "*Religion* refers to systems of general compensators based on supernatural assumptions." "*Compensators* are postulations of reward according to explanations that are not readily susceptible to unambiguous evaluation." "*Supernatural* refers to forces beyond or outside nature which can suspend, alter, or ignore physical forces."[30] One flavor of this theory might be called the *new economics of religion*, which stresses the fact that people often treat compensators as rewards, thus according them value and making them salient for economic exchange and for any other kind of human behavior that can be analyzed in economic terms, such as multiplayer games.[31]

Little notice has been given to the fact that religion is not the only sphere of life oriented toward compensators. The same is true for spectator sports, theater, movies, television dramas, novels, and music. Sports fans rejoice in the victories of their teams almost as if they themselves had won, apparently gaining subjective status comparable to that of religious sect members, feeling they are better people for their association with the athletic god that they adore. Clearly, people gain vicarious feelings of satisfaction, exaltation, and enlightenment from experiencing powerful fictional narratives.

Around the year 2000, the new discipline called *cognitive science* added three major ideas that could be integrated with the New Paradigm. All start with the recognition that human cognition is a complex set of functions in the human brain, which were shaped by biological evolution, primarily under the conditions of life hundreds of thousands of years ago. In those ancient days, humans learned to cooperate and to anticipate the dangers and opportunities around them. Furthermore, they learned to plan, which required a mental template for goal-directed action. Finally, the brain developed a huge capacity to store information, some of it temporarily holding short-term memories of the immediate past to keep the individual well orientated in the current situation, able to act energetically on the basis of knowledge of the immediate situation. Yet planning, cooperation, and the increasingly complex behaviors required by technology also required long-term storage of more abstract knowledge. Briefly stated, here are the three religion-relevant ideas from cognitive science:

1. *Mind reading:* The human brain possesses a set of functions that models the mind of an animal or other person, which evolved to permit complex, appropriate action with respect to prey, predators, and partners. This set was so important for human survival that it is hyperactive, imputing consciousness and intentionality to many complex natural phenomena that are not really conscious. This hyperactivity predisposed people to believe in supernatural beings.[32]

2. *Narrative:* In order to be able to plan effective action to achieve goals that could not be achieved immediately, and to communicate these plans to each other, humans developed a reliance upon narrative as a mode of thought. A narrative describes a person who has a goal and interacts morally with other people to move toward that goal, overcoming obstacles in achieving a series of subgoals, to the ultimate attainment of the goal. This narrative form of cognition predisposed people to believe that the world is

meaningful, and to understand meaning in terms of stories like the legends of a religion.[33]

3. *Memory:* While a full understanding of memory still eludes science, it seems that memories of specific momentary situations or brief scenes of action are stored in something just beyond short-term memory, as records of memorable episodes. The *episodic memories* that endure and have impact are connected to strong emotions. Less emotionally tinged *semantic memories* store a variety of kinds of facts, from the meaning of a word to the location of a local natural resource, learned through repetition. Different kinds of religion appear to use different kind of memory. Emotionally intense religious sects rely upon powerful episodic memories, such as a conversion experience. Established denominations, with their intellectualized theologies, rely more heavily upon semantic memories, which are strengthened gradually over time by the repetition provided by rituals.[34]

These and other ideas from cognitive science improve the basis on which we can understand religion, but they do not yet explain religion, as it developed over many centuries in urban-centered, agriculturally based ancient nations. This can be accomplished only by incorporating theories of communication and the construction of formal organizations based on social and economic exchanges, as the New Paradigm does. Individual cognition does not in itself explain such essential features of religion as the emergence of the priestly role, the development of complex doctrinal systems, the creation of religion-focused artworks, conformity to moral and ritual expectations, and the alliance between church and state. Nor can the purely cognitive theories explain secularization in the modern world, or the organized opposition to secularization that one finds among the societies dominated by the Judeo-Christian-Islamic tradition.

Secularization can be defined in several ways, depending on the facts one wants to explain and one's theoretical predispositions. An extreme definition would be: secularization is the death of religion. A more moderate definition is: secularization is the disestablishment of religion, removing it from a dominant position in the structure of society but not endangering its existence. An example of the latter is a marvelous journal article by Talcott Parsons published back in 1964, "Evolutionary Universals in Society."[35] When I came to know Parsons personally, he seemed very much like a parson to me, a mild-mannered but very powerful minister who offered to lead students to their philosophical salvation. He argued that religion was one of the very first institutions to evolve in human social evolution, of permanent importance in establishing the basis of morality, but of decreasing significance as other institutions evolved to take over some of its subsidiary functions. Although not entirely convinced by this argument, I greatly respected its sophistication. After all, our advanced brains could evolve only after we had complex digestive systems, and while the human appendix is vestigial, the stomach certainly is not.

Aware of Parsons's work, but approaching the question from a different direction, Stark and I developed a *homeostatic* model of secularization. In *homeostasis*, the overall structure and function of a system remain constant, while numerous minor changes occur within it. Especially among highly educated segments of the population, science and the cosmopolitan viewpoint produced by interaction with different cultures erode faith. In addition, members of the societal elite have less need of many specific compensators, such as the subjective social status that membership in a religious sect confers. Thus, families that ascend in social status tend to secularize. However, in a constant circulation of the elites, other people are dropping in social status, and thereby developing increased need for religious compensators. Entire denominations secularize as their leadership gains status in secular society, but the result is religious schisms, in which sects break away from denominations and revive religious faith. Society "runs in place," containing much movement but making no progress, as secularization is balanced by revival and religious innovation.

When Stark and I developed this perspective, we were also aware of a very different cyclical secularization theory proposed back in 1937 by Pitirim Sorokin.[36] As it happens, Sorokin founded the Harvard Department of Sociology, which Parsons later dominated, and Sorokin felt that Parsons had even betrayed him in the academic status game.[37] Like some other European right-wing social theorists, notably Oswald Spengler,[38] Sorokin argued that every successful civilization in based on a distinct set of ideas, which define it in distinction to other civilizations and give it strength, but which inevitably erode over the centuries. In its youth, a civilization is *ideational*, asserting that reality is spiritual rather than material. Often, the civilization is created by a radical group, perhaps even military conquerors, who demand faith in the particular ideals that justify its rise. Once a newly risen civilization is secure and prosperous, its ideals slowly shift, even over the span of a thousand years. It becomes more *sensate*, believing that reality is whatever the sense organs perceive. Its aims are physical or sensual, and it seeks to achieve them through exploiting or changing the external world, as our own civilization does through godless science and technology. Eventually, though, Sorokin argued that the sensate phase of a civilization ends in collapse, followed by a bloody period of chaos that may last many centuries, until a new civilization arises at the beginning of its own ideational phase.

The three MMOs described above nicely illustrate the fundamental issues in the debate between Parsons and Sorokin. Like Parsons, *Lord of the Rings Online* asserts that religion can serve as the universal, enduring support for morality, offering optimism even during times of great social turmoil. Like Sorokin, *World of Warcraft* assumes that civilizations fall, as well as rise, while faith and faithlessness are both parts of the historical dynamic. Human society in WoW has disintegrated, as its elite lost faith and used religious institutions merely as convenient tools, whereas the Elves split into two factions, Night Elves, who are like a fundamentalist religious sect, and Blood Elves, who are the extreme in technological secularization. Meanwhile, the Orcs are just beginning to establish their own civilization, just emerging from tribal shamanism and not yet quite ready to erect temples. *Dark Age of Camelot* takes an even wider view, contrasting three civilizations at about the same stage of development, but based on different beliefs. Thus insights about the competing social-science theories can be gained by empirical research inside these virtual civilizations.

Research Methods

My chief research methodology was to explore the gameworlds by playing them with the primary goal of learning rather than winning, but winning was a requirement for exploring their more advanced virtual territories. In my previous research in *World of Warcraft*, fully 2,400 hours were invested in running twenty-two avatars of every race and class. A few other games tabulate data about hours played: *Star Wars Galaxies* (in which I invested 618 hours), *Lord of the Rings Online* (479 hours), *Tabula Rasa* (305 hours), *EverQuest II* (262 hours), *Rift* (214 hours), *Gods and Heroes: Rome Rising* (194 hours), *Warhammer Online* (105 hours), *Sacred 2: Fallen Angel* (46 hours), and *Guild Wars* (44 hours). Other MMOs described here lack timers, but I estimate that my investment in each of those ten was greater than one hundred hours, and often significantly greater: *The Matrix Online, Dark Age of Camelot, Age of Conan, Pirates of the Burning Sea, Pirates of the Caribbean, Final Fantasy XI, Star Trek Online, Dungeons and Dragons Online, Fallen Earth*, and *Star Wars: The Old Republic*. In the case of seven games that required reconnaissance but not exhaustive exploration, I took an avatar up to level 25: *Aion, Faxion, Perfect World, Forsaken World, Runes of Magic, Lineage II: Goddess of Destruction*, and *Elder Scrolls IV: Oblivion*. Solo-player games tend to be short, but some of them I only sampled, while completely finishing these four: *The Da Vinci Code; Chronicles of Narnia: The Lion, the Witch, and the Wardrobe; Star Wars Episode III: Revenge of the Sith*; and *Constantine*.

On the level of the mechanics of data collection, a prime technique was taking tens of thousands of screenshot pictures of the display on the computer screen, especially capturing all the text and fundamental actions of each significant quest arc. In the case of very popular games, many online data resources were also used. For example, WoWWiki (http://www.wowwiki.com) is a very extensive

encyclopedia of *World of Warcraft* information, while Wowhead (http://www
.wowhead.com) provides details of all the quests, both of them based largely on
volunteer input from players. Of course, I would never rely entirely on these
sources, but always observed the quest or other virtual experience myself. On occasion I would use database systems associated with the game to do a census of
avatars or gain other systematic data suitable for statistical analysis.

In some gameworlds, notably *World of Warcraft*, I was a very active member of
guilds or comparable groups of players, and benefited from the experiences of my
associates. Indeed, a medium-sized WoW guild I myself founded in the spring of
2008 was still in existence four years later. However, the need to spend time
taking screenshots and maneuvering my avatar into situations where useful information would be available rendered me a somewhat unhelpful team player, so I
had to use online forums, blogs, and the other data sources to gain a full appreci-
ation of the social implications. In some of the MMOs, reading the in-game text
chat was especially useful. One excellent example was the help chat in *Fallen
Earth*, which was often moderated by a very competent employee of the game
company, and where experienced players provided advice for inexperienced ones.
In several MMOs, my avatar joined a guild that had a very active text chat,
learning more from what the guild members discussed with each other than from
going on game quests with them.

In the experimental scientific method, research is carefully designed to test
hypotheses logically derived from theories. This study did not use that method,
but employed an approach that I believe gave comparable results. Rather than
just wandering around in the virtual worlds and seeing what happened by chance,
I very carefully planned out what my avatar would do and where it would go, to
gain desired data. This meant that I had to begin by doing some reconnaissance,
both inside the gameworld and in online information sources, and develop avatars that would have appropriate abilities and personalities for the particular lines
of research they would undertake. Having the theories discussed in this chapter
in mind, I identified nine distinct areas of the social science of religion that could
be the framework for organizing the data, suitable for analysis in terms of the
theories. The following chapter sets computer gaming in the wider contest that is
sometimes called the modern *culture wars*, especially in the struggle between traditional religion and secular humanism. The nine chapters that follow it each
focus on one aspect of religion that social scientists seek to understand, and an
appendix briefly describes the forty-one gameworlds on which this book is based.

The nine topic-focused chapters are not merely a convenient way of organizing the research findings, nor just an analytical framework, but nine high-level
scientific quests that motivated and guided the research from the beginning. In
gamer lingo, strings of connected quests are called *quest arcs*, and they have some

of the sacred quality of Noah's Ark and the Ark of the Covenant, providing a sense of deeper meaning. The four *World of Warcraft* avatars mentioned in the first paragraph of this chapter were on sacred quests, the first two to gain greater abilities that would allow them to accomplish new quest arcs, and the last two in the process of doing two more specific missions, which had been formally assigned to them by quest givers in the gameworld. So that was the primary research methodology that guided my ethnography, discovering all the specific missions I need to undertaken to triumph in nine great quests that had been assigned to me by the gods of science.

We naturally but naively think religions are about gods, so the first of these meta-quests is "Deities," reported here in chapter 3. In Judeo-Christian-Islamic societies, gods are spoken of in the singular and capitalized: God. When Durkheim argued that God was a metaphor for society, representing the unity of adherents, he implicitly favored monotheism because it represents unity, either of one people as in Judaism or of all people as in Christianity and Islam, under a single Lord. Some scholars believe that monotheism encouraged the emergence of science during the Renaissance and afterward, because it assumes that all of nature was created by one deity according to one law that can be discovered through research.[39] But humanity is not unified, and nature seems to be a chaos of conflicting forces. Thus, monotheism expresses a utopian ideal, but harsh reality may better be described by polytheism in which multiple deities compete. The computer games described here are about winning, and thus about competition, but with the paradoxical promise that all players can win. From the "winner take all" perspective of chess or tennis, this seems unnatural—even supernatural—and one way it can be accomplished is by letting every player triumph over nonplayer characters, in a fictional struggle between virtual gods, even sometimes fighting against deities.

Chapter 4, "Souls," contrasts the Judeo-Christian notion of a unitary, immortal soul with the Indo-European idea that each being has multiple finite aspects which can be represented by different avatars. So-called Turing machines, early digital computers, were designed according to the soul principle, and a degree of unity is provided to the human mind by the limited capacity of human short-term memory.[40] However, modern cognitive science views the brain as a collection of rather separate modules, each assembled from submodules composed of individual neurons, and similarly modern sociology views humans as collections of distinct roles. In gameworlds, devoted players exhibit the psychological concepts of *protean self*, as they shift from avatar to avatar, and *multiplex self*, as they run multiple secondary avatars simultaneously. Given the human ability to play the role of being another person, and the almost endless possibilities provided by virtual world technology, in the future many people will experience ancestor veneration avatars (AVAs). To do so, one merely creates an avatar for a gameworld based on a deceased relative and uses the perspective of that relative while playing the game. This interesting opportunity suggests that abandoning the primitive notion that humans possess unitary, immortal souls may liberate us to explore a number of rewarding spiritual alternatives.

If gods fade out of existence, and souls disintegrate, the chapter on priests considers a very different but parallel consequence of disbelief. Priest avatars, or avatars with similar functions like clerics or mages, exist in most fantasy gameworlds, yet many of the aspects of real life that motivate religious professionals are lacking. Permanent death is generally absent, so nobody needs to officiate over funerals, and the absence of families limits the need for marriage ceremonies. Religions, however, are prominent in the story lines of MMOs, so priest characters must inhabit the many virtual cathedrals and temples. The chief social role of virtual priest avatars is as healers, typically in team combat where the priest supports a warrior who directly engages the enemy. In the real world, women are more religious than men, but men dominate the clergy, while in gameworlds an unusually high fraction of the priests are female. Only rarely do games include very elaborate religious rituals, and the ones that do tend to be unpopular. These observations suggest that the erosion of belief in postmodern culture may also erode or at least transform the roles played by professional clergy. Suspension of disbelief may allow game companies to make a profit, but the priesthood may go out of business.

Shrines are the homes of gods, and the chapter with this title covers all forms of sacred architecture, including churches, cathedrals, temples, and monasteries. Religions differ in terms of how strictly they separate sacred objects and places from profane ones, with animists believing that everything has a sacred quality, and dualists being strict separationists. Many gameworlds make a clear distinction in terms of their mythologies, identifying some rocks as shrines, but not all. In technical terms, game designers distinguish the *display model* that produces the visual image from the *world model* that determines how the avatar can interact with it. For example, the image of the many stones making up the wall of a temple is a single graphic that belongs to the display model, while the programming that prevents the avatar from walking though the wall is part of the world model. This is akin to the distinction that architects make between form and function, although ideally form follows function. In gameworlds, a third factor combines with form and function, namely, the narrative that is expressed through written text and the actions of meaningful story lines. Thus a virtual shrine or temple can evoke the supernatural through visually resembling something sacred in the conventional world, by being spoken of in the narrative as religious, and by functioning in the game to provide a measure of transcendence from the material world.

Chapter 8, "Morality," considers the central function of religion in sustaining a code of behavior for members of the society that adheres to the particular faith. In social science, one major approach is criminology or the broader sociology of deviance, and concepts from this field can illuminate dimensions of the gameworld even though faith is probably not a powerful determinant of behavior by avatars. As it happens, during the seven years I taught at the University of Washington, my biggest class was Social Deviance, where I was inspired by the interest expressed by five hundred to seven hundred students per year. The class covered religious deviance, a field my research then concentrated in, as well as providing an introduction to criminology and to the social science of mental disorder, the field in which I had taken my graduate exams. A key theme of the chapter naturally is the standard academic conceptualization of how religion and morality relate to each other. Morality evolved to support the success of one's own family or tribe, by building a partnership among tribe members. But it is problematic in a world where separate tribes compete to the death over limited resources, as is the case in many gameworlds and may become the case in the wider world that humans inhabit.

The chapter "Cults" examines how religion sets standards for behavior and belief—indeed how religion comes into being. Every religious tradition began as a cult, such as the one Moses led out of Egypt, or as a cultlike sect that broke away from an existing group, as Christianity did from Judaism. Indeed, the descriptions of very early Christianity found in the New Testament makes them seem very similar to the two modern communal cults, the Process and the Children of God, about which I wrote two books.[41] Consider Acts 4:32, "And the multitude of them that believed were of one heart and of one soul: neither said any of them that ought of the things which he possessed was his own; but they had all things common." Cult movements are deviant religious organizations with novel beliefs and practices, and fictional ones abound in the gameworlds. Real-world cults can be analyzed in terms of the new supernatural compensators they create through intense social implosions, or through the methods they use to absorb new members. However, both real and fictional cults can be considered total works of art, comparable to the grand operas about Pagan gods written by Richard Wagner, but experienced as a realm of real life by cultists and gamers alike.

Religion has many roots, but the taproot reaches into the grave of every deceased friend or family member, and draws from the depth psychology of our own personal fear of dying. Ultimately, religion is about meaning that transcends mortality, so a gloomy chapter on death (chapter 10) prepares this book for its more optimistic conclusion. Much of the action in computer games involves killing, causing the deaths both of players' avatars and of nonplayer characters. But death in MMOs is not permanent, because in almost every instance the deceased character can return to life. Popular games do not explicitly employ the Hindu concept of *samsara*, referring to an endless cycle of birth, suffering, death, and reincarnation—yet as a practical matter the nonplayer characters are trapped in this tragic pattern. Huge cemeteries, individual graves, and splendid tombs abound. A few memorials for actually deceased persons can be found. In some games, the player's avatar can be one of the Undead, supposedly having experienced an entire life before the player began the game, and now existing in a form not unlike a corpse. The games may trivialize death, but an argument can be made that religions do the same, by pretending that it is less horrifying than it really is.

To end the book on a positive note, the final chapter concerns quests. In a very real sense, this chapter uses games as a vantage point from which to debate whether life has meaning. Competitive games have goals, both small ones and large ones, collecting points of various kinds on the way toward winning. A superficial meaning of the word *meaning* comes from translation of one word into another, for example connecting the German word *Spiel* to game, or stealing a Latin word for game to create the adjective *ludic*. But humans want *meaning* to have a deeper meaning—referring to some transcendent purpose. One way they do this is through seeking to achieve goals in life, which can range from the very simple goal of having lunch to vastly richer goals such as creating a good society for our children to thrive in, thereby giving both the struggle and the accomplishment a significance to human beings. The purposeful nature of human questing translates not only to the acts performed by the person but to the features of the surrounding world that play roles in the quest. Thus, humans invest meaning in life through their questing, whether or not gods already did so. Along the way, players lose some games, and death is the ultimate defeat. The ultimate victory is to play eternally.

Conclusion

This book does not claim that multiplayer online games will supplant religion, but that many of religion's historical functions have already been taken over by other institutions of society, in the process of secularization, and games will play a role in the further erosion of faith. Quite apart from what psychological and social functions games may play, they provide a vantage point from which to consider changes happening in the wider culture and to celebrate human creativity. Thus fantasy is not a perfect substitute for faith, but it has some advantages. One is freedom, because a player can decide from moment to moment which game to play, which avatar to play inside it, and within certain limits what goals the avatar should seek. Precisely because religion has traditionally oversold its value to humanity, and such value as it has may decline as many competing cultural institutions arise, fantasy need not simulate faith. Indeed, to describe secularization as the erosion of religious faith is too negative a way to define it. We might better say: secularization is a form of cultural progress that liberates the playful human imagination.

2 THE CULTURE GAME

The larger world surrounding the online gameworlds has some of the qualities of a game itself, and this fact relates directly to both religion and the gameworlds. The form the relationship takes can be described in terms of the well-established method of training military officers known as *war games*. This book and its topic are enmeshed in a *culture war*. The two sides are not clearly drawn, but on one side we can vaguely see conservative forces that want to preserve traditional American culture including old-time religion, and on the other side radical forces that are exploring alternative cultural options connected to new technologies. One battlefield in this war is federal funding of scientific research, which in recent years has included computer games. Thus the admittedly minor battle over federal funding of game-related research is like a tabletop war game, recapitulating on a smaller scale the huge culture war waging in society at large.

Of course the word *war* is an exaggeration here, because people are not really being killed, although significant financial resources are threatened. From the perspective of the gameworlds, war is an appropriate metaphor, because many of their backstories involve wars, yet no real blood is shed. Critics of the current political process in the United States and many other nations decry the flagrant use of deceptive rhetoric by politicians and their habit of accepting donations from vested interests that do business with the government. Yet both of these "misbehaviors" are what one might expect if politics were a complex game in which deception and influence trading were standard features of the set of rules.

This book concerns gameworlds, so it is not the proper place for a detailed analysis of the current political scene, from the formal perspectives of political science and political sociology. Given that I wrote this book exactly a half century after I first registered to vote, perhaps I can be forgiven for offering an ordinary citizen's perspective on how the political landscape has changed in the United States. I remember hearing Senator Strom Thurmond speak, just when he was switching from the Democratic Party to the Republican, in opposition to some aspects of the civil rights movement and in loyalty to the Old South. Whatever one may think of the man's politics, he was a remarkable relic of the past, as symbolized by the fact he was still serving in Congress at the age of 100. Abraham Lincoln, it will be recalled, was a Republican, and while both modern parties support racial equality, many southern conservatives shifted as Thurmond did from Democrats to Republicans.

As a sociologist of religion, I have watched the religious realignment of the two parties with some interest. At the height of the civil rights movement, many of its leaders were clergy, Reverend Martin Luther King, Jr., being only the best known. A few leaders on the political left continue that tradition, but a powerful connection between the evangelical movement and the Republican Party has arisen in recent decades. Many Republicans today believe that the following cultural commitments naturally harmonize with each other: free markets, limited government, strong national defense, and religious conservatism. An entire book could be devoted to a serious analysis of how or whether these four really fit together, rather than being a temporary coalition of logically unrelated ideologies, brought together by accidents of history. However, at the moment the free-market Republican goal of reducing the costs of government combines with the cultural traditionalism of "the religious right" to form the basis of opposition to government-supported research on games and virtual worlds.

Of course, the political dynamics are very different in other countries. Many of the games covered by this book were developed in Asian nations, or by international companies with Asian investment, and some of them incorporate diluted versions of Asian religious traditions. In earlier publications, I have examined a number of gameworlds created by European companies, and a few are mentioned in these pages. By the standards of the United States, both Asia and Europe are relatively secular regions of the world. The Americas are a much more religious region of the world, including most nations south of the United States. This point raises an interesting fact: information technologies in general, and online games specifically, have become popular in Latin America more slowly than the economic prosperity and educational level of its middle classes would have predicted. I sense that Latin America is catching up, as illustrated for example by the increasing number of articles in the Spanish-language version of *Wikipedia*, and it will be interesting to see if the recent introduction of MMOs into Mexico and South America will lead to the creation of new games more in harmony with Catholic perspectives.

It is important to note that the most popular MMOs are in the fantasy category, which inevitably means they have nonstandard supernatural content. As of December 29, 2011, the MMO blog MMORPG.com listed fully 543 games. Included were many that were defunct, had not yet launched, emphasized real-time strategy rather than role playing, or were very minor browser-based games, yet the list provides a good general picture of the MMO universe. For example, 84.9 percent of the 543 MMOs included player-versus-player combat, 5.7 percent did not, and the situation was uncertain for the remainder. In terms of the genre of the game story, fantasy MMOs were by far the most common with 62.2 percent, followed by sci-fi with 17.1 percent. The other categories were historical (9.2 percent), real life (5.2 percent), sports (3.7 percent), superhero (1.5 percent), and horror (1.1 percent). This book includes a few sci-fi and historical games which have religion-related content, as well as many fantasy games. The fraction of solo-player videogames and computer games devoted to fantasy is lower, because many of them are based on adventure movies or other nonsupernatural media content. But fantasy dominates the online MMO universe, and thus virtual worlds tend to possess deviant supernatural assumptions.

Religious Tension

The concerns that religious conservatives have about electronic games are clearly stated on a website called Christian Spotlight's Guide 2 Games.[1] A large number of reviews have been posted on the site, which is based on "a Christian world-view," "to assist gamers and parents in making wise decisions in their choice of electronic games." The reviews were written by a variety of people who actually played the games and had some background as videogame players. Indeed, many of the reviews are quite sophisticated, assessing the pros and cons of a game in a balanced and clear manner, so visitors to the site can make up their own minds. Reviewers share three general areas of concern: (1) sexual content that they consider inappropriate for youngsters and in extreme cases for adults as well, (2) gratuitous and graphic violence that may disturb children and provide a bad model for adult behavior, and (3) non-Christian religious or magical content that contradicts their religious views. The third of these is most relevant here.

Checking Christian Spotlight near the end of 2011, I found reviews of five of the games covered here, written by four different reviewers, each of which had a section describing problems with the *spiritual content* of the game. The following excerpts clearly suggest a tension between traditional Christian faith and the supernatural assumptions in the games:

Elder Scrolls IV: Oblivion: This game is quite spiritual, just not in a good sense most of the time. Members of the Dark Brotherhood speak of the "Night Mother," and a deity by the name of Sithis that they often refer to as if he's a god. The Night Mother turns out to be a ghost. There are numerous references to the gods, typically referred to as "the 9," and you can visit any of their temples to pray to a specific god to have your attributes fixed if they are hurt, or you can have diseases cured. In the beginning of the game you are confronted by the emperor of Cyrodill (the land the game takes place in) and he speaks of how the gods brought you two together and he asks what your sign is. You must then pick a specific star layout that you apparently were born under which then gives you a special ability. Throughout the game, especially in the Dark Brotherhood, you see occult like shrines.[2]

Guild Wars: Prophecies: Magic, magic, and more magic, some gods, and more magic. The game revolves around the ability to use magic. You can cast fireballs, throw ice shards, call lightning, or use the dark arts of necromancy to raise the dead to destroy your opponent. While it isn't said where the power of the magic comes from, it's fairly obvious that the source is spiritual as most magical abilities are called forth by certain movements or sayings. The storyline involves some talk about gods, but it's with a lowercase 'g' and isn't spoken of very often. For the most part NPCs dedicate "whatever" to "such and such god," and some areas of the map are named for a god, like "Grenth's Footprint."[3]

Legend of Zelda: Ocarina of Time: Some magic items, mention of gods, one character is a fairy. Other characters are shown using magic, plot deals with an item considered holy. . . . Sadly, this game is pretty murky in terms of spirituality. The plot of this game first involves hunting for a familiar item to Zelda fans: the Triforce. In the plot, this item was created by the gods of Hyrule and can grant the wishes of whoever owns it. On the subject of gods, this game features three goddesses who are credited with the creation of Hyrule. These three are later shown being prayed to at the end of the game.[4]

Sims Medieval: Hero class Wizard casts spells, looks into crystal ball, Hero class Priest(s) can pray, player is understood as deity, Grim Reaper appears.[5]

World of Warcraft: Lots of magic in this game: from auras to ranged damaging ice novas, resurrection spells, etc. In addition, you see many characters and NPCs (Non-player characters) which seem to have evolved half way between two species. There are also ghosts that linger in some quests, and when you die, you become a ghost and your object is to run back to your body to be revived.[6]

In terms of standard conceptualizations in the social science of religion, the problems boil down to two issues: (1) promotion of non-Christian religions, and (2) favorable depiction of magic. These two problems may not cause much worry for members of liberal Christian denominations, nor for believers who make a strict distinction between their faith, which is real, and fiction, which is not to be taken seriously. But a considerable body of social-scientific research indicates that these people are not the ones who sustain the religious world. Rather, religion gains its strength from the strongest believers: sects, clerical orders, fundamentalists, and evangelicals. Their faith operates in significant *sectarian tension* with the secular world, and they draw their neighbors and family members away from secularism through their social bonds and by saturating the wider culture with their ideas.[7] Today, however, modern technologies have become not only the medium for global communication but a force pulling in the opposite direction, away from ancient religions.

Over the past twenty years, a vast social science literature has used questionnaires to study people's use of the new information and communication technologies, although many important questions have still only been touched upon rather than studied deeply. During the period 2000–2004, the General Social Survey administered a battery of questions about website use to a reasonably representative sample of the American public. Table 2.1 reports some results of tabulating a few of them against the standard GSS question "How often do you attend religious services?" At least 2,300 respondents answered this question plus each questionnaire item about use of the web. Anyone who wants to explore these issues more deeply, perhaps through more elaborate statistical methods, can access the data online.[8]

For our purposes, the most interesting one of the website usage items concerns "games you can play on your computer." Table 2.1 reveals that 41.0 percent of respondents who never attend religious services have consulted a game-related website in the past month, compared with only 32.1 percent of those who attend services at least once a week. The people who never attend church are a variegated collection, including not only strict Atheists but also elderly people or others with mobility problems, and people who lack friends or family who might draw them into church. The better comparison group of nonreligious people consists of those who attend once a year or less often, as their rate of attendance could be explained simply by an occasional wedding or funeral in church. Fully 44.4 percent of them visited a game-related website at least once in the past month, 12.3 percentage points higher than those who attend religious services most frequently.

The question about games does not specify what kind, and the popular games at the time included very abstract games like Tetris, sports games, and many varieties other than the narrative games that feature in this book. Thus we would not necessarily expect to see a very strong negative correlation between church attendance and visiting game sites, but the pattern we do see is substantial. The positive correlation between church attendance and visiting religion-related websites is indeed much stronger.

Table 2.1 Frequency of Religious Attendance and Visiting Websites

	Never	Once a Year or Less	More than Once a Year to Monthly	More than Monthly but Not Weekly	Weekly or More Often
In the Past 30 Days, Visited a Website about (2000–2004 GSS):					
Games you can play on your computer	41.0%	44.4%	43.4%	40.3%	32.1%
Religion/church related	6.5%	9.5%	14.0%	28.5%	42.2%
Sexually explicit material	19.3%	16.4%	13.5%	6.1%	4.4%
Science	43.5%	41.0%	35.9%	37.5%	32.2%
Music/concerts	48.4%	49.5%	48.4%	46.2%	36.4%
Visual art/art museums	21.7%	25.6%	24.9%	24.1%	19.7%
Health and fitness	47.0%	52.0%	53.2%	54.8%	51.4%
Personal home pages	29.3%	24.9%	28.6%	24.3%	22.4%
Sites related to your work	51.0%	55.8%	57.1%	58.4%	56.4%
Played Online (2000–2002 GSS):					
Play a game with someone on another computer?	24.1%	25.1%	18.9%	20.8%	14.1%

The seven other topics do not exhaust the full list, but were selected because they help us understand the meaning of the negative correlation between game sites and religion sites. Church attendance appears to discourage visiting sexually explicit sites more strongly than it does game sites, but again on the basis of the GSS data we cannot say exactly how strong the religious hostility specifically to fantasy games might be. Interestingly, church attendance is also negatively correlated with visiting science, music, and art websites. However, we do not see much evidence of this negative religious pressure on websites about health or work, or personal websites. Had the pattern been identical for all seven other topics, we might have concluded that religious people make much less use of the web, and this could possibly have reflected social class differences rather than cultural differences. But that is not what we see, and the data are consistent with the theory that highly religious people have a tendency to reject secular culture in general, including that most recent addition to American culture, computer games.

The bottom row of table 2.1 shows an item from a different battery, which was included in just the 2000 and 2002 GSS surveys and reflects data from 1,637 respondents. Among people who seldom attended church, 25.1 percent had played a game with a person on another computer, compared with only 14.1 percent of respondents who attended church at least weekly. The most recent data reflected in table 2.1 date from a few months before *World of Warcraft* launched in late 2004, and online gaming has evolved greatly since then. Thus, we will need new studies, incorporating batteries of more sophisticated questions, to chart the current and future tension between religion and computer games, let alone to explain it.

One useful questionnaire dataset actually dates from a year earlier than the earliest GSS data reported in table 2.1, and thus fully a dozen years before I completed writing this book. With support from the National Geographic Society, a team headed by James Witte and including me carried out a huge online questionnaire study in 1999, called Survey2000.[9] Large numbers of respondents were recruited through National Geographic's worldwide readership and through educational institutions. The system for administering the batteries of items was very sophisticated, selecting subsets of respondents at random to get one of a number of topical modules, so the dataset is huge in terms of numbers of questions as well as numbers of answers. Survey2000 contained a series of questions about leisure activities, one of which was "playing video games." Table 2.2 shows that adult videogame players were slightly less likely to participate in religious groups and to like hymns and gospel music. The large number of respondents makes it possible to control for other variables. For example, the results are very much the same if one samples only people age 18–29 and separates the males from the females.

Since I managed federal funding for the General Social Survey for the better part of a decade and was part of the Survey2000 team, I am in a good position to

Table 2.2 Videogames and Religion Variables in Survey2000

	Playing video games?		
	Never	Sometimes	Often
Participate in religious groups?			
Not at all.	64.0%	65.6%	71.2%
Am a member.	17.3%	18.4%	15.8%
Am an active member.	18.7%	16.0%	12.9%
Total	100.0%	100.0%	100.0%
Respondents:	21,382	19,132	6,575
Hymns and gospel music?			
Like it very much.	9.2%	7.9%	7.1%
Like it.	27.8%	24.8%	20.1%
Have mixed feelings.	34.5%	35.1%	33.1%
Dislike it.	15.5%	17.4%	19.3%
Dislike it very much.	8.3%	9.9%	14.8%
Total	100.0%	100.0%	100.0%
Respondents:	16,863	14,989	5,205

compare their samples of respondents. The General Social Survey administers the questions through an at-home interview and recruits respondents to match the general noninstitutionalized population as closely as is practical. Survey2000 was able to reach a much larger sample of respondents, but one that was less representative of the general population. However, the most obvious bias of Survey2000 is that all of its respondents were computer users who already by 1999 were comfortable responding to an online questionnaire. This means that any religious-secular differences would not be merely the result of later adoption of the Internet by religious people, and thus for once a sampling bias works in favor of good social science, rather than against it. While lacking a perfect comparison with the general population, I am struck by how many of the Survey2000 respondents report no involvement with religious groups.

Clearly, great opportunities exist today for online surveys specifically designed to assess the differing orientations toward fantasy games of people having different religious views, and even to explore over time how participation in fantasy gameworlds might change an individual's religiosity. For example, a questionnaire including a battery of items measuring conventional religiosity could also list twenty online activities, including "play *World of Warcraft* or a similar online fantasy game." However, since the topic of this chapter is culture, it is worth noting that questionnaires are a favorite tool of sociologists, but research on culture is more central to anthropology which makes much less use of sample survey methodologies. Indeed, the method used most intensively in this book is precisely ethnography—not merely doing the sociological method of participant observation by actually playing the game, but focusing on the culture of the games while playing them, which is more properly called *ethnography*.

Cultural anthropologists do not merely observe "the natives" performing rituals, while doing scientific ethnography. They also rely upon *native informants*, members of the culture who are willing and able to communicate the custom of their tribe to the anthropologist. A particularly apt example was E. E. Evans-Pritchard, who enlisted natives as research assistants—almost as spies—to obtain secrets he could not have obtained himself.[10] Particularly in my earlier research on *World of Warcraft*, I often benefitted from insights offered by other players, and for this book I read extensively in forums, wikis, and blogs where thousands of players report their thoughts and experiences. Thus, I benefited from many native informants who belonged to the Gamer tribe. What about the rival tribe of Antigamers? We can thank Senator Tom Coburn and some of his Republican colleagues for having served as the functional equivalent of native informants, by at least beginning to articulate their opposition to the emerging secular gaming culture.

The Political Arena

In MMOs, battlegrounds designed for player-versus-player combat are often called *arenas*, and Washington, DC, is in many ways indistinguishable from one of these contest instances. Neither in political Washington nor in *World of Warcraft* does one see real blood spilled, and there are qualities of culturally defined game to both. In December 2010, Republican senator Tom Coburn of Oklahoma issued a report, *Wastebook: A Guide to Some of the Most Wasteful Government Spending of 2010*.[11] It lists one hundred wasteful expenditures of the US federal government, highlighting the ten he and his staff consider the most egregious. Number 6 is "Studying World of Warcraft and Other Virtual Games—(Irvine, CA) $2.9 Million." On January 1, 2011, the Fox News cable channel, in its morning roundup program *Fox and Friends Sunday*, publicized this antigame claim, saying "three million dollars" were wasted studying *World of Warcraft*.

Coburn's one-page condemnation begins, "Most people have to work for a living; others get to play video games." There is an accompanying illustration that is the cover of Bonnie Nardi's book *My Life as a Night Elf Priest: An Anthropological Account of World of Warcraft*.[12] Footnotes link to the website of the National Science Foundation, specifically to abstracts of two grants, one for $100,007 to Professor Nardi, and one for $2,997,936 to Walt Scacchi, a colleague of Nardi at the University of California, Irvine. The abstract for Nardi's grant, which is in the public domain, explains that the grant was exploratory in nature, and states its scientific motivation clearly:

> This exploratory study will analyze and understand the ways in which players of World of Warcraft, a popular multiplayer game, engage in creative collaboration. World of Warcraft is a massively multiplayer online role playing game with ten million players worldwide. The proposed research is novel in locating creativity in the context of collaboration in a distributed online space. Most creativity research is laboratory based. It takes the individual as the unit of analysis. This research will examine creativity as a collaborative act, and will investigate creativity in a distributed online context.
>
> The research will focus on modding—the creation and distribution of player-created software modifications that extend the game—as an act of creative collaboration. What is the effect of collaboration on creativity? What motivates players to maintain engagement? How does the game software itself support or hinder collaboration? What interaction tools do players use to undertake creative collaboration? What can be learned from creative collaboration in games about mediated collaboration in general? Can these principles be translated to other environments such as work, or does the very context of "play" have inherent qualities that cannot be easily translated?
>
> The increasing confluence of work and play in games and virtual worlds is a topic of growing interest in industry and the military. The practices of millions of young people are being shaped by participation in multiplayer games. Players will take these practices into the workplace and military service. Investigating how creativity is enabled by collaborative online practices is vital to our understanding of how work and military service can be reshaped to encourage and sustain creative activity in these arenas.[13]

Scacchi's grant was not a study of *World of Warcraft*, nor indeed of any other game, but a large research project on "decentralized virtual activity systems."[14] Nardi is a co–principal investigator on it, and indeed UC Irvine is a center of research on virtual environments, where faculty members often collaborate on a variety of projects. By December 2010, the grant's abstract had been augmented with fifteen literature citations, including essays about games both Nardi and Scacchi had contributed to the peer-reviewed online journal *First Monday*. Both are extremely active researchers in the broad new research areas of virtual environments, in which games are just a subfield, and both had independently contributed chapters to the 2010 book I edited on the subject, *Online Worlds*. It is also the case—and public knowledge—that I managed review and funding of these two grants. I should note that under current government rules, editing a book does not give the editor a conflict of interest with the authors, and editing *Online Worlds* was appropriately done outside my government responsibilities and restrictions.

Nardi's chapter, "Culture and Creativity: *World of Warcraft* Modding in China and the US," was written in collaboration with Yong Ming Kow, a graduate student in information and computer sciences who is interested in how modding culture can shape the future of software development more generally.[15] *World of Warcraft* permits users to write mods in the Lua scripting language, with technical restrictions that prevent people from altering the game to their own competitive advantage. In my own research I often used the CensusPlus mod that allowed me to count how many avatars of different kinds were online at any given moment, for example to chart the population changes over a period of weeks when *World of Warcraft* added a new virtual continent.[16] Modding is an example of open source software creation, and a very important topic in computer science. Given the fact that China and the United States are competing currently for economic and technological power, and *World of Warcraft* modding is done in different ways in the two countries, it would seem that $100,007 was a good investment in Nardi's exploratory grant.

Scacchi's chapter, "Game-Based Virtual Worlds as Decentralized Virtual Activity Systems," is an example of the way that innovators have been adapting game technology to "serious" purposes.[17] People who have not extensively experienced the new virtual world technology find it difficult to imagine the implications of this revolutionary technology, and therefore it may seem frivolous to them, or they may even be repelled by it. Cultural conservatives may associate games with gambling, a vice they have good reason to oppose. Indeed, the *Pirates of the Caribbean* MMO, which seems aimed at children, requires the player to win at poker and blackjack at virtual gambling tables. One thesis of this book is that people dedicated to existing cultural traditions probably should oppose virtual world technology and the games within it. But Scacchi's work is a very serious exploration of the positive uses of the technology, and his chapter offers two examples. The first is *DinoQuest Online*, a game-like system for teaching elementary school children and the general public about paleontology and the life sciences. The second example is a mod of an existing game that transformed it into a training tool for workers in high-tech semiconductor factories.

It should not be assumed that Senator Coburn was alone in his antagonism to federal support of game-related research, because three other leading politicians supported his efforts: 2008 Republican presidential nominee Senator John

McCain, House Majority Leader Eric Cantor, and Congressman Darrell Issa. In August 2010, Coburn and McCain had jointly issued *Summertime Blues: 100 Stimulus Projects that Give Taxpayers the Blues*.[18] Number 39 was titled "Research: Marketing Video Games to the Elderly (Raleigh, NC and Atlanta, GA)—$1.2 million." This title was an extreme misrepresentation of the research being criticized, which could hardly have been unintentional given that Coburn and McCain cite a *Time* magazine article that reported more fully on the research, titled "Can Gaming Slow Mental Decline in the Elderly?"[19] This is a very serious research question in cognitive science and mental health, but actually the research project was broader, involving information technology other than games, which the senators' staff must have seen when they read the abstracts on the NSF website. The research was supported by a pair of collaborative NSF grants actually titled "Improving Older Adult Cognition: The Unexamined Role of Games and Social Computing Environments."[20] As in the cases of the Nardi and Scacchi grants, I managed review and funding, in accordance with appropriate NSF peer review procedures. All of the information reported here is in the public record, and I take very seriously my obligation to preserve the confidentiality of NSF review.

The following February, after the Republicans had captured the US House of Representatives, the study was disparaged again in the heated debate over the not yet decided federal budget for the fiscal year that had started the previous October. The new chairman of the House Oversight Committee, Darrell Issa, introduced an amendment to the funding bill, saying, "None of the funds made available by this Act may be used by the National Science Foundation to study whether video games improve mental health for the elderly."[21] Strictly speaking, videogames are electronic games that play through a television set, and games played on computers are not video games, although the studies funded by these grants used a Nintendo Wii for part of the work, which is a videogame system. However, the cognitive dimensions of mental functioning studied do not relate to the strictly psychiatric notion of "mental health" versus illness. In other words, the amendment was incompetent as guidance for science funding, but was raw political rhetoric uttered in the heat of a culture war. Issa's amendment was not adopted, but it was clearly a move in the culture game.

Late in 2010, Representative Eric Cantor launched an online system where citizens could use keywords to search the NSF awards database to identify grants they felt should not have been funded.[22] Cantor suggested trying these keywords: "success, culture, media, games, social norm, lawyers, museum, leisure, stimulus," and offered two examples, both of them game-related: "Recently, however NSF has funded some more questionable projects—$750,000 to develop computer models to analyze the on-field contributions of soccer players and $1.2 million to model the sound of objects breaking for use by the video game industry." As the public grants database reports, I was not the person who managed review of either of these grants.

Writing in *USA Today*, Dan Vergano offered the facts about Cantor's two examples, under the accusatory title "How Some Politicians Stumble on Science." After checking with NSF, he reports,

> The soccer study turns out to be computer scientists studying how remotely connected teams form to conduct "nanoscience, environmental engineering, earthquake engineering, chemical sciences, media research and tobacco research." And the "breaking things" study turns out to be acoustics experts "pursuing fundamental advances in computational methods while solving several particularly challenging sound rendering problems," so that the U.S. military, among others, can create more realistic combat simulators for troops.[23]

The results of the "breaking things" study, which was actually called "Sound Rendering for Physically Based Simulation," could be applied to games, and also could have many other applications, but the study is fundamental research at the intersection of computer simulation and acoustics, developing methods to synthesize the sounds produced by many kinds of physical events.[24]

Vergano may have been wrong, or at least incomplete, when he implied in his title that incompetence—or political cynicism—was responsible for the public criticism of research studies by politicians. It is possible, although evidence is lacking, that opposition to game research partly reflects the worldly asceticism that Max Weber said marked traditional Protestantism, and the new gaming culture defies many Protestant traditions.[25] The prominence given to Nardi's book in Coburn's December 2010 report—with its cover picture of a Night Elf priest from *World of Warcraft*, hints at an awareness that a culture war is in progress, and a significant fraction of the public is prepared to scorn elves and cultic priestesses in favor of well-established religion.

The publisher had asked me to read Nardi's manuscript and published part of my response on its back cover: "World of Warcraft is the best representative of a significant new technology, art form, and sector of society: the theme-oriented virtual world. Bonnie Nardi's pioneering transnational ethnography explores this game both sensitively and systematically using the methods of cultural anthropology and aesthetics with intensive personal experience as a guild member, media teacher, and magical quest Elf." It is worth noting that she played the game on her own time, as I did for my own book on *World of Warcraft*, and neither of us used tax money to do so. Her government grant was specifically for the part of her research comparing the use of the new technology in China versus in the United States, a worthy research project whatever side one takes in the American culture war, and it was entirely legitimate for her to recapitulate portions of that research in her book.

The cover of Nardi's book was also featured in a report about alleged waste and abuse, *The National Science Foundation: Under the Microscope*, issued May 26, 2011, by Senator Coburn.[26] The senator is entirely correct that all government agencies must serve taxpayers efficiently, and any waste is to be deplored. However, he advocates terminating funding for the social sciences at NSF and greatly reducing educational efforts, which can be explained as an expression of his position in the culture wars. The social sciences, of necessity, call into question all the standard institutions and doctrines of society, although hopefully without any distorting bias against any of them. All human cultures are problematic, including the new cyberculture to which gameworlds belong. For many years, the evangelical Christian groups that are a big part of Coburn's constituency have warned against the many videogames they consider sacrilegious, and as this book makes clear the fantasy religions in the gameworlds are only very seldom Christian, and very frequently Pagan in nature.[27]

It is revealing that while Coburn's report on NSF especially targets the social sciences, the examples given chiefly concern human-centered computing, online social media, and games. My own position on the cultural battlefield is suggested by the fact that of all program officers managing grants criticized by Senator Coburn, I manage by far the largest number, which anyone can discover by inspecting the online grant abstracts he cites. There is much to praise about efforts to reduce waste in government, and I welcome Senator Coburn and his supporters to read this book. If they wish, they can conceptualize it as a travelogue of an alien nation with which they are currently at war.

The Lay of the Land

Given that computer gameworlds have become a political battleground, it is worth charting this contested territory, from the perspective of the attackers. Shortly before this book went to press, Senator Coburn issued another Wastebook, so this section will use four reports from his office, to catalog all the game-related government investments his staff criticized. While many of the examples were NSF grants, some received funding from other agencies. Not infrequently, the grant itself was not really about games, or only partly about them, but here I will consider all the examples in the four reports that Coburn's staff categorized in terms of computer games. The point is not so much to rebut the criticisms leveled against particular government-funded project as to sketch the wide range of scientific questions that game research can explore, and to identify many of the ways in which games can be valuable for society. Any particular scientific research project is capable of failing, and transformative research is typically risky. Sufficient information will be provided here so that the reader can check the final results of any of the projects, many of which were very far from conclusion when I wrote these pages.

Coburn's reports may or may not interpret information correctly, but they provide hundreds of references, often in the form of links to websites belonging to the funding agency or to the university or other organization that received the funding, including links to the online abstracts of the NSF grants listed in table 2.3. All NSF grants have unique seven-digit identifier numbers, which are generally given in Coburn's reports, and the online database of all grants allows one to search by this number or by keywords in a description of the grant. Anybody in the world can access this database at http://www.nsf.gov/awardsearch/, and all of the information reported here is in the public record. I have already quoted the abstract of one of Nardi's grants, and every grant has such an abstract. As in the case of her grant, many also list publications related in some way to the grant. Each abstract also gives contact information for the principal investigator. Imagine—and this is certainly a fantasy—that a grant had been given to Robert E. Howard to write his Conan stories, on which the *Age of Conan* MMO was based. His contact information might be given as: Robert E. Howard rehoward@conanuniversity.edu. To find his academic home page, one merely enters into Google: "Robert E. Howard site:conanuniversity.edu." I did this for all the real grants listed here, in order to learn more about the project.

Table 2.3 begins with grants I have already discussed. I should note that the four Coburn reports also list a large number of grants to study online social networking, and looking them up in the online database reveals they tend to be made by the same programs and managed by the same program directors as the game-related research projects. Thus, cultural traditionalists believe that the new forms of online social life that have become so important in postmodern American culture—and so financially significant worldwide—are frivolous or subversive of traditional values. The two collaborative grants about older adult cognition are listed separately, because while they support the same project, they were made to different institutions with two coequal principal investigators, Anne McLaughlin at North Carolina State University and Maribeth Coleman at Georgia Institute of Technology.

Following the McLaughlin and Coleman grants in the table is a very successful project carried out by a remarkably productive team of researchers that studied the social and economic dynamics of the MMO with which I begin the next chapter, *EverQuest II*. Anyone who explores Noshir Contractor's website, or

Table 2.3 Grants Relating to Gameworlds and Avatars in Senator Coburn's Reports

Coburn's Description	Official Title	Grant ID	Investigator	Institution
Studying World of Warcraft and Other Virtual Games	Creative Collaboration in an Online Game	0829952	Bonnie Nardi	University of California, Irvine
Studying World of Warcraft and Other Virtual Games	Decentralized Virtual Activities and Technologies: A Socio-Technical Approach	0808783	Walt Scacchi	University of California, Irvine
Research: Marketing Video Games to the Elderly	Improving Older Adult Cognition: The Unexamined Role of Games and Social Computing Environments	0905127	Anne McLaughlin	North Carolina State University
Research: Marketing Video Games to the Elderly	Improving Older Adult Cognition: The Unexamined Role of Games and Social Computing Environments	0904855	Maribeth Coleman	Georgia Institute of Technology
What are the group dynamics like in the online video game EverQuest 2?	Virtual Worlds: An Exploratorium for Theorizing and Modeling the Dynamics of Group Behavior	0729505, 0841583	Noshir Contractor	University of Illinois at Urbana-Champaign; Northwestern University
What are the group dynamics like in the online video game EverQuest 2?	Virtual Worlds: An Exploratorium for Theorizing and Modeling the Dynamics of Group Behavior	0729421	Jaideep Srivastava	University of Minnesota, Twin Cities

Question	Title	Grant	PI	Institution
What are the group dynamics like in the online video game EverQuest 2?	Instrumenting Behaviors and Attitudes in Virtual Worlds	0628036	Dmitri Williams	University of Illinois at Urbana-Champaign
What are the group dynamics like in the online video game EverQuest 2?	Instrumenting Behaviors and Attitudes in Virtual Worlds	0628072	Daniel Hunter	University of Pennsylvania
What is the relationship between online virtual world users and their avatar?	The Avatar-Self Relationship: An Exploratory Study of Identity Negotiation in Second Life	0848692	Ulrike Schultze	Southern Methodist University
Where is the line between work and play in online virtual worlds?	Productive Play: The Convergence of Play and Labor in Online Games and Virtual Worlds	0744197	Celia Pearce	Georgia Institute of Technology
How do people interact in digital worlds?	Transformed Social Interaction in Virtual Environments	0527377	Jeremy Bailenson	Stanford University
How do people interact in digital worlds?	Exploring the Behavioral and Facial Similarities of Humans and Their Virtual Representations	0741753	Jeremy Bailenson	Stanford University
How do people interact in digital worlds?	Virtual Worlds: Scalability and Content Creation	0835601	Vladlen Koltun	Stanford University

(continued)

Table 2.3 (*continued*)

Coburn's Description	Official Title	Grant ID	Investigator	Institution
Can you trust other people in virtual worlds?	Virtual Civility, Trust, and Avatars: Ethnology in Second Life	0942997	Eiko Ikegami	New School
Can avatars in online virtual worlds become more socially engaging?	Virtual Environments and Behavior	9873432	Jack Loomis	University of California, Santa Barbara
Can avatars in online virtual worlds become more social engaging?	Explorations of Virtual Environments as a Methodological Tool in Social Psychology	9872084	James Blascovich	University of California, Santa Barbara
Can avatars in online virtual worlds become more social engaging?	Advanced Training Institute in Social Psychology: Immersive Virtual Environment Technology	0129717	James Blascovich	University of California, Santa Barbara
Can avatars in online virtual worlds become more social engaging?	Virtual Environment Technology and Eyewitness Identification	0219399	James Blascovich	University of California, Santa Barbara
Can avatars in online virtual worlds become more socially engaging?	Using Virtual Environment Technology to Understand and Augment Social Interaction	0205740	James Blascovich	University of California, Santa Barbara

Can avatars in online virtual worlds become more social engaging?	Design and Evaluation of Socially Engaging Avatars	0915472	James Blascovich	University of California, Santa Barbara
Can avatars in online virtual worlds become more social engaging?	Design and Evaluation of Socially Engaging Avatars	0914965	Zhigang Deng	University of Houston
A Recession-Inspired Video Game	Values at Play: Integrating Ethical and Political Factors into System Design	0613867, 0924088	Mary Flanagan	Hunter College; Dartmouth College
Does playing FarmVille on Facebook help people to make friends and keep them?	The Role of Social Network Sites in Facilitating Collaborative Processes	0916019	Nicole Ellison	Michigan State University
Zoo Receives Federal Funding to Develop Online Video Game "Wolfquest"	WolfQuest: Learning through Gameplay	0610427	Grant Spickelmier	Minnesota Zoo Foundation
What would it have been like to attend the 1960s New York World's Fair?	Interconnections: Revisiting the Future	0840297	Lori Walters	University of Central Florida
Taxpayer Money Pays for "RapidGuppy" Cell Phone Game	Experiencing Evolution: Integrating Mobile Gaming and Multimedia to Extend Informal Evolution Education	1111627	David Reznick	University of California, Riverside

reads publications that resulted from the research, will see that there really was a set of four grants, one of which acquired a second grant number when Contractor changed universities, involving a team of four principal investigators. Visiting their individual websites reveals that the team has been publishing around one scientific article per month, and that a large number of students and other researchers have been creatively involved. For example, the website of Dmitri Williams, who is now at the University of Southern California, lists a huge number of game-related academic publications, in which this leading young scholar has collaborated with a vast team of people with overlapping specialties.[28]

Like Nardi and Scacchi, Williams contributed a chapter to *Online Worlds*, focusing on one of his main research questions: To what extent do people use avatars to explore alternate identities?[29] One can easily see why this topic might disturb some conservatives, because they do not believe people should possess ambiguous gender, multiple personalities, and assumed names. Williams is not an advocate for such things but a scientific researcher who seeks to understand the facts about how people express themselves through the new technologies. Many of the other researchers listed in table 2.3 also study the relationships between avatars and their users, including Celia Pearce and Jeremy Bailenson, who also contributed chapters to *Online Worlds*.[30] Each of them takes a somewhat different approach to this complex topic, including developing design principles and new techniques that will be valuable for the computer and communications industries.

The grant titled "The Role of Social Network Sites in Facilitating Collaborative Processes," with Nicole Ellison for its principal investigator, does not even mention games in its abstract, let alone naming Farmville. Rather, it is a study centering on Facebook, having a very solid scientific focus:

Collaboration, when it works, optimizes the contributions of individuals, often resulting in better decisions, outcomes, and experiences than individuals working alone. Social network sites (SNSs) offer new opportunities for collaboration due to their social and technical affordances. SNS profiles enable the display of identity information, which can act as a social lubricant and help individuals initiate conversations and find common ground. Within SNSs, contact lists lower the transaction costs associated with interaction. Finally, SNSs enable access to a larger pool of individuals (and their wider and more diverse knowledge base) while also providing a context in which social capital processes serve as a mechanism for encouraging collaboration, advice-giving and information-sharing. This project will develop and test a model of SNS-enabled collaboration motivated by the following research questions: What forms of collaboration are enabled by SNSs? How do the features of SNSs affect these processes? Who uses these sites to collaborate and why?[31]

Of course one of the ways Facebook links people together is by offering games like Farmville, many of which are social, and this fact is mentioned in publications resulting from the grant.[32] Bonnie Nardi, Nicole Ellison, and Ellison's co-principal investigator, Clifford Lampe, have argued that Senator Coburn and his staff lacked a sophisticated understanding of social science, and secondary reports about science in the popular press often impart erroneous impressions in the minds of the general public as well as politicians.[33] But it also seems to be the case that the senator's staff did not contact any of the scientists whose work they attack, never seeking solid information about what the research really entailed or giving the scientists the opportunity to respond to criticisms. Rather, they treated each attack on a scientific study as a move in a game, seeking to gain advantage for their side in a political contest. Bluffing, misrepresentation, and bullying can be good tactics in many games, and it may be the case that all political parties engage in them.

The grants listed at the end of table 2.3 concern educational applications of gaming technologies. Both the Spickelmier and Walters grants are managed by my colleague Arlene de Strulle, who contributed a chapter to a reference work I edited, *Leadership in Science and Technology*. Writing with Joseph Psotka, who has extensive experience with training games produced for the military, she explores not only the potential of computer games and virtual reality (VR) to educate people for life in the world of the future but also the barriers that have prevented educational institutions from realizing this potential:

> Whether to counter misconceptions, provide access to normally unperceivable phenomena of Earth's systems and processes and inaccessible environments, or immerse students in exciting, motivating adventures with incidental but important meaning, games and VR technologies offer unprecedented educational opportunities. These opportunities may never fit into the existing framework of education unless current approaches to the use of educational technologies change. VR and games can stretch and shape students' minds in ways that have not yet been explored by educators in large-scale implementations. This is disruptive technology at its core.[34]

The four Coburn reports also criticize three game-related projects funded by agencies other than NSF. Political conservatives often list the Commerce Department among agencies that ought to be shut down, because they do not believe government should do anything that might favor one private enterprise versus another, and this may be why Coburn criticized the Commerce Department for supporting development of the videogame industry in Massachusetts.[35] A grant to the International Center for the History of Electronic Games to preserve classic games may seem frivolous to many taxpayers,[36] but this criticism could be leveled against any use of taxpayer money for museums, or any "recreational" facilities such as national parks and sports stadiums. Indeed, it is quite reasonable to argue that government should not invest in culture in a multicultural society, especially not in a free-market, egalitarian society that makes no distinction between "high culture" and "popular entertainment." However, electronic games are an important part of our culture that may not be preserved for future generations without special effort.

Conservatives, as well as people of other political persuasions, worry whenever computer technology is used to change human behavior, and this may be part of Coburn's opposition to funding from the National Institutes of Health for a game to combat obesity by teaching good nutritional practices. However, the official description of the project makes it sound like political action on behalf of President Obama, specifically mentioning his wife: "Virtual Sprouts: Web-Based Gardening Games is an interactive and simulated version of the First Lady's Organic Garden in a game-based environment that will target subjects from low income, minority populations in Los Angeles, including children ages 8 to 11, their parents, other family members, teachers and the community."[37] A December 2010 report, *Designing a Digital Future*, from the President's Council of Advisors on Science and Technology and issued directly from the Obama White House, says researchers should work in this area:

> *Games for learning, and immersive environments*: Develop and evaluate "serious games" that combine the engaging experience of electronic games with a serious educational purpose. Create immersive environments that can emulate situations in which students apply what they have learned. Devise tools to make the development of games and environments easier, cheaper, and more practical for teachers.[38]

Thus there are many reasonable criticisms of public support for games research and education, including the simple fact that one team in the current political game promotes such projects. While I am prepared to argue that the research is necessary, and that the educational applications are promising, the key point here is that the value of the new technologies is contested. The best place to seek the radical perspective the conservatives oppose is not in the Washington political arena but in the gameworlds themselves.

The Final Frontier

Most games described here belong to the fantasy genre, rather than to the adjacent science fiction genre, which has less interest in the supernatural. But science fiction provides a good perspective on secular alternatives. Many scholars, including many with training in one or another branch of religious studies, have remarked upon the religious significance of the *Star Trek* tradition.[39] It been expressed in several computer games, of which two will be described here: *Star Trek Deep Space Nine: The Fallen* and *Star Trek Online* (STO). In their introduction to *Star Trek and Sacred Ground*, a collection of essays by a dozen authors all writing about this topic, Jennifer Porter and Darcee McLaren explain: "An underlying and consistent theme of the *Star Trek* series is the presentation of rational scientific humanism as an alternative to religious faith. A new theme, notably found in episodes from the *Deep Space Nine* and *Voyager* series, explores the potentially positive value of religion."[40] These words were written before the fifth *Star Trek* series, but some authors in the volume additionally explore some of the motion pictures. All authors agree that the early *Star Trek* episodes strongly expressed secular humanism and often criticized religion, but they suggest two different but mutually reinforcing reasons for the moderate shift that occurred later in *Star Trek*'s history.

First, *Star Trek* originally expressed the visions of one man, Gene Roddenberry. I met him at a conference sponsored by a secular humanist group, the Committee for the Future, back in 1972, but my perspective on his ideology comes primarily from watching most of the episodes when they were first broadcast, and from reading much more recent publications. Clearly, he was a critic of religion and possessed great enthusiasm for the potential of science and technology to transform human life for the better. He died in 1991, and his influence over the series had already attenuated to some degree even before his death. But even during his tenure as "Great Bird of the Universe," like other commercially successful television programs, *Star Trek* adjusted to match the perspective of its audience.

Second, public admiration of science and technology may have peaked with the Apollo missions to the moon and declined afterward, even as religious sentiments became important again in public culture—at least in the United States, where *Star Trek* was produced. The authors who suggest this idea do not go deeply into the sociology of modern religion, so they do not present compelling evidence. However, their thesis is rather complicated because the religions shown in *Star Trek* tend to be fictional faiths belonging to extraterrestrial cultures, rather than popular faiths in contemporary culture. *Memory Alpha*, a high-quality *Star Trek* wiki, does have an article on Christianity, which lists several episodes mentioning this religion. A very few episodes include direct references. In some cases the link is very weak—for example, to the presence of a Bible being among the books on a bookshelf. Other cases are perhaps incongruous, such as the scene in which the agnostic engineer Scott plays "Amazing Grace" on his bagpipes at the funeral of the Vulcan science officer, Spock, who definitely was not a Christian.[41]

In the *Star Trek* mythos, the frontier of exploration is seemingly outer space, yet the technological means of spaceflight in this tremendously influential region of popular culture is unrealistic in the extreme. Not only do we not know how to travel faster than the speed of light or beam somebody directly from an orbiting spaceship to the surface of a planet, but all the discoveries of physics indicate that these feats of magic are impossible in our universe. A deeper reading of *Star Trek* suggests that the final frontier is not really outer space but the human soul, as the stories really concern self-discovery, interpersonal conflict, and tensions between mutually alien cultures. How this mythos relates to religion can be seen in the differences between four cultures—human, Bajoran, Vulcan, and Klingon. *The Fallen* is a solo-player game dating from 2000 that depicts a hunt for three sacred orbs associated with the planet Bajor, and *Star Trek Online* (STO) is an extremely complex massively multiplayer online game that I studied from its launch in February 2010 as it developed over its first two years, and which includes Bajoran, Vulcan, and Klingon characters. The episodes of the television series *Deep Space Nine* take place in the years 2369–2375; STO is precisely set in the year 2409; and the entire mythos claims to depict the real human future.

Although several different species belong to the United Federation of Planets, the roughly thousand *Star Trek* stories tend to revolve around humans, with an occasional alien who very closely resembles humans. Except for rare visits to San Francisco, where Starfleet headquarters is located, we see almost nothing about future terrestrial society outside Starfleet, and Starfleet itself is an overwhelmingly secular institution. Some of the stories revolve around religion, but chiefly in two very secular ways. First, when Starfleet encounters a religious culture, it is almost always a primitive one, while the culture represented by Starfleet itself appears to lack religion. Second, on occasion Starfleet encounters what appears to be a God, but it always turns out to be a nonsupernatural member of a technically more advanced society. The most striking and frequently encountered example is Q, a superior being from the Q Continuum who has the power to change human reality with a sweep of his hand, yet he himself has all the foibles of a human and belongs to a society of many Qs not very different from ordinary people. In the rather marvelous novel *I, Q*, all reality begins to go literally down the drain.[42] Q himself is traumatized by what is happening, but in the end he discovers that no superior being is at fault, but the Q-like avatar of an ordinary human.

The Bajorans are central to the *Deep Space Nine* series, the third of five television manifestations of *Star Trek* and the only one that emphasizes long story arcs connecting many episodes. The planet Bajor has just been liberated from occupation by the fascist Cardassians, and the deep Bajoran religious traditions were intensified by the agonies they suffered under Cardassian rule. Although Bajor had developed interstellar flight several centuries before humans did, they had not expanded far, and their society remained focused on their home planet with its ancient culture. The TV series and *The Fallen* take place soon after the human-dominated Federation had taken over a Cardassian space station, which they renamed Deep Space Nine and moved to a newly discovered wormhole into another universe, which they discovered near Bajor. Early episodes of the TV series reveal that Bajoran religion is based on actual facts, but which the Federation interprets as resulting from contact with an advanced technological civilization, not so advanced as Q but still far beyond their own abilities, rather than from contact with supernatural beings, as the Bajorans believe.

Four episodes of the first season of *Deep Space Nine* focused on Bajoran religion, and the last of them, "In the Hands of the Prophets," is especially noteworthy. Biologist Keiko O'Brien—a Japanese woman married to an Irishman and thus representing humans in general—has established a school for the dozen children on the space station. She teaches them about the wormhole, describing it as the technological creation of an advanced species of extraterrestrials, whom Commander Sisko, the commanding officer of Deep Space Nine, has met but who remain mysterious. *Memory Alpha* begins its summary of the episode thus: "Vedek Winn Adami, a Bajoran religious leader, visits Deep Space Nine. She finds Keiko O'Brien's school, and denounces her for teaching about the Wormhole in a scientific way, instead of teaching the Bajoran religious view that the Wormhole is the Celestial Temple and the home of the Prophets. She calls Keiko's teaching blasphemy, and drives a rift between the Bajorans on the station and Starfleet."[43] Vedeks are the 112 leaders of Bajoran religion, and Winn Adami was cynically leading a fundamentalist movement in order to become *kai*, the Bajoran equivalent of pope. After a debate in which Keiko refuses to abandon science in her teachings, Winn orders a follower to firebomb the school, proving how deceitful she is by convincing the follower to suffer the consequences while escaping them herself. This critique of religion is softened by the presence of another Vedek, Bareil Antos, whose faith is much more liberal.

Over the past ten thousand years, nine orbs appeared in the skies over Bajor. Because this was when Bajoran science was still undeveloped, the orbs were given religious significance. Calling them the Tears of the Prophets, the Bajorans believed they were sent to guide Bajor along the paths of wisdom, gifts from the supernatural prophets who dwelled within the Celestial Temple. The orbs did indeed possess power, but derived from advanced science rather than magic. The goal for a player in *The Fallen* is to control three additional orbs, associated in Bajoran lore with the Pah-wraiths, who were enemies of the prophets in ancient times and may have represented a breakaway faction of the extraterrestrial culture that created the wormhole. As *Memory Alpha* explains, "*The Fallen* focuses on the quest to find the lost orbs of the Pah-wraiths capable of releasing the 'fallen gods.' The Cardassians, the Dominion and the Bajorans are all eager to obtain the artifacts for their own purposes—and only the Federation stands in their way."[44]

The gameplay consists of finding one's way through mazes, figuring out how to unlock gateways, battling enemies along the way, and picking up various resources. To get the most out of the game, one plays it three times, experiencing the environments in different ways as three different characters: Sisko the human, Worf the Klingon, and Kira Nerys the Bajoran. The first two stages experienced by Kira communicate the religious significance for her people. Her story begins at a monastery on Bajor, and its second scene take place in a ruined temple. *Memory Alpha* is the wiki for canon *Star Trek* culture relating to the television series, while *Memory Beta* is an almost equal wiki covering noncanon lore beyond the fictional history of the television programs. *Memory Beta* outlines the first scene:

> Major Kira Nerys, during this time, was meeting with an old friend from the Bajoran Resistance called Obanak Keelen who lived at a monastery on Bajor. Obanak had become the leader of the heretical Cult of the Pah-Wraiths who believed that the Pah-Wraith were the True Prophets of Bajor. They also advocated that the Prophets were false gods who had abandoned the Bajorans in their time of need. Obanak asked Kira to put pressure on the Vedek Assembly to allow the cult to explore an ancient temple on Bajor's moon of Jeraddo. The monastery was attacked at this point by the terrorist group known as the Kahl-taan who had been secretly sent by the Vedek Assembly to deal with the heretical cult. Communications were damaged while enemy troops were beamed into the monastery. Eventually, Kira managed to restore communications with her runabout and transport the cult members off the planet and return to Deep Space 9.[45]

Obanak is an interesting character, and reflects one of *Star Trek*'s main strategies for building human interest into the stories—giving rich personalities to the characters who cause trouble. He is a friend of Kira, who is the most significant female character in *Deep Space Nine*. She had been a freedom fighter during the harsh Cardassian occupation of her planet and has strong attachments to Bajor's ancient religion. However, many episodes place her in the difficult position of dealing with competing factions within Bajoran religion, and she may have doubts stemming from the fact that the supernatural Prophets did nothing to prevent the Cardassian conquest of her planet. Obanak is a leading monk, called *prylar* in Bajoran, but he has concealed important facts about his actual status in the conflicted world of Bajoran religion:

> Prylar Obanak served in the Bajoran Resistance during the Cardassian Occupation of Bajor, during which time he became a friend of Kira Nerys. The occupation, however, shook his faith in the Prophets, making him vulnerable to conversion. This ultimately took place while he was working on a mining project on the Bajoran moon of Jeraddo, where he encountered one of the three orbs of the Pah-wraiths. Through the orb, the Pah-wraiths instructed him to locate the other two orbs in order to open their own Celestial Temple. Obanak did not reveal his possession of the orb, however, instead claiming he had been converted after reading a tablet in which the Pah-wraiths apparently predicted the occupation.[46]

One of the reports Kira wrote inside *The Fallen* praises her friend: "Let me make one thing clear, Obanak Keelen is a good man. During the occupation, Obanak fought with as much skill and courage as any cell leader in the Bajoran resistance. Obanak's attack on the Cardassian prison camps at Maar'saan saved tens of thousands of Bajoran lives. We fought together as comrades during the war." The second scene takes Kira, Sisko, and Worf to the temple on Jeraddo, without knowing that Obanak had obtained one of the three orbs there, collecting artifacts and making a copy of a mysterious mural that includes information about the orbs. After many battles and maze explorations, the game ends as Obanak performs a ritual uniting the orbs, giving him immense power, but ultimately locking him inside the new wormhole they create. Thus, Obanak is a tragic figure, in the classical sense of the term, basically good but being corrupted by hunger for power, in the grip of ancient passions and religious ideology.

The Vulcans, represented by Spock in the original *Star Trek* series, are a technologically advanced society that like the Bajorans refrained from aggressive penetration into portions of the galaxy already occupied by other civilizations. In order to limit violence, they have developed a culture that emphasizes control over their own emotions, and some of the rituals through which they do this have a quasi-religious quality. One is reminded about the debate here on Earth over whether Confucianism should be classified as a religion or as an ethical philosophy, because of its emphasis on developing wisdom rather than worshiping supernatural beings. A few episodes of the last TV series, *Enterprise*, take place in

P'Jem, a Vulcan monastery that can be found in *Star Trek Online*, but the place seems more like a spiritual retreat than a cathedral. A key Vulcan ethical principle is IDIC—Infinite Diversity in Infinite Combinations—which has some affinity to cultural relativism in anthropology because it celebrates the value of non-Vulcan cultures and thus encourages noninterference in the affairs of other societies, including primitive ones. The Federation enshrined this principle in the Prime Directive, which prohibits Starfleet from behaving like the navy of an aggressive colonial power, thus encouraging respect for religious societies, without acknowledging that their beliefs might possibly be true.[47]

The Klingons are depicted as a technologically advanced but culturally primitive feudal society, whose religion seems designed to encourage brutal conquest of other societies. They have nothing comparable to IDIC or the Prime Directive, and their religious traditions were bloodthirsty in the extreme. *Memory Alpha* explains:

> The Klingon Empire was founded some time in the 9th century by Kahless the Unforgettable, who performed many heroic feats including the unification of the Klingon people when he killed the tyrant Molor. Kahless came to be revered in Klingon society to the point of near-deification, and many aspects of Klingon culture came to revolve around an emulation of Kahless' life.
>
> Ritual was a very important element in Klingon society. While the Klingons were not a religious people as such, they did believe that deities existed at one time. However, Klingon warriors supposedly slew their gods as they were considered to be more trouble than they were worth.
>
> The Klingon afterlife was supposedly divided into two branches. The dishonored were taken to Gre'thor aboard the Barge of the Dead, a vessel captained by Kortar, the first Klingon. Kortar was supposedly the one who had originally killed the gods who created him and was condemned to ferry the dishonored to Gre'thor as a punishment. Once in Gre'thor, the dishonored were watched over by Fek'lhr, a vaguely Klingon-esque figure.
>
> Those who die honorably supposedly went to Sto-vo-kor, where Kahless was said to await them.[48]

The *Star Trek Online* quest arc that most centrally involves Klingon religion is "The Fek'Ihri Return," which I completed with my Klingon starship captain, Korbette. (Note that the exact spelling of Fek'Ihri is open to debate.) Inspired by the *Star Trek: Deep Space Nine* episode "The Sword of Kahless" and the earlier *Star Trek: The Next Generation* episode "Rightful Heir," this arc imagines that ancient enemies of Kahless have somehow returned from the dead to seize the Klingon Empire by stealth or force. A Klingon sword, called a *bat'leth*, is a two-handed scythe-like weapon, and Kahless is said to have crafted the first one over a thousand years ago. STO describes the four quests thus:

1. Blood of the Empire: Strange energy signals herald the return of the dread Fek'Ihri and your crew must fight to defend the homeworld.
2. Destiny: Stories say the Sword of Kahless is needed to defeat the Fek'Ihri. You will need the assistance of powerful allies to find it.
3. Afterlife: The Barge of the Dead awaits its newest passenger . . . you!
4. The Gates of Gre'thor: Storm the gates of Gre'thor and descend into the underworld. You will need to face Fek'Ihr himself to survive!

"Blood of the Empire" begins with a spaceship battle followed by a difficult land battle to reach the Shrine of Kahless on a planet in the Boreth system. There Korbette meditated and fell into a trance, awakening on the Barge of the Dead. This ship of the dead was clearly inspired by the Greek myths about Charon, the ferryman who conveys the souls of the dead to Hades. On the ship she confronts the Ferryman, who says: "I am the first Klingon ever to draw breath. In my day I was more powerful than even the gods. But they grew jealous of my might and scorned me. I could not allow this insult to my honor to pass, so I slew them. In punishment for my sin, I must spend eternity here. My task is to take the souls of the condemned to Gre'thor. All those who die in dishonor come to me." Note how different Klingon religion is from Christianity. The gods are merely powerful beings, having no moral superiority, yet dishonor is a sin that inevitably will be punished. There is no talk of mercy or humility.

Korbette reveals her own fearlessness by liberating the slaves from their oars, and defeating Herron, Lord of the Dead. She commands the ship to Gre'thor, where the souls of the dead assist her in breaking through the gates. At this point, Korbette faces three specters that represent the three chief concerns that motivated Klingon religion, which are rather different from the Ten Commandments of Judeo-Christianity or the eleventh Christian commandment, "Love thy neighbor." Each is personified by a gigantic warrior, each of whom explained what he represents before seeking to destroy Korbette:

COWARDICE: I am the shadow of fear. I am the dark hand that clutches your heart and closes your throat before battle. I am the doubt that forces you to flee. I am the anguish of the damned who die in their beds.
DISHONOR: I am failure, and I am regret. I am the challenge not given. I am the falsehoods that drip from your tongue like poisoned honey. I am the insult accepted without response, and the warrior who dies in captivity.

TREACHERY: I am the blade in the back. I am the whispered rumor that destroys honor. I am an alliance with an enemy. I am the victory won without honor. I am the plot that harms a fellow warrior, and the soul sold for latinum.

Latinum is the most valued currency of the Ferengi species, who are interstellar merchants for whom the chief commandments are Rules of Acquisition, three of which read: "Never allow family to stand in the way of opportunity"; "Never place friendship above profit"; and "Home is where the heart is, but the stars are made of latinum."[49] Thus, the faith of the Klingons contrasts completely with the avaricious philosophy of capitalism, represented by the Ferengi, and expresses the ethic of a bloodthirsty feudal society. This does not imply that the Klingons are unified, because their competing clans, or *houses*, carry out a form of limited warfare within Klingon society. Other missions in *Star Trek Online* concern this internecine struggle, but "The Fek'Ihri Return" concerns their unification under Kahless.

The next enemy defeated by Korbette was the resurrected spirit of the enemy of Kahless, Molor. Then she meets Kahless himself, who praises her: "I see the change in your heart, Captain. You have faced Cowardice, Dishonor and Treachery and lived to tell the tale. You have looked Death in the eye, and not been cowed. I am honored to fight at your side. You are truly one of the greatest warriors of your age." Together they must face the leader of the reborn Fek'Ihri, and in explaining this, Kahless notes: "Whether this abomination was spat out of the fiery pits of Gre'thor or created by an unholy use of science is of no matter. It must die."

STO leaves open the questions of whether all of this arc of battle was real or whether parts of it were hallucinations or a dream brought on by meditating at the Shrine of Kahless. The ultimate victory was real, and Korbette was rewarded by Chancellor J'mpok of the Klingon High Council. As in the television episode "Rightful Heir," Kahless may not have been a supernatural resurrection of the original hero, but a technological clone of him. In any case, the entire religious culture of the Klingons is radically different from Christianity, as well as from the secular humanism of Starfleet.

Something well in excess of a thousand of the missions available in *Star Trek Online* were created not by the game designers but by players, using a marvelous software system called the Foundry. One of them perfectly captures the Starfleet perspective. My Starfleet tactical officer, John Bainbridge, was the 921st person to complete "The Return to Terra Nova," created by a player who called himself Kirkfat. "Terra Nova" was an episode of *Enterprise*, the fifth *Star Trek* series, originally broadcast October 24, 2001. It tells the tale of the first human colony outside the solar system, which broke contact soon after it was established and suffered a devastating asteroid impact that forced their descendants to live in caverns, where they have forgotten their ties to Earth. Archer, the commander of the Enterprise, struggled to reestablish ties to the planet and convince them to migrate to the "overside" from their caverns, in order to escape the long-term effects of this disaster. In Kirkfat's mission, a distress call sent John to Terra Nova on a science vessel called the USS *Durkheim*, commanded by Captain Maxwell Weber, clearly references to pioneer sociologists of religion Émile Durkheim and Max Weber.[50]

The planet now is a theocracy, led by a renegade anthropologist from Earth named Kurtzan—presumably named after the renegade trader Kurtz from *Heart of Darkness* by Joseph Conrad[51]—who has recently died, just when his followers urgently needed medical supplies. John encounters a couple of dozen people kneeling at the base of a great pyramid and bowing before him as he approaches. Elder Nadeline rejoices:

> Blessed are the prophecies. The Archers come again. Lord Kurtzan will now make the great ascent. Our faith has been redeemed. . . . We praise you, holy Archers. . . . What is dug on the sacred stones now sees the light of the overside. The Archers return to walk the path of the Novan people, to leap the carved rocks, and to make the great ascent. We cherish the Archers' great climb. We pray for the descent of the serums.

In the ascent of the pyramid, John is required to read two sacred stones, then enter the temple at the peak, where he finds the body of the anthropologist beside his message urging medical help for the Novans: "I pray that you also preserve the Novan religion. It may be full of fallacies, but it has unified and inspired the Novans to continuing living on the 'overside.' It has been a source of cultural progress and technological advance. It has become the essence of their culture." John delivers a sacred stone to the suppliants, plus the needed medicine. He beams out the body of the anthropologist, who had become the Novans' god, and whom they now believe had indeed magically ascended to heaven, because the technology of teleportation was not yet part of their culture. This player-created mission clearly implies that humans will be intensely religious only if their culture has regressed to a primitive stage of development.

Conclusion

The great game currently being played between fundamentalist religion and secular humanism will not be won or lost for many years, but the current round seems to be a draw. Federal funding of games research continued at the point in time when this book was completed, yet its future remained very much in doubt. In the wider scheme of things, this may be insignificant, yet it illuminates the potentially decisive culture wars that may determine the course of human history, for better or worse. Also illuminated is the contrast between faith and fantasy, the key theme of this book, foreshadowing the related themes that define the following chapters. If secular humanism were to triumph ultimately, its last moves in the struggle would be like those of a chess match. Perhaps both bishops would be toppled, followed by a final assault on the opponent's king. His name, incidentally, is God.

3 DEITIES

Gods perform many functions in human culture, but prominent among them are *compensation* and *conceptualization*. As the New Paradigm in the sociology of religion explains, gods serve as the exchange partners of last resort, the superhuman helpers we beg for assistance when all else fails. When Napoleon asked astronomer Pierre-Simon Laplace why he did not mention God in his writings, Laplace supposedly replied, "I had no need of that hypothesis."[1] Sociology offers many data-supported hypotheses about religion, but none of them require the actual existence of gods, and an unneeded hypothesis is functionally equivalent to a false hypothesis. Religious beliefs are compensators, based on supernatural explanations, and as such they serve not only to pacify frustrations or fears but also to conceptualize the universe. Each of many gods can personify a particular moral concept or natural force. The compensatory function of gods is emphasized in monotheism, and their conceptual function is emphasized in polytheism, but both are important in both. Because the goal of fantasy gameworlds is providing never-ending adventures within a complex narrative that transcends mundane reality, they tend to be polytheistic, postulating a pantheon of deities that play different roles, none of which monopolize the action, as a single god would do, or treat the player like a pawn in a god game.

Readers who have never explored an online fantasy gameworld may find it difficult to imagine the experience. *EverQuest II* (EQII) will provide a good in-depth introduction, both because it is a high-quality classic example and because gods play important roles in it. Released in 2004, it is the sequel to *EverQuest*, which was launched quite early in the history of MMOs, in 1999. EQII is a fully three-dimensional visual environment, in which the user runs an avatar through a series of adventures usually organized in quests, which are assignments given the avatar by a quest-giver nonplayer character (NPC). The world of EQII is called Norrath, and it is a vast world indeed. Over the years, EQII has been improved and expanded, and it remains visually quite impressive, offering at the time of my research late in 2010 a vast virtual world consisting of thirty-four zones possessing a wide range of environments, plus many additional areas, including twenty-seven "shared dungeons" and at least eighty major "instances" attached to the huge zones.[2] An explorer experiences Arctic ice in Everfrost, desert heat in the Sinking Sands, and every other kind of somewhat realistic setting from jungles to cities. The different lands are islands, including three fantastic archipelagos in Overrealm, where the islands float not in the sea but in the sky.

Travel within a zone is accomplished in several ways, the simplest of which is walking. Between some locations, it is possible to ride more swiftly, borrowing a horse, bird, or magic carpet. At great expense, it is also possible to buy a mount for currency earned inside EQII through completing quests or looting the bodies of fallen enemies, by buying special in-game currency for real-world dollars, or in the case of cute dragons used in some advanced areas simply by completing a series of high-level missions. Travel from one island to another is done by means of teleportation, only possible at certain key portals. Some portals appear to operate on the basis of a fantastic technology, whereas others have a religious basis.

Long ago, the gods abandoned Norrath, leaving its people to fend for themselves as whole continents were shattered. Then through Faydark and the Butcherblock Mountains they crept back and tried to regain their lost status as lords of all the lands. One was a goddess named Tunare, the Mother of All, who had situated teleportation rings of stone, slightly smaller versions of Stonehenge, at points distant from the other portals. As an EQII wiki explains, "With the return of Tunare, Her Druids have rediscovered the secret of travel to Her sacred stone rings. The problem was never in their training of the prayers of transportation, but in the rings themselves! The High Priestess has brought the Mother's teachings back and with it the ritual to re-consecrate the stone rings."[3]

To explore Norrath, I needed an avatar. In general, I find it useful to create a character whose interests and personality fit the environment and the kind of exploration I intend to conduct. This practice really began decades ago when I carried out covert ethnographic research inside a number of real religious movements, notably two that were historically related to each other, Scientology[4] and the Process Church of the Final Judgment.[5] Subsequently, both groups were happy when they saw my publications, but they had not realized I was studying them, and thought I was an ordinary member. This research was done around 1970, prior to the development of academic norms against covert observation, and it is not clear I was any less a real member than all the other members, who were using the groups for their own selfish purposes. Thus, I had developed role-playing as a standard sociological research technique, involving concepts like *reflexivity*, the realization that all social science is conducted from the unique perspective of the researcher, but that perspective can be adjusted to produce the best research results.[6]

To study the ambivalent relationship between gods and humans in EQII, I decided to base my avatar on a real person in my own family whose life was closely related to religion, yet who had a legitimate grievance against God. Her name was Cleora Bainbridge, and she was born on November 8, 1868, in Cleveland, Ohio. Her father, William, was a Baptist minister, and her mother, Lucy, later became the head of the Woman's Branch of the New York City Mission Society. Cleora was named after Lucy's living mother and dead sister, thus symbolizing the way naming connects people across generations and bridges between life and death. Young Cleora would have experienced a great adventure exploring the world in 1879–1880, when her parents traveled fifty thousand miles to visit Protestant missions throughout Asia and wrote influential books about missionary work.[7] However, she did not live to experience much of life, dying only a little past her first birthday from what her death record called "water on the brain."[8]

Little remains of baby Cleora outside her grave beyond a single photograph, her father's comment she was a "naturally strong and healthy child,"[9] and a poignant short story written by her mother which contains no real information about her daughter but expresses her mother's profound grief: "The Christian parents could in submission say, 'It is well, since God wills it so,' but the mother's heart was aching still for the earthly presence. She longed for a sight of the sunny face and the sound of the prattling lips so still. Heaven seemed too far away, and a long weary way ere she should reach it. How apt the sorrowing Christian heart is to forget the daily toil for Jesus, and 'look too eagerly beyond.'"[10]

If it were possible to resurrect Cleora, 140 years after her untimely death, I imagine she would be very ambivalent about deities, and that ambivalence might reveal itself in her choices. In creating Cleora in *EverQuest II*, the first choice was her *archetype*, whether she is to be a fighter, a scout, a priest, or a mage. Given her connection to religion, she had to be either a priest who heals other avatars or a mage who is well adapted for solo exploration, using magic for both offense and defense. Among mages, there are six class specializations: wizard, warlock, illusionist, coercer, necromancer, and the one she became, conjuror, which avoids the evil connotations of the other mage specializations and allowed her to explore interesting interactions with secondary avatars. The next choices were sex and race. It had already been decided she would be female, and the six available races were Human, Barbarian, Gnome, Erudite, the feline Kerra, and Half Elf. I chose the last of these, as another expression of Cleora's ambivalence, half human and half elf. Or, as a frequently told Norrath joke says, "Half Elves are now only 49.99999% Elves."

I had her photograph in mind as I made the final adjustments to her appearance, and I gave her red hair knowing that was the color of her mother's hair.

A novel published by her father when she would have been fifteen centers on a fifteen-year-old girl named Cleora. He wrote:

> Her hair was golden, her teeth perfect, and her emotions, as with those of her complexion, played over her features like sunbeams upon the clouds of the morning. "What an intelligent and interesting daughter you have," was frequently said to the fond parents. She was a real mother's child, already showing the same common sense and personal magnetism. Life being spared, she was sure to make her mark with both head-work and heart-work, and to become more and more attractive, while others were losing their charms.[11]

Life being spared! In the novel, Cleora became an overseas Protestant missionary, yet the book got her father in a good deal of trouble, because in its pages he satirized the self-serving behavior of some real missionaries he knew. Given that both of Cleora's parents wrote fiction in response to her death, and one of them portrayed her as a saint adventuring through a world of woe, I felt they would not mind me sending her on new adventures through *EverQuest II*, where much of the deeper meaning comes from satirizing religion.

Return of the Norrath Gods

When Cleora first entered Norrath, in the frigid northern islands, she began to notice that people she met (that is, nonplayer characters) were mentioning deities, almost in passing, during conversations about action and adventure. She learned that the area had been blessed by a god named Mithaniel Marr, but she heard more about a god named Brell. When Cleora offered to help Battlemaster Golben, he exclaimed, "Thank Brell!" Dolur Axebeard referred to dying as "going to see Brell," and Belka Thunderheart called life after death being "seated at Brell's table." Another time, Dolur spoke about how the Orcs burn the flesh of piles of their soldiers' dead bodies: "And sure as Brell is my maker, dreadful skeletons rise up out of the piles, ready to fight again." Belka referred to the glacier surrounding them as "Brell-forsaken ice." "Brell guide ye, Cleora," Dolur blessed her. However benevolent Marr might be, Brell seemed an especially interesting god.

On Cleora's behalf, I checked one of the wikis devoted to EQII and learned that Brell Serilis was also a very demanding god, dominating the lands under the surface of the earth:

> Followers of the Duke of Below find true happiness in the caves, caverns and tunnels that permeate the belly of Norrath, but this is one of few

points upon which all followers of Brell can agree. The Runny Eye Clan of goblins claim he is their father, much to the disgust of the dwarves of Kaladim who are certain that only the dwarves are the true children of Serilis. The vicious gnolls of Split Paw disagree entirely, for was it not Brell who sculpted them out of the sacred Clay of Cosgrove?[12]

Thus, three different races had competing Brellian sects, each convinced it was the chosen people of this subterranean deity—Goblins, Dwarves, and Gnolls. Another EQII wiki provided more of Brell's history, suggesting that a fourth race, the Kobolds, were also originally Brellian:

Brell Serilis was first to come to Norrath during the Age of Scale, and from his Plane of Underfoot, a dark realm of vast caves and endless tunnels, he quietly created a magical portal to a cavern deep in the belly of Norrath. Through this portal the Duke of Underfoot seeded the depths of Norrath with all manner of creatures. Brell then returned home, sealing his portal within a labyrinthine chamber of mystical Living Stone. During the Elder Age, he created the Dwarves as part of the gods' plan to keep watch over the dominant dragonkind. Later, Brell returned to create the gnomes, resembling dwarves to some extent, yet more wiry and gnarled, consumed with tinkering with devices more so than their cousins. It was due to Brell's abandonment of the Kobold race that some of them turned to worship of Rallos Zek through one of their own elder shamans Rolfron Zek, who Rallos made into the demi-god of despair.[13]

Ambivalent Half Elf that she was, Cleora did not rush to declare allegiance to a god, nor to leave her training grounds in the Arctic wastes to explore the wider world. Finally, after reaching experience level 25, she flew on a gryphon to the Butcherblock Mountains, a temperate zone where she developed her skills in gathering resources like minerals and herbs from the environment, battling a range of enemies, and gaining strength and diversity in magic spells. At level 26 she briefly visited the chief metropolis of Norrath, Qeynos, then visited for a time in Willow Wood, the suburban village where Half Elves lived. There she began her education in crafting, sampling all the major professions to transform raw material into manufactured objects. A crafting apprentice begins as a general artisan, then specializes in one of three main classes, followed by one of three subclasses: craftsman (carpenter, provisioner, woodworker), outfitter (weaponsmith, armorer, tailor), or scholar (alchemist, jeweler, sage). Given her reflective personality, she became first a scholar, then a sage, specializing in scribing spell upgrades useful for priests or for mages like her.

She was very excited to meet Daelyn Twinstar, the Half Elf Mentor, who first asked which of her parents was an Elf. Cleora replied that her mother was an Elf, and her father a Human. Daelyn explained this implied Cleora was a sentimentalist, and she was quick to agree. To help Cleora understand what it meant to be a Half Elf, Daelyn sent her to do jobs for two local residents, paying close attention to how they treated her. Both of them spoke harshly to her, but only one of them seemed motivated by prejudice against Half Elves. Daelyn explained, "It is true we are oft-judged because of our race, but we tend to share that trait ourselves. . . . We tend to assume humans and elves will look down upon us, and we tend to see examples of this even when it is not true." Daelyn then sent Cleora to help a male Human and a female Elf who were in love with each other, who may have held excessively positive stereotypes of the other's race, but in any case cherished rather than despised the differences between them.

Cleora returned to the Butcherblock Mountains, and only after reaching experience level 30 did she have a long conversation with Philosopher Rhime, the local deity historian, about which god she should follow. A level later she made her decision and went to Bronlor Stormhammer, Conservator of the Underfoot, to declare her allegiance to Brell. He told her the story of his own personal "epiphany," acknowledging that a spiritual experience was unusual for a technology-oriented Dwarf like himself. Bronlor was working deep underground when a cave-in trapped him hopelessly. For the first time in decades he prayed, and at first nothing happened. Just when he was about to surrender to despair, a Gnoll shaman saved him, saying that some intuition had inspired him to dig in Bronlor's direction. He concluded: "I can't explain it, but I believe the Duke saved me that day so that I may serve as his tool in these times. He is eager to find those still faithful to him. Remember, all that you stand upon and all that you see is built upon the earth. Let the Underfoot also serve as the foundation in your life."

Enthusiastically, Cleora undertook the first mission for Brell Serilis, the Duke of Below. "Building a Foundation of Devotion" required her to collect four samples of sacred ore, inside four very difficult labyrinths deep underground. Cleora was able simply to run past all the hordes of hostile monsters because she had already reached a much higher level of experience than a neophyte disciple of Brell would usually have achieved, and the mission instructions claimed it could be done at level 20. She concluded that followers of Brell would need to group into teams, yet given that members of a group of friends might choose to follow very different gods this seemed unlikely. Her rewards included a humble altar of Brell, which she set up in her home back in New Halas on the northern glacier.

The second quest for Brell, "Prospector of Lost Faith," first required Cleora to announce Brell's return to seven groups of enemies across Butcherblock Mountains, which was actually quite easy at the beginning, given Cleora's ability to sneak carefully around obstacles. But then she was required to complete a series of extremely difficult steps to retrieve the Chalice of Hope from deep within the Orc stronghold, Crushbone Keep. Supposedly, this could be accomplished at level 35, but as a solo quester Cleora failed at level 45, plunging her first into hopelessness, then into disgust at Brell's excessive demands. After gaining a degree of enlightenment from religious monks of the Ashen Order, at level 65 she returned to Crushbone Keep, retrieved the Chalice of Hope, and received as her prize a jewel that would have been valuable to an avatar at level 35 but was quite valueless to her at level 65. When next in New Halas, she gave the jewel back to Brell at his altar, and contemplated whether she should pray for him to give her something in return. Thinking he had treated her badly by assigning quests that were far too difficult to her, she concluded that bowing before him would be a humiliation she did not deserve.

The third Brell quest, "The Anguished Children of the Duke," required Cleora to retrieve three totems belonging to his worshippers among the Kobolds, a hostile race whose language she had learned but toward whom she felt no sympathy. This turned out to be rather easy at level 65, given that it was a level 55 quest, and she had fully expected Brell to make it too tough for her. Her visible reward was a nearly useless Underfoot Attendant, a bundle of rocks in the form of a little man who followed her around and watched her battles without offering her any aid. She named him Lithic, thought he was cute if useless, and concluded there was no point doing any more quests for Brell. The fourth quest would have involved restoring lost Brellian artifacts to his Dwarf worshippers, and the fifth would have restored the Underfoot Cathedral. Cleora concluded that gods were too selfish to adore.

Late in her long series of adventures, deep in the wilds of Kunzar Jungle, Cleora encountered an extreme religious cult called the Tabernacle of Pain. Considering that Brell seems to be a somewhat sadistic god, she decided to join the cult to see what she could learn about the meaning of pain. To prove her mettle to the lizardmen of the Tabernacle, she hunted around Snake Eye's Hunting Camp, killing ten tyrannosaur-like trakanasaurs and fourteen sasquatch-like jungle quatchas. Success in this mission allowed her to enter the Tabernacle's island in the Venom Flow River, where numerous members of the cult were practicing martial arts. A senior Clay Shackle monk explained the system to her. The cult was organized in a series of ever more demanding levels of combat power, called castes, each one gained by accomplishing a two-stage trial. The first stage involved various feats performed in the jungle, but the second stage always involved defeating a member of the caste in the combat ring at the center of the island.

The feat for the Trial of Clay was simple, merely breaking twenty-five clay pots situated near the shore around the perimeter of the island, trying not to aggravate the monstrous leeches in the river while doing so. Her first opponent was Glazjo Roughscale, an enhanced level 74 member of the Clay caste. Since Cleora had reached level 78 at that point and was allowed to use her fire elemental pet, Brand, she was confident and did indeed vanquish him. She needed to be careful, however, because she had read in a wiki, "If you are a pet class, then YOU must strike the death blow, not your pet."[14] She hoped that joining the Clay caste would give her valuable religious teachings, perhaps from secret scriptures, but other than the necessity of enduring and inflicting pain, she learned nothing. She gained a magic bracelet, called the Clay Shackle, so she pondered whether it might be teaching her the lesson that religion was a form of bondage.

The first part of the Trial of Stone required Cleora to hunt down Cluckatrice, a dominant member of the cockatrice species, which she accomplished easily. Tvzik Maul, an enhanced level 75 member of the Stone caste, proved much tougher than Glazjo Roughscale, and on her first attempt Cleora was defeated in the combat ring. Recognizing she needed to develop her skill and strength, she left for a time and undertook missions for various tribes. At level 80 she returned, first seeking an audience with the highest-ranked leaders of the cult, grandmasters Raakaz and Kaybal of the Tynonnium Shackle, but they refused to speak with her. On her second attempt, she vanquished Tvzik Maul, but it was a difficult struggle. She hoped to learn something of the cult's doctrines when she was admitted to the Stone caste, on the theory that this caste must be devoted to Brell, the god so often represented by stone. But again, no wisdom was given her.

The Trial of Rock began when a senior Rock Shackle monk directed her to break through a rock training wall on the beach. It did not fight back but was tremendously durable, so both she and Brand soon ran completely out of power. Her solution was to dismiss Brand back to the netherworld where he lived when not serving her, then recall him, doing this twice because on each return his power was restored. After a very long effort they crashed through the wall. She pondered how easily her power had been exhausted, and how near she had come to defeat the second time she faced Tvzik Maul, but she returned to the combat ring to face Maz Seriz, an enhanced level 76 member of the Rock caste. For a while the battle went well, and using Brand deftly, plus her own mage spells, she was able to beat her opponent down to less than a quarter of his original health without taking any damage herself. But she had exhausted all her power. Maz Seriz turned away from Brand and attacked her, quickly defeating her.

There was only one possible conclusion: she would need to surrender to Brell and beg his help, if she was going to stand any chance fighting her way into the Rock caste. Although it was possible to gain experience above level 80, all the way to 90, her current form of existence in the world limited her experience to 80, and thus set limits on both her health and her power, and so going off and doing a few dozen missions to build experience would be impossible.[15] She traveled all the way back to her home in the northlands, to pray before the altar of Brell Serilis she had set up in her living room. She had done this many times before, but previously she had always stopped just short of asking Brell for help. This time, she took from the altar two charges each of Earth's Vigil and Forgehammer. On her way back to the Tabernacle of Pain, by mistake she triggered Earth's Vigil, realizing only then that the first charge would be lost in ten minutes, so she flew on her dragon the last few miles to face Maz Seriz before this protective spell wore off. She used every skill she possessed, and in the middle of the battle hit him with Forgehammer, which stunned him for a very long time and ensured her victory. Thanks to Brell!

Again, Cleora learned nothing from the monks of the Rock caste, but one belonging to the next level of the order, the Copper caste, did tell her a little. Above the Rock caste, progress through the castes takes years, and one must usually wait for the departure of a member of the Copper caste before aspiring to join it. As the first half of her trial, he told her to kill a large number of mistgoblins, to collect ten pendants from their shamans. The Tabernacle was stockpiling these pendants, which were made from the discarded scales of the dragon Severilis, in hopes they could be used as a weapon against him some day. This was not an easy task, because earlier Cleora had learned how difficult it was to penetrate at all into goblin territory, but she did complete it quickly. Rather than rushing into the combat circle on the Tabernacle's island, she prepared herself carefully. Significantly, she did something she had never done before, changing the system of abilities she had gradually built over all her previous time on Norrath, maximizing her conjuror skills and her shadow abilities for the battle to come. Also for the first time she practiced briefly summoning an additional secondary avatar, a brute named Goneker, using the Communion spell. Then she returned to face her Copper Shackle opponent.

The battle was so fierce, and her concentration on managing her many magic spells so intense, that she never really knew the identity of her adversary. As soon as he appeared in the ring, she cast Blazing Avatar II on Brand, to give him more ability to do damage, told him to attack, and then quickly cast Vehement Skin IV, to increase his resistance to damage. She then cast three magic spells in quick succession that relate to the three elements other than earth: Roaring Flames IV and Aqueous Swarm V, which produced temporary secondary avatars of fire and water, and Winds of Velious II, an air spell. Next she loosed Goneker on her opponent. None of these actions, with the possible exception of Winds of Velius, would draw the enemy's attention to her, because each involved a secondary avatar that would draw anger upon itself. Then she cautiously started firing other spells: Crystal Blast VIII, Ice Storm VII, Fiery Annihilation VII, Petrify V, and Earthquake V, pausing occasionally to restore health to Brand with Heal Servant VII. Eventually Brand died, unfortunately, and when the opponent sank lifeless to the area floor, Cleora herself was low on health and power. But with Brell's help she had triumphed, because her last remaining charges of Earth's Vigil and Forge-hammer had provided the margin of victory.

A senior Bronze Shackle monk explained to her that the first task for his caste was an incredibly dangerous mission to penetrate deep into the City of Mist and retrieve the Amulet of the Jade-Fist for the Tabernacle. Cleora consulted a wiki and discovered that this task was impossible for her, because the amulet was in a jar upon which sat a super-duper enhanced level 77 Toris Phantom, surrounded by other enemies. The wiki said the only way it was even conceivable to get the amulet without having a group of friends to help was if one had the Feign Death (FD) ability, which she lacked: "Those with FD, good timing, and a suicidal need to solo can drop dead on the harvest, leap back up, and complete the gather in time to get the update. Remember, you have to pop back up before the NPC's get back to spots they were standing before they attacked you, or else they will aggro you as soon as you stand up. Immediately FD'ing again will allow survival with some luck. You can also FD then fear to give yourself a few extra seconds."[16]

Reluctantly, Cleora refused to accept the mission from the Bronze monk. She returned to her home, where she offered up to Brell all the shackles she had earned from the Tabernacle, destroying them on his altar. In return, he gave her just enough favor to get two charges of Earth's Vigil. She pondered her gains and losses, concluding that she still did not understand what value the gods were to Half Elves like herself, and where in the confusing world of Norrath she could ever gain full understanding of her existence.

Pantheons

Gameworlds tend to have polytheistic religions, which may seem archaic yet possesses a certain logic even in the modern world. Over three decades ago, I published *Satan's Power*, a book about the Process, a polytheistic, psychother-apeutic, communal cult that conceptualized its four deities as ideal personality types: Jehovah, Lucifer, Christ, and Satan. I wrote, "The duality *Jehovah:Lucifer* described two alternate social approaches to human life, rather similar to the *Apollonian:Dionsyian* dichotomy of Nietzsche, or the familiar *cold:hot, rigid:flexible, conservative:liberal* dichotomies of common language."[17] Christ, in this typology, was the unifier, whereas Satan was the separator. This unusual theology asserted that Christ was not Jesus but a god who sought to bring the stern female principle Jehovah together with the permissive male principle Lucifer, in a marriage to overcome the conflict between them. In so doing, Christ risked becoming the victim of their divine dispute. Satan, in contrast, sought to drive Jehovah and Lucifer further apart, and to isolate Christ from the other divine principles. In so doing, Satan happily split herself into higher and lower fragments.

The overall conception of the system was that God had broken himself into innumerable fragments, the large chunks being the gods and the small splinters being the people, *in order to play a game*. The group spoke of life explicitly as the Game of the Gods. In a grand cycle of explosion and compression, the Christian principle of unification was in the process of resolving all conflicts in order to reassemble God. Later, God would fragment again, in the *eternal recurrence* of which Nietzsche writes.[18] Thus, one advantage of polytheism is that it can present an ontology—a well-ordered system of concepts that organize our thinking about existence—personifying the fundamental categories or forces as deities. Here we shall examine three gameworld polytheisms, but others will appear throughout this book.

In *EverQuest II*, fully fourteen deities have returned to Norrath—one actually consisting of a committee of six avatars—and about a dozen others lurk elsewhere and may arrive at any time. We have already seen the names of three of them, Marr, Tunare, and Brell. The whole pantheon of present deities is listed in table 3.1, arranging them in three groups according to the game's definitions of moral character, which I call the god's *valence*: good, neutral, or evil. The table gives the name and location of the prophet for each god, plus the deity's qualities, including relations with other gods, as given in the EQII wiki.[19]

Each of these gods represents something meaningful to humans, but not usually entirely pleasant. In looking through the list, or by actually doing quests for these gods as Cleora did, one gets a correct sense that the pantheon is an incoherent mess, in which each deity has a distinctive character but an overall conceptual structure is lacking, aside from the obvious difference between good and evil gods. Religion seems to be the area of human culture which EQII satirizes more savagely, and if its view is factually correct, then faith is a farce.

The six deities in *Sacred 2: Fallen Angel*, a solo-player fantasy game, are organized in a much more coherent intellectual structure, as outlined in table 3.2. The descriptions of the gods are taken from the character-creation display at the beginning of the game, while the descriptions of the divine gifts are taken from the instruction manual. When starting a new character, the user first selects which of six characters to run—Seraphim, High Elf, Dryad, Temple Guardian, Shadow Warrior, or Inquisitor—and then which of two paths the character will follow. The Campaign of Light will restore balance to the world of Ancaria, which is in danger of being ruined by uncontrolled use of a magical technology involving a principle called the T-force. The Campaign of Shadow will fully unleash the horrible possibilities of T-force and lead to war. Depending upon the selection of a character and one campaign or the other, various gods can be

Table 3.1 The Pantheon of Deities in *EverQuest II*

Deity	Valence	Prophet	Qualities
Mithaniel Marr	Good	Sir Bayden Cauldthorn in Old Kelethin	The Truthbringer; governs the Plane of Valor. Ally: Karana. Enemies: Innoruuk, Cazic-Thule, and Bertoxxulous
Quellious	Good	Pacificator Merrek in Butcherblock Mountains	The Tranquil, a child goddess who wanders in search of Peace. Ally: Rodcet Nife. Enemies: Rallos Zek and Innoruuk.
Rodcet Nife	Good	Bainyn Fairwind in North Qeynos	The Prime Healer; fights disease and death, is generous and humble. Allies: Karana and Quellious. Enemy: Bertoxxulous.
Tunare	Good	Kurista in Old Kelethin	The Mother of All; rules the Plane of Growth. Allies: Karana and Rodcet Nife. Enemy: Bertoxxulous.
Brell Serilis	Neutral	Bronlor Stormhammer in Butcherblock Mountains	The Duke of Below; offers true happiness in caves, caverns, and tunnels. Ally: Bristlebane. No enemies currently in Norrath.
Bristlebane	Neutral	Tobel Patadash in Enchanted Lands	The Trickster; pursues mischievous fun at the expense of nearly all else. Not clear about having true allies or enemies, other than considering all other deities to be laughingstocks.
Karana	Neutral	Askr in Timorous Deep	The Rainkeeper, the power of storms, both the rain that gives life and the sandstorms or hurricanes that take life away. Allies: Mithaniel Marr and Tunare. Enemy: Bertoxxulous.
Solusek Ro	Neutral	Civean Il'Pernod in Butcherblock Mountains	The Burning Prince; rules the Plane of Sun and derives power from his father, Fennin Ro, who rules the greater elemental Plane of Fire. No allies or enemies.

The Tribunal	Neutral	Justinian Theo in Timorous Deep	The Council of Justice, six deities who rule the Plane of Justice where those guilty of crimes against the universe are imprisoned. No allies or enemies.
Anashti Sul	Evil	Plumetor Dul'Sadma in Sinking Sands	The Former Prime Healer, sentenced to nonexistence by the other gods when she unwittingly released undeath upon the inhabitants of early Norrath. Successor: Rodcet Nife. Allies and enemies: uncertain.
Bertoxxulous	Evil	Hrath Everstill in Gorowyn	The Diseased; rules the Plane of Disease, a dark land dotted with geysers of ooze and rivers of pus. Allies: None. Enemies: Many.
Cazic-Thule	Evil	Danak Dhorentath in Butcherblock Mountains	The Faceless; causes terror, pain, misery, violence, torture, living sacrifice. Allies: Rallos Zek and Innoruuk. Enemy: Mithaniel Marr.
Innoruuk	Evil	Xilania Nevagon in Greater Faydark	The Prince of Hate; preaches that hate is a creative force able to overpower any opponent. Allies: Rallos Zek and Cazic-Thule. Enemies: Quellious and Mithaniel Marr.
Rallos Zek	Evil	Tychus Zeksworn in Butcherblock Mountains	The Warlord; promotes victory for the strong and death to the weak. Allies: Innoruuk and Cazic-Thule. Enemies: Quellious and Bertoxxulous.

Table 3.2 The Pantheon of Deities in *Sacred 2: Fallen Angel*

Deity	Valence	Divine Gift	Description of the God	Description of the Divine Gift
Lumen	Exclusive Light	Dazzle	God of Light. He makes all things visible. He is a healer and knows what has been and what will be.	The God of Light lets light beams shoot from the character. Opponents are petrified and damaged and might even burn.
Forens	Light	Inspiration	Goddess of Philosophy and Wisdom.	The power of philosophy makes the character deflect almost all attacks back to the attacker for a certain time.
Kybele	Light	Infusion	Goddess of Nature. She is the patron of fertility and life, of flora and fauna.	Nature itself grants the character and all allies part of its life force. The character is instantly healed, and the effect of current afflictions is reduced.
Testa	Shadow	Will-o-wisp	God of Science. He is the spirit who brings life to dead and mechanical things.	The God of Science fills the character with energy, making him shoot out T-energy balls that heal allied units and damage opponents for a while.
Kuan	Shadow	Kuan's Breath	God of War. He protects the soldiers and grants them the determination necessary to persist in battle.	The God of War confuses all nearby opponents, making them attack each other.
Ker	Exclusive Shadow	Sakkara	Goddess of Evil. She is the destroyer, and the guardian of darkness.	The Goddess of Chaos calls upon a powerful, magically shackled demon who fights for the attacker. But the shackles won't hold forever.

selected. A character of the Seraphim type can follow only Light, and must select among the three Light deities: Lumen, Forens, or Kybele. In contrast, an avatar of the type Inquisitor must follow the Shadow path and one of the three Shadow deities: Testa, Kuan, or Ker. The four other kinds of avatar can select either campaign. An avatar of these types on the Light path cannot worship Ker, and one on the Shadow path cannot worship Lumen. However, one of these avatars can worship any of the remaining deities, regardless of chosen path.

A divine gift is an especially valuable distinctive ability, obtained through allegiance with the associated deity, and conceptualized in supernatural terms. My avatar was a Shadow Warrior who had chosen the Light Campaign and the nature goddess Kybele. The "divine gift" provided by Kybele is Infusion, which increases the life regeneration rate in recovering from a battle. As my avatar advanced in experience by accomplishing many quests, thus facing ever more powerful enemies, his divine gift could increase in effectiveness. As I checked the statistics at experience level 18, Infusion, when triggered, instantly heals the avatar for 637 health points, then 393 points per second for ten seconds. But this cannot be done again for fully 650 seconds, or nearly eleven minutes.

Inhabitants of Ancaria select one god from the pantheon of six, and may not even believe in the existence of the other five. Notably, in the Realm of the Seraphim, nonplayer character Sophia (wisdom) proclaims, "There is but one God. You may have heard differently, that there are many Gods such as Kybele, Lumen, Ker and so forth. But those are all mere aspects of the One True Creator, and we Seraphim were his angels." She goes on to lament that her God long ago left the world, disgusted by the behavior of its people, leaving the Seraphim frustrated, withdrawn, but slightly hopeful that some day he might return. She sends the player's avatar to Liosilath, mentor of avatars, who scoffs, "What! The world, the universe, and the whole lot—made by one Creator! Well, she's entitled to her opinion, but I think it's nonsense."

Lumen is clearly named after the Latin word for light, as found in *illumination*, a word that can mean *enlightenment* with both physical and religious implications. It also connects to the Judeo-Christian parable in which existence begins when God says, "Let there be light." Kybele just as clearly derives from the Greek. Often spelled *Cybele* in English, she was the Earth Mother goddess of nature among the Phrygians, but was worshiped by Greeks and people of other nations as well. In exploring Ancaria, an avatar discovers six "books," really short tracts describing each of the gods. The first of these belongs to Kybele, suggesting that her religion is the oldest, despite the fact that other gods may claim to have been the creator. Kybele's tract described her cult: "Followers and priests of Kybele have erected countless memorial shrines all over Ancaria, although many of them are hard to recognize as one. The church of Kybele does not emphasize grandiosity. Instead, they prefer chasteness and humility, which is consequently reflected in all her shrines. Worldly possessions do not mean anything to Kybele, for the only real and most valuable treasure in the world is life."[20]

In Khorum, a desert town probably named after Karakorum, the capital of the Mongol Empire, my avatar met Kybele's servant Lia. She gave him the blessing of the goddess, then instructed him to convert five apostates back to the faith, after they had failed to attend "mass." Note that Mass is the word for a major Roman Catholic ceremony, but the culture of the town seemed Arabic, given the desert environment, the architecture and clothing, and the names of many characters. The first apostate regained for Kybele, Asad, enthusiastically recited this chant:

> We are the earth.
> We are the rhythm of day and night.
> We are the movement of the earth as it turns on its axis and dances around
>   the sun.
> We are the weight of the earth.
> We are the speed of the earth.
> We are the history of the earth.
> We are evolution, from the humble mosquito to the mighty whale and
>   the labyrinth of the mind.

This chant expresses the modern Gaia concept of Earth as a living being, regarded simultaneously from scientific and religious perspectives.[21] The last phrase, *labyrinth of the mind*, comes from a Christian memorial by Tennyson that begins:

> Strong Son of God, immortal Love,
> Whom we, that have not seen thy face,
> By faith, and faith alone, embrace,
> Believing where we cannot prove;
>
> Thine are these orbs of light and shade;
> Thou madest Life in man and brute;
> Thou madest Death; and lo, thy foot
> Is on the skull which thou hast made.
>
> Thou wilt not leave us in the dust:
> Thou madest man, he knows not why;
> He thinks he was not made to die;
> And thou hast made him: thou art just.[22]

The second apostate, Basim, confirms that the earth is a living organism, as stated in the Gaia hypothesis. The third, El-marees, proclaims that all things are part of the great unity, and we are the children of "our Mother Earth." The fourth, Fayr, says that the transformation of all people into a unity within "Kybele's design and consciousness" will still preserve individuality. The fifth, Rasul, announces, "Death and life, in all their myriad forms, are one within the unity of nature. It is impossible to rebel against nature or act out of turn." Thus, just as the Trinity is a mystery for Christians, transcendence of the dichotomy between free will and predestination is a mystery for the followers of Kybele.

The connection of Kybele to the ancient cultures of the classical world reminds us that real religions were not very different from today's fictional polytheisms, an observation reinforced by the MMO *Gods and Heroes: Rome Rising*. When I initially studied this very interesting, high-quality gameworld in 2010 by running a soldier avatar named Andivius up to level 25, it had not yet been released to the public.[23] I was one of the small group of testers allowed to explore Rome in the third century BC, in a closed beta version of the unfinished game. The beta-tester nondisclosure agreement would have prevented me from writing about it, but on March 4, 2011, the developers of *Gods and Heroes* lifted the prohibition against reporting what I saw, and as soon as the game was released to the public in June 2011 I returned to study it further, through taking a mystic avatar named Aspera up to the maximum level, level 30.[24] Created by a pair of small companies, the first of which went out of business before completing the job, *Gods and Heroes* faced great challenges coming to completion and drawing subscribers, but its intellectual content is among the best I have experienced.

In addition to several towns, *Gods and Heroes* presents a huge and really marvelous virtual model of the city of Rome, including the temples of fully fourteen deities. Each temple has a colossal statue of the god or goddess, as traditionally represented, and most have a below-ground chapel with a smaller version of the statue, where an NPC offers quests for followers of that particular deity, and occasionally participates in quests for followers of other deities. Completing the special deity quests builds favor with the deity, as does performing libations and gaining experience ranks, conferring special abilities on the avatar. Table 3.3 lists these temples, the gender of the deity, the section of the city in which the temple is situated, and the type of avatar and avatar's assistant associated with the deity. The table also includes brief descriptions of the first eight deities, taken from the game manual, and three counts I made of players' avatars in-game, admittedly of rather small populations.

When I created Andivius, given that he was a soldier, I had a choice between only two deities he might serve, Mars and Minerva. I selected Minerva, and this set the particular line of abilities Andivius could gain as he progressively did

Table 3.3 The Pantheon of Deities in *Gods and Heroes: Rome Rising*

Deity	Gender	Description	District in Rome	Avatar Type	Avatar's Assistant	Number of Avatars		
						Beta	SPQR	Census
Mars	Male	Mighty, fearsome god of war	Vallis Murcia	Soldier	Phoenix	33	24	101
Minerva	Female	Goddess of wisdom and war	Vallis Murcia	Soldier	Gorgon	24	12	67
Jupiter	Male	Supreme leader of the gods who presides over laws, social order, and justice	Colosseum	Gladiator	Eagle	48	28	79
Fortuna	Female	Goddess of victory and fate	Colosseum	Gladiator	Pegasus	22	7	50
Bacchus	Male	God of wine and intoxication	Palatinus	Mystic	Centaurus	14	8	40
Trevia	Female	Goddess of sorcery and magic	Palatinus	Mystic	Empusa	34	31	76

Pluto	Male	Dour and gloomy god who rules the underworld and the souls of the dead	Capitolium	Priest	Cerberus	30	14	53
Juno	Female	Solemn and regal goddess; defends virtue and moral values; presides over childbirth, marriage	Capitolium	Priest	Sphinx	13	12	28
Apollo	Male		Caelius	(Scout)	unknown			
Diana	Female		Caelius	(Scout)	unknown			
Mercury	Male		Viminalis	(Nomad)	unknown			
Nemesis	Female		Viminalis	(Nomad)	unknown			
Neptune	Male		Forum	none	none			
Vesta	Female		Forum	none	none			

missions for Minerva that increased his favor with her. Chief among them was gaining a gorgon who could serve as a secondary avatar assistant during fights. Aspera selected Trevia, goddess of the crossroads, rather than Bacchus, god of inebriation, in part because Trevia with her three heads seemed far more supernatural, and because she liked the idea of making careful decisions at crossroads in life, rather than lurching toward a stupid future in a condition of stupefaction. Eventually she gained Empusa as the secondary avatar appropriate to Trevia, who briefly at moments of crisis would help drain the life from enemies. Each class of avatar has a choice between male and female deities; both have their temples in the same district of Rome, and each deity offers a particular assistant to the avatar. The *Gods and Heroes* interface is designed for six classes of avatar, but Scout and Nomad were not available during the period of my research.[25]

The last three columns of table 3.3 show the distributions of avatars across eight gods in three samples, data derived by manually searching the in-game team-building system. The first set of data was all 218 members of the one guild—called the Ares Olympians "tribe"—that existed in the beta test on November 21, 2010, and to which Andivius and essentially all other avatars belonged. The second is the total membership on July 21, 2011, of the largest tribe (136 members) on the Mars server, SPQR, to which Aspera belonged. And the last column is the total number found in ten scans of all 494 avatars currently online for at least one scan, done over July 14–21, 2011, on all three servers: Mars and Bacchus in the United States and Apollo in Europe. Presumably, selecting an avatar type was more important to players than selecting a deity, but it is worth noting that only one goddess, Trevia, was more popular than the corresponding god—the disreputable Bacchus.

There are at least two ways polytheism can develop, although the two often mix together, as in the case of Roman religion. First of all, when ancient tribes merged into kingdoms, the new state needed to harmonize their respective religious cultures. One way was to find correspondences, like Jupiter = Zeus, but another way was to collect different gods into a pantheon, such as adopting the Etruscan goddess Minerva as part of the Roman pantheon. Second, multiple gods may be interpreted within an overarching intellectual system in which each represents a concept. These can be aspects of humanity, such as Venus = Aphrodite = love and Mars = Ares = war. Or they can represent aspects of nature, such as Jupiter = Zeus = sky, Neptune = Poseidon = sea, and Pluto = Hades = underworld. None of the parallels were perfect, and some were rather imprecise or even speculative. Jesus was occasionally identified with Hermes, for example, who was often depicted as carrying a sheep on his shoulders, as was Jesus, the Good Shepherd. More traditionally, the Greek god Hermes was identified with the Roman god Mercury.

There exist several social-scientific theories for why monotheism historically replaced polytheism, although they manifestly do not apply to Asian religions, given that popular Hinduism remains polytheistic, and the ascended beings of Buddhism are not gods in the Western sense.[26] One general class of theories is political, considering monotheism to be a tactic used by Western elites to consolidate power during an extended period of social chaos in which they could not rely upon the endurance of secular institutions. Western civilization inherited its traditional view of God from its feudal past. The Lord in heaven was the ultimate justification for the power exercised by the lord of the manor. The duke had a king above him; the king had an emperor, and the emperor had a god. To challenge the lowest of these authorities was to challenge the very stability of the universe. However, it would be wrong to see this ideology as merely a tool for oppression of peasants by aristocrats. To the extent that the system worked smoothly, it conferred meaning on every status within the society, and all aspects of life supported hope that faith could triumph over the limitations of human existence. How well this all worked is a question for historians of the particular time and place.

For James O'Donnell, two factors combined to motivate the transition from Paganism to Christianity.[27] One was the reliance of Paganism upon magic, because the different gods and lesser spirits were believed to serve different functions and could be encouraged to do so by appropriate rituals or sacrifices. The other factor was Christianity's intolerance. The usual story is that Christians were persecuted by Pagans—proverbially thrown to the lions in the arena—yet the opposite is equally true. Paganism was a complex society of deities, and thus of subcultures and faiths, whereas monotheism was a dictatorship by one god. When asked his religion, a Pagan philosopher might have quipped, "I am a republican," meaning that he preferred a diversity of celestial powers, rather than blind obedience to only one. Perhaps humans in general would prefer a balance between polytheism and monotheism, different members of society in different circumstances preferring one extreme or the other, yet a god that goes to war against all the others will either win or lose, and perhaps by chance the god of the Christians won and exterminated all the others, committing mass deicide.

Rodney Stark has argued that Christianity triumphed because it was more benevolent, encouraging people to be nicer to each other, whether tending the sick, dealing kindly with strangers, or supporting strong families.[28] This may be true, and many Christians have long believed something like this, yet this theory leaves open the question of why something like Christianity was not the first religion, never requiring the ancient world to go through a polytheistic period in the first place. In the earlier theory book written in collaboration with me, Stark had endorsed the notion of religious evolution, and like O'Donnell had made the decline of magic an important factor in the equation.[29] Over time, general compensators would come to predominate over specific compensators, as well-established religious institutions found magic to be hazardous for faith because its value could be disproven. The logical end of the process was not monotheism, however, but dualism: one good god representing all rewards, and one evil god representing all costs. The last stage in the triumph of monotheism would be Pollyannaism, a blind hope that only good exists and every seemingly bad event is but a scene in a good drama—a bump on the road to heaven. However, the trend from many gods to two to one need not stop there, and the next number in the mathematical sequence is zero.

A very different explanation suggests that the specific polytheisms that existed in the Roman Empire were in a process of decay two thousand years ago, and thus vulnerable to mystery cults coming from the conquered but unassimilated civilizations of the eastern empire. Whatever the benefits of monotheism, this perspective considers the decline of Paganism to be something approximating a historical accident. The following remarkable paragraph written by Jérôme Carcopino depicts beautifully the malaise of late Roman religion:

> One great spiritual fact dominates the history of the empire: the advent of personal religion which followed on the conquest of Rome by the mysticism of the East. The Roman pantheon still persisted, apparently immutable; and the ceremonies which had for centuries been performed on the dates prescribed by the pontiffs from their sacred calendars continued to be carried out in accordance with ancestral custom. But the spirits of men had fled from the old religion; it still commanded their service but no longer their hearts or their belief. With its indeterminate gods and its colourless myths, mere fables concocted from details suggested by Latin topography or pale reflections of the adventures which had overtaken the Olympians of Greek epic; with its prayers formulated in the style of legal contracts and as dry as the procedure of a lawsuit; with its lack of metaphysical curiosity and indifference to moral values; with the narrow-minded banality of its field of action, limited to the interests of the city and the development of practical politics—Roman religion froze the impulses of faith by its coldness and its prosaic utilitarianism. It sufficed at most to reassure a soldier against the risks of war or a peasant against the rigours of unseasonable weather, but in the motley Rome of the second century it had wholly lost its power over the human heart.[30]

Alienation from the Gods

Several gameworlds, like *EverQuest II*, imagine that the gods have departed this world, perhaps after devastating conflict they waged against each other. One of many other examples is *Lineage II: Goddess of Destruction*, the 2011 Westernized version of a 2003 Korean MMO. With the good results of Cleora in EQII in mind, I created an avatar named Lizbeth after my father's older sister, Elizabeth, who like Cleora died in infancy, surviving less than a week. Like Cleora, she needed to belong to a class that would be ambivalent about gods, so the best choice was a Dark Elf. The game manual explains: "Dark Elves excel at the dark arts, including death magic and shadow empowerment. Dark Elves were once part of the Elf race. They split off to pursue their worship of Shilen and dark magic, but Shilen proved to be too evil, and the Dark Elves now stand on their own"[31] The first two nonplayer leaders of the Dark Elf Guild that Lizbeth met expressed this point in their own words. Magister Talbot said, "Now that our gods have abandoned us, it's down to us to get stronger. Otherwise, we as a people will be a mere footnote in the annals of time." Grand Master Xenos put it this way: "We Dark Elves have no Gods to believe any more. That's why we need to try harder."

Many gameworlds that possess gods keep them at a distance from the avatars. The extreme case may be the religion of the Holy Light in *World of Warcraft*, practiced by Humans and in varying degrees by several other races, which contrasts with the Elune religion of the Night Elves.[32] The Holy Light is an abstract set of ethical principles, completely lacking in personality, mythology, or symbols, supporting the values of respect, tenacity, and compassion. The Light is not remotely like a person, and represents a thoroughly demythologized religion, the last step in a historical process of secularization before atheism. Elune, the Moon Goddess of the religion of the Night Elves, is very much a deity, specifically female, represented entirely by female priestesses, and having qualities like those of Kybele, both Mother Goddess and Mother Nature.

Dark Age of Camelot possesses many of the superficial attributes of religion, and the first chapter already mentioned some of the Christian symbolism in the Albion realm, without clear references to Jesus or the Bible. The religion of the Norse in Midgard provides an even more clear example of distance between an avatar and its god. I ran an avatar named Reitsche up to level 35 of 50, on the rarely used cooperative server Gaheris, where realm-versus-realm warfare did not exist and she could thus explore any territory appropriate to her experience level. There was no need to take her any higher, because the Norse mythology all came in the lower levels.

In Hafheim, Reitsche took training from Freja of the Valkyrie Order about how to develop a special power called Odin's Will. One manifestation of it, Odin's Faith, could protect her against magical damage. Odin's Retribution could damage several enemies at once, if they stood directly before her, and Odin's Restraint could slow their movements. Odin, of course, is the king of the Norse gods, called Wotan by some overcivilized Germans. In that village she helped many crafters who could manufacture useful items from raw materials, but some-how the trade of a tailor or blacksmith did not seem a proper way for a Valkyrie to pass her time. As the game's guidebook explains, "Females only need apply to be the handmaidens of Odin. Brandishing spears, shields, and sword, Valkyries also have a unique spell line called Odin's will that includes cone-shaped area of effect spells, direct-damage shouts, and buff shears."[33]

For one mission north of Ulvastad, Reitsche disguised herself as a Vendo, one of the bear-men, to sneak into their encampment to overhear what the ghost wolf named Spirit Emissary said to them: "Greetings, chosen children of Fenrir! Your master smiles upon your deeds! The end times draw near and the land must be prepared for the final days when the Vendo will be lifted up! . . . You must prepare the way by driving out the trolls and the Vikings from this land!" Fenrir, it will be remembered, was the monstrous father of the wolves who will kill Odin at Rag-narok, the cosmic battle that ends the reign of the gods.

Just inside Jordheim near the Mularn gate, Reitsche met Brienda, the Valkyrie trainer, who gave her a new weapon and explained, "This is the work of Odin and Thor. Our gods speak to us through four mighty oracles called the Visindakonar." Several of these "vision wives" had prophesied dangers to come, but Visindakona Magna had remained silent, with the implication that when she spoke a great warrior would be given a crucial mission to perform. From this time onward, Reitsche always wore a helmet framed by wings, feeling this proclaimed her Viking identity, plus reminding friend and foe alike that Valkyries fly above the battle, conveying heroes to Valhalla in preparation for Ragnarok. However, Reitsche's actual missions did not directly concern the Norse gods, nor plucking dying heroes from the battlefield, but centered on a rather minor part of Norse mythology, the Tomtes.

These originally were benign household spirits in Sweden, similar to dwarves and to many people's image of the elves who help Santa Claus. However, they could get nasty when someone frustrated them, and the Tomtes of Svealand had become very nasty indeed. For many years, the Tomtes had Svealand to them-selves, but the Norse moved in from Grenlock's Sound. At first, each group cau-tiously kept its distance from the other. Then one of those minor events occurred on which the wheel of history so often turns. A settler woman left her campfire to get some firewood, leaving a freshly baked loaf of bread next to her empty water skins. A Tomte approached the fire, ate some bread, and was amazed at how deli-cious it tasted. Soon the bread was gone, and the Tomte noticed the water skins and decided to repay the woman by filling them with water. The next night, the woman intentionally left out a second loaf of bread and a broken cooking pan. In the morning, she discovered that the bread had disappeared but the pan had been repaired. The settlers and the Tomtes still kept their distance, but developed a mutually beneficial relationship. Unfortunately, this changed when the number of settlers grew explosively, and they began to crowd the Tomtes out of their ancestral land. Reitsche's main quest line was a series of efforts to keep them from returning.

Frankly, the main line of quests against the Tomtes was theologically rather bland, and it would have been much more interesting to be involved directly in conflict among the Norse gods, or in their fierce battle against giants, dwarves, and other competing supernatural beings. This plan was brilliantly fulfilled by one of the most highly praised solo-player games, *God of War*.[34] At the beginning of this game, we learn that a Spartan warrior named Kratos is ready to seek death as the only escape from madness. For years he had been a servant of Ares, the god of war, until Ares tricks Kratos into killing his own family, hoping thereby to transform him into the perfect warrior. The theme of the game, and of its successors, is building the killing abilities of Kratos still further, so he can take vengeance against Ares.

In a somewhat timid manner, the other gods help Kratos, because they feel that Ares has been too hungry for the power that must be shared among them all. The instruction manual presents a scene titled "Gathering of the Gods," which begins:

ZEUS: I have gathered you here on this holiest of grounds to discuss the fate of a mortal whose actions I sense could have grave implications to all of us here on Mount Olympus.

ATHENA: My lord, my father, it is Kratos of whom you speak. I have been his patron goddess these last 10 years as he has fought to stave off madness and earn our forgiveness.

ARES: The man is a fool. He turned his back on a gift so—

ZEUS: Enough, Ares. I know what he has done. And, might I add, I know why he did it. You should be ashamed.

Step by step during his odyssey, each of the other gods gives Kratos a magic power, beginning with Poseidon's Rage which enables Kratos to defeat the hydra. It was very common for videogames of the period to be constructed in a series of levels, each of which culminated in a battle with a boss. *God of War* gave that plan a new twist, because Kratos also experiences a series of boosts to his power, each conferred by a friendly god. This illustrates a key advantage of polytheism for fantasy: It naturally supports stories that take place in a series of chapters. Parallel to that segmentation of the narrative, polytheism is also *polythemism*: each deity represent a different theme, as Poseidon represents the sea, and the three-headed hydra is a sea monster. The question then becomes what themes exist in human life that need expression as gods. Perhaps people differ in their life themes, and for some the themes are grim indeed. Early religions often conceptualized supernatural forces as mythologized animals like the hydra, often blurring the line between beast and deity. In *Gods and Heroes* the hero sometimes battles gigantic three-headed dogs, and the devotees of Pluto have Cerberus at their beck and call. Indeed, seeking salvation from a god, rather than from our own dogged determination, may be barking up the wrong tree.

Conclusion

God is a dog. Yes, dogs exist, while gods do not, yet gods are in part a personification of nature, and dogs are parts of nature that have been domesticated by humans, giving them unnatural roles to play and uncanny meanings. God dogs our steps, constantly reminding us to follow our culture's moral code, and representing humanity's dogged determination to reach unreachable goals. We personify dogs by giving them names, like Fido for fidelity, or Checkers, the game-named political donation that tested Richard Nixon's fidelity. One of the most famous dogs was fictional, like a god, and named for a god. He is Pluto, the cartoon pup created by that noted plutocrat, Walt Disney. The first member of human society to reach heaven was Laika, the Russian dog whose name in Russian refers to the language of the dogs—namely, barking. She flew into orbit on Sputnik 2 in 1957, and was allowed to die there because no provision was made for bringing her back from the jaws of death. Each dog has his day; each god, too. Yet dogs will still be with us, even after the last god has slouched to that doghouse of rejected deities, Valhalla.

In fantasy gameworlds, there are often many gods, both to represent many competing fictional tribes and to play different roles in the lore justifying all the hundreds and thousands of quests. High-quality gameworlds tend to have deep mythologies, and thus to attribute distinct meanings to the competing gods. Indeed, the best way of conceptualizing the polytheism of many games is that a polytheistic universe is one characterized by conflict, and conflict is the hallmark of computer games. As it is a silly play on words to say that "God is a dog," theology is a very serious play on words that seeks to extract meaning and comfort from a universe that is both chaotic and horrifying. In a gameworld, the player can seize control over the chaotic horror, successfully complete meaningful quests, and achieve a form of gradual transcendence by ascending the levels of experience and thus of power. There has yet to be designed a gameworld in which the highest-level players ascend to become the gods who create the new quests, perhaps because the real gods of the games are the game designers, who like traditional gods resent any mere mortal who seeks to join their pantheon.

4 SOULS

The example of Cleora in the previous chapter suggests that avatars can be the vehicles to convey a considerable weight of human meaning. They may even illuminate what it means to be a person, in a manner very different from that offered by traditional religion, which often conceptualized a human as a spirit or soul. The superstition of the soul falsely believes that there is a unique, unitary self within every human being, and that self is somehow immortal. The issue of immortality will be covered in the chapter on death, and here the focus will be on the integrity of the individual person.

Avatars, in traditional Indo-European religions, represent aspects of a god or other transcendent being. The fact that we use the Hindu word *avatar* should not blind us to the fact that other religions in this vast tradition possess similar concepts. When Europa was abducted by Zeus, he came to her in the form of a white bull, for example. Had Judaism been an Indo-European religion, we might speak today of Jesus as an avatar of Jehovah. Monotheism is very uncomfortable with the idea that God can fragment, because the logical conclusion of fragmentation is polytheism. Similarly, monotheism may not be hospitable to the theory that the individual person also comprises many subpersons that can at times function autonomously. In ancient Egyptian religion, there were not merely many gods but also many semiautonomous parts to the soul. The salient fact about avatars in Indo-European religions is that prominent deities tended to have several of them, each expressing a distinct aspect of the gods' nature.

A very modern way to think about such issues is to frame them in terms of artificial intelligence (AI), including the simple forms that are common in gameworlds. Most of the "people" in those worlds are not avatars at all but nonplayer characters of a variety of kinds. I find the enemy NPCs especially interesting, and I often try to "reverse engineer" them in my mind, trying to figure out how their programming code is structured to allow them to function as they do.

Often, one of my low-level avatars has stood on the seacoast of Westfall in *World of Warcraft*, where obnoxious amphibious humanoids called Murlocs swarm. Some stand in one place; others seem to walk on predetermined courses, but others seem to wander within some invisible boundary. I can easily conjure in my mind a programming routine that cycles through a loop every second or so. It knows where the Murloc was a second ago, and it knows where the Murloc is now. One part of the code checks whether the Murloc has reached the boundary of its territory. If the Murloc has reached the boundary, the program invokes a "turn in a different direction" subroutine, which calls up a random number to determine a new course, but checks to make sure that new direction is away from the boundary. If the Murloc is not at a boundary, the program calls up a random number that has a small probability of making the Murloc change course anyway. Somewhere in that code is a routine that checks to see if an enemy (namely my avatar) has come within a range of X virtual meters. If so, the Murloc goes through an animation sequence expressing surprise followed by rage; it emits a disgusting gurgling shout, and it runs at top speed toward my avatar.

Then begins the battle. A complex set of algorithms determines how much damage the Murloc and I do to each other. I unleash my attacks mostly by hitting keys or clicking icons, whereas the Murloc's program has a standard battle loop. Some NPC enemies have very complex alternative attacks, mostly selected by random numbers within a set of predefined choices. The more sophisticated ones are able to decide which opponent to strike, if two or more opponents are battling it. In some cases, the simple AI routine seems to have a primitive form of machine learning, it which it responds either to the enemy who has done damage to it most recently or to the one that has done the most damage since the battle began, while others simply stick with the first opponent until it has been killed. Murlocs have lines in their code that cause them to run away if they have been severely damaged, then walk sideways a distance, before returning to the fight. This is fiendish, because if their path takes them near another Murloc, the new one follows them, adding a fresh opponent to the battle.

Once the design concepts for a Murloc have been established, writing the programming code is easy, because it follows standard computer science practices, in a form that is called *rule-based reasoning* when it is applied to more advanced artificial intelligence problems.[1] Contemporary digital computers are Turing machines, named after AI pioneer Alan Turing.[2] A Turing machine has three parts: (1) store, (2) executive unit, and (3) control. In more familiar contemporary terms, these are: (1) memory, (2) central processing unit, and (3) program. Instructions from the program tell the CPU to move data from one memory register to another, along the way often transforming the data—for example, adding together the numbers in two registers and putting the result in a third.

A Turing machine is perfectly deterministic, giving the same result each time the program is run, unless so-called random numbers are incorporated in the algorithm. Even random numbers are deterministic, although producing results the user could not have predicted, because at best they put the time from the computer's clock into an algorithm such as taking the remainder from the result of dividing two long integers, one of which was seeded from the clock, and the other of which was a prime number. Turing effectively offered a theory of the human mind, in which the central processing unit is the self, performing executive functions for the brain. The philosophical issue of whether humans possess free will becomes a technical question of where the brain's random numbers come from, and how they factor into its algorithms.

It was convenient for the first several generations of digital computers to be designed as Turing machines, both because of the relative ease in applying the methods of mathematical logic to them and because of the practicalities of building microelectronic components that could be combined in a modular manner, as a relatively small number of mass-produced computer chips, one of which is the "soul of the machine," the CPU. One of the most admired books about the social process of creating computers is *Soul of a New Machine* by Tracy Kidder.[3] It describes the frantic efforts of a team to create a new computer, motivated not by greed for money but by the desire to *play pinball*. That is, if the team succeeds, its reward, as in the game of pinball, will be to be allowed to play the game again, creating yet another newer computer. On one level, the soul of the machine is the spirit of the team of humans that built it. Yet they themselves are functioning like a Turing machine, following the algorithm to build one machine after another, each with greater speed and memory than the previous one, but designed according to the same principles. However, other computing paradigms exist, including massive parallel processing in neural nets.

I have published a good deal of work using neural nets of different kinds, but of course I programmed them on conventional computers, which meant that the whole program was run by a CPU.[4] However, if computer were built from the ground up for massive neural nets, there need not be any CPU. A common term for this is *parallel distributed processing*.[5] The actions of the computer would be the result of interaction among millions or billions of semiautonomous units, perhaps specialized in terms of function, but none of them serving executive functions over all the others. AI pioneer Marvin Minsky has argued that the human brain consists of a very large number of units—each represented by a large number of individual neurons—a *society of mind*, as he calls it.[6]

For over a century it has been widely known that damage to portions of the brain can erase memory and affect personality.[7] Today, leading cognitive scientist Paul Bloom argues that the obsolete notion of the unitary immortal soul is the most intense point of contention between religion and science.[8] Extreme cases, such as the few individuals in whom the connections between halves of the brain have been severed, give the most striking evidence of how self and awareness can become fragmented.[9] Yet even in apparently normal people there is considerable evidence against the naive notion of a unitary self.[10] Perhaps the illusion of a self reflects the very limited capacity of human short-term memory, or some mechanism associated with visual perception.[11]

It is clear to anyone that long-term or semantic memory is not only vast but structured in some way, allowing one human to play the role of another human. Indeed, one of the more interesting cognitive science theories of religion is that belief in gods represents hyperactivity of the human mind's ability to think in terms of another being, and to infer consciousness in any complex system.[12] Believing that a storm is the wrath of Thor thus may be the same cognitive error as assuming that the whirlwind of memories and desires in the human mind reflect the will of some internal supernatural being, the soul. Thus, Bloom and some of his colleagues in cognitive science argue that many popular conceptions of reality come from applying a relatively small number of mental models to a diversity of aspects of reality that they may not really fit.

As all the MMOs illustrate, humans can easily play roles, constructing separate persons within themselves that function only in a particular context. Religion also provides examples, not only in exotic examples such as spirit possession[13] but even in the most orthodox traditions. Moses, it will be recalled, was a man with two identities, Hebrew and Egyptian, who experienced a fragmented life. As an infant he floated down the Nile toward a completely unexpected childhood; as an adult he fled his homeland for an alien society, and later the Red Sea parted so he could lead the original Exodus. When capitalized, "Mosaic" refers to his religious tradition, but when written in lower case, it means a work of art assembled from many small pieces. The term *mosaic* originated in a different religious tradition, as an expression of the Muses who exemplify the arts in ancient Greek culture. The online identity of an MMO player is similarly fragmented, across multiple avatars and multiple dimensions within each. To a significant degree, this is also true for every human being in ordinary life.

In ancient Greek mythology, Proteus was a sea god, who like water could change his shape, but who also could prophesy the future. Forty years ago in an essay titled "Protean Man," Robert Jay Lifton argued that modern people were becoming ever more mutable, jostled by the rapid rate of historical change and by constantly changing social demands to play a variety of often contradictory roles.[14] Lifton was aware of the deep historical roots of his concepts, but he was especially energized by the recent history of totalitarianism and the Nazi Holocaust. Another writer of that period, the protean actor Robert Shaw, dealt with a similar issue in his novel and play *The Man in the Glass Booth*, which concerns a man who was simultaneously a Nazi and Jew.[15] On a deep metaphoric level, we all are both Nazis and Jews, criminals and victims, lust and intellect, and the moral challenge is to channel our mutability. We are all changelings, and if we properly understood this fact, we could use the rapidly changing technology to liberate ourselves without oppressing others. Computerized role-playing games are a training ground for exploring these issues.

Star Selves

This is the story of three Jedi knights: Obi-Wan Kenobi, Anakin Skywalker, and Simula Tion. The first two of these science-fiction priests are characters from the *Star Wars* movies and will be examined as they play their roles in the solo-player game *Star Wars Episode III: Revenge of the Sith*.[16] The third Jedi is one of the four main characters I ran in the massively multiplayer online role-playing game *Star Wars Galaxies*. Anakin Skywalker was the apprentice of Obi-Wan Kenobi, and their relationship was central to the movies and to *Revenge of the Sith*. Simula Tion never met Kenobi, but did visit his house on the planet Tatooine, shortly after his death. On the jungle moon Yavin 4, she encountered Luke Skywalker, the son of Anakin. On the planet Naboo, she once observed a military ceremony conducted by Darth Vader, without realizing that he had once been Anakin Skywalker.

Two different actors played Obi-Wan Kenobi in the movies. Alec Guinness played him in the original 1977 film. Despite the fact that the character died before the end, his disembodied spirit played cameo roles in the 1980 and 1983 sequels. Then, Ewan McGregor played the role in the three prequels, produced decades later but set in the fictional universe decades earlier. Anakin Skywalker was played by six actors in the six movies. Jake Lloyd was Anakin as a boy in the first prequel movie; Hayden Christensen played him as a young man, and once Anakin had been transmogrified into Darth Vader, his physical form was usually played by David Prowse but in some action scenes was played by Bob Anderson, and his voice was by James Earl Jones. In the 1983 film *Return of the Jedi*, when Darth Vader was briefly unmasked as he was dying, Sebastian Shaw played him. I played Simula Tion in *Star Wars Galaxies*, but I also played engineer Algorithma Teq, bounty hunter Socio Path, and a Wookiee entertainer named Guzzlebooze. When I did the solo-player game, I also acted as both Obi-Wan Kenobi and Anakin Skywalker, although on the very small stage of my television set. Thus, even before the story begins, we get a sense that multiple identities overlap, and there is no one-to-one correspondence between person and character.

Obi-Wan Kenobi is a rather stable character, but Anakin Skywalker went through profound transformations that could be described in terms of psychiatry, morality, or group loyalty. Thus, Obi-Wan Kenobi represents stable detachment from the world's chaos, whereas Anakin Skywalker represents unstable passions that respond to the problems of the world and ironically aggravate them. As the movies conceptualize it, the universe is bound together by the Force, and a very few Force-sensitive individuals are able to draw magical powers from it. Superficially, one asks whether they will use this power for good or evil. The movies are more subtle than this, speaking of the Light Side and the Dark Side of the Force.

Star Wars Episode III: Revenge of the Sith, a game based on the movie of the same name, is a non-Christian religious drama.[17] The *Star Wars* stories concern the Jedi, akin to Zen masters, who possess supernormal powers based on their knowledge of the Force. They must cultivate an almost Zen Buddhist detachment from the world, lest they be seduced to the Dark Side to serve their own personal desires rather than the spiritual needs of the galaxy.[18]

In electronic games, personalities are not only emulated, they are also augmented. Over time, avatars gain skills, and the mythology of the particular world may define their powers in supernatural terms. In the *Star Wars* mythos, Jedi have the unique ability to channel the Force, that mysterious energy field that no one outside their priesthood can handle. In the videogame, Force Power can move some physical objects and attack enemies, but also becomes depleted with use and must be replenished from supplies that are found through the environment. As the PlayStation 2 version of the game manual explains, there are seven Force Powers:

1. Force Push: Quickly press the R1 Button to perform a Force Push. A wide wave of energy knocks back multiple enemies and causes damage.
2. Force Grasp: Press and hold the R1 Button to lift the target into the air, and move the Left Analog Stick in the direction you want to throw it, then release the R1 button. You can throw enemies or objects around you. The target takes damage, along with any enemies it hits.
3. Force Stun: Press and hold the R2 Button to stun several droids (if they are clustered together). After a moment of concentration and after enough Force Power is used, the droid(s) will remain stunned for a short while and you can finish them off or deal with other threats.... If used on weak-minded humanoids, they are tricked into fighting for you for a short duration.
4. Force Lightning: Press and hold the R2 Button to electrocute enemies, effectively stunning them and doing continuous damage. You can continue to send bolts until the enemy is defeated or your Force Meter runs out.
5. Saber Throw: Press the L2 Button to throw your lightsaber, damaging all enemies and objects in its path. The longer you hold down the L2 Button, the farther your lightsaber will fly. The lightsaber automatically returns to you after making a curved flight arc.

6. Force Heal: Press and hold the R3 and L3 Buttons . . . to heal yourself using the Force. This ability uses a lot of Force Power and drains the meter very quickly, so use it wisely.
7. Force Speed: Move the Left Analog Stick twice in any direction to receive a temporary speed boost. While using Force Speed perform combos to create powerful attacks.

Proper use of the Force was central to the *Star Wars* saga—not which buttons to press on the controller but what purposes the Force may be used to achieve. However, the tension between the Dark and Light sides is not the only dimension relevant to personality and represented in the movies and gameworlds. A second dimension is the degree to which the individual person—whether the game player or character in the stories—is a natural-born hero, innately superior to the vast majority of other people and characters. In the first of the prequels, Obi-Wan Kenobi meets Anakin Skywalker when Anakin is still a small boy, and recognizes that the Force is strong in him. But Anakin may already be too old for Jedi training, because he already experiences passion, notably love for his mother and resentment at being a slave boy. Later, when Anakin has become a young man, he falls in love with Queen Amidala, but love is incompatible with being a Jedi. Then Anakin seeks to liberate his mother from her slavery, only to watch her die from torture because he came too late. The *Revenge of the Sith* game does not emphasize this background, but it provides the human explanation for why Anakin turns to the Dark Side and becomes Darth Vader, the formidable villain of the series. A key factor is that Anakin gains a new mentor, the future emperor of the galaxy, who seems to empathize with Anakin's feelings. Note that Anakin is an unusual person, not only because of his Force sensitivity and passions, but because he holds extremely high status in the galaxy, as do all his immediate associates.

When I explored *Star Wars Galaxies*, nine classes of avatar, called paths, were available: bounty hunter, commando, entertainer, Jedi, medic, officer, smuggler, spy, and trader. The last of these was the starting point for one avatar, Algorithma Teq, because I wanted her to become an engineer who could build droids. My first avatar was Simula Tion, a Jedi. On the path-selection screen in the character-creation module, this was the description of her path: "Jedi are Force Sensitive beings that can use their Force power to over-come and control their enemies and can master the art of fighting with a lightsaber. Force Sensitive individuals feel a connection to the energy that surrounds all living things and binds the galaxy together." The remarkable thing about this description is that it says nothing about the Jedi being a religious order.

Like *Lord of the Rings Online*, *Star Wars Galaxies* faced the considerable challenge of being true to an existing legend, while giving freedom to the player to experience the fantasy world in new ways. The solution for *Lord of the Rings Online* was to situate the action at the same time as part of the well-known story, even letting the player interact with key characters at several points in the narrative, but carefully sending the player off on special missions that used the territory and ethos of the existing legend yet not duplicating specific missions from the legend. *Star Wars Galaxies* took a different approach, setting its action immediately after the events of the original 1977 movie. At that point in the *Star Wars* legend, the Jedi had been eradicated, and there may have been only one of them left in the galaxy; namely, Luke Skywalker, son of Anakin. Thus, the religion was extinct at this point.[19]

However, players would want to be Jedi, and the game creators struggled at first to resist this, and then to accept it. When the game launched in June 2003, only after months of effort could a few especially stalwart players become Jedi, but then in November 2005 a major redesign of the game allowed any player to begin the game with a Jedi avatar.[20] This, of course, violated the official legend, because hordes of Jedi did not exist at that point in the history of the galaxy. But it also was anomalous in terms of the Jedi identity itself. The account of Obi-Wan Kenobi and Anakin Skywalker tells the story not only of the last days of the Jedi order but also of the intimate relationship between master and student that shaped the character of each Jedi. Later in the mythos, Luke Skywalker underwent very brief training from Obi-Wan Kenobi, then longer but incomplete training from Yoda, a senior Jedi who was in hiding on a swamp planet. Yet Simula Tion received no such training and had no mentor. Because she began her life as an adult, we did not get to see her early years, but once she entered the world her advancement occurs without the intimate relationship with a master required for a true Jedi.

Once Simula Tion reached the desert planet Tatooine, the character from the mythos who had the greatest impact on her life was not a Jedi but the repulsive giant slug Jabba the Hut. Already when she was at level 5, he was trying to employ her. A Jedi named Nos'lyn did appear briefly at various points in her progress, giving her the robes that serve as a uniform for a Jedi padawan, or student; a force crystal from which she gets an educational mission; and later a lightsaber. The Jedi lesson was called "Anger and Harmony," sending her to a ruined village where the Dark Side of the Force had perverted all creatures, and to an oasis where the Light Side produced tranquility. A later Jedi quest required collecting crystals from within dark caverns, in order to upgrade the lightsaber, but this was an equipment upgrade rather than an epiphany. To gain the Mark of the Hero, she demonstrates altruism, honor, courage, and intellect in a series of difficult missions, but religion was not necessary for success.

Eventually, I took four different avatars up to the level 90 experience cap in *Star Wars Galaxies*, but all four died when this gameworld shut down on

December 15, 2011. Five days later, *Star Wars: The Old Republic* launched, a story-focused MMO from a different company, so I immediately created four different avatars in it, using a different role-playing strategy. Each of them was based on a science fiction author whose works I admired: Edgar Rice Burroughs, Robert A. Heinlein, Isaac Asimov, and Alfred Bester.[21] The last of these is less well known outside the science fiction subculture, but is somebody I knew personally. We had been on a panel at a regional science fiction convention, devoted to invented religions in science fiction, where I had teased him for writing religious scripture, in the form of two remarkable novels, *The Demolished Man* and *The Stars My Destination*, each of which combined one form of psychoanalysis with one form of parapsychology.[22] He died in 1987, but was resurrected as a fictional character in the science fiction television series *Babylon 5*, played by Walter Koenig, who also had played Chekov in the original *Star Trek* series, and in a trilogy of novels based on the series, written by Gregory Keyes.[23] In *Babylon 5*, he was the evil head of Psi Corps, comparable to Darth Vader, so in this complex series of roles-within-roles, I made him a member of the Sith order who rivaled the Jedi.

At their peak, the Jedi were the most influential religious order in the galaxy, although if one sets aside the fact that they were officially involved in the galactic government, they had many of the features of a magical cult. In many ways similar to Scientology, the real religion created by science fiction author L. Ron Hubbard, the Jedi Order is a self-defined elite group who seeks to lead humanity using a combination of religion and science.[24] In general, the sociology of religious movements finds that the small groups disparagingly called sects or cults by non-members offer compensatory social status to members.[25] Whatever their status in the wider social system, members can feel they are superior because they alone follow the one true religion, and because they have set up an alternate system of honor in direct competition with the secular status system. The relevance to gameworlds is that they also confer a sense of special status on the player, for mastering the complex interface and rules of play, for gaining increasing status in the hierarchy of levels, and for becoming first the member and later the leader of a guild of fellow players. A very interesting feature of some classes of character in many gameworlds is that the player can have two or more avatars, one having power and status over the others.

Simple Secondary Avatars

Most MMOs allow some or all of their classes of avatars to have assistants, which can be called *secondary avatars*. Some of them are defined in naturalistic terms, such as the pet possessed by a hunter in *World of Warcraft*. Others are defined in supernatural terms, such as the minion of a warlock in the same MMO. A hunter gains a pet by finding a suitable animal in the wild, taming it, feeding it, and training it. When killing an enemy, a warlock can cast the *drain souls* spell that steals a soul shard from the enemy, which can be used to summon a demon to do the warlock's bidding. In action, the hunter's pet and warlock's demon serve similar functions, often being used as a *tank* to hold the attention of an enemy, while the hunter shoots bullets or the warlock casts harmful spells, both standing at a safe distance from the enemy. Four MMOs will illustrate the range of religion-related secondary avatars here: *Lord of the Rings Online* and *Age of Conan* illustrate simple secondaries with very limited user control, whereas *Dungeons and Dragons Online* and *Guild Wars* illustrate much more complex control systems.

My main *Lord of the Rings Online* avatar, Rumilisoun, had acquired three pets by the time she had reached an advanced level: Beorn the bear, Poe the raven, and Lamhainn the lynx. Each had its own characteristics, although only one could be active at a given time, and she tended to go questing with Beorn at her side. In the *Lord of the Rings* mythos, heroes represent transcendent good against profound evil, and they strenuously avoid using magical powers. Nothing is ever said about God, yet the implication is that the heroes serve a divine purpose. As an Elf lore master, Rumilisoun seeks knowledge, guards wisdom, and wields ancient secrets as if they were magic. Her craft serves Nature, and draws upon natural powers that have religious implications, although they are seldom explicitly described in religious terms. Over time, she learns the languages of the different animals, and when she became a *friend of bears*, her understanding of their speech allowed her to call one from the wild to assist her.

When operating both Rumilisoun and Beorn, the computer interface offers two separate sets of controls, and Beorn's consists of clickable icons in a conveniently placed bar. Some of the icons made him take particular actions in a fight, and could be triggered at the exact moment when they were needed. A collection of such special actions would be gained over the course of time. For example, *roaring challenge* made Beorn roar at the enemy, causing it to attack him, while *rage* put Beorn into a rage, attacking the enemy fiercely. Most of the icons set general rules for Beorn's behavior, which he would then follow autonomously as events unfolded:

> Aggressive Mode—Your pet will enter combat when valid targets are detected.
> Passive Mode—Your pet will not enter combat unless commanded to.
> Guard Mode—Your pet will enter combat to defend you or itself.
> Attack—Your pet will attack your currently selected target.
> Follow—Your pet will move towards you and then act according to its mode.

Stay—Your pet will stay in its current position unless its mode requires combat.

Assist—When enabled, your pet will attack targets that you attack.

Thus, secondary avatars are typically *semiautonomous*, using very simple artificial intelligence techniques to allow them to interact with the changing environment without constant direct control from the user. This reinforces the perception that they are distinct entities, possessing an identity separate from the avatar and the player, even though their computer code is part of the same program as that of the avatar and, indeed, of the environment as well. Secondary avatars have lower status than the primary avatars, so they may increase the player's sense of social status. Most obviously, they expand the expression of the player's personality, enabling a *multiplex self*. A protean self changes from moment to moment, depending upon the circumstances, while a multiplex self expresses multiple dimensions of the person simultaneously.

Eridanos, my necromancer avatar in *Age of Conan*, illustrates how there may be multiple secondary avatars with supernatural qualities. As *AoCWiki* explains:

Necromancers summon and command the undead, and they are legion. Their ghoulish minions are capable of tearing men apart or casting their own death magic. The rotten corpses of the dead follow wherever the necromancer leads. Evil and twisted Necromancers bring the cursed and dead back from beyond the mortal realm to do their bidding. The dark magic wielded by necromancers ranges from the unholy to pestilent corruption and the freezing touch of death. Through careful study they can develop the ability to call corpses from the earth to rise up and surround a foe or even attain lichdom, turning themselves into terrifying undead archmages.[26]

Eridanos himself seems to have been a resurrected spirit. *Age of Conan* starts every primary avatar in the same area, facing the same challenges, after being washed up on the same beach. Not only Orastes, my Aquilonian priest of Mitra, but also Boadicea, my Cimmerian shaman, and Atlantea, my Stygian priestess of Set, were forced to complete essentially the same quests up to level 20. I then took Orastes to level 50, and the other two to level 30. Once Orastes reached level 50, I gained the right to create a new character at that level, skipping all the repetitive quests at lower levels. Thus Eridanos, starting his adventures with high-level abilities, was already the master of secondary avatars when I started running him.

He had a choice of which minions to work with, up to a total of six, with one high-power minion taking the place of two lower-power ones. Thus, sometimes he had four, and at other times six. For the sake of variety more than magical effectiveness, he operated six different ones when he retrieved a relic from Atlantis called the Phoenix of the North in a heavily defended ice cave in the Eiglophina Mountains, after killing a witch named Mithrelle. The selection screen in the user interface describes them:

> Arcanist—spells have a chance of augmenting the attacks of its master and brethren with extra damage
>
> Mage—spells inflict a small amount of splash damage around their primary target
>
> Corruptor—basic melee attacks, which have a chance of inflicting additional unholy damage with each attack
>
> Harvester—melee attacks have a chance of bestowing mana and stamina upon their master's team
>
> Life-stealer—melee attacks have a chance of stealing life and transferring it to the necromancer and their associates
>
> Mutilator—basic melee attacks which have a chance of inflicting bleeding wounds. If enough bleeding wounds are inflicted, melee attacks against the victim cause a small amount of extra slashing damage

The selection screen calls the arcanist and mage *undead sorcerers*, and the four others *mindless undead minions*. The sorcerers cost two pet points, whereas the others cost one point each. Eridanos had eight points to distribute, so he could, for example, have gone into battle with two arcanists and two mages at his side. However, the melee minions were useful because they would rush up to the enemy, hopefully confusing it. The *Age of Conan* wiki notes the lack of complexity in operating minions: "The player can set aggressive, defensive and passive modes but other than that they will only attack your target and can't be individually controlled."[27]

Each minion contributes only a little to the necromancer's powers. As the description for sorcerers says, "Sometimes an apprentice does not meet their master's measure, but that does not mean they cannot serve." Functionally, each minion is not very different from other avatar enhancements, like armor and spell-enhancing buffs, except that they are represented on the computer screen as a separate human character. They automatically modify the complex algorithm that causes damage to the enemy, without requiring extra work on the part of the player. When the primary avatar is running across the terrain, the minions follow, spreading out a little bit and finding their way around obstacles. In combat, the sorcerers stand back and hurl magical spells, while the melee fighters bunch together near their target.

Complex Secondary Avatars

Dungeons and Dragons Online (DDO) has a much more complex system for operating secondary avatars, allowing both fine control and a degree of autonomy. Sagittarius, my avatar in DDO, was a ranger, which meant that, like Rumilisoun, he could have an animal pet. His pets, a hyena and a lioness, were rather stupid, however, and not as versatile as Beorn. But he could also use very sophisticated mercenaries, called *hirelings*, who had the same fundamental abilities as players' avatars of the same class. DDO is primarily a very large set of dungeons, or *instances*, in which it usually requires a team of players to complete a set of missions that often take two hours. Hirelings are substitutes for fellow players, the expedient for solo players and for sociable players whose friends do not happen to be online at the moment. DDO is a free-to-play, pay-to-win game, in which no monthly subscription is required, and hirelings really work for the game company. They must be rented by a player, either with virtual coins earned by completing missions inside DDO or with points that must be bought in an online store for real dollars.

For each hireling there is a hotbar holding ten icons, and clicking one either gives a specific command or sets the general behavior of the agent. Four of these are actions that only the particular hireling can perform; for example, a cleric may have one icon to give significant healing to a selected wounded ally, and another one to give minor healing to all members of the party. Six icons are the same for all hirelings: 1 toggles between stand still or follow the primary avatar, 2 summons the hireling to the avatar, even over a long distance, 3 sets the hireling to behave autonomously, 4 engages defensive mode, the hireling responding only if it or the primary avatar is attacked, 5 engages passive mode, the hireling doing nothing, and 6 has it interact with a target.

The last of these might, for example, have the secondary avatar pull a lever in one of the many dungeon mazes, when two widely separated levers must be pulled simultaneously to open a gate. The hireling follows the primary avatar to one lever, is told to stand still, and the user right-clicks the lever to select it as the hireling's target. The primary avatar then walks to the second lever and activates it, while the player clicks the hirelings' sixth icon to tell it to interact with the first lever. These combined actions open the gate, something that one avatar could not do alone.

One mission carried out in the ruins of Threnal illustrates how complex the action of a simulated team can become. Buried deep beneath the earth for five hundred years, the Library of Threnal has just been entered by archaeologists. An ambitious man named Coyle is seeking an ancient manuscript that could give him magical powers, but he has kept this reason for entering the library secret. In

DDO, he is represented as an autonomous nonplayer character, as are two assistants who accompany him. They stand in the central book repository of the library, responding as waves of monsters of different kinds enter from random directions. As soon as Coyle sees a monster, he attacks it, and his assistants follow his lead. Unfortunately, this will result in his quick death, and the goal of the mission is to keep him alive for fifteen minutes.

Sagittarius rented five hirelings; two were cleric healers, and three were warriors with different attack modes to give them a range of chances against different monsters. On ordinary missions, he often instructed all his hirelings to support him in defensive mode, which means they heal him and attack only enemies who have harmed him. This time, he gave the three warriors instructions to act autonomously, which means they immediately attack enemies they detect. Thus, when monsters approached, six members of the team attacked them: Coyle, his two assistants, and three of the hirelings. The two cleric hirelings stood passively watching the battle, only reacting on those rare occasions when Sagittarius took damage, or when given specific instructions. Sagittarius set his own attention on Coyle, and, whenever Coyle took damage, instructed one of the clerics to heal him. In the pause after one attack and before the next, Sagittarius would rapidly use the clerics plus his own limited healing abilities to restore the health of any members of the team who needed it.

Notice that the nine-member team included three agents who could not be controlled at all, three secondary avatars who were set to function autonomously but could have been controlled, and three characters (counting the primary avatar as well as two secondaries) under the direct control of the player. Given that groups of attacking monsters came from random directions, and the behaviors of the AIs were influenced by their exact locations in relation to the others, even very simple programming produced a remarkably complex result.

Guild Wars has an even more complex system for managing secondary avatars, which evolved along with the game during its early years. This gameworld has a unique payment method, charging for each major expansion as a separate game but then requiring no payment to play online, and each part covers distinct virtual geography. I purchased the first three units bundled together as *Guild Wars Trilogy* and developed three avatars, one in each, but capable of traveling across all three territories. The virtual geography in *Guild Wars* is rather constrained, indeed constituting effectively a vast set of mazes, which allows it to manage localities as instances, where separate groups of players will not encounter each other even if they are in the same place. This allows *Guild Wars* to offer many small scripted dramas, experienced at different times by different players, in which friendly nonplayer characters join the avatar's team. Only in cities and major outposts do all players currently online encounter each others' avatars.

There, different players are encouraged to team up for group quests, but when a player cannot find suitable partners, or wishes to play solo, it is easy to recruit nonplayer characters' allies as *henchmen*.

The best example for present purposes is a mission called "Divinity Coast," which was completed by Venator Strenuus, my ranger avatar who began in the second part of *Guild Wars Trilogy*, which is called *Factions* and takes place in a fantasy version of China. There are twenty levels of experience in *Guild Wars*, and at this point Venator had reached level 15 and joined a theocratic military order called the White Mantle that worships the Unseen Ones. The Divinity Coast instance includes villages under attack from hordes of evil spirits, as well as religious shrines that perform miracles, and the main task is to take a relic called the Eye of Janthir to a fishing village where it can be protected. In this remarkable mission, Venator led fully five different kinds of secondary avatars: pet, henchmen, hero, ally, and the Eye of Janthir itself.

Venator's pet was a playful tiger which he had tamed long before, using his Charm Animal spell. It would accompany him, defend him, and attack whatever target he did. If it died, he had a spell to resurrect it. Pets gain experience, as they hunt alongside their owners, and they can gain a small number of special skills. The user can set one of three behavior modes—attack (aggressive), guard (defensive), and heel (passive)—and change these in the midst of action. There is an option to name the pet, but Venator never gave his tiger the honor of a name.

For this mission, Venator used four henchmen: Alesia (healer), Stefan (fighter), Orion (mage), and Dunham (enchanter). When in a city or major outpost, all the available henchmen line up near the exit, and the player can select them through a module in the computer interface. Unlike the mercenaries in DDO, they do not cost anything, but when virtual gold is looted from an enemy corpse, they take their shares. They do not have individual control panels, but the user can place a flag on the terrain—even at some distance from where the primary avatar is standing—and the henchmen will run to that point. In action, each behaves as if it were the avatar of a player with the specified role. Stefan would run toward the selected enemy to engage in melee combat, while the others would stand back and perform their distinctive roles.

Nightfall, the third part of the trilogy, added heroes to the mix, and by buying the whole package I was able to give my avatars a robot-like golem hero named M.O.X. The avatar I started in *Nightfall*, Helen Augusta, eventually had three heroes, each of which could be handled separately, but Venator used just this one. A hero is almost exactly like a second primary avatar and along with henchmen can be sent into battle even while the primary avatar remains aloof from combat. M.O.X. had a rather full set of controls, complete with icons for whatever skills I wanted to put on his action bar, and he progressed up through the same levels of experience, attributes, and skills as any primary avatar. For each hero, there is a separate flag that can tell it where in the vicinity it should go.

Justiciar Hablion was the first nonplayer ally with whom Venator interacted in "Divinity Coast," and he served as a quest giver, first instructing Venator to cleanse himself in the Fountain of Truth on the top of a hill, then giving him the Eye of Janthir. The mission did not consist simply of delivering the Eye safely to its destination, but also using it to identify five villagers who have the magical aptitude to study with the Grand Masters at the Temple of Unseen. As these villagers are identified, they join the party as allies. They are passive and contribute little to progress, yet delivering all five safely to the goal earns a bonus for the mission.

The Eye of Janthir is a tall, translucent tetrahedron, described by many players as a pyramid. It contains an eye, rather like the Masonic eye in the apex of the pyramid on the back of a US dollar bill. The mission turns out not to be so much rescuing the Eye of Janthir as using it in a religious ritual called the Test of the Chosen, conducted each year at the Summer Solstice by the White Mantle, as a kind of entry exam to its esoteric university. The Eye floated over Venator's head, taking no part in the combat, but functioning as a secondary avatar whenever it came near friendly villagers, judging them. It knocked most of them to the ground, as a sign of rejection. The chosen five it sanctified, and caused them to express joy:

> "And my brother said I wouldn't amount to anything. Ha! Who's laughing now?"
> "I can't wait. This is the most important day of my life."
> "I knew it. I always knew I was gifted."
> "I wonder if I'll get my own room in the Grand Temple."
> "I've always dreamed of studying with the Grand Masters."

To the extent that secondary avatars act autonomously, we conceptualize them as distinct persons, yet all nonplayer characters who serve a given primary avatar are in varying degrees expressions of the player. An interesting worldwide phenomenon is the tendency of people to give person-like names to boats and occasionally to other vehicles. Several ships have been named *Queen Elizabeth*. The B-29 aircraft that dropped the atom bomb on Hiroshima was named the *Enola Gay*, after the pilot's mother. Thus, there is historical precedent for personifying technology. Secondary avatars illustrate the potential complexity when segments of computer code and graphic images represent aspects of a person.

The situation becomes even more complex when the symbolism encompasses multiple other people. For example, I named my main avatar in *Rift* after my grandmother, Mildred Sims, adjusting the name slightly to make it more mythic: Mildryth. At different points in her progress up the fifty experience levels in this gameworld, she had one or another sprite-like secondary avatar flying around her head and offering considerable help in combat. In naming them, I tried to think what my grandmother would have wanted. The answer was obvious: her two daughters. So I named one Audie, the nickname of my aunt Audrey Sims Rohn, and the other Bobbie, the nickname of my mother, Barbara Sims Bainbridge. As children, we are the secondary avatars of our parents, and after their deaths we can continue to serve occasionally as their avatars.

Ancestor Veneration

Many people give little thought to the personality of an avatar at the point they create it, although the gameworlds covered here offer many choices in designing the avatar's appearance, starting with his or her gender. The key decisions, however, are what *World of Warcraft* calls *race* and *class*. The different races begin their sagas in different geographic locations with different cultures, as well as having different appearances, so their early questing experiences will be quite different. Class determines some of the most important skills the avatar can develop, although other skills can be decided upon later in the avatar's life. Superficial appearance and specialized skills define significant dimensions of a person, but are not the same as personality. The one other attribute decided when an avatar is created that might express personality is the name. Invariably, MMOs prevent assigning a name that is already in use on the particular server, and some impose a limit of one word for a name, rather than two or more. Players vary greatly in their name-creating habits, but often they do seem to be expressing their image of who the avatar is going to be.

For *Pirates of the Caribbean Online*, based on the Disney fantasy movies set around the year 1700, I created an avatar named Lionel Wafer. This name seems a little silly, but perhaps suggesting a personality lacking a sense of humor and not really capable of heroic accomplishments. Yet I chose the name because it belonged to a real historical personage, a remarkable man who served as the doctor of the Caribbean pirates and published an astonishing 1699 autobiography that despite its extremely fantastic content is generally considered to be quite accurate.[28] One of my four avatars in *Age of Conan*, Orastes, was based on a remarkable character in one of the original Conan stories, as we shall see in the following chapter.

At times, I fashioned an avatar to express a cultural archetype, the most prominent examples being Catullus in *World of Warcraft* and Rumilisoun in *Lord of the Rings Online*, both of whom achieved the top experience levels in their respective gameworlds, and both of whom published essays under their own names.[29] Catullus, of course, was the name of a prominent ancient Roman poet, but I crafted the avatar's personality to include not only the cynical hedonism of the poet but also the engineering ability that allowed the Romans to conquer their world. This avatar belonged to the Blood Elf race, who reminded me very much of dissolute Roman aristocrats. Rumilisoun I imagined to be the granddaughter of the Elf scholar Rúmil, who in the *Lord of the Rings* mythology invented writing. Because her name is pronounced with an emphasis on the second syllable, Rumilisoun lacks the accent over the first vowel, a small reflection of the fact that she is a pedantic scholar, interested in documenting the war raging around her, but not willing to participate fully in the fellowship of good battling evil.

In the previous chapter, Cleora showed how an avatar could serve as a memorial. Given all the possibilities for self-expression and cultural exploration in online role-playing games, it seemed to me that it would be worth exploring in a new direction, creating a number of avatars based on deceased members of my own family. This began with my second *World of Warcraft* character, Maxrohn, whom I named after my uncle Max Rohn. My first avatar in this gameworld was a Human mage I named Aristotle, imagining that he was a philosopher exploring the fauna and contrasting cultures of his world, just as the real ancient Greek named Aristotle had done. New Human characters always begin at Northshire Abbey, not a very hospitable institution for a mage, and they soon visit Stormwind City, where there is a rather spectacular cathedral. Given my background in the sociology of religion, I soon realized I would need to create a Human priest avatar to explore fictional religion in *World of Warcraft*, and Maxrohn was the result. My uncle, who had died some time before, was an Episcopal priest who had served in the Bahamas and Virgin Islands, and whom I always thought of as something of an adventurer. So I very much had my uncle in mind as I ran this avatar for over seven hundred hours.

For this study, I created eighteen major avatars based on deceased relatives. I had known two-thirds of them personally, such as in the cases of Williamwheeler in *Warhammer Online*, based on my father, William Wheeler Bainbridge, and Junellen in *Aion*, based on his mother, June Ellen Wheeler Bainbridge. Others were historical figures I knew through family lore and through their extensive publications. The earliest, Edmund Bainbridge, was probably born in 1702 (or 1692 depending on the source you believe). I knew about him because a genealogist hired by our family had uncovered various facts about his life.[30] Edmund Bainbridge was my real great-great-great-great-great-great-grandfather, and I imagine that at age eighteen he voyaged to the Caribbean in search of wealth and adventure.

This is not so fanciful as it might seem, because he was a man of strong character, who later in his life had a relationship to the British Empire not very different from that of some pirates of his day. In 1747 he was indicted for rioting and high treason by the British government in New Jersey, listed first among the criminals who rioted first at Somerset and then at Amboy,[31] and was described by authorities as "one of the captains of the western rioters."[32] The dispute concerned whether farmers like Edmund owned the land they had been working for years, often holding what they thought were legal deeds to their properties, or whether it belonged to "proprietors" who had received titles to vast sections of land from the king. In his vast, four-volume history of the struggle for liberty in the early history of the United States, Murray Rothbard reports:

> In July, one of the most serious of the riots broke out in Perth Amboy, the main center of the resident Eastern proprietors. John Bainbridge, Jr., had been arrested for taking part in the Somerset County outbreak and was imprisoned in Perth Amboy jail. At this point, a rescue party of 150, armed with clubs and led by Edmund Bainbridge, Simon Wyckoff, and Amos Roberts, appeared at the courthouse, knocked down the sheriff and the mayor, broke open the jail, and jubilantly rode off with the prisoner.[33]

Most of Edmund's life, apparently, was spent in farming, but it was easy to imagine he had voyaged to the British part of the Caribbean as a young man, had adventures, and returned to New Jersey only after suffering a business failure. One of the points I discovered while running the eighteen family avatars was that real human beings really do have adventures like those in videogames, just not very often. A related point is that we must understand that the real past was a very alien environment, including features that seem fantastic today. In Edmund's case, online research revealed that he had owned a slave, named Negro Nellie, who featured in a famous law case.[34] At Edmund's death, Nellie was inherited by his daughter, who freed Nellie, but one of her brothers sued, saying that Nellie was family property and should belong to him. The court indeed freed Nellie, as part of the final eradication of slavery in northern states. It may be an exaggeration to say truth is stranger than fiction, but not much of an exaggeration.

The stories of two of the other family members who became avatars can illustrate the ways in which real lives can parallel adventure games, and this pair of "brothers" features prominently in the concluding chapter of this book. William Bridgebain in *Tabula Rasa* was based on my grandfather, William Seaman Bainbridge, and Consuelo Seoane in *Pirates of the Burning Sea* was based on his brother-in-law, Consuelo Andrew Seoane, who had married William's sister Helen. After my grandfather's older sister, Cleora, died, his parents adopted Helen, who became his younger sister—and I used Helen as one of my *Guild Wars* avatars.

As mentioned in connection with Cleora in the previous chapter, when he was a boy of just nine, my grandfather accompanied his parents on a fifty-thousand-mile research tour of American Christian missions across Asia. Helen, who was younger, was deposited with my grandfather's maternal grandfather and paternal grandmother, who had married each other after the deaths of their first spouses. Thus, by the time he was ten, my grandfather already had experienced enough adventures for a lifetime, in Japan, China, India, and the Middle East. We don't actually know where Helen was during that trip, because the 1880s census does not list her living with her grandparents, and she once vehemently remarked, "I hate grandmothers!" Note the complexity of social relations among these people, another indicator of the problematic nature of the self.

William Seaman Bainbridge became a world-famous surgeon, beginning his career by taking a rich insane patient to rendezvous with Kitchener's army on its way to the battle against the Mahdi in Khartoum, Sudan. In 1915, he convinced the mayor of New York City to support him in a fact-finding tour of surgical procedures used on wounded soldiers on both the German and French sides of the western front in World War I.[35] Once the United States had entered the conflict, he found being the chief surgeon on the largest hospital ship rather boring, so he simply gave himself new orders to complete a book-length study of surgical procedures by visiting the most advanced French hospitals, including on the battlefront. At one point the British arrested him on suspicion of being a spy, but connections back in Washington made them release him.

He was always fascinated by military technology, assembling a collection of gas masks, for example, and trying out new airplanes at every opportunity. Although he never learned to operate any kind of vehicle himself, not even a car, he forced one Allied pilot to fly him far over the German lines, and in a later incident was the only passenger in a light plane over the English Channel when the engine quit, but the pilot was able to glide back to a French beach. In 1923, he aggressively examined the crisis in the German Ruhr and Rhineland, which were under French and Belgian occupation, and his virulently anti-German report was instrumental in preventing American aid to the suffering German children.[36] During that particular adventure, he communicated back home in code, using the cable address "Bridgebain, New York." When I needed a medically oriented avatar to become a biotechnician in the science-fiction gameworld *Tabula Rasa*, I naturally thought of my grandfather and of "Bridgebain," which in a sense was my family's first email address. Later, when I saw that medical technology was central to the postapocalyptic gameworld *Fallen Earth*, I resurrected Bridgebain and made him my first avatar to reach the top experience level in two different virtual worlds that were highly relevant to his own real-world experience.

Despite what might seem to be a feminine first name, which refers to the "consolation" offered by the Virgin Mary, Consuelo Andrew Seoane was the most masculine of men. He fought in the Spanish-American War on the side of the United States in the Caribbean, and was of Spanish extraction, so I naturally thought of him when preparing to create a Spanish officer avatar for *Pirates of the Burning Sea*. His last name was pronounced see-OH-nee, which does not sound very Spanish, and we called him "Uncle Con." At the Siege of Santiago, a Mauser bullet pierced his right lung, and he carried the slug inside him for the rest of his life.[37] I believe his connection to the Bainbridge family came through a friendship he developed with a surgeon and senior officer at the battle, Louis Livingston Seaman, who was my grandfather's cousin and later had his own adventures embedded in the Japanese army during the Russo-Japanese War, on a quest to learn about their medical practices.[38] When the Philippine Insurrection broke out the following year, Con was promoted to second lieutenant in the 41st US Volunteer Infantry, and once again he served with Louis. On the assumption that he was fluent in Spanish, the former colonial language of the Philippines, Con was offered a top position handling maps and trail finding. Hiding the fact that he did not actually speak Spanish, he frantically studied textbooks, and the army never realized they had been tricked.

Con's greatest adventure began in June 1909, when he and naval doctor Joseph "Snake" Thompson posed as naturalists interested in reptiles and beetles and set out upon a two-year espionage tour against Japan. Their mission would have brought instant death if the ubiquitous police ever realized they were American spies. Con was particularly worried by the fact that Snake hid a camera in a secret compartment of the creel in which they carried specimens. Beginning their tour in Hong Kong, they traveled through the Ryukyus and Okinawa, the length and breadth of Formosa (Taiwan), spied for seventeen months in the home islands of Japan, then briefly investigated Manchuria and Korea. They used false identities, pretending to be South African Afrikaners, and gained credibility with the Japanese by arranging to be repeatedly insulted by British diplomats, who despised their opponents in the Boer War which had ended just seven years earlier.

Con and Snake examined dozens of potential invasion points, memorizing as much as they could and using a code to insert a few crucial facts into an apparently harmless naturalist's diary. For example, when they viewed the Sendai Temple they wrote that there were 135 steps in the approach, referring actually to the total number of artillery field pieces they had seen in the area. Another time, references to fifty-four green polypedates and seventy-eight tadpoles meant five four-inch guns and seven eight-inch guns. In the spring of 1911, Con returned to the Philippines, where he expanded the notes and recollections into a massive report on the costal fortifications of Japan, including many charts, complete with detailed plans for invasion if American relations with Japan ever degenerated into war, as Con was sure they would.[39]

These real adventures are very much like the fictional adventures in a fantasy MMO, consisting of a series of quests, trekking across vast territories studded with potentially lethal enemies, in the context of a backstory concerning major conflict between societies having vastly different cultures. Of course, few people really have adventures like this. For an exploratory study, examining the potential of gameworld avatars as vehicles for ancestor veneration, however, they were ideal. Often, the first scientific study of a new question employs very unusual means, but as knowledge is gained the subsequent studies become progressively more normal. Here, it was extremely useful to me that my own family included some fantastic adventurers—all of whom also were intellectuals who wrote books and articles expressing their understanding of their own experiences. Considered the other way around, my family has long been obsessed with making real life conform to the expectations of extreme fantasies.

There is no reason why every family cannot construct its own mythology, with a style appropriate to the particular lineage, as a way of cherishing each other and remembering the dearly departed. In the past, only aristocratic families claimed this privilege, and it is a telling fact that the most prominent fantasy gameworlds are feudal societies. As an expression of its fanciful approach to life, my family has a coat of arms, although since we lack a feudal estate it is not clear what substance this symbol has. Several versions exist, with the common feature that the shield is decorated with three battle-axes with the blades facing left. In the version used by my immediate family, the weapons are separated by the battlements of a fortress, in the shape of a right angle with the point upward enclosing one ax below, and partially separating with its point the two axes above. Over the shield there is not a helmet but a goat standing on green grass. Given the tradition of naming the eldest male in our family William, as a child I wondered if this were a "Billy goat," and the whole thing might be a "goat of arms." The Latin motto below the shield certainly seemed serious: "Dum spiro, spero." This means "While I breathe, I hope." Given that I was asthmatic as a child, this seemed both apt and encouraging. We no longer live in a feudal society, so it would seem appropriate for every family, however humble it might be in the wider social structure, to have such symbols, and to behave within the home and inside virtual worlds in an aristocratic manner.

This point connects directly to the theme of this book, because ancestor veneration was one of the original functions of religion.[40] As all the Williams in my family illustrate, as part of a custom many preliterate societies also practiced, we often remember people of the past by giving their names to new people when they enter the world. Perhaps the distinctive feature of ancient Egyptian civilization was its cities of tombs, and the estimated hundred million mummies buried in the sands, yet all that veneration was extremely costly. One of the great economic advantages of the great monotheistic religions that succeeded Paganism was that they required far less veneration of deceased ancestors. God up in heaven was taking good care of their souls, so we here below did not need to worry much about them. This observation raises a very serious question that both Atheists and social scientists of religion have failed to recognize: If God does not exist, what obligations do we have toward deceased relatives?

Duties aside, most of us want to remember our lost loved ones, to think about them, possibly learn lessons from their lives, and to deal with our feelings about them in a manner satisfactory for our own psychological well-being. After my own experience of running eighteen avatars based on deceased family members, I can say that this new method of veneration is very efficient and reasonably satisfying. Presumably one wants to spend many hours in the game-world anyway, so it costs nothing to pattern an avatar on a lost loved one. If one's grief is especially acute, this may be a painful experience, and thus inadvisable. But once one has gained a degree of emotional detachment from such a loss, there is the opposite danger of forgetting the person. While running a veneration avatar, one's consciousness of the dearly departed will fluctuate, sometimes very powerful in one's awareness and sometimes very far in the background. Especially if the avatar's situation fits the personality of the family member, as certainly was the case for William Bridgebain and Consuelo Seoane, then there can be a sense of rightness, a fusion of identities that is extremely satisfying.

At a higher level of abstraction, a very radical possibility exists. Perhaps a veneration avatar really is a reincarnation of the deceased person. If a human soul is a dynamic pattern of information, logically separate from the person's body but going out of existence when it dies, then a similar dynamic pattern of information might to some degree really be that soul. The fact that it lacks much of the information that had been locked in the deceased person's brain, and now is being emulated in low fidelity by another brain, certainly sets limits on this possibility. But if religion ceases to fulfill the human need for transcendence of death, such an idea deserves consideration. In any case, absolutely no technological advances are required at this point to allow millions of people to run avatars through gameworlds based on their deceased relatives. Here I have expressed the idea and carried out a reasonably successful demonstration study. All that is required now is a cultural shift to grant a degree of respect to people who choose to create veneration avatars.

Conclusion

Soul does not equal sole. The related concepts of protean self and multiplex self both suggest that humans are collections of fragments, just as each biological organism is an assembly of atoms, molecules, and cells. In online environments, including but not limited to gameworlds, that complexity is evident. One of the areas of most intense scholarly debate concerns how much the players of games really identify with their characters, and the extent to which most players actually become engrossed in the roles.[41] These twin questions are reflected in the two terms commonly used: *avatar* (an expression of the user's fundamental identity) and *character* (a role played in a drama that may be remote from the user's own identity). It may be that for most players today a gameworld is just a shooting gallery, where they can indulge their aggressive instincts on virtual targets, without any deep significance, while only a few neurotics actually play roles. However, we are still early in the history of gameworlds, and as the rest of society evolves or disintegrates, they may take on increased and increasingly diverse significance.

The idea of ancestor veneration avatars is a simple but radical one, which could compensate humanity to some degree for the loss of religion. But many other radical ideas may be developed in the coming years. As I ran multiple sets of secondary avatars, it occurred to me that this experience may be a harbinger of how we might manage a diversity of machines and virtual agents in the future, personifying intelligent mechanisms in order to make it easier to interact with them. Work teams later in this century may be conceptualized as hybrids of humans, robots, and disembodied artificial intelligence agents, each with its own role to play, more or less humanized depending on function and circumstances. Ancestor veneration avatars are a logical example to emphasize here, because of their connection to religion. They remind us that religion compensates humans for the loss of loved ones, as well as compensating for the inability to achieve desired goals, and indeed much of the passion connected to faith is like the Passion of Christ, a memory of suffering, longing, and hope personified in an avatar.

5 PRIESTS

Given the connection between fantasy fiction and religion, many gameworlds provide a player the opportunity to have an avatar that is a religious professional. However, many of the functions of clergy in the physical world are lacking, because the life contingencies for an avatar in a virtual world are quite different from those of a human being in the physical world. In most popular MMOs, an avatar cannot really die, so there is no need for psychological compensation in the face of death. Sickness is cured by potions, rather than soothed by prayer. Morality is enforced by the rules coded into the software, and by social pressures within long-lasting groups like guilds and tribes, rather than by sermons and fear of divine punishment. Avatars never have children, so Sunday school is unnecessary, and even marriage is missing from most gameworlds. However, religious architecture is quite common, and most worlds contain cathedrals, temples, or shrines. Given the near ubiquity of gods, logically there must be clergy, but it is not clear what they would do in their churches, and whether they have any role mediating between the other avatars and the deities.

Following the principle that suspension of disbelief is not very far from belief, we can wonder why the real world has priests at all. In popular fiction, as well as in authentic anthropology, the ancestor of the priest is the witch doctor—or, as professionals prefer to say, a *shaman*. There are two extreme but plausible theories about shamans: (1) they are crazy, and (2) they are frauds. When I developed a detailed analysis of these ideas in the context of developing formal models of cult formation, I came up with a third model, but it was really only a combination of the first two, watered down so that many members of a group contributed to the development of supernatural ideas, in a patchwork of many tiny episodes of insanity and deception.[1]

A huge social scientific literature exists, much of it influenced by psychoanalysis but also based on extensive anthropological evidence, explaining how psychopathology produces shamanism.[2] Indeed, the psychoanalytic movement depicted all magic and religion as projections of neurotic wish fulfillment or psychotic delusions. Ironically, the same may be true for psychoanalysis itself, and the movement had many of the qualities of a magical cult.[3]

Julian Silverman offered an especially cogent five-step *psychopathology model* of how a person becomes a shaman: (1) the individual is beset by an irresolvable personal problem involving self-esteem; (2) the individual becomes preoccupied with this problem and withdraws from social life; (3) in this isolation, the individual experiences sensory deprivation which produces psychotic symptoms even in a previously normal person; (4) in this altered state of consciousness the individual receives what later is defined as a religious vision; and (5) the individual cognitively reorganizes this experience in positive, religious terms and seeks to convince other people to adopt the vision.[4] This happens to fit most of the stories of messiahs, including Moses, Buddha, and even Jesus, who was tempted by Satan on a mountaintop, as well as modern messiahs who have been studied closely.

The fraud theory has not received much scholarly attention, although logically religion could be included as a subtopic in some future reorganization of the field of criminology. In my own statement of the three models, I called this the *entrepreneur model*, to avoid emphasizing the crime of fraud, because it seems that many legitimate businesses in capitalist society exaggerate the benefit of their products and services, and flimflam may be an essential feature of the job of salesman. Clearly, religion is often a *confidence game*.

A religious entrepreneur observes from close contact with existing groups that religion can be a profitable business, and that new cults must have a supply of novel compensators. If entrepreneurs acquire appropriate trade skills working in an existing cult or similar supernaturally oriented trade, then it will be possible for them to go into business for themselves. However, it is difficult to invent effective new religious compensators, so these frauds tend to commit a second crime—namely, plagiarism, adapting existing religious culture by relabeling and by mixing together previous products. Of course, most small businesses eventually fail, even though some enjoy considerable local success for a while, and only a few become major corporations with extensive monopolies, as Christianity and Islam have done. Once the original founders have passed away, there is nobody left to diagnose as psychotic or convict of fraud, but the social movements that survive retain these dubious qualities.

Two interconnected processes contributed to the evolution of shamans into priests, over the period of many hundreds of years. First, as Stark and I emphasized in *A Theory of Religion*, the emergence of church-like bureaucracies made religious professionals become more defensive, making ever fewer claims about their magical powers.[5] A family brings a desperately ill grandmother to a shaman, who goes through a mumbo-jumbo dance and proclaims a cure, but the grandmother dies. Now the grandfather gets sick. Clearly the family is not going to bring the grandfather to the same shaman, but they might try another witch doctor who uses different mumbo-jumbo. Indeed, anthropologist E. E. Evans-Pritchard documented how strenuously witch doctors attempt to keep aspects of their craft secret from each other to maintain their competitive edge.[6] Once shamans band together into a formal organization, their fates become entangled, and they cannot afford to let one of their colleagues make magical claims that are too easily disproven. So the more solidly established a religious organization is, the less emphasis it will give to magic.

Second, and functioning as the context for the first development, society as a whole becomes progressively more complex over time, and its institutions undergo extreme differentiation.[7] This entails the division of labor, in which work becomes organized into an increasing number of specialized categories.[8] One consequence for religion is that more and more of its ancient functions are taken over by other professions. A priest is no longer needed to officiate over a wedding, because a secular justice of the peace can do it instead. Laws are enacted by legislatures, rather than being inscribed in holy books or brought down from mountaintops by messiahs. Art and literary culture become enshrined in secular colleges and profit-making entertainment industries. Healing is done by medical doctors, who even take on the precarious task of providing useless treatment to people who are fated to die. To some extent this benefits religion, because it no longer is forced to perform controversial functions, but this cultural differentiation also erodes its reason for existence. As in the case of medicine, many of the secular institutions provide compensators, such as the arts emphasized here, thereby destroying religion's traditional monopoly over them.

Today at least, religion remains a viable business, although one may debate whether its practitioners are well paid. Clergy do indeed get paid for their labors.[9] When religion backed away from magic, it also had to back away from lavish rewards for its professionals, because their customers began to notice the opulent lifestyles of the head priests, a hint that the clergy might be rapacious hucksters. Churches found a clever trick to elude this trap, officially moving the wealth to the church as a collectivity and presenting priests as impoverished altruists. Yet in an established denomination, the clergy experience great lifetime security, including good medical care, and live often in architectural complexes in which their home may be modest but other areas serve as extensions of their living space. In some denominations, they get to parade around in splendid clothing during their narcissistic public rituals. All those benefits constitute payment for their services, so they are rich not only in spirit but in effective material and social wealth.

What social role can clergy play in virtual worlds where the avatars lack the need for compensators? The modest answer is: a support role in group battle. Traditionally in MMOs, when groups of players cooperate to battle hordes of enemies, especially in completing missions that cannot be completed by solo players, there are three primary roles. The *tank* stands toe-to-toe with an enemy, wearing heavy armor to protect against the enemy's attack, monopolizing the enemy's attention while doing a modest amount of damage in return. The *DPS* (damage per second) role requires an avatar to stand outside the range of the enemy's attacks and shoot arrows, bullets, or magic spells to do more damage to the enemy. The *healer* also stands at a distance, but using healing spells to counteract the damage done to the tank. In MMOs, clergy are primarily healers.

The first thing to notice about this traditional arrangement is that the healer plays a secondary or even tertiary role in a social group. Without the tank, healing is useless. I have actually found the priesthood a somewhat difficult role, because one must avoid any action that might *aggro* the enemy, which means drawing the enemy's fire by aggravating it. Healers have very feeble armor, so even if they are frantically healing themselves, they are easy to conquer. This can be a big disadvantage in solo play. The fact that clergy are healers in group play does connect to religion in the physical world, because religion is among the very most social of human activities. Although the conventional game literature does not emphasize the point, it seems likely that the healers perform another function—serving as an audience to applaud the accomplishments of the warriors they are healing. Real-world clergy may perform this function as well, because they not only castigate sinners but also praise saints.

To understand the healer's role, it is also necessary to understand its computational character, what might be called the *mechanics* of the role. A set of quantitative variables is associated with each avatar, quite a large number of them in some cases. The key variable is often called *health*, because if the health variable reaches zero, the avatar loses the battle and is often considered temporarily dead. The term *hit points* is also used, signifying the amount of damage an avatar can sustain before losing the battle, or the amount of damage an enemy does with each sword thrust. The D in DPS stands for the number of hit points of damage. The act of healing an avatar entails restoring lost health or hit points. This can be done by casting a spell, or by providing a potion which the avatar's user can imbibe whenever needed. It is also possible to cast a *buff* spell that temporarily increases the maximum amount of hit points an avatar can have, or the rate at which health regenerates. In most gameworlds, but not all, health naturally restores over time, but not fast enough to keep the avatar alive during combat.

The most popular gameworlds have far more than three kinds of avatars, in order to encourage players to run many avatars for different purposes and to gain different interesting experiences, so the three primary functions of tank, DPS, and healer are varied in complex ways across different *classes* of avatar. Priests are the primary healers, whose chief function is to support the avatars of other players during combat, perhaps taking on secondary healing functions by providing magical potions outside of combat as well. In *Dungeons and Dragons Online*, similar characters are called *clerics*, and clerics are a subclass of priests in *EverQuest II*. When I studied *World of Warcraft*, to explore the doctrinal differences, I created a priest in each of the seven WoW races that had them: In the Alliance: Human, Dwarf, Night Elf, and Draenei; in the Horde: Troll, Undead, and Blood Elf. The three other races lacked priests. In two, the Horde's Tauren and Orcs, shamans serve religious functions, although Trolls and Draenei have them as well. Druids also have religious functions among the Tauren and Night Elves. The tenth race, the Gnomes, place their faith in science and technology, although their Mages and Warlocks wield some magical powers. In the expansion that occurred after I finished my research, some Gnomes were inducted into holy orders, but frankly I doubt they would be good in that role, given their lack of spirituality.[10]

A Failed Priest

This is the story of Orastes, wayward priest of the god Mitra, who suffered mightily because he failed to follow his priestly calling as a healer. He was a character in *The Hour of the Dragon*, one of the Conan stories by Robert E. Howard, and I used him to explore much of *Age of Conan*, a gameworld set in Howard's fantastic Hyborian Age.[11] The Conan stories are brilliant but brutal, and at times they border on pornography. *Age of Conan* is milder in this regard, but intended only for adults. In combat, red blood splashes across the screen, and some episodes are sexually tinged. Howard was a remarkably talented writer, but he was also arguably insane and psychologically dependent upon his pathological mother. When he was six years old, he and his mother agreed that they would die together. At age thirty, upon learning that his mother had only a few hours to live, he shot himself.[12] Thus Orastes is a symbol of pathology, both because he betrayed his priestly vows, and because such vows themselves may not be entirely normal.

Orastes became conscious, lying on a beach in a strange land, half dead and missing half his memories. He knew his name and sensed he was no longer a young man, but he had no idea what events and decisions had constituted his life. He remembered being on a ship in a storm, and calling out to the god Mitra as the vessel disintegrated in the lashing waves. As he sank into the deep, words had come to his mind: "Their god is one of justice, security, and liberty and their priests are ready to fight to ensure these freedoms and battle against oppression, tyranny, and villainy." Yes, he must have been a priest of Mitra himself, but he had forgotten the incantations, rituals, and skills. The last thing he recalled deep beneath the waves, his lungs filling with water, was the sunken city Atlantis.

Coughing out the seawater, Orastes sensed a man kneeling beside him, saying something about doom rising in Hyboria to the west. The man explained that this beach was part of the pirate haven called Tortage, in the Barachan Isles. He said his name was Kalanthes and urged Orastes to find a seer named Nadini in the nearby city, but to be careful because the chains he still wore marked him as a slave and thus as a victim to the whim of anyone more powerful than he. A few steps along the path, Orastes encountered someone who was in no position to threaten him, a beautiful woman named Casilda who had been hung by her wrists in a scavenger's camp. Freeing her, he tried not to be distracted by her beauty, as they fought their way through the jungle. At the city gate they parted, but Casilda promised to reward him later for saving her, in a very personal way.

Once he had his bearings in Tortage, Orastes visited the seer Nadini, first convincing her he was not a spy for Strom, the leader of the Red Hand pirates. She told him to close his eyes and said, "You bear a sinister mark on your flesh, an omen of destiny, that pains me to look upon it. But as to your past? Why, you have the features and grace of the noble Aquilonian people. Aquilonia itself is the bastion of civilization in this indecorous age. Tell me, what ghosts of memories play out behind your closed eyes?" Only indistinct images, perhaps of some magical icon, floated in the mists of his deranged memory. For further insight, Nadini sent Orastes to Belesa, a missionary of Mitra who hid in the basement of the town's inn and plotted against Strom.

Belesa greeted him with encouraging but perplexing words: "The light welcomes you!" Yet it was night time, and the flickering flames of primitive oil lamps hardly penetrated the darkness. Then he remembered that Mitra was the sun god, often portrayed as a bright disk with sunbeams emanating from it. When Orastes explained that his mind had been consumed by darkness, Belesa promised to lead him along a path toward enlightenment. To earn insight, he must combat evil. That required defeating Strom and his Red Hand minions, who had become agents of a much more powerful yet still shadowy wickedness.

A series of preparatory quests reminded Orastes that the world was an amalgam of the natural and the supernatural, in which cold steel and hot lightning often combined to spill warm blood. He saved Ninus, the local priest of Mitra, from attackers, and obtained medicine for a Stygian boy at his temple named Si-Khu. The boy told him that something sinister was brewing in Stygia, where the wicked priest Thoth-Amon was both raising an army and seeking ancient scrolls. Arias, an agent of the Cimmerian barbarian Conan who had seized the throne of Aquilonia, told Orastes the boy's father had been cursed by something called the Mark of Acheron, and this triggered the realization that Orastes himself had been cursed by it as well. Awareness of an appalling truth dawned. Orastes had been cursed in order to prepare his body to become possessed by the reincarnated soul of an ancient Acheronian, to serve in Thoth-Amon's army, but his near drowning in the ruins of sunken Atlantis had destroyed that demon. Now, if he could only obtain the Phoenix Medallion, a good antidote to the evil Mark of Acheron, he could regain his lost identity.

Nadini tells Orastes that all history is a series of toil-filled days that end in destruction. "Atlantis drowns and salt water chokes ten thousand throats. Acheron burns and holy fire peels the flesh from a million bones. The ages turn, and we come to a cave. An altar stands untouched. Upon it, a medallion rests." An Atlantean artifact, the Phoenix Medallion permits rebirth and thus liberation. Strom seeks it to escape bondage to Thoth-Amon, but he does so by enslaving the common people. Conan might use it to prevent Thoth-Amon from invading Aquilonia. Orastes might use it to restore his memory and begin a new life of justice, security, and liberty.

First, Arias explains, an army of slaves bearing the Mark of Acheron must be destroyed, so they cannot serve either Strom or Thoth-Amon. This can be accomplished by a single brave adventurer, if he combines a strong sword arm with the forces of the very earth itself. A Thoth-Amon assistant, the witch Mithrelle, performs a magical ritual every night to calm the raging volcano that stands just beside the army's camp. If Orastes can disrupt the ritual, the volcano will erupt and pour molten lava over the cursed army. The essential ingredient is the blood of a virgin, so Orastes must obtain blood from a sexually experienced woman and somehow substitute it without Mithrelle's knowledge in the very center of the enemy encampment. Casilda willingly contributes a vial of her blood, thus shaping the history of the world on the basis of her own very personal sexual history.

Orastes kills dozens of Acheronian-possessed warriors on his way to the high mountain altar, and before Mithrelle arrives he replaces the vial of virgin blood with Casilda's red seductive liquid. Mithrelle conducts her ritual, pouring the blood over the body of the virgin and the corpse of a man. Like an angry earth god, the volcano erupts, and Orastes runs for his life as balls of fire blast his enemies.

Next, Orastes must kill Strom, who prepares to flee the city to join Thoth-Amon, and seize the Phoenix Medallion. Then Kalanthes reappears to impart further wisdom. He proves to be a priest of Ibis and enemy of Thoth-Amon, and has been watching Orastes to see if he could be decisive in the war that was brewing. He tells Orastes to seek further guidance from the sorceress Scyra in Tarantia, the capital of Aquilonia. She tells him that he actually holds only one of four fragments of the Medallion, the Phoenix of the West, and he must over a very long series of quests obtain the other three. Each one restores some of his lost memory and power.

Orastes obtained the first fragment of the medallion when he reached level 19 in questing experience, and was allowed to attempt each of the other fragments after attaining additional levels. Between these epic adventures, he would wander through Aquilonia, Stygia, and Cimmeria, undertaking smaller missions more or less indirectly related to the coming war. At level 30, Scyra sent Orastes to get the Phoenix of the South in the ironically named Blessed Caves in Stygia, which required scaling a high cliff, killing many Black Ring cultists, and facing both the Arch Mage and a monster called the Blood Defiler Guardian, before escaping by leaping into a subterranean river. The two remaining fragments can be obtained at levels 50 and 60. The Phoenix of the North is in an ice cave in the Eiglophian Mountains far past Cimmeria, and it is guarded by Mithrelle, who must be killed to reach it. The Phoenix of the East is guarded by the demon Har-Shebes in a cave beside Thunder River, but obtaining it does not end the series of heroic quests.

The Atlantean god contained within the Phoenix Medallion must be released during a purification ritual in a grotto called Crom's Rock in the Field of Chiefs, in Lacheish Plains in Cimmeria. There, Thoth-Amon personally kills the suppliant, then the Atlantean god resurrects him, saying:

> Your destiny is almost complete, Avatar. My people interred me within the amulet until the day the Grim Grey God walked once more. That day is coming. My powers are as dead as my people, but I can still give you one gift. Immortality. Where Acheronian sorcery kept you in eternal death, let Atlantean magic even restore you to life. I die now, die the true death. The circle is complete. May the young gods watching over this world keep you safe, Avatar. May they guard you against the Grim . . . Grey . . . God. . . .

Orastes never faced the Grim Grey God at level 80. He was content to regain many memories, and ponder the meaning of life in a world where gods at any time may erase reality and time gradually fades the blood ink in which our lives are written. What did Orastes have to remember? Once upon a time he had committed a heinous crime, better forgotten but unforgettable because he was a character from one of Howard's best-known stories. In that tale, he had obtained the Heart of Ahriman and used it to restore Xaltotun to life, an Acheronian sorcerer who had been dead for three thousand years.[13] Xaltotun nearly became dictator of the world, before Conan destroyed him. Unable to erase his sin and become the benevolent healer that a priest should be, Orastes turned his back on Mitra's civilization and rode off into oblivion.

The Path of Healing

Robert E. Howard once explained, "The gods of yesterday become the devils of tomorrow."[14] Conan may be prehistoric, but in a very real sense he represents a post-Christian past. For the better part of twenty centuries, Christians portrayed Pagans as cruel and licentious. Howard took the stereotype of Paganism promulgated by its Christian opponents and reversed the moral values, relishing exactly what the Christians reviled. Several of the fantasy worlds described in this book draw heavily upon European Pagan traditions, as filtered through Christianity, but this is the one example that reverses the positions of good and evil, within a specifically Christian framework.

Howard belonged to a school of post-Christian horror writers, of whom H. P. Lovecraft is most famous and with whom Howard enthusiastically corresponded. Both authors published in the influential magazine *Weird Tales*, and they shared the view that reality is much weirder than ordinary people imagine. Lovecraft put this point thus: "All my tales are based on the fundamental premise that common human laws and interests and emotions have no validity or significance in the vast cosmos at large."[15] This is not very far from the psychoanalytic view that humans fail to understand the distorted nature of their own personalities, and that religious faith is a symptom of psychopathology.[16] In his story about the ancient supernatural being Cthulhu, Lovecraft expanded on his weird thesis:

> The most merciful thing in the world, I think, is the inability of the human mind to correlate all its contents. We live on a placid island of ignorance in the midst of black seas of infinity, and it was not meant that we should voyage far. The sciences, each straining in its own direction, have hitherto harmed us little; but some day the piecing together of dissociated knowledge will open up such terrifying vistas of reality, and of our frightful position therein, that we shall either go mad from the revelation or flee from the light into the peace and safety of a new dark age.[17]

This may be true for the science of history, because some of its findings seem to imply that human life is futile. Atlantis, Acheron, Aquilonia—all gone and most forgotten. The Renaissance was haunted by memories of the fall of classical civilization, and at the beginning of the industrial age Gibbon's *Decline and Fall of the Roman Empire* set new standards for erudition and analysis of the death of cultures.[18] In the turbulent twentieth century, social historians like Oswald Spengler and Pitirim Sorokin contemplated the imminent fall of our own civilization. Spengler argued that every civilization is based upon a great idea and dies when the potential of that idea is exhausted.[19] Sorokin tried to explain why such a formative idea would inevitably become exhausted, but held out some slim hope that it could be revived in a cycle of decay and restoration lasting centuries.[20]

Priests of the different races in *World of Warcraft* belong to different religious traditions that are at different points in Sorokin's cycle. Human religion is beset by decay, whereas Orc religion is just becoming established. The Elves have suffered schism into two groups, the secular Blood Elves and the Night Elves who hold tight to their fantasy faith. Night Elves worship the lunar goddess Elune. This is a good example because it highlights the religious roles that women play in WoW, and thus connects this chapter to a common topic of discussion in the sociology of conventional religion, the somewhat contradictory gender differences in piety and power. My Night Elf priestess, Lunette, loved to visit the Temple of the Moon in Darnassus, the capital city of Teldrassil, the large island where all Night Elf avatars begin their careers. Teldrassil, like the Norse world-tree Yggdrasil, is actually an immense tree, and like most Night Elf architecture the temple includes trees. In the center of the temple stands a colossal statue of Elune, the moon goddess, holding up the moon, from which flow streams of light that bless and heal her worshippers below. All Night Elf priest trainers are female, although male avatars can become priests.

Priests in WoW do not gain their calling from any kind of direct communion with a deity but from training by *priest trainer* nonplayer characters, like one in the temple who would train Lunette. The training does not involve study or meditation, but is conducted by casting a magic spell perceived as a flash of light, in return for money. Similarly, Lunette's healing powers do not require prayer, or even drawing moonbeams down from Elune, but simply expending some of her supply of mana to accomplish a technical act of healing. This is a key point about religion in virtual worlds: The priest's powers do not require faith in the supernatural, but are reliable technical skills in a world where nature functions differently than in our world. Thus, while WoW religions seem to be pale fantasies compared with real-world religions, their ability to accomplish miracles is undeniable, while that of real-world religions is open to debate. When Lunette wants to resurrect a comrade who has been killed on the field of battle, she simply employs her resurrection skill, and the comrade is ready to fight again.

One way to understand the special role of priest is by comparing it with other roles that employ magic. *Final Fantasy XI* (FFXI) is remarkable for its large number of role specializations, fully twenty of them, many of which have supernatural powers. These are not all permanent classes, as in *World of Warcraft*, to which a character is assigned at birth and forever destined to remain within, but jobs that can be acquired in different combinations. The most priestlike is the White Mage, described thus on its page in the FFXI wiki: "With the ability to utilize the most potent spells from the Cure, Regen, Raise, and Bar Spell families, White Mages are the premier healers in the game, and are nearly indispensable when forming a party."[21] It is one of the six standard jobs, the others being Black Mage, Red Mage, Monk, Warrior, and Thief. The other fourteen are extra jobs, gained by completing special quests that become available at level 30 of experience. All twenty are listed in table 5.1, arranged in terms of their relationship to the supernatural, with the descriptions offered on their pages of the FFXI wiki.

Table 5.1 Censuses of Jobs in *Final Fantasy XI*

Job	Description	9 a.m. Census	9 p.m. Census
	Mages		
White Mage	Armed with the most efficient recovery spells, White Mages can ensure a party's survival in the most dire of situations.	11.5%	9.5%
Black Mage	Through devastating magic spells, Black Mages bring tremendous firepower to the battlefield.	10.0%	10.6%
Red Mage	Red Mages are called the Jack of All Trades by many for their abilities to cast White Magic, Black Magic, and fight with swords and daggers.	14.7%	12.2%
Blue Mage	A Blue Mage can employ the legendary arts of the Aht Urhgan Immortals, a unit of elite imperial special forces.	4.6%	3.8%
	Mage-like Warriors		
Paladin	Paladins specialize in close-range combat, just like Warriors. However, through long hours of spiritual training, paladins have acquired the ability to cast White Magic spells, making them even more valuable on the battlefield.	4.6%	4.7%
Dark Knight	Dark Knights are powerful damage dealers who have the capability to further their damage by using select Black Magic spells.	3.5%	2.9%

(continued)

Table 5.1 (continued)

Job	Description	9 a.m. Census	9 p.m. Census
Scholar	Extensive knowledge of ancient martial theory granted Scholars the ability to wield dual schools of magic, between which they would alternate depending on the situation at hand.	1.1%	0.7%
	Others with Special Powers		
Summoner	These heretic mages have unlocked the secrets of the forbidden magic of Vana'diel by creating a pact with the Avatar known as Carbuncle.	5.2%	3.9%
Ninja	Strict training in the forbidden arts of the Far East have transformed the Ninja into cold, hard killing machines.	4.4%	4.7%
Monk	With their bodies that double as deadly weapons, Monks attack enemies with explosive strength.	4.6%	5.3%
	Other Jobs		
Warrior	Specializing in the arts of battle, Warriors are masters of all aspects of melee combat.	6.1%	5.7%
Thief	Specializing in covert actions, Thieves aim for the perfect opportunity to attack the enemy.	6.9%	8.5%

Beastmaster	Based on their knowledge of beasts, Beastmasters can charm the beasts of Vana'diel to fight alongside them or obtain items that summon beasts through the Call Beast job ability called Familiars.	3.2%	3.9%
Bard	A Bard uses songs as the job's main advantage to boost the party's stats.	4.7%	3.7%
Ranger	With unparalleled tracking abilities and skill with the bow and arrow, rangers are experts in the field of hunting.	1.4%	2.1%
Samurai	The Samurai job focuses on the mastery of weapon skills and skillchains.	4.8%	6.3%
Dragoon	With their lances in hand and their faithful wyvern by their sides, Dragoons surprise their enemies with their extraordinary jumping abilities.	1.7%	2.9%
Corsair	Descendants of the dauntless pirates that once scourged the seas of the Near East, Corsairs rely on the "Hexagun" (a multi-barreled handgun) and elaborate luck-based abilities to alter the stakes of battle.	2.2%	1.4%
Puppetmaster	These wandering performers entertain crowds and confound their enemies with a customizable puppet known as an "automaton."	1.0%	1.4%
Dancer	Dancers are front-line healers who execute Waltzes and Sambas to heal and create beneficial effects, and perform Steps to inflict negative effects upon the enemy.	3.7%	5.9%
TOTAL		100% (2,071)	100% (1,323)

The table shows results of a population census I carried out on one of the instances of FFXI, the Fenrir server, on Saturday, September 4, 2010, using the gameworld's information system for finding avatars to recruit to a team. FFXI is notable for being an international game, including easily accessed phrase books translating between English, French, German, and Japanese, allowing people who speak different languages to cooperate on teams. It is also notable for working across platforms, not only on personal computers but also PlayStation 2 and Xbox. Given its international character, each server serves the entire world. With this in mind, I did two censuses on that day, one at nine in the morning eastern daylight time, and the other at nine in the evening. Given the time zone difference, the earlier census picked up many of the Japanese players, while the later census concentrated on North American players.

The two censuses show that white mages are among the most popular jobs but account for only around a tenth of the job distribution. While white mages are the analog to priests in other gameworlds, they are conceptualized in *Final Fantasy XI* as avatars who use magic for healing, rather than as religious professionals. Dancers, the last job in the table, also heal, but without the use of supernatural powers. It is unclear whether monks really have supernatural powers, because their advanced abilities may just represent expert martial arts training. It is worth noting that FFXI is a Japanese game, designed for an international audience but coming from a country in which the Judeo-Christian tradition that defines religion for Western social scientists never achieved great popularity. However, the online gaming culture is very international, leading to many parallels across games. The paladin in FFXI is a combination warrior and white mage, while in WoW, paladins are a class of warrior priests.

Gender in the Priesthood

World of Warcraft is so central to the universe of MMOs, and so huge in scope and human population, that it affords vast opportunities for quantitative research. For example, we can learn more about the meaning of the priest role by comparing priests with members of other classes, in terms of key variables like the gender of the avatars, which like class is determined at the moment the avatar is created. I ran fully seven priest avatars through WoW, one of them all the way to level 80 in the Horde when that was the maximum possible, and a second to 75 in the Alliance, because seven races offered the opportunity to be a priest and gave somewhat different cultural backgrounds. Any class can be either gender, and gender is an especially interesting variable in religion. On the one hand, women are more often deeply religious, while clergy are more often male, indeed exclusively male in several religious traditions.

I cannot argue that we will learn accurate facts about gender differences in real religion by examining *World of Warcraft*. Rather, we will find something that illuminates the gender significance of the clergy precisely because of a difference between the game world and the surrounding world. Priests in WoW have the real power to do something effective: they can heal. Priests in the real world merely pretend to do something effective, mediating between their parishioners and the nonexistent gods. Whatever valuable secondary functions priests may perform in conventional churches, such as providing comfort or organizing community activities, their chief function is supporting the illusion that their costly fantasy is real. Thus clergy are more frequently males for the same dual reason that criminals often are—men more often play public roles in the wider society, and men more often exploit people outside their immediate families. That is not what priests in WoW do.

The following paragraphs will focus on the gender pattern across WoW classes, with a focus on priests, and, for comparison, on the most different class, warriors. To begin with we need to see the context in which the data were collected. The first of three datasets is based on the Horde guild that my level 80 Blood Elf priest, Catullus, joined. It may be the most successful guild in WoW, and was chosen for that reason: Alea Iacta Est (AIE) in the Earthen Ring realm (Internet server). The name echoes Caesar's words when he crossed the Rubicon, "the die is cast." This famous quote suggests the long heritage of games in which chance plays a prominent role, but it also implies that the real world can be conceptualized as a game. The AIE guild was formed in association with a popular and long-running online podcast, *The Instance*,[22] which has offered a wide-ranging half-hour or longer discussion of *World of Warcraft* issues nearly every week since January 6, 2006.

Most WoW guilds are small, and a typical successful guild might have fewer than a hundred members, but AIE always had more than ten times that number during the time I studied it. Quantitative data about AIE were obtained from WoW's Armory online database, which offered data on all 3,179 AIE avatars level 10 or above when the data were collected in 2008.[23] One may well ask how representative AIE is, or whether it has an atypical membership. Rarely, a guild is dominated by, or even entirely composed of, avatars of one type. For example, on July 10, 2008, the Ladies of Destiny on the Scarlet Crusade realm had 214 members, 204 of which were female. Ladies of the Night on the Bladefist realm had 135 members, all but one of them female. A Scarlet Crusade guild named the Darkspear consisted of one hundred Trolls. On the Earthen Ring realm, the Blood Elf Brotherhood consisted entirely of Blood Elves, while Gnome Nation was nine-tenths Gnomes, and the Dwarven Alliance consisted two-thirds of Dwarves and one-third of Gnomes.

Most guilds had diverse membership, however, and this was certainly the case for Alea Iacta Est. Aside from sheer size, the most obvious way it is unusual is that its members are part of a vigorous communication system that reflects and influences WoW culture more generally. AIE has a newsletter, as well as being connected to the podcast, and it stages many special events such as raids, marches, craft fairs, contests, parties, formal decision meetings, and celebrations of dates like its anniversary and New Year's Eve. Members are unusually knowledgeable about WoW culture and the implications of decisions about shaping their avatars. Thus, it is especially valuable as a source of information about WoW culture and society, but must be balanced by samples of avatars obtained in a very different manner.

Therefore, I did a census of all avatars online at any point during Saturday, January 12, 2008, on two contrasting other realms, Emerald Dream and Scarlet Crusade. To do this, I employed a piece of open-source add-on software called CensusPlus, which works directly through an avatar logged into WoW itself.[24] Emerald Dream and Scarlet Crusade were well-established realms, both having been in existence for more than a year, and in the same time zone. All three realms employed in this study are RP, or "role playing" realms, with an officially expressed but unenforced preference for taking the mythology seriously and staying in character at least much of the time. The difference between Emerald Dream and Scarlet Crusade is that the former is a player-versus-player (PvP) realm, in which players outside the newbie starter areas attack each other at will, creating a much more violent climate than in normal realms where players cannot fight each other unless both agree to do so.

Repeatedly through the twenty-four hours of the sampling day, I ran the CensusPlus add-on program, which tallies a census of all avatars online at the moment in a given faction. I did so using two WoW accounts and two computers, plus having two avatars in each realm—one Horde and the other in the competing Alliance faction—because the program can be run only while operating an avatar of the given faction and realm. The number of avatars totaled fully 22,851, of which 12,051 were on Emerald Dream and 10,800 on Scarlet Crusade, with the full range of experience levels from 1 through 70 that existed prior to the Lich King expansion in November 2008 that took the top to 80. CensusPlus did not report the gender of avatars, so I needed to take subsamples of avatars and manually look them up on the Armory. Randomly, 1,517 avatars were selected with experience levels 20–39, excluding a few who were involved in the subsidiary arena competitions, which are common at level 70 but tend to involve only very specialized "twink" avatars at early levels. The range 20–39 was chosen because such players have left the newbie zones and selected their professions, but still have a long way to go before completing their climb up the latter of experience. The second subsample consisted of all 1,664 level 70 priests and warriors for whom later data could be obtained, focusing on warriors as well as priests because this hypermasculine class provided the greatest contrast with the somewhat feminine priest class.

When a player creates a new avatar, the key decisions are selecting class, gender, and race. It is important to note that there are absolutely no differences in the capabilities of male and female avatars in WoW. Other things being equal, a warrior woman is just as powerful as a warrior man—although she tends to appear smaller—and she can wear the same armor, wield the same weapons, and move as swiftly. We can speculate that other players respond to female avatars somewhat differently, although this remains to be proven. Any differences in the behaviors or accomplishments of avatars of the two genders must, therefore, be the result either of differences in the skill or personality of the player, or the cultural stereotypes of male and female roles held by players about their avatars.[25]

In WoW, the stereotypical tank is the warrior, and the chief healer is the priest, but other classes can play these roles to a greater or lesser degree.[26] Paladins are explicitly a mixture of warrior and priest, but perhaps a little better in the tank than healer role. The general consensus expressed on the chief WoW-oriented wiki is that the DPS role is equally well played by the mage, who can cast spells from a distance, and the rogue, who hurls knives, but the mage may have an advantage over multiple enemies, while the rogue can sneak up on a single enemy without being detected.[27] Druids are rather balanced avatars, able to tank as well as heal. The other three classes available at the time—hunter, shaman, and warlock—operate with assistants and thus can function rather like questing groups during solo play without the need to involve another player. This is most obvious in the cases of hunters and warlocks who have pets (hunting animals) and minions, respectively, secondary avatars that can act like a teammate. Shamans also have assistants, although immobile ones called *totems*.

The class of a WoW avatar has considerable implications for other attributes, notably the armor the avatar can wear and the professions that are most valuable. Priests rely upon spells to protect themselves, and they are limited to wearing feeble cloth armor. In contrast, warriors can wear plate metal armor, but lack protective spells. While some armor can be bought from vendor NPCs or looted from dead enemies, much of it is manufactured by players from virtual raw materials, using crafting professions. Players may share these products with guild mates or sell them to other players through an elaborate online auction system. The tailoring profession makes cloth armor, and blacksmithing makes plate metal armor. The cloth required by tailors is readily acquired from defeated enemies, but the metal for a warrior's armor must be mined from remote lodes using the mining profession.

Because an avatar can have only two of the main professions, many in all classes specialize in the crafts required to make their own armor. Thus, in the first

Alea Iacta Est dataset, 54 percent of priests practiced tailoring, and the number is almost identical, 53 percent, in the Two Realms dataset. Among warriors in AIE, 71 percent practiced mining and 37 percent did blacksmithing. In the Two Realms dataset, the proportions are 73 percent and 53 percent. Mining provides the raw materials for two other professions, engineering and jewelcrafting, so the economic value of mining makes it the most popular profession overall.[28]

The second most popular major profession among priests is enchanting, practiced by 41 percent of them in AIE and 36 percent of them in the Two Realms. Enchanters obtain various magical substances, either buying them from vendors or generating them by disenchanting articles looted from enemies, then use them to magically enhance objects such as their own cloth armor. In addition, enchanters can make magic wands, which are the most effective weapon priests wield.[29]

WoW's creators do their best to fine-tune the system so that no class has a net advantage over another, so it is worth noting that gender is not strongly or consistently associated with success in playing the game. By September 30, 2008, 21.8 percent of the male AIE avatars had reached level 70 of experience, compared with 22.1 percent of female avatars. The mean male level was 41.1, compared with 42.6 for female avatars. The random subsample of lower-level avatars allows us to compare the rapidity of progress by the genders, because both CensusPlus and the Armory record an avatar's experience level, but the Armory data were collected between forty-one and fifty-six days later. On average in the Two Realms dataset, each of the 807 Emerald Dream avatars advanced 0.21 experience levels per day, compared with 0.19 levels for the 710 Scarlet Crusade avatars. In both realms, female avatars were slightly slower in climbing up the experience ladder than male avatars: 0.20 levels per day compared with 0.22 in Emerald Dream, and 0.18 compared with 0.20 in Scarlet Crusade. So gender differences in achievement are slight.

As table 5.2 shows, there are substantial differences in which classes the two genders choose to play, especially with respect to priests and warriors. Across all three comparison samples, male avatars are more than twice as likely to be warriors as are female avatars, and about half as likely to be priests. Apparently something about the culture of the AIE guild makes female avatars more likely to be warlocks and less likely to be druids, whereas in the Scarlet Crusade realm female avatars are more likely to be druids. Other gender ratios are fairly consistent across samples, and the extreme gender differences in the propensity to be warriors or priests suggests that the power of gender stereotypes in the wider society is at work in WoW.

We noted that warriors and priests represent the clearest contrast in the social roles the avatar plays in combat groups. A warrior is aggressive, getting right up in the face of the enemy, and courageous in withstanding the enemy's lethal power. A priest is supportive, nurturing, and frankly vulnerable in battle. Experienced players on a team expect the warrior to take punishment on their behalf, but they tend to

Table 5.2 Gender and Class among 4,696 *World of Warcraft* Avatars

Class	Alea Iacta Est Guild			Emerald Dream Realm			Scarlet Crusade Realm		
	Female	Male	M/F	Female	Male	M/F	Female	Male	M/F
Druid	6.1%	10.6%	1.74	10.3%	9.3%	0.90	16.2	9.4%	0.58
Hunter	17.7%	18.5%	1.04	17.2%	16.8%	0.98	17.8	18.2%	1.02
Mage	12.2%	9.7%	0.80	13.0%	10.4%	0.80	12.6	9.6%	0.76
Paladin	11.7%	8.8%	0.75	12.6%	11.2%	0.88	11.1	12.5%	1.13
Priest	**15.0%**	**8.0%**	**0.54**	**11.9%**	**5.9%**	**0.49**	**8.3**	**5.0%**	**0.61**
Rogue	8.5%	10.4%	1.22	11.5%	15.9%	1.39	9.5	10.1%	1.06
Shaman	5.2%	10.0%	1.92	5.7%	4.8%	0.83	8.7	9.8%	1.13
Warlock	20.8%	10.8%	0.52	11.5%	11.5%	1.00	10.7	13.6%	1.27
Warrior	**2.9%**	**13.2%**	**4.61**	**6.1%**	**14.1%**	**2.30**	**5.1**	**11.8%**	**2.30**
Total	100.0%	100.0%		100.0%	100.0%		100.0%	100.0%	
Cases	905	2274		261	546		253	457	

protect priests, who in return can heal them and even resurrect them from death. In the abstract, warriors and priests exhibit role differentiation and division of labor in avatars well adapted to group cooperation. In my own experience of running avatars of all these kinds, hunters, warlocks, paladins, and druids are more autonomous, the first two because they and their secondary avatars are already self-contained teams, and the latter two because their abilities are balanced and multifaceted. This suggests that avatars may vary in terms of how much they are sociable versus individualistic, quite apart from the aggressive-nurturant dimension.

Existing sociological literature offers a range of perspectives from which to analyze the huge difference in the propensity of female avatars in WoW to be priests rather than warriors. One dimension of explanation is differences in orientation toward violence and physical risk taking, because males more commonly commit violent crimes or engage in physically aggressive sports,[30] and greater female affinity toward religion may be the result of aversion to risk taking.[31]

Another dimension is implied by the fact that in WoW priests are healers, and women traditionally are the more nurturant gender.[32] Sociability is a dimension of variation among people, and women are widely believed to have more need for interpersonal relationships.[33] However, it has also been argued that males are more group-oriented, because their hunter-gatherer ancestors hunted in groups and relied for their very lives upon their fellows.[34] In WoW, however, both warriors and priests are highly specialized, and thus rely upon fellow team members to do the tasks they cannot. Imagine a warrior and priest questing together; if either fails to play his or her professional role, both die. Quite apart from the personality trait of sociability, the division of labor binds people together into networks of exchange and mutual reliance. Cooperative behavior, therefore, has both innate and instrumental causes.

Another measure of gender differences in *World of Warcraft* is provided by *talents*, a class-specific ability that costs one talent point (an avatar earns one talent point for every experience level gained after level 9). There is no good reason other than laziness or indecision why a player would not immediately update the talent points right after leveling. However, of 1,522 avatars in the level 20–39 dataset, 16.8 percent had been tardy in updating their talents. Given the largely incorrect stereotype that WoW players are teenagers, and teenage boys are proverbially irresponsible, it is interesting to see that male avatars do not score worse on this measure than female ones. In fact a slightly larger fraction of female avatars have failed to update their talents, 17.1 percent versus 16.7 percent, but this is an insignificant difference. Only ten of 1,663 level 70 priests and warriors do not have the full 61 talents available to them; four of these have 59 or 60 and the remaining six may represent failed avatars or bad data. Perhaps nobody reaches level 70 without a high degree of conscientiousness.

For each class, there are three separate talent trees, in which the most powerful talents are not available until the avatar already possesses many lower-level ones belonging to the same branch. Thus, there is some incentive to specialize in one or another, although a player is free to select low-level talents across any combination of the three. In the cases of priests and warriors, one talent tree is generally regarded to be best for solo play, one for team play, and the third combines both. This makes talents a reasonable measure of the social division of labor. As the WoW wiki explains, "The Discipline Priest is the jack of all trades, but master of none.... The Holy Priest stands proud among the best healing classes in the game."[35] Shadow priests have the most damaging spells, and thus are best suited to solo play. Among warriors, "protection talents are generally very useful for Main Tank group work, allowing the Warrior to put up with more punishment than otherwise possible."[36] Arms talents are the most diversified, whereas Fury talents are best for PvP duels against other players. Thus, avatars that emphasize Holy priest or Protection warrior talents are best for their respective roles as healer and tank.

To get a simple measure of specialization, I identified all the cases in which an avatar had more than 30 points in a given talent tree. All but two of 740 level 70 priests having 61 talent points were specialized, by this measure, and 46 percent of the priests were Holy healers. All but one of 914 warriors were specialized, and 40.8 percent of the warriors were Protection tanks. Among female priests, 49.3 percent played the traditional healer role, compared with 42.7 percent of male avatars. Note that this gender difference in performing the priest role is on top of the already great gender difference in selecting the role in the first place. This finding reinforces the hypothesis that the traditional female nurturant role expresses itself in female WoW avatars.

The prediction for warriors is more complex. Both Arms and Fury specializations prepare a warrior for solo play, and nurturance is not featured by either kind. Indeed, playing the social tank role is most analogous to healing for priests, so one would predict that female warriors would be more willing to tank, just as female priests are more willing to heal. This is exactly what we find, because 48.4 percent of female warriors are Protection tanks, compared with 39.3 percent of male warriors. Even when they have stepped outside the traditional feminine role and become warriors, female WoW avatars are more willing to play a cooperative social role than are male avatars.

Ancient Egyptian Rituals

Few gameworlds give priests the full range of duties that clerics have in the real world, but *A Tale in the Desert* (ATITD) comes close. Set in ancient Egypt, ATITD lacks combat and nonplayer characters, emphasizing instead puzzle solving, and most of the puzzles have strong social dimensions. Users must perform such mundane but realistic tasks as collecting straw to make mud bricks and growing vegetables to feed to sheep in order to get mutton, oil, leather, and dung. Over time, a user builds a system of machines for processing flax to make fabric, potter's wheels and kilns for making clay jugs, and workbenches for glass and metal products. In so doing, a beginner needs extensive help from advanced users, because many of the necessary raw materials are unavailable to beginners. In *A Tale in the Desert*, players build ancient Egypt nearly from scratch, then after about two years, they start over from the beginning in a new *telling* of the tale. My ATITD avatar, Renhotep, participated in the fourth telling.

Many of the tasks are group rituals—such as deity worship, vigils, and even weddings—so membership in cooperative social groups is absolutely essential. The social-science theory that fits this virtual Egypt best was developed by anthropologist Bronislaw Malinowski in his study of the Trobriand Islanders, who built their seagoing boats in group rituals and used them to sustain noneconomic but symbolic trade with fellow Argonauts on other islands.[37] This theory says that in any society, *technology is embedded in social rituals*, and the economic rationality of engineering may be only secondary to its culture-constructing properties.

"Principles of Worship" illustrates a social ritual oriented toward the ancient Egyptian deities. Two aspirants must bring various sacrificial items to the ceremony and complete the complex actions within twenty-five minutes. This requires preparation, coordination, and knowledge, so typically a third, more senior person organizes everything and directs the two aspirants, serving as a senior priest. My avatar, Renhotep, joined a special guild, Worship World, in hopes they would help him, but instead he learned through a more diverse Helping Hands guild, in which Hatun Kisi, a level 35 woman, wanted to conduct this ritual. She introduced him to Darky, a level 9 man, and together the three of them collected the required items.

At the sacred altar in Shabbat Ab, they began the "Ritual of Initiation." Under Hatun's close direction, Darky placed a small diamond on the left pillar of the altar, and Renhotep placed a piece of twine on its right pillar. They meditated, and the twenty-five-minute clock began counting down. For Renhotep, the crucial steps that required running a distance were dropping a beetle down a mine and learning the new skill of Ritual Item Construction at a School of Architecture for a cost of 10 linen, 200 firebricks, and 100 oil, all of which he supplied himself. Darky lit a ritual torch in the deep desert and placed camel milk in a grassy field near water. Hatun had scouted all these locations ahead of time, so she rushed hither and thither guiding the two aspirants. All the while they chanted:

"Praise Horus, King of Egypt!"
"Praise Isis, whose seed is forever fertile!"
"Praise Osiris, who was Reborn like the Scarab!"
"Praise Thoth, the Magician who created Science!"
"Praise Ra, of the Blazing Eye!"
"Praise Bastet, who teaches grace and elegance!"
"Praise Amun, who gives us reason to celebrate!"

"Principles of Worship" is the first step in a series of religious rituals that constitute the Discipline of Worship, and "Test of the Vigil" is the second. Renhotep had built his compound on the east bank of the Nile in Saqqarah, near a crossroads, and he helped members of a local Saqqarah guild conduct this test at an altar in their compound just east of where he lived. The first step was to gather the materials necessary for a ritual bonfire. Since Renhotep had been doing much construction at his compound on the Nile, he was able to provide many firebricks from the kilns he had built weeks earlier. He also did what any novice could have done, gathering vast piles of wood from nearby trees, but he had to rely upon more advanced neighbors for the silver bowl and the flax seeds crushed to make oil. He and a neighbor took turns watching the fire as it burned and waiting for a vision. After a few minutes a mystic voice announced the nature of the first sacrifice.

Periodically, the voice would tell them to place one or another item into the fire, somewhat at random but starting slowly and with a fairly common item. Most of Renhotep's neighbors had set up their compounds near the altar many months before, and they had a variety of items already stored away. A guild storage facility was also nearby. So when the mystic voice demanded a particular item be sacrificed, one or another ancient Egyptian would shout "I've got one" and run home to get it. Very quickly, Renhotep passed the "Test of the Vigil," but the team kept the fire going as long as possible to earn increased stature within the society of the Nile.

Renhotep did not go further in the Discipline of Worship, but the ATITD wiki explained the six further steps. "Path of the Pilgrim" requires a group of seven players to voyage across the desert tithing at shrines.[38] "Test of Festivals" involves collaborating with others in a series of rituals to fully satisfy these gods: Isis, Osiris, Bastet, Ra, Maat, Hathor, and Thoth.[39] "Test of Beacons" demands doing an extremely complex series of actions seven times to summon and anchor an altar.[40] "Test of Leavened Bread" has teams compete in baking holy bread dedicated to a god whose identity is learned during the ritual, and giving the bread to a specific type of person also announced only after the beginning.[41] "Remembrance Ceremonies" are group sacrifices performed at specified discipline monuments.[42]

The initial instructions for "Test of the Humble Priests" says, "Humble yourself before five of twelve Gods. The faithful will not choose their gods—rather, the gods will choose them. Begin by performing a Ritual of Humility, by yourself, at a common altar. Place candles on the left and right pillars, signifying enlighten-ment. Place a small diamond on the left focus to provide clarity, and a jug of water on the right focus, showing purity of spirit. Light the candles in the order placed. Further instruction will come to those enlightened." The twelve gods are Amun, Geb, Hathor, Heket, Maat, Nut, Ptah, Set, Sobek, Tayet, Tefnut, and Thoth. Five are assigned at random, and groups of players must complete the appropriate devotion ritual for each of them.[43]

The marriage ritual is part of the Discipline of Harmony. This series of challenges concerns developing social bonds with other Egyptians. The first step is "Principles of Harmony," in which one must formally introduce oneself to eleven different avatars, beginning with initiates of all six other disciplines: Art and Music, Architecture, the Human Body, Leadership, Thought, and Worship. The five remaining introductions require finding very advanced avatars: an initiate of six or more of the seven disciplines, the grandson of an Oracle, the granddaughter of an Oracle, the legacy of a Sage, and a Grand-legacy. By the time I finished my ethnographic research, Renhotep was an initiate of all seven disciplines, so he would have qualified for the first of the rare-avatar introductions. After completing "Principles of Harmony" and reaching level 7 of general experience, Egyptians earn the right to marry, and a successful marriage allows both parties to pass a Discipline of Harmony goal and gain an experience level. More about this remarkable institution can be read at a University of Harmony, one of the many types of schools scattered across the landscape:

> Marriage in Egypt is a private affair. A man and a woman, two women, or two men, each of whom has been in the land at least 24 hours should find an altar. One spouse places a medium diamond on the left focus, the other places one on the right. Five close friends witness the marriage by medi-tating at the altar. Points for the marriage are the number of weeks of that marriage times the number of Tests that your spouse passed during the marriage. Your marriage score is the sum of points for such marriages. Couples are aware of each other's accomplishments, may use each other's possessions, AND MAY EVEN LOG IN AS ONE ANOTHER. Divorce in Egypt is quick and easy.

Renhotep attended the wedding of Albertine, a level 12 woman, and Cronus, a level 14 man, also attended by six other avatars, at the same Saqqarah altar where he experienced "Test of the Vigil." An ordained priest is not strictly required, but the ceremony begins when one person plays the role of cleric, meditating upon an elaborate altar to purify it of any lingering residue from past ceremonies. One of the partners to be married places a medium diamond on left pillar of the altar, and then the other places a second medium diamond on the right pillar. Quickly, five witnesses meditate upon the altar, and sacred music announces that the pair is now a unity.

At the end of the research, Renhotep visited the Pyramid Lake University of Leadership to check the current census. He was one of 1,089 citizens at that moment. Note that this is only one–twelve thousandth of the number of subscribers possessed by *World of Warcraft*, but *A Tale in the Desert* is not a mass-market game. It is a kind of virtual utopian community, sociologically very significant despite a low population. Table 5.3 lists the seven disciplines and the numbers who had been initiated or reached more advanced levels of expertise in each. The table describes the task to become an initiate. More tasks are required to become students, and to ascend to even higher levels.

The sculpture required to pass "Principles of Art and Music" is a uniquely designed creation, assembled out of whatever materials the artist wants. Renhotep built his at the crossroads near his house, in the form of a tall ankh symbol, the Egyptian cross, crux ansata, or life hieroglyph. He set it up near the road, first making the underlying structure with the required boards, rope, and linen, then positioning bunches of straw, starting with three vertical ones, one atop another, for the shaft of the ankh. Two horizontal bunches went right and left to form the cross piece, and six turned at angles to form the circle at the peak. He named his sculpture "It Was Life, but Is No More," referring to the transformation of grass into straw, and ancient Egyptians into mummies.

Conclusion

Role does not equal roll. In gamer terminology, this statement is approximately false. When players create new avatars, they are said to *roll* them. This term comes from the original tabletop version of *Dungeons and Dragons*, in which creating a new avatar involves rolling dice. In the games described here, there is no random element in creating a new avatar, so players merely select which predefined *role* they wish to play. Thus, in the early history of role-playing games, role did equal roll, but no longer. However, selecting a role has great consequences for the course of every subsequent battle, setting the probabilities of every tiny outcome even when chance also plays a role. The priest or cleric role, we have seen, possesses an extreme mixture of similarities to and differences from the traditional role of clergy.

Table 5.3 The Seven Disciplines of *A Tale in the Desert*

Discipline	Initiates	Students	Higher Ranks	To Become an Initiate
Architecture	586	318	146	Build a compound (workplace building), and expand it to at least sixteen sectors.
Art and Music	899	52	6	Build a sculpture, open it for judging, and receive twenty-one "interesting" votes or tear it down.
Harmony	717	148	61	Formally meet initiates of the six other disciplines plus specific more advanced types of characters.
Human Body	714	132	200	Find thirty-five different species of plant life within twenty minutes.
Leadership	893	39	3	Convince twenty-one people to sign your Leadership Initiation Petition.
Thought	679	43	15	Build an Empty Hand Puzzle and have seven people solve and rate it, or solve three recently recognized puzzles.
Worship	452	189	92	With a partner and a spiritual guide, within twenty-five minutes perform a complex ritual for the gods Horus, Isis, Osiris, Thoth, Ra, Bastet, and Amun.

Magic actually works in gameworlds, rather than being a fantasy, so the relation of clergy to magic is much closer than in the real world. Because gameworld magic is neither a lie nor a compensator, there is no reason for clergy to distance themselves from it. Indeed, because many priestly functions are missing from most gameworlds, clergy are required to embrace magic. *A Tale in the Desert* is the exception that proves the rule, because despite being marvelously inventive and well designed, it is highly unpopular. The key to understanding these mysteries is the realization that gameworlds lack compensators precisely because they are compensators. The entire virtual world gives pleasure because it allows players to live out their fantasies, so there is no need to set aside some portion of the content to be taken on faith.

6 SHRINES

On a remote hilltop in the Barrens zone of *World of Warcraft* stands the Shrine of the Fallen Warrior. During the first major scientific conference to be held inside a gameworld, in May 2008, a pilgrimage of scholars paused there on their trek from the Orc city, Orgrimmar, to the Tauren city, Thunder Bluff.[1] They knelt in prayer or meditation, each according to his or her own faith or philosophy, then they danced wildly in celebration of life. An angel spread its white wings over the shrine, upon which lay the green corpse of an Orc, clutching the hilt of a great longsword in his motionless hands. The shrine commemorates the short sojourn on Earth of artist Michel Koiter, who had died while helping to create *World of Warcraft*, and the dead Orc is his avatar. His brother wrote, "A hero's enduring spirit transcends many worlds beyond our own."[2] Yet, as Shelley wrote about the monument for the pharaoh Ozymandias, "Boundless and bare, the lone and level sands stretch far away."[3]

In memorials, temples, and sacred groves, humans seek to transcend the harsh limitations of material existence, yet they do so by shaping and interpreting physical structures. Indeed, humans habitually conceptualize all kinds of abstractions in physical terms. Heaven is above our heads, and hell is below our feet, yet both are spiritual conditions. "Dependent" people literally hang down like pendants around the necks of upstanding, high-status, overbearing people. Physicists have gone beyond the old metaphor that time is the fourth dimension to imagine string theories in which perhaps seven other dimensions may somehow be curled up so we cannot see them, and yet dimensional thinking may be nothing more than a set of spatial metaphors, based on our familiarity with graph paper. Not to be outdone, psychologists describe the human personality as a five-dimensional OCEAN measured by Openness to experience, Conscientiousness, Extraversion, Agreeableness, and Neuroticism.[4] The objects in gameworld territories are like hieroglyphs in papyrus scrolls, symbolizing much through their form and placement.

In his book *Gardens of the Gods*, Christopher McIntosh offers principles for analyzing the sacred space of religiously oriented formal gardens, employing concepts that can be adapted to sacred spaces in general. He suggests their symbolic language has a common structure with three ingredients—three "parts of speech." First, a garden has *form*, distinguished not only by its outline but also by the internal divisions, which can be distinguished by alternatives such as symmetrical versus asymmetrical and linear versus curved. Second are the physical *objects* arranged within this form, which include hills and ponds. Third are the *plants* themselves, which are accorded special meaning either directly through the names and labels attached to them or indirectly by their arrangement in relation to other symbolic objects and shapes.

A similar three-factor framework can be applied to virtual sacred spaces. The first would be the same: the physical arrangement of the boundaries and objects that constitute the space. In McIntosh's scheme the second and third are distinguished by the fact that the distinctive purpose of a garden is to cultivate plants, so his third category is the plants themselves and the second is the other objects, in which he even includes any animals that may have been intentionally added to the environment. In a virtual world, the distinctive property of a sacred space is that it can actually house supernatural objects, persons, and forces. Thus, the third category would be anything that was deemed to have actual supernatural properties. The second category then becomes residual, all those objects in the environment that do not have supernatural powers, even if they may in some way symbolize transcendence. For example, an altar that performs a supernatural function when clicked with the user's mouse is in the third category, whereas one that has no function is in the second category. Thus, in a virtual sacred space, the three parts of speech are: *form*, *natural objects*, and *supernatural objects*.

However, to follow the linguistic metaphor of parts of speech, all three of these are nouns, different instances of the same part of speech. Can we identify three verbs, to expand the metaphor into a second plane? Perhaps these three are analytically useful: *symbolize*, *imitate*, and *serve*. When one thing symbolizes another, it stands in place of it in a meaningful sentence. A grave represents death, for example. But a virtual grave also may visually imitate a physical grave in the "real" world. And it can serve to commemorate the deceased person, or serve as the door to an underground vault, as is often the case in *The Legend of Zelda*, or as a treasury that can be looted of valuable goods as in *Sacred 2*. As the functions a virtual object serves can vary in virtual worlds, so can its symbolism and appearance. A patch of dirt in a grassy field may symbolize either a rude grave or a small garden, yet what it imitates is simply a patch of dirt. Or the life of an artist like Michel Koiter could be symbolized either by a patch of dirt in a grassy field or a glorious shrine on a mountaintop. So even though the categories overlap and meanings often correlate, it can be worth distinguishing the deeper meaning an object symbolizes from its sensory connections to the real-world object it imitates, and distinguishing both from the functions it serves in the game narrative.

McIntosh observes that a garden of the gods is most typically a representation of paradise, and in considering any sacred space a good starting point is to discern whether the entire environment is a metaphor for something else. Next, key features of form may be identified, such as how the center of the space is marked or not marked, whether there are symmetries such as the four points of the compass, and how doorways and other entrances are treated. If the center of the space represents transcendence, then an entryway represents transition or transformation. Internal walls and other barriers become a labyrinth if they are numerous and complex, and maze-like structures can represent the difficult paths of decision encountered in life or during a religious pilgrimage to transcend the ordinary barriers of life. In describing one religious maze, he says, "The winding path represents life's journey, with the wrong turnings representing sins and mistakes. The path leads symbolically through death and then into the garden of paradise."[5]

The battle cry of "modern architecture" in the twentieth century was "Form follows function." This doctrine discouraged nonfunctional decoration and assumed that form and function were the only two variables in the equation of design. Arguably, a third variable is meaning, which may often be confounded with either form or function. Furthermore, in virtual worlds, form may diverge quite far from function, because the *display model* that produces the visual image can be different from the *world model* that determines how the avatar can interact with it. The apparent origin of the "form follows function" doctrine was an essay written just before the dawn of the twentieth century by the architect of Chicago skyscrapers Louis Sullivan. But when he enunciated this principle, it was embellished by poetic language:

> Whether it be the sweeping eagle in his flight, or the open apple blossom, the toiling work horse, the blithe swan, the branching oak, the winding stream at its base, the drifting clouds, over all the coursing sun, *form ever follows function*, and this is the law. Where function does not change, form does not change. The granite rocks, the ever-brooding hills, remain for ages; the lightning lives, comes into shape, and dies in a twinkling.[6]

Everything seen in a virtual world is artificial, so in a very real sense it is one of McIntosh's gardens. The fact that Sullivan embeds his design principle in poetic images of nature hints at a creationist view that everything in the world was designed by a deity, whether Jehovah or Mother Nature. Thus, this chapter will need to consider the sculpted geography of the entire world, especially when it seems to have some overall sacred significance, as well as the architecture of local cathedrals, temples, and monasteries.

Deciphering Four Churches

The solo-player game *The Da Vinci Code*, based on a movie that in turn was based on a novel by Dan Brown, depicts four religious sites: Saint-Sulpice in Paris, Temple Church and Westminster Abbey in London, and Rosslyn Chapel in Scotland. The moviemakers naturally wanted to film at each of the four sacred sites, but they were forced to use filmic tricks when Saint-Sulpice was not available. Refused permission to film at Westminster Abbey, the moviemakers used Lincoln and Westchester Cathedrals instead. Both cathedrals received considerable criticism for apparently supporting this heretical endeavor, and both posted explanations on their websites, Lincoln publishing a sermon against the film and Winchester holding an exhibition debunking the story. Both Temple Church and Rosslyn Chapel gave permission to film on site.[7]

However, the video game depicts all four genuine churches, not perfectly accurately, but with many correct details. Some of the departures from authenticity were simplifications to reduce the game developers' workload, but others were aesthetic, as when frequently more colorful stained glass was placed in the virtual windows than exists in the real ones. In all three media, the story combines secret codes with religious heresy, assuming that beneath surface appearances lurk hidden truths that conventional religious organizations have sought to suppress. Thus, symbolism exists on many levels, and cracking one code merely unlocks another encrypted message. Depicting the churches fairly realistically accomplishes two things. First, it anchors an otherwise wild narrative in an authentic setting that facilitates the suspension of disbelief. Second, the rich visual recreation of sacred spaces facilitates a sense of immersion on the part of the player.[8]

This was true even when I set out to write these paragraphs. I had completed the game four years before but had not saved my data and now wanted the freedom to explore the four enigmatic churches without having to worry about fighting enemy monks or arduously working my way once again through all the levels of progress. Several websites gave me the three codes I needed: "vitruvian man," "clos luce 1519," and "phillips exeter." Entering these into the game at the beginning gave my avatar infinite health, the ability to kill an enemy with a single punch, and freedom to roam the levels at will. Two other secret codes gave me all the virtual objects the avatar would have collected along the way.

When developers are creating a game, they need to be able to conduct tests running avatars through specific situations, so they build such codes into the programming. Just before commercial release, they disable most of them, but they found that leaving a few in could be a valuable marketing ploy. A few weeks after a game has launched, when sales have dropped, they allow the codes to spread online, from one fan to another, rebuilding interest and possibly inspiring friends of players to buy the game. This is not done with MMOs, which are designed for long-term subscriptions, but something analogous takes place with respect to virtual world geography. Some locations required for quests are very difficult to find, and the first player who succeeds can gain fame by posting the coordinates online.

The fundamental premise of *The Da Vinci Code* is that Jesus and Mary Magdalene had a child, and a secret sect called the Priory of Sion has preserved her family line even to the present day, when the heir of Christ is a police cryptographer named Sophie Neveu. At the scene of her grandfather's murder in the Louvre Museum she meets Robert Langdon, professor of religious symbology at Harvard University. Harvard, of course, is a place that represents supreme erudition, and a longstanding debate between myself and Christopher McIntosh concerns whether Oxford University is a superior symbol to Harvard University, given that one of us attended Oxford and the other Harvard.[9] With this book I am happy to say I have published with both of their presses.

Very quickly, Neveu and Langdon team up on a search for the Holy Grail, while fleeing from the police and from what appears to be Opus Dei, a real organization associated with the Roman Catholic Church. The motive of the enemy is to suppress the truth that women are equal to men in the sight of God, and that the current avatar of Christ is in fact female. Sophie does not know the story of her own origins, and Langdon knows only some superficial information about the Priory of Sion. However, they are well prepared to unlock the secrets contained in many puzzles and codes, given their professional backgrounds in cryptography and symbology. The first puzzles relate to the *Mona Lisa* and other works of art by Da Vinci, but the fundamental premise of the story is that a vast number of physical objects encode esoteric meanings.

The game differs from the movie and novel in three main ways. First of all, there are many more puzzles to be solved, giving the player many hours of pleasant perplexity. Second, at each virtual location there are several enemies to fight, which are easily mistaken for members of one sinister sect. Third, a fictitious order of the church is involved, rather than the real organization Opus Dei as in the film and book. Until rather late in the novel, it appears that Opus Dei has committed murders, but in fact this organization was not guilty, although it is depicted in extreme terms. *The Da Vinci Code* is a work of fiction, but it received considerable criticism from some in Christian quarters, who perceived it to be a serious critique of orthodoxy, from a cultic and feminist perspective.[10]

In 2006, Opus Dei found it necessary to post a point-by-point refutation of the novel's claims on its website, mentioning that a number of spokesmen were prepared to give lectures on the topic to local audiences. One section of the refutation is especially relevant to sociological analysis: "In various places, The Da Vinci Code describes Opus Dei as a 'sect' or a 'cult.' The fact is that Opus Dei is a fully integrated part of the Catholic Church and has no doctrines or practices except those of the Church. There is no definition or theory—whether academic or popular—that provides a basis for applying the pejorative terms 'sect' or 'cult' to Opus Dei." Indeed, by definition the Roman Catholic Church cannot have sects, because a sect is a completely independent organization within a loose religious tradition.[11] The Catholic Church may have "orders," but Opus Dei does not use that term for itself, preferring "personal prelature" or simply "organization."[12]

The game refers to the group as Manus Dei rather than Opus Dei, thus distancing the story from direct criticism of real Catholic organizations, and it adds a radical subgroup that is responsible for all the wicked behavior. The game instructions describe them:

> Manus Dei—This conservative and highly regulated sect of the Church values discipline and strict following of the rules above all. They have little tolerance for other religions and their practice of corporal mortification (self-flagellation to absolve their sins and keep pure) is looked down upon by the upper echelon of the Church. Though their practices have always been a point of contention, recently it has become a high profile issue and the Church has been considering Manus Dei's removal from their stable of recognized sects.
>
> Sanctus Umbra—The seedy underbelly of Manus Dei, Sanctus Umbra is only a whispered tale passed on as a legend from the early 1930s. Rumors speak of a group of monks trained by Manus Dei in the ways of the ancient Hassassins (or assassins) from their youth. Their ability to blend with shadows is said to be uncanny, and their thirst to inflict God's vengeance, insatiable.

"Hassassins," it must be noted, were Islamic, not Christian. A medieval Shia sect that today is sometimes compared with al-Qaeda, the Hashāshīn became the subject of many exaggerated stories in Christendom. Marco Polo, for example, told the story of their leader, the Old Man of the Mountain, who ruled a terrestrial paradise where young men were trained to be assassins for God.[13] About Manus Dei, a knowledgeable online reviewer named Nate Ahearn commented:

> Whether they were trying to differentiate the game from the movie by switching the name of the faction of the Catholic Church—known as Opus Dei in the novel and film and Manus Dei in the game—or if it was

simply because of the immense amount of the pressure that the real life group had put on the film makers, it's still a nice change of pace; at least for someone who has already plodded through all things *Da Vinci*. Why they felt the need to add in another sub-group, the Sanctus Umbra, within Manus Dei (a group that is completely absent from the book and movie) is beyond me but at least it's one more thing that separates the game from the rest of *The Da Vinci Code* world.[14]

While Opus Dei means *work of God* in Latin, Manus Dei means *hand of God*. *Sanctus Umbra* is a little perplexing. *Sanctus* is Latin for holy, sacred, or inviolable. It is a well-known adjective in the masculine nominative case, or, more technically, a participle from the verb *sancio*, meaning to confirm or make sacred. *Umbra* means shadow or shade, and can be found in the common English word *umbrella*, "little shadow." Umbra is the nominative form of a feminine noun, or if the intention was to make the final *a* long, it would be ablative case suggesting something like "by shadow." Thus, unless the phrase refers to becoming holy by means of a shadow, it seems to be ungrammatical. Inside the game itself, the phrase is translated Holy Shadow, but in proper Latin that would have been Umbra Sancta, putting the feminine ending on *sanctus* and perhaps reversing the word order to improve style. Either the game designers were not Latin scholars, or they created a deeper sexual symbolism by mixing masculine and feminine genders. The top ten translations for *sanctus* in Google Translate are: holy, sacred, saint, consecrated, chaste, hallowed, venerable, morally pure, saintly, and virtuous.[15] The top ten for *umbra* are ghost, shadow, shade, darkness, dark, dusk, obscurity, night, phantom, and spirit. When challenged by the whole phrase, Google Translate generated "The Holy One of Shadow."

In the book and movie, a sadomasochistic Manus Dei monk named Silas goes to the Saint-Sulpice church in Paris, to unearth the secret of the Holy Grail's location, but Neveu and Langdon do not go there. In the game, however, the player's avatar is usually Langdon, but sometimes Neveu, so Langdon does visit Saint-Sulpice to solve many puzzles and battle hordes of monks. The novel claims the church was built over the ruins of "an ancient temple to the Egyptian goddess Isis,"[16] and is imbued with feminine symbolism. Dan Brown described its superficial design thus: "Saint-Sulpice, like most churches, has been made in the shape of a giant Roman cross. Its long central section—the nave—led directly to the main altar, where it was transversely intersected by a shorter section, known as the transept. The intersection of nave and transept occurred directly beneath the main cupola and was considered the heart of the church . . . her most sacred and mystical point."[17]

However, he explains further, this conception is superficial, and the actual most sacred point is elsewhere, where a mysterious Egyptian obelisk stands at the end of a brass meridian line in the floor, which the novel calls the Rose Line. This is something like an occult *ley line*, with tremendous significance that only someone who knows the feminine, Pagan nature of the sacred site could understand. Beneath the sign of the Rose supposedly is buried the keystone that holds the secret of the Grail's hiding place. Dan Brown did not invent all this fantasy, but derived much of it from *The Templar Revelation: Secret Guardians of the True Identity of Christ* by Lynn Picknett and Clive Prince,[18] one of many books that belong to a growing library of unorthodox religious speculation that blends Christianity with Pagan and New Age notions.

The *Wikipedia* article on Saint-Sulpice devotes much space to refuting all these speculations, noting there is no evidence there ever was an Egyptian temple on the site, nor that the fictitious Priory of Sion ever headquartered there. The obelisk and brass line exist, but were installed in the eighteenth century to use the sun shining through the transept window to calculate the date of Easter.[19] In the novel, the idea that the keystone is hidden at Saint-Sulpice is actually a ruse, and Silas finds only a decoy bearing the inscription "Job 38:11." The middle of that verse alerts Silas that he has been duped: "Hitherto shalt thou come, but no further." In the game, when Langdon inspects the flagstone Silas broke to uncover the decoy, he comments that whoever smashed it must have found the keystone hidden beneath. Thus, many secret codes tell lies. Later in the game, at the other end of the line on the floor, he must enter the month and day when an eclipse of the sun occurred, to earn a "station of the cross statue."

The circumference of the church, working clockwise from just left of the main entrance, contains the fourteen Stations of the Cross. The player may stop at each one in turn, inspect it, look upward at an artwork depicting the scene, and receive a brief narration describing that step in the journey of Jesus to his crucifixion. The traditional Stations of the Cross are not entirely scriptural, a few being added in the Middle Ages, and the Roman Catholic Church began using a purified version in the year 2000.[20] For example, three involving women are not described in the Bible: Jesus meeting his mother (station 4), Veronica wiping his face with her famous veil (station 6), and his mother being the one who removes his body from the Cross (station 13). The game narration for Veronica's station is longer than others, correctly noting that the Bible does not mention it, but implying that the apocrypha and other unorthodox sources are correct in mentioning it. At the thirteenth station, the game narration says scholars still debate exactly what happened to the body of Jesus, but asserts that both Marys, his mother and his wife, were present when it was removed from the Cross.

The second sacred place in the game is Temple Church in London, the original portion of which is circular, and which even after a rectangular section was added does not approximate the shape of a cross. In the novel, a symbologist colleague of Langdon's calls the Temple Church *pagan to the core*: "'Pantheonically pagan!' Teabing exclaimed. 'The church is round. The Templars ignored the traditional Christian cruciform layout and built a perfectly circular church in honor of the sun.' His eyebrows did a devilish dance. 'A not-so-subtle howdy-do to the boys in Rome. They might as well have resurrected Stonehenge in downtown London.'"[21]

The website of the church acknowledges the connection to the Templars, but not to Stonehenge or other pagan monuments: "The Church was built by the Knights Templar, the order of crusading monks founded to protect pilgrims on their way to and from Jerusalem in the 12th century. The Church is in two parts: the Round and the Chancel. The Round Church was consecrated in 1185 by the patriarch of Jerusalem. It was designed to recall the holiest place in the Crusaders' world: the circular Church of the Holy Sepulcher in Jerusalem. It is a numinous space—and has a wonderful acoustic for singing."[22]

Saint-Sulpice was a decoy, but the Temple Church was a mistake, resulting from misinterpretation of one of the clues. In the game, many puzzles take place there, however. A scroll must be deciphered, and a hidden key found, before the avatars can even enter the church. A remarkable scene in the game, absent from the film and book, requires Langdon to escape from a storeroom in which his enemies have locked him. To do so he must rummage through the junk in the room to find tools to unlock the door. Many boxes of Bibles get in his way, and those holy books provide absolutely no escape from his plight. For those who want to experience the church remotely, its website links to a virtual tour, consisting of panoramic displays that can be rotated and zoomed, from three different viewpoints, including the center of the round nave.[23]

The correct interpretation of clues took the team to Westminster Abbey. As in the novel and movie, the game finds the chief clues to the whereabouts of the Grail in the symbols on Newton's tomb, but the game also requires solving five puzzle poems on scrolls, involving memorials to Chaucer, Shakespeare, and other notables. So the first religious site was a decoy, the second was an error, and the third was a clue. The fourth, Rosslyn Chapel, was the goal, and the hiding place of the Grail.

Among the elements of the most significant puzzle in Rosslyn are four sculpted angels on the rear wall, named Hope, Truth, Faith, and Courage. After several steps, Langdon and Neveu find three disks, called Daisy, Lily, and Rose. A gate they must pass through is decorated by the Star of David, which the myths interprets as a male triangle (point upward) merged with a female triangle (point downward). All six points of the star are labeled with virtues, and they ignore the three male ones: Loyalty, Wisdom, and Strength. Placing the flower disks in the correct feminine places opens the gate. For Neveu, this leads to recognition of her own sanctity, because this was, after all, a gate coded for women. For Langdon, solving the last puzzle satisfies his intellectual curiosity, but does not offer transcendence.

Cathedrals, Temples, and Churches

Before they are anything else, virtual worlds are simulations of places, and their environments typically include much architecture. Amid castles, farms, business buildings, and homes can be found religious structures, sometimes among the most prominent features on the countryside, or the focal points of cities. Their significance varies by the nature of the fantasy that defines the game. At one extreme, *Lord of the Rings Online* is such a total but abstract religious allegory that churches would be out of place, just as they would be in the Garden of Eden. If all the world is a sacred place, no architecture within it can be distinctively sacred.

On the other hand, locations in gameworlds serve practical functions for gameplay, so they cannot ever be entirely sacred. A good example is the headquarters of the Jedi on the planet Tython in *Star Wars: The Old Republic*. As the game's wiki explains, Tython was the original home of the Jedi, where their founders had discovered the Force: "It was on this world that the brightest and best philosophers, priests, scientists, and warriors came together to discuss their discoveries involving the enigmatic, mystical Ashla (light side of the Force). They established a Forge initiation ceremony that would eventually lead to the invention of lightsabers after they faced threats from beyond Tython. . . . Eventually dissidents who used the Bogan (dark side of the Force) rose up, sparking the Force Wars. This conflict left Tython in ruins and even though the Ashla-centered group was victorious, both groups were forced to leave."[24]

With the passage of thousands of years, history became legend, and legends were forgotten. Then the Jedi returned to Tython to rediscover their ancient heritage. In a recent war, the main Jedi temple on Corescant, the capital of the Galactic Republic, was destroyed, so they built a new one on Tython, within walking distance of the very ancient ruins of their original temple. Although called the Jedi Temple, it is more like a small college town, providing a range of services for the students and faculty who work there. A few quests take place in the ruined temples, and the new one is the main training ground for young Jedi.

The Jedi Order has nothing to do with Western monotheistic religion, but, as noted in chapter 4, has affinities with Asian martial arts cults and possesses a philosophy not very different from Zen Buddhism. Therefore, there is no artwork depicting a god or messiah and no cathedral-like worship space.

The most prominent symbol is an ornate dodecahedron levitating in the two-story entrance hall. Like a college, the temple has two academic lecture rooms, although the instructor in one is bathed in mysterious light and levitating in the air. The temple includes a council chamber and several offices that can be entered only when the player is on a suitable mission. Two large circular rooms could be used for mass gatherings, although one has tables like those in a cafeteria. The other is being used by few small groups for their various purposes, is dominated by a hologram of a planet, and could on occasion be used for mass meditations. The temple complex includes a market, where only weapons and armor are sold, a cantina where avatars may rest when the player does not need them, a lightsaber training area, and a landing area for a space shuttle. Outside the main entrance are two training areas where students may fight simulated battles against the robots called *droids* in *Star Wars* lore. It should be noted that, in their pure form, Eastern spiritual practices like Zen Buddhism do not make a distinction between sacred and profane, and this Jedi Temple does not as well.

Final Fantasy XI illustrates well the range of variations in the degree to which virtual spaces are considered sacred. The central territory of the world called Vana'diel is ruled by three competing but allied city-states, Bastok, Windurst, and San d'Oria. They differ in political system, the races that inhabit them, and their histories. They are united in their opposition to the Goblins and other forces of chaos that swarm around their lands. Each of the three city-states is based on a different cultural principle, and religion is significant in only one of them. The Republic of Bastok, built by a race called Humes and clearly intended to represent humans, is an industrial society, complete with mines, factories, technological laboratories, and ugly gray pollution. A second race has made its home there, the Galka, who are used as manual laborers and harbor some resentment about their lower-class status. Science and technology take the place of religion, so there is no religious architecture.[25]

Windurst City is also home to two races, the Tarutaru who built the city and the feline Mithra hunters who help connect the city to the surrounding natural environment. The Tarutaru speak in a childish, stilted, and at times inscrutable manner. Only after doing a few missions for them does the player realize that Windurst is modeled on the campus of a university, and the Tarutaru are academics in the humanities. As arrogant intellectuals, the Tarutaru often seem silly, but in fact they possess great power because they have mastered magic. The central structure of the city is Heavens Tower, a temple where all of the governmental functions take place, where several quests begin or end, and where at the very pinnacle the mystic Star Sibyl rules through her prophecies. Magic rather than religion connects this city with the supernatural realms.[26]

San d'Oria is the home of the Elvaan race, and it is modeled on a walled feudal city, combining European medieval and Asian styles. All the structures are made of heavy, gray stones, not unappealing, but looking very solid. A dynasty of kings has ruled for five centuries, supported by two classes of warriors, the Royal Knights, who defend the nation's borders, and the Temple Knights, who defend the city itself and maintain tranquility within its walls. The two are rivals, each led by one of the princes of the royal family, and this rivalry suggests the tension between secular and religious institutions of medieval society. The San d'Oria cathedral is an imposing structure near the most prominent public buildings of the city, and its leadership appears to have some independent power, as well as connections to the Temple Knights. Its religion is monotheistic, worshipping a female deity named Altana, the Dawn Goddess. After she created the world, she wept five tears, and when each splashed upon the ground it generated one of the five races.[27]

The religious architecture in *EverQuest II* consists of many structures strewn across the vast landscape of Norrath, but given the large number of gods and the fact they were so long absent from Norrath, we should not expect to find a monolithic cathedral representing an established state church. In Qeynos, a major city, two different supernaturally oriented factions can be found, one representing mages and the other representing priests. The Concordium, or Masters of the Arcane, have their headquarters in the Tower of Three. There, a hooded figure named Bellengere the Three observes, "If knowledge is power, and power corrupts, then it is only logical to presume that knowledge corrupts." He goes on to explain that this syllogism is incorrect, because power need not corrupt if it is wielded with caution to avoid corruption. Thus, members of the Consortium have the duty to gain all arcane knowledge before evil forces seize it to give themselves absolute power.

The Tower of Three is a remarkable stone structure, frankly ugly in form, surrounded by its own moat, although it is easy to swim across if one does not want to walk across the short bridge over the water. The most bizarre features of the tower are two massive secondary stone towers, one square in cross section and the other hexagonal, which are supported in the air halfway up the main tower by flying buttresses. The main tower is octagonal, and there may be some arcane numerological significance to these integers: 4, 6, 8. Its interior is mysterious, centered on a pool of water. The floor is tiled in squares, circles, and arcs where the circles overlap, with an extension out over the pool to allow one to stand at its center. Three massive dragon-like gargoyle statues glower down, separated by walls colored like dark skies flecked with clouds and highlighted by stars. Instead of a ceiling, the open space extends far, far upward, almost to the top of the tower, lighted by four chandeliers, each with four flames, which make the blue letters of inscriptions in an exotic language glow.

The faction of priests is called the Celestial Watch, or Defenders of the Divine, described thus in Norrath lore inside the game:

> The Celestial Watch is a religious society made up of disciples of the now absent gods of benevolence and light. This order honors all good deities and is an extremely spiritual congregation. Members watch the skies for the return of their gods, preaching diligently that the deities of old are not gone forever. The Celestial Watch is a selfless organization that ministers to the physical and spiritual well-being of the good people of the Kingdom of Qeynos. It sometimes undertakes missionary crusades to distant lands to spread the word of the righteous.

The Celestial Watch has its headquarters in the Temple of Life, which is an open-air body of water, called the Pool of Jahnda, surmounted by a rotating structure that looks rather like a flying saucer.[28] It levitates above four stone supports, apparently rising on power injected into the water from four devices that reach down into the water from the supports. Some players have speculated that one of the good gods, Rodcet Nife, the Prime Healer, could be an extraterrestrial, and this saucer might be the vehicle in which he came to Norrath.

The priests and medics standing around the Pool of Jahnda confirm that it is dedicated to Rodcet Nife, and they seek aid in performing his healing arts. Templar Calmarath, standing at the bottom of the stairway leading down to the pool, fumes against those who turn the priests' sacred power away from healing toward killing, "claiming to spread the word of the gods all the while soaked in blood and other remnants of war!" When asked to explain, he fumes that a priest should heal the wounded and give comfort in the face of death, not cause wounds and death. "Clerics bring the word and lessons of the gods to the faithful, not go running around reveling in combat. We should be guides and guardians of the soul, not weapons of war." Thus, it makes sense that the most sacred place for priests should not be a cathedral, expressing the power of a military alliance between church and state, but a healing pool, at the site where a divine healer brought mercy to this war-torn world.

As we saw in chapter 3, Norrath has druidic stone circles, resembling the real-world Stonehenge, and many other game worlds do as well. *World of Warcraft*, for example, has four alchemical stone circles representing earth, air, fire, and water. The most realistic depiction of the original Stonehenge is found in *Dark Age of Camelot*, along with an unrealistic version of Hadrian's Wall, and a collection of places made famous by the Arthurian legends, beginning with Camelot itself.

When I created a friar to explore Albion in DAoC, I named him Glastonbury to link him to one branch of the legends with which I was especially familiar, centering upon the town of Glastonbury west of London. This is an area rich with stories, both Pagan and Christian in nature. A cone-shaped hill overlooking the town, dramatically called the Tor, was apparently an Iron Age religious site, and the serpentine pathway leading to the top may have been a ritual maze for sacred processions.[29] Glastonbury Abbey was a major center of the Catholic Church from the Norman Conquest in 1066 until it was sacked by Protestants in 1539, and a sign erected for tourists there suggests it was the burial site of King Arthur.[30]

A legend promoted both by the local tourist agency and by esoteric religious groups held that Jesus as a teenager accompanied Joseph of Arimathea to Glastonbury, and Joseph returned after the crucifixion to establish the very first Christian church there.[31] As outrageous as this idea may seem, it has lodged in English folklore, and was expressed in a beloved hymn by poet William Blake:

> And did those feet in ancient time
> Walk upon England's mountains green?
> And was the holy Lamb of God
> On England's pleasant pastures seen?[32]

While there is no Glastonbury inside DAoC, for a time one of the game's Internet servers was named Glastonbury, and there is a location called Wearyall. This refers to Wearyall Hill, near Glastonbury Abbey, where visitors could see a thorn tree supposedly descended from the one that sprouted magically from the staff of Joseph of Arimathea, when he thrust it into the ground after carrying it all the way from Palestine. There is good reason to doubt the authenticity of the tree, although the local myths suggest it was continually replanted from cuttings, necessitated most recently in December 2010 when vandals hacked the limbs off. In Vetusta Abbey, just west of the north gate of DAoC's Camelot, can be found a nonplayer character named Brother Joseph, the most recent of a long line of Josephs who watched over the Wearyall Tree at the Isles of Avalon. He explains to anyone who asks, "We do it in honor of Joseph, who placed his staff in the ground and said aloud that he was tired. From his staff grew a mighty tree."

Five hundred years later, in this mythic conception, King Arthur was the last defender of a Christian kingdom against Pagan invaders from the Norse lands, and his death marked the temporary triumph of darkness over light before the monks at Lindisfarne established a toehold for Christianity on the other side of Britain over a century later. In this variant, the Arthurian legends seek to ennoble England's slide into darkness after the Roman departure, and to explain why England should remain a fundamentally Christian nation rather than seeking to revive the indigenous faith that built Stonehenge and sculpted the Tor.

Legends serve purposes for the people who create, transmit, and modify them. Consider the discovery of Arthur's tomb. In 1184, the abbey suffered a catastrophic fire. Apparently as part of the repair effort, a real Iron Age burial was found on the site in 1191, and the abbot jumped to the conclusion that this was King Arthur's tomb. Sometime in the following century, the names *Jesus* and *Maria* were chiseled into the wall of the abbey, perhaps merely to serve as a place for pilgrims to stop and pray, but some believed it was to mark the spot where these two historic personages had actually stood. As Chaucer reports in his *Canterbury Tales*, religious pilgrimages had become big business, and we can interpret these legends as advertising for a tourism game that is still played over the same landscape today.[33]

The old stories tell that Arthur went to the Isles of Avalon to die, and some claim that this means Glastonbury. It is not an island today, though it is partially surrounded by marshy ground and so by great stretch of the imagination might have been something like an island in olden times. The nearby hamlet of Cadbury has long been a claimant to being Arthur's Camelot, and surprising archaeological excavations carried out in the late 1960s revealed it was occupied during the correct time period, with much more impressive fortifications than the rival Camelots. The Arthurian legends serve the interests of local business groups, many tiny mystical groups in the area, and ultimately to some extent British national identity. Given the unavailability of documentary evidence, reasonable people are free to believe that Cadbury was Camelot, and Arthur was buried at Glastonbury.[34]

The Meaning of Substance

The word *substantial* can mean significant, as well as solid. Yet gameworlds are anything but solid, despite their significance. The definition of *virtual world* followed in this book is very broad, including a wide range of computer games and videogames that have a world-like quality. There must be an environment designed to appear at least roughly like a real location, in which the user can take actions over time that have consequences, in interaction either with real human beings represented by avatars or with nonplayer characters that resemble humans and animals. Most important are massively multiplayer online fantasy gameworlds, but solo-player and strategy games also have a world-like quality and may address religious questions.

Visually, the relationship between the player and the avatar is suggested by the different ways the computer graphics display the scene. Some gameworlds use what is loosely called the *isometric* perspective, looking down on the scene from a set position, or, in the case of *Sacred 2* or *Daemonica*, a third-person position that can be adjusted only slightly. This is typically the case in strategy games like *Rome: Total War* that lack an avatar that might define the appropriate perspective. A very different approach, followed by *Battleground Europe* and many other shooter games, is first-person perspective, seeing the environment only through the eyes of the avatar. Many high-quality modern gameworlds allow a variety of perspectives, smoothly shifting from a distant third-person perspective to a first-person perspective. Experienced MMO players find that a third-person perspective is usually best, because it allows the player to see more of the environment than the avatar could actually see, such as a tiger sneaking up from behind. Players may switch to first-person perspective when inside narrow passageways or when running along the narrow edge of a wall or wooden beam.

The sacred design dimension of gameworld applies not only on the small scale to a particular temple, but often on a much wider scale, to the design of the territory over which the game is played. *Faxion* is a case in point, because the zones representing the Seven Deadly Sins circle Purgatory City. Heaven is conceptualized as being above the land, and hell below it, but both can be entered only by teleporting from one spiritual plane to another. Purgatory anchors the whole world, providing a training ground for new players, as well as a conceptual center for the other zones. Constructed of massive, cathedral-like buildings built from gray virtual stone blocks, it is actually rather attractive in design, with elaborate carvings arching over doorways and an occasional statue of a gargoyle or dragon. The city and the seven zones are bisected by the river Styx, and new players enter not far from the docks where Mediterranean-style sailing ships presumably delivered them after departure from the lands of the living.

In all of the gameworlds, much of the action consists of running long virtual distances or, for advanced avatars, riding a horse or other mount. Traveling a distance costs time, and in *World of Warcraft* it might take a high-level avatar a full hour to run from Undercity to Booty Bay. A low-level avatar would take much, much longer, being killed repeatedly along the way. Some of the worlds allow travel along certain routes by ship or aircraft, and a few give high-level avatars flying mounts. But a common mode of transport over long distances is teleportation, depicted in various ways by different worlds. In *The Matrix Online*, an avatar can teleport between public telephone booths, but only if the avatar has once walked to the destination. The metaphor is that the avatar is information that can be transmitted over wires, even virtual ones. In *Gods and Heroes: Rome Rising*, avatars teleport between statues of the flying horse Pegasus, but, again, only after once taking the trip by virtual foot.

The fact that travel takes time and effort suggests one human meaning for distance: it represents investment. It is meaningful also for the fact that distances separate areas that individually have separate meanings. *Warhammer Online* is notable for the number of quests that require running a long distance, battling past a line of enemies, and performing a ritual at an altar or shrine. If religion were purely spiritual, the same ritual could have been performed just as well at home, but the mythos of the gameworld requires travel to a sacred spot.

Some places are sacred because of an event that occurred there long ago, and gameworlds based on existing legends can exploit this to great advantage. *The Lord of the Rings Online* depicts all the territories visited in the first two volumes of Tolkien's great work, including many tiny details. For example, *The Hobbit* describes a scene in which three trolls are turned to rock by the rising sun, and they can still be found there in the gameworld, as can the "slimy island of rock" where Gollum lived.[35] From *The Fellowship of the Ring*, the gameworld took not only the distinctive cities of the Humans and Elves, Bree and Rivendell, but key buildings in both that can actually be entered and experienced as if they were real, including the Prancing Pony Inn and the House of Elrond.[36]

A three-step quest arc in *Warhammer Online* illustrates the potential futility of investing physical objects with sacred meaning. A High Elf officer in the Shining Guard named Deliaren Swordsinger had sent a patrol into the Broken Dunes, under the command of Chaethis Runehand, a woman to whom he apparently had a strong attachment. The patrol had not returned, but Deliaren could not search for it because he had to remain at Mathrin's Watch to command his unit, so he sent my avatar, Williamwheeler. He found the corpses of the patrol, but no blood of enemies on their blades. This clue told him that the enemy were shadow wights, who did not bleed because they were already desiccated corpses, so he killed seven of them and reported the death of Chaethis to Deliaren. Handing Williamwheeler a piece of jewelry, Deliaren moaned, "There is nothing for it now. I cared for her ... perhaps not enough. I cannot bear to look upon her token any longer! Please, take it to the place she loved most in life. It is not far, I know she would want it. . . . Chaethis, I am so sorry." The place was a small shrine overlooking the northern sea, but the altar had long before shattered into two rough blocks of stone, and nothing magical happened when he placed the token upon it. The name of this quest arc is "Futility."

Home as Temple

Many MMOs, but not, for example, *World of Warcraft*, allow people to rent homes or guild halls, where avatars may place many pieces of furniture, trophies, and artworks they earn or buy during the course of their questing. A tour of many homes in *Star Wars Galaxies* revealed very little evidence that anybody collected religious artifacts, perhaps reflecting the ambiguity of the Jedi cult in that gameworld, whereas many religious artifacts were available in *EverQuest II*. Cleora had fully sixty items on display in her small apartment at New Halas, including an oversize glacial statue of an Ice Maiden, an Iskar throne, and a statuette of Queen Antonia Bayle that would shout inspiring slogans on command. Among arguably religious items on display were a tiny painting of the sun god; a huge painting of Firiona Vie, the Avatar of Growth; and Cleora's own future tombstone. Among her stored collections was a complete set of the fifteen Thullosian tribal idols, although Cleora had to admit she had bought them from other players, rather than questing for them herself. Similarly, she had purchased altars for all fourteen of the returned gods of Norrath, intentionally selecting ones that had been crafted from scratch by other players, which she displayed in her loft room.

The altars were all different in appearance, although the ones belonging to gods in the same category were similar to each other. Brell Serilis was one of the neutral gods, and the bases of all their altars were lumps of rock shaped rather like large armchairs, supporting a donation bowl on a wooden tray. Placed on the tray in Brell's altar was a representation of what appeared to be a city gateway, with gold-tipped columns on either side, framing two crossed symbols of Brell's under-earthly nature: an ax and a pick. The altars for Solusek Ro and the Tribunal were similar, but in place of the crossed digging tools, Solusek Ro's had a crown and pike, while the Tribunal's had a mace or scepter. Bristlebane's altar was somewhat different, lacking the model gateway but displaying juggling balls and a dagger, and decorated with a fool's cap.

The altars of the five good gods were identical wooden tables, with extremely gaudy stands for legs, supporting a pair of uplifted golden hands as well as the donation bowl, but with slight differences of shape or decoration. The simplest were those of Quellious and Karana, which differed only in whether the hands were together or slightly apart. In the altar of Mithaniel Marr, the hands were reaching for a sword. Hands held a golden crown in the altar of Tunare, flanked by green leaves representing her connection to Nature. A golden disk levitated above the hands of the altar for Rodcet Nife, gently bobbing up and down. It bore his symbol of a healing hand.

Skulls dominated the altars of the five evil gods, supported above similar twelve-sided tables on central pillars. All the skulls glowered over golden donation bowls and had golden eyes. The tables for Cazic Thule and Bertoxxulous were similar, as were the supports for the skulls, but the former was flanked by four clenched fists, and the latter by two scythes. The other three shared a different style of table with reddish supports for the skulls, but a different symbol atop each. The altar for Ralos Zek sported a battle-ax, whereas the one for Anashti Sul had a peacock scepter, and the altar of Innoruuk carried the face of a beast. In addition to these altars, Cleora had a complete collection of decorative shrines for all fourteen deities, which differed from the altars in being smaller, having lighted candles, and performing no supernatural functions. Like the crafted altars, the shrines had been constructed by carpenter avatars of players.

Most players of *EverQuest II* undoubtedly are not obsessive altar collectors, because each avatar can have a connection with only one deity. In Cleora's case, that was Brell Serilis. She actually owned four Brell altars, of four different types. She had earned her humble altar from questing for Brell, and bought the three others from other players. The blessed and imbued ones differed in being adorned by lighted candles, but the only functional difference among the four is the cost in favor of obtaining any particular benefit from Brell, as shown in Table 6.1. Like the crafted altar, the imbued altar had been made by a carpenter avatar, but one with a higher skill level. The blessed altar had been obtained by a brave player by killing one of a number of powerful enemies in the high-level dungeon, Castle Mistmore, or under similar dire circumstances. As the table suggests, she actually used only the imbued altar, because she got a better deal, each blessing or miracle costing her less favor with the god.

Cleora collected altars in *EverQuest II* in order to study them for this research project, but Aspera had a mix of motives for collecting minions in *Gods and Heroes: Rome Rising*, and for rebuilding the ruined temple on the estate where they lived. Sociologist Alvin Gouldner described classical Greek and Roman society as a contest system, in which each man competed for status against all others.[37] This may be somewhat true of all societies, and especially true of feudal societies, but classical civilization was fundamentally a contest, winning it not only vast territories for centuries but also a special place in world history. Appropriately, Johan Huizinga's influential book about the human propensity to treat life as a game bears a Latin title: *Homo Ludens*.[38] Scholars sometimes call game studies *ludology*, deriving this English word from Huizinga's Latin.

Social status, in a contest society, is a position in a power hierarchy. For one person to have high status, many others must have low status. Rome was not merely a plutocracy, in which wealth was the primary token of status, because it was essential for a high-status person to have authority over the lower-status people. This was not just a factor after the assassination of Julius Caesar and the establishment of the empire, but before, under the republic, as well. To be a Roman citizen was a mark of status in a hierarchy, as was to be a landowner, dominating the other people who lived on the land, whether they be slaves, or noncitizen freemen.

The role of religion ran parallel to the state, but was only loosely connected to it. Political leaders served religious functions under the republic, but religion was diverse and polytheistic. As the transition of the state from republic to empire occurred after the death of Julius Caesar, the transition of religion from republic to empire occurred centuries later, after the death of Julian, the last Pagan

Table 6.1 Functions of Brell Serilis Altars in *EverQuest II*

Ten Benefits	Effect of the Blessing or Miracle	Favor Cost from Different Altars			
		Humble	Crafted	Blessed	Imbued
Five Blessings					
Patience of the Smith	Increases crafting skill and combat luck	750	629	600	569
Stature of Serilis	Protects against physical, heat, and cold attacks	875	734	700	664
Earth's Vigil	Increases maximum health and power, and their regeneration outside combat	1000	839	800	759
Pick of the Duke	Summons a secondary avatar and raises mining skill	1125	944	900	854
Brell's Hammer	Summons 2 Brell's Hammer, which increases many statistics of the avatar	1250	1049	1000	949
Five Miracles					
Rift from Below	Inflicts crushing damage on nearby enemies	1125	944	900	854
Brell's Favor	Increases progress and durability substantially	1312	1102	1050	997
Forgehammer	Stuns target; inflicts divine damage	1500	1259	1200	1139
Armies of the Underfoot	Summons a limited pet to aid the avatar	1687	1417	1350	1282
Protection of Brell	Mitigates physical damage and heals members of one's group	1875	1574	1500	1424

emperor, and establishment of the dictatorship of Christianity. Thus Rome experienced not one but two "Julian transitions." *Gods and Heroes* takes place long before either of these transitions, but religion plays a key role in the status system, and each avatar ascends a status ladder of a particular god or goddess.

In the form that was released in June 2011, but not in the earlier closed beta-test form I studied in November and December 2010, each avatar is an aristocrat who owns an estate, and each estate has a temple to the particular deity chosen for that avatar. However, the estate was devastated during recent conflict, followed by thievery and even forgery of a false document purporting to show that the land was owned by one of the thieves. Early quests allow the avatar to regain possession of the estate and reconstruct the villa and the military barracks, but more work is required to restore the temple, and to replace many of the estate's personnel who were killed.

From the very beginning, an avatar in *Gods and Heroes* does not function alone, but has a minion helping out in the many battles. At experience level 11, a second minion is added, and a third at level 21, and I believe a fourth would have been added at level 31, but the game stopped at level 30 when it was released. Many quests earn the loyalty of additional minions, and others can be hired for money. In each case a *pactum* is signed by both parties, establishing a legal leader-follower relationship. When called upon, the minion must do the avatar's bidding. In return, the minion is allowed to live on the avatar's estate when not accompanying the avatar on quests. Because the number of minions that can accompany the avatar is limited, and the possession of minions denotes status, eventually hordes of minions inhabit the estate. While all the land and architecture of the estate expresses the status and power of the aristocratic avatar, the temple sanctifies that authority.

The situation in the early closed beta was simpler. Andivius, my beta-test avatar, was a warrior with a small camp rather than a large estate; had he returned after the game was formally launched, he would have had an estate. His resting minions could actually be seen at camp, although this was not initially the case for the estate. The avatar I ran through the released version, Aspera, was a mystic aristocratic woman who used magic spells rather than swords in combat. Her name comes from the ancient Latin expression *ad astra per aspera*, "to the stars through difficulties." And she did indeed cause and experience many difficulties, while *aspiring* to high social status in both secular and religious circles. She was a follower of Trevia, goddess of sorcery and magic, who was the least human in form of the Roman pantheon, and who had mystical connections to death.

When Aspera first visits her estate, she meets Flamen (priest) Merula, standing before the ruined temple. Together they pray to Trevia, and then Merula suggests Aspera offer aid to the priests in either of the two secondary cities,

Ostia or Aricia. When Aspera accepts this quest, immediately wooden scaffolding appears around the heavily damaged columns of the temple, showing that reconstruction has begun. At the small pantheon at Aricia in the Alban Hills zone, Caesonia Larta tells Aspera to help Attia Phillipa, a poor woman of the town who had lost everything to treachery.

Attia Phillipa laments that her father had died, followed soon after into death by her mother, whom some strange force had driven into raving madness, and the documents proving that Attia should inherit the state had vanished. Her powerful uncle has laid claim to the estate, and her only hope is to find the lost will her father had written. Incongruously, she tells Aspera to kill three rats and place their carcasses on three offertories at the cemetery south of Aricia. Perhaps Attia is also falling victim to raving madness, but Aspera complies. Once the third rat has been sacrificed, the ghost of Attia's mother appears, summoned from Hades. She explains that she was murdered by her brother-in-law, who placed a rabid bat in her bedchamber while she slept. Her dying act, as the madness of rabies destroyed her mind, was to hide her father's legal documents in a flowerpot in the room in the bathhouse that has three statues. Giving them to Attia ends the quest, but begins Attia's sadistic revenge, as she plans to make her uncle suffer before destroying him. Returning to Caesonia Larta, Aspera is told to pray to Trevia's statue in the pantheon, is lifted into the air by a bright light of apotheosis, and receives a new Trevian power, the spirit shroud which reduces damage suffered in combat.

Immediately, Aspera returns to her estate to tell Flamen Merula what happened. At the beginning of their conversation, the estate's temple is still a ruin, but with wooded scaffoldings around the columns, which are in the process of reconstruction. She instructs Aspera to visit the Trevian temple in Rome and speak with the flamen Tifia Silexia. There, in the sanctuary beneath the public part of the temple, Flamen Tifia Silexia sends Aspera to find an acolyte named Scilaea who was spying on bandits in Vinetum. Scilaea tells Aspera that the bandits have formed an alliance with the Techinists to steal Scrolls of Medea, extremely sacred objects for the Olympian religions. Often called Telchines, these mysterious beings may be remnants of a preclassical Mediterranean religion, which the Greeks and Romans connected with evil technological magic, and whom the Olympians sought to destroy. After several more steps, taking Aspera first to the tomb of the Latins in Alba Longa, then to a smugglers' den in Tyrrhenian Shores, she retrieves the scrolls and experiences a second apotheosis in the Temple of Trevia at Rome.

The result for her estate's temple is completion of the work restoring the columns, removal of the scaffolding, and beginning of the next stage of reconstruction. By the time she had reached the top level of experience available, 30, Aspera had rebuilt most of her estate, although the far end of the temple still had scaffolding around the area where the high altar was being rebuilt. She commanded a total of forty-one minions and twenty-four other servants on her estate. She could hunt deer and rabbits in her forest and swim in the lake with a dolphin. She could also play with cats and dogs, including one hound she had acquired by completing a comedy quest that had required her to interview dogs and cats throughout this fantasy virtual world about the guilt or innocence of that particular beast. As with her minions, some of whom had disreputable pasts, the crucial fact was their submission to her authority, not their religious orthodoxy.

Many other opportunities occur in *Gods and Heroes* for a hero to serve a god, with the result being more status for the hero but without obvious improvement to the temple on the hero's estate. For example, in the Alban Hills zone there stands an apparently abandoned Etruscan temple, dedicated to the gods of that north Italian people whose language and culture were very different from that of the Latins. A quest giver named Mettia Socellia explains a sacred mission called "A New Pantheon: Glory of the Celestials": "The glory of the Olympians is unmatched—Rome's continued victories over her heathen neighbors proves this. As Rome's borders expand, the question is posed—what do we do with the sacred objects of the conquered? Effigies of their erroneous gods are not fit for worship, but if the proper rituals are performed, the temples of our enemies can be reconsecrated."

The Roman priests had brought a statue of Jupiter for the reconsecration of the temple, but it had been stolen by bandits, so the first task was to battle into their camp and retrieve it. However, when it was placed on its pedestal just outside the entrance to the temple, it was consumed by magic flames. An Etruscan demon still possessed the temple, and the Roman hero needed to exorcise it. Vetranius, a nearby mystic, said that exorcising the demon would require two owl talons, stygian essence taken from eight undead corpses, and burning ichor that can be obtained only deep within the caverns behind the temple of Vulcan. Aspera assembled these ingredients, and then entered the Etruscan temple accompanied by two of her minions, defender Leontia and healer Drusilla. She threw the magical materials into the sacred flame, calling forth the demon, which the three of them quickly destroyed. The quest series concluded with these words from Mettia Socellia: "To combat darkness, it seems that sometimes darkness must be invoked. You have danced with the infernal gods but emerged to the light and in the process sanctified a new temple for the glorious Olympians. For this glorious act, may the gods fill you with their power."

Conclusion

An altar can alter. When we enshrine a religious principle in a physical object, such as a block of stone called an altar or a plot of earth called a cemetery, we change it superficially by applying symbols and arranging other objects around it.

But in so doing, we also change it deeply, through the meanings we attribute to it. It becomes an anchor for our thoughts, or a channel for our hopes. Because spatial reasoning is so central to the way humans think, and computerized virtual worlds can fool us into thinking they are three dimensional, the games described here can be powerful tools for thinking about novel spiritual alternatives. Yet they are especially vulnerable.

Many of the games possess complex mapping systems, sometimes having the ability to mark a spot, either by clicking on its representation or entering a waypoint command into the text chat system. In *Star Wars Galaxies*, for example, on the planet Tatooine, "/way-4773,-3009" guided you to the empty home of the late Jedi master Obi-Wan Kenobi. Except that now the entire gameworld, like lost Atlantis, no longer exists, so no one will ever go "there" again. While informed speculations abound, we really do not know what Stonehenge meant to the people who built it, yet it has been one of the world's most meaningful landmarks for thousands of years. The ephemeral places in virtual worlds lack that substantial quality, yet fleetingly they can be quite meaningful, within the world's lore and the experience of those who visit it. Arguably, the very fact they are not physical makes them better symbols of transcendence.

7 MAGIC

In the New Paradigm theory of religion, magic differs from religion in that it has narrower scope, providing very specific compensators, like hope for a cure from a specific disease, whereas religion provides general compensators, like hope for eternal life.[1] Social scientists have often pointed to another difference, the fact that religion seeks help from supernatural deities by propitiating them, whereas magic seldom deals with gods, behaving like a form of impersonal technology, for example through alchemy that manipulates supernature just the way chemistry manipulates nature. When it does seek the aid of supernaturals it forces them to comply, rather than begging their aid. In his classic study *The Golden Bough: A Study in Magic and Religion*, Sir James George Frazer argued: "In so far as religion assumes the world to be directed by conscious agents who may be turned from their purpose by persuasion, it stands in fundamental antagonism to magic as well as to science, both of which take for granted that the course of nature is determined, not by the passions or caprice of personal beings, but by the operation of immutable laws acting mechanically."[2]

This is certainly true for magic in gameworlds. Only in rare cases are deities at all involved in the process of preparing or utilizing a magical power. The favor of a deity is central to *Gods and Heroes*, and peripheral to *EverQuest II*, but absent from *World of Warcraft* and most others described here. Furthermore, virtual world magic follows very strict laws, often very simple ones. However, these laws have little connection to the laws that Frazer believed he had found in his scholarly study of real-world religion. Part of the difference can certainly be attributed to the contingencies of a fast-paced game playing on a computer. For example, when a mage in a gameworld casts a spell, the player merely clicks the icon for that spell on a toolbar. No time is taken to type in laboriously a long set of magic words. But another cause of the difference may be that game designers worked not from anthropological scholarship but from modern stereotypes of magic spells, such as depicted in the "Sorcerer's Apprentice" sequence of Disney's 1940 high-culture animation *Fantasia*. There, Mickey Mouse learns a magic spell before he is advanced enough to handle it properly. The spell is easy to cast, but hard to control. In the gameworlds, much attention is given to the arrangement of many spells in a hierarchy matching the avatar's progression up the levels of experience in the game.

Frazer said there were primarily two forms of magic, based on distinct theories he called the Law of Similarity and the Law of Contact. The first of these connects very directly to how human cognition works. We represent things in our mind as concepts, and arrange concepts in terms of similarity. If we cannot achieve our goal for some real thing by manipulating it, we manipulate the concept as symbolized through some other thing. A crude example is making a voodoo doll that represents our enemy, then sticking pins in it to cause real harm to the enemy. Philosopher of semantics Alfred Korzybski argued that humanity often got into trouble because it believed in fallacies that arose in the still primitive organization of our minds. Among his proclamations were: "The word is not the thing" and "The map is not the territory."[3]

Magic following the Law of Contact assumes that any object that has ever been in contact with an enemy can be used to cause magical harm to that particular enemy, but not any other. Burning the enemy's hat will cause the enemy to burn, and that voodoo doll will be more effective if it contains hair from the enemy or, as in *Pirates of the Caribbean Online*, if the doll is touched once to its target. Frazer noted that the two forms of magic can be combined, and that it is also possible to make finer distinctions.

For example, we could construct a new typology of magic by cataloging all of the kinds of metaphors that humans commonly use. As of July 9, 2011, the *Wikipedia* page for "Figures of Speech" lists four fundamental rhetorical operations, seventy-three linguistic schemes for changing the pattern of words in unexpected ways, and eighty tropes that change the meanings of words.[4] A trope often used in actual magic is *synecdoche*, using a part of something to stand for the whole, as a hair to represent the enemy. This is a special case of *metonymy*, alluding to something by referring to something related to it, which exactly follows Frazer's Law of Similarity. With a stretch of the imagination, any type of metaphor could give rise to a form of magic, not to mention *paralipsis*. The end of the previous sentence was in fact an example of paralipsis, and this book makes heavy use of *paronomasia*, especially in the conclusions of chapters. If need be, one could look paralipsis and paronomasia up in the dictionary, but it might be preferable to employ them as a magical incantation without worrying about such details as what they actually mean.

Alternately, contemporary cognitive science can serve as the source of magical ideas, especially in its growing catalog of common human cognitive errors. A good starting point would be the three cognitive theories of religion introduced in chapter 1: *mind reading*, *narrative*, and *memory*. The first of these begins with the observation that hyperactive human empathy imputes consciousness and intentionality to many natural phenomena that are not really conscious. In his anthropological study *Sorcerers of Dobu*, Reo F. Fortune reports that farmers on Dobu Island off New Guinea attribute poor crops to magic by neighbors that has caused their vegetables to walk away into the neighbors' fields.[5] Ambulatory vegetables are uncommon in gameworlds, but many have a few here and there to add spice to the roster of enemies. Walking trees are part of the Middle Earth mythos, so some can be found in *Lord of the Rings Online*, and others lumber across various regions in *World of Warcraft* and *Gods and Heroes*. (The use of "lumber" here is a case of paronomasia.) A very large fraction of the fantasy games personify the four elements of Western alchemy—earth, air, fire, and water—whether as enemies or as helpful secondary avatars.

The magical application of narrative marks every fantasy gameworld and every quest within it. A virtual world is not "real," and the avatar's accomplishments within one are therefore not fully real either. Achievements in a game can be compensators for lack of achievement in the "real world." Arguably, they can become real if other people take them seriously and honor the player for them. The human mind evolved its narrative abilities to plan complex lines of action and to communicate about them in service of group survival and biological reproduction. If reaching the top level of experience in a gameworld contributes nothing to survival or reproduction, then it is fundamentally valueless. However, if survival and reproduction are already assured, then humans may as well spend their time on whatever gives pleasure, and gaining subjective social status in a gameworld, perhaps by beating an NPC enemy using a powerful magic spell but with no other people present to applaud, can be worthwhile. In the journal *Sustainability*, I have argued that virtual status symbols such as a lavish mansion in a gameworld are far less destructive than the conspicuous consumption of owning one in the real world, which wastes significant natural resources.[6] So, under the right circumstances, virtual can be better than real, and magic achieves real results.

The memory theory of religion notes that two kinds of memory support two kinds of religion, so the same is true for magic. Semantic memory, requiring repetition and somewhat lacking in emotion, is the basis for low-tension, mainstream religion. It is also the cognitive basis for Frazer's Law of Similarity, because it is the semantic similarity between two memories that allows one thing to be the magical substitute for another. Episodic memory is much more emotional, connected to intense experiences such as religious conversion and fundamental to fundamentalist religious sects. But religious conversion is magical, because research tends to show that it does not really change a person, but typically represents symbolic rededication to the individual's existing faith. People do switch religious denominations, but in a process called *affiliation*, not *conversion*, and primarily in response to changes in social relationships, rather than as transformation of the self.[7]

What could be more magical than baptism with holy water to wash away one's sins? In many of the games, such as *World of Warcraft*, a priest takes training every couple of levels of experience from an NPC functionary in the religious hierarchy, paying a set price in virtual money. Rather than reading a textbook or listening to lectures from the mentor, the priest simply stands still and allows a sudden magic spell to be applied by the trainer, instantly giving the priest a new supernatural ability. Each such conversion experience is real, in the context of the gameworld, and a high-level priest may have experienced a hundred of them.[8]

A different way of analyzing gameworld magic is in terms of preexisting genres of fantasy literature. In 1978, I carried out a quantitative study of science fiction literature by administering a questionnaire to participants at IguanaCon II, the 36th World Science Fiction Convention (worldcon), in Phoenix, Arizona. This happened to be the worldcon where *Star Wars* won the Hugo Award for best dramatic presentation, and thus it marks a turning point in the history of science fiction. Analysis of the data identified a fantasy cluster of authors that could be assigned to subcategories, including sword-and-sorcery, horror-and-weird, general fantasy, and science fantasy.[9] The author who correlated most strongly with sword-and-sorcery was Robert E. Howard, and of course the gameworld *Age of Conan* is directly based on his work. The leading writer of horror-and-weird was H. P. Lovecraft, whose work powerfully influenced *Dungeons and Dragons Online*. The highest correlation for general fantasy was J. R. R. Tolkien, whose work was the basis for *Lord of the Rings Online*. The science fantasy category provided the conceptual basis for magic in all the worlds.

As it consolidated in the pages of fiction magazines in the 1940s, science fantasy consists of stories set in a universe where the laws of nature are very different from those found on our world. But those laws are just as rigid as the laws of physics and chemistry we experience. Thus, magic that contravenes natural law is just as impossible in those fantasy worlds as it is in our real world. The differences lie in the particular laws of nature that apply. In a sense, magic is impossible in both worlds. However, what is natural for the other world is supernatural in ours, so we tend to call it magic erroneously.

The authors who led the science fantasy movement in the 1940s were not personally influential on the games, but they developed a rationale that applies to them well, and that has multiple connections to post-Christian religion. For example, they published in *Astounding Science Fiction* and *Unknown Worlds*, two magazines edited by John W. Campbell, Jr., in a circle of authors including L. Ron Hubbard, who applied many of their ideas in creating the real-world religion Scientology.[10] A series of stories called *The Incomplete Enchanter* by historians

L. Sprague de Camp and Fletcher Pratt presented with the greatest rigor the theory that magic was simply the technology of worlds in which the natural laws were different, and de Camp went on to become the chief force behind the revival of Conan after Howard killed himself.[11] *Gather, Darkness!* by Fritz Leiber is the most perfect of many novels that imagined technology becoming so dangerous that the leaders of the world covertly reverted to a medieval form of society, in which science was hidden within a religious order until such time as it was safe to make it public again.[12] Indeed, any real magic that broke the laws of nature would be so dangerous that new laws would need to be instituted to prevent it.

Taboo Magic

If Cleora was a poor believer, living in a world with low-quality gods, and Orastes was a poor priest who escaped from a demented story by Robert E. Howard, Rumilisoun was a poor magician precisely because she perfectly embodied J. R. R. Tolkien's ethic that one must resist the temptation to use magic, even for good causes. She was a fine scholar like Robert Langdon, and also an Elf, which made her doubly aloof, in *Lord of the Rings Online*. The four races there are the same ones featured in *The Hobbit* and Tolkien's ring trilogy: Hobbits, Humans, Dwarves, and Elves. The Humans represent Tolkien's view of the human race, basically positive but not carrying much symbolic meaning. Each of the three others represents an accentuation of certain human characteristics. The Hobbits are modest, unambitious, and very uncomfortable with technology. The Dwarves, in contrast, are rather aggressive and love engineering; they do not get along at all well with Elves, and cooperate with them only out of necessity. Elves are bookish scholars who are immortal so long as they stay away from danger and strife; they are more enthusiastic about nature and the humanities than they are about science and technology.

The story of *Lord of the Rings* concerns an impending war, in which Sauron is assembling an invasion army of Orcs and Goblins, against which the four allied races must defend themselves. Sauron is a fallen angel comparable to Satan, and he seeks the power of the one ring that can rule all the other magic rings, a clear metaphor of evil technology. That ring had fallen into the possession of the Hobbit Bilbo Baggins, who bequeathed it to his nephew Frodo Baggins, who must somehow summon up the courage to take the ring deep into the accursed territory of Mordor, where it can be destroyed forever. In *Lord of the Rings Online*, a few Dwarves have gone over to Sauron's side, resonating with his enthusiasm for technology. The Elves are collecting as many of their historical records as they can before migrating westward, away from the war zone, and it is an open question how many of them will join with Hobbits, Humans, and the remaining Dwarves to fight against Sauron's evil army.

Elves in the Tolkien mythos stress scholarship over technology, which is represented metaphorically by magic. Rumilisoun entered Middle Earth in Ered Luin, a country split between the Dwarves and the Elves. After completing low-level quests, she crossed the River Lune eastward into the Shire, where the Hobbits dwell. She soon visited the Human city Bree, made her way through dangerous lands farther eastward to the beautiful Elven redoubt Rivendell, and also explored the cold lands of the north. She bought a cottage at a convenient location southeast of Bree, before trading it in for a big house back in Ered Luin, and joined a kinship whose lodge was in the western district of the Shire. Using Elrond's library in Rivendell, she developed her intellectual skills to achieve *supreme* rank as a scholar, then realized that her research could not be completed without a hazardous expedition through the Mines of Moria and Lothlórien deep into Mirkwood.

LOTRO conceptualizes environmental pollution in Christian terms as moral pollution, without explicitly using Christian words or symbols. Many lands and creatures have been blighted, but in keeping with the quasi-religious nature of the mythos they tend to be described as sinfully corrupted rather than chemically tainted. Rumilisoun battled corrupted salamanders across the islands of Tyl Ruinen, then used a draught to cleanse the cursed statue that had been causing the corruption. The quest "Touch of Corruption" required collecting a dozen spider venom pouches carried by Orcs in the Kinsfell, with which they coated their arrows and swords, and superficially this seems like a case of nonsupernatural chemical pollution. However, poison-tipped weapons are immoral, and the Orcs turned to many immoral technologies under the vile influence of their demonic leader, Sauron. Many other quests, for example, require destroying Orc siege engines, but the player never uses one against the Orcs. "Corruption from Fornost" concerns bears who have been corrupted by the bite of the Barghest, which is a traditional monster from north English folklore, often depicted as a dog or a bear that has been possessed by an evil ghost. As the instructions for "Glinghant Corrupted" explain, pools of water have been tainted by "foul spirits of corruption led by a grisly demon called Nengon."

A series of quests near the Haunted Inn in the advanced Mirkwood region illustrates LOTRO's fundamental concepts of the relationship between nature and technology. Mirkwood was added to LOTRO in a major expansion on December 1, 2009, and it was not at first possible to reach the inn because it lay beyond a wall defended by the Orcs. One of the limitations of MMOs is that they have tended to present static worlds in which large historic events could not occur, largely because new players needed to have the same experience as earlier players. Both WoW and LOTRO have recently experimented with ways to circumvent this stasis, allowing players to participate in historical transformations.

Notably, LOTRO adds quests every couple of months that tell additional "books" of epic stories, and completing a series of quests in western Mirkwood beaches the wall and allows access to large new eastern territories, including the Haunted Inn at Audaghaim.

The inn overlooks a ruined village that was destroyed years ago in some great disaster. There Rumilisoun and her bear companion, Beorn, battled ghosts on a gloomy hill of ash and charcoal. A quest sends the player to read the headstones in Audaghaim's graveyard in search of clues about why the area is haunted by Oathbreakers. Oddly for such a small town, four people died within days of each other, but supposedly for different reasons: "natural causes," "illness," "took his own life," and "fell to his death." A fifth gravestone is blank. The next quest in the series requires the player to interview those few haunting spirits who are willing to speak, while defending against the murderous attacks of all the other spirits. One ghost says, "Progress is a wonderful thing, is it not?" Another remarks, "Audaghaim is a peaceful village; we townsfolk want for naught." Another denies there is any trouble in this peaceful town. However, the player acquires strange coins from the ethereal corpses, which turn out to be "tokens of fealty to the Necromancer." A battered book found in the ruins chronicles the exact period, but the pages for the week on which the four people died have been torn out, and the player finds a sinister shrine to the Necromancer in the woods. Returning to the blank headstone in the graveyard, Rumilisoun encounters the ghost of the record keeper of Audaghaim who had written the book, and she learns the full truth.

Seeking technical solutions to the problems of life, the people of Audaghaim had pledged devotion to the Necromancer, who represents science and engineering. They hoped to gain comfortable, trouble-free lives in return. Four members of the village protested, so they were killed and buried under deceptive gravestones. The record keeper failed to stand with them in opposition to this false progress, but he wrote the truth in his journal, so he also was killed. "Yes," his ghost says, "the Necromancer came and promised much, and we saw the opportunity for progress and prosperity." But the immediate result was murder of the dissidents, and the long-term result was the death of the entire village.

LOTRO is ambivalent about nature, as Christianity is. The text introducing a quest called "The Search for a Remedy" says, "There is a phenomenon that often happens in nature in which remedies grow hand-in-hand with poisons. Weeds that harm can often be found nestled amongst leaves that cure." The traditional Christian explanation is that our environment is not the Garden of Eden, and our own sins caused us to be cast out into a world where we have knowledge of both good and evil. This is another way of saying that salvation cannot be achieved in this world, whether by technology or more ecologically benign means, but only in another, supernatural world.

Thus, LOTRO is also ambivalent about magic. In creating Rumilisoun to be my primary LOTRO avatar, I imagined she is the granddaughter of Rúmil, the Elf in Tolkien's mythology who invented writing, that she like him was an erudite scholar and historian, and that her only interest in the War of the Ring was documenting it for Elrond's library. The ending of her name was taken from *Alisoun*, a common name for remarkable women in Chaucer's *Canterbury Tales*.[13] Given her orientation toward history, I made her a Lore-master, which is a class of avatar very similar to the magic-wielding mage in many other gameworlds, the role that Cleora played in *EverQuest II*. The LOTRO game guide explains: "The Lore-master wields ancient secrets to confound his enemies and aid his friends. His knowledge of ancient lore allows him to confuse and stun foes, as well as to protect against the dark powers of the enemy. The Lore-master is also capable of calling animals to his aid. . . . The Lore-master will be the closest you can come to being a powerful spell-slinger."[14]

A mirror image of the LOTRO cosmology is *Runes of Magic*. As the name implies, magic is the focus of this MMO, but magic emerges in parallel with the social disintegration of the world. The instruction manual for this MMO focuses on how to operate the game, including the magical abilities avatars gain within it, treating magic as merely one form of technology. The supernatural narrative is provided only in an appendix:

> A long time ago, the god Ayvenas created a book in which he captured the shape of the world and recorded the origin of life. The book's name was "Taborea." Ayvenas realized his creations were weak, so he placed incarnations of himself into Taborea to teach his people various skills and abilities. Before long, the people grouped themselves according to characteristics. The world's races were born, and the legend of creation was written.
>
> Time passed, the races evolved, and Ayvenas was glad to see calm and stable growth. One day, while writing in the book of "Taborea," a thought crossed Ayvenas' mind: "What would his world be like if it was imbalanced?" Without his knowing, Ayvenas' thought was recorded, and Taborea began to change. . . .
>
> Ayvenas was stunned when he realized his creation—Taborea—had slipped from his control. He decided to tear apart the chapters of the future and scatter the fragments throughout the land. He wanted to give the power of the world to the people so that they could shape Taborea's future.

While many social scientists in our own world view religion as the descendant of magic, this evolutionary pathway is reversed in *Runes of Magic*, where magic evolved from religion. LOTRO forces avatars of different races to collaborate, pretends that good avatars would never resort to magic, and depicts a clear battle between good and evil. Like most other fantasy MMOs, *Runes of Magic* celebrates the disintegration of religious consensus because it liberates the individual player to enjoy a diversity of stories, some of which may satisfy the wicked desires hidden deep within the player's heart.

Principles of Magic

The most important general principle to note about magic in virtual worlds is that it works. Rather than being merely a collection of specific compensators, it offers real rewards, but by means that seem impossible from the standpoint of the natural laws that govern the normal world we all live in. The best example through which to explore the implications of this principle is *The Matrix Online*, a now-defunct but rather marvelous gameworld based on the trilogy of *Matrix* movies.[15] The films tell the story of Neo, a computer hacker who discovers that the apparently normal city he lives in is really a computer simulation. Picked up by a group of humans rebelling against the machines that operate the city, he undergoes training that has affinities with Asian religious disciplines and gives him ever greater power to hack the city's program through sheer willpower, while playing a Christ-like sacrificial role in bringing the machine rule to an end.

The *Matrix* mythos drew heavily upon postmodern philosophical ideas, most explicitly the writings of Jean Baudrillard, who suggested that reality had become obscured behind a maze of ideological metaphors.[16] However, the European intellectual background was much broader than the work of one rather poetic Frenchman, because Baudrillard drew on traditions of existentialism, Marxism, and psychoanalysis, all of which raised serious doubts about whether the images of reality we possess have any objectivity. These secular ideologies in turn reflect ancient religious views that some deeper reality must exist beneath the world of appearances, or in some way above mundane assumptions as the very word *super-natural* implies—a realm above the natural.[17]

In the twentieth century, chemistry and physics reinforced this view that the world of appearances is not real, by developing a model of unseen phenomena alleged to be more fundamental: atoms, molecules, and forces. The city depicted in the *Matrix* movies, and directly experienced in *The Matrix Online*, offers another model in which the fundamental reality is composed of data manipulated by a computer program. The ability to hack the code is equivalent to magic power. However, in both nuclear physics and computer science, full knowledge of the system does not offer the power to change natural laws. Rather, it provides a more accurate understanding of those laws in order to use them to one's own advantage.

There is no god in the city, although there are four churches in its slums. The city is divided into fifty-two neighborhoods arranged in four main districts representing four levels of danger and difficulty: Richland, Barrens, International, and Downtown. The first two are slums, the third is a Chinatown, and the last is the business district and home of the ruling class. There are Congregational churches in the Camon Heights and Mara neighborhoods, both in the ironically named Richland poor district. There is a First Unified Church in Sobra Shores, and a Church of the Disciples in Manssen Park, both in Barrens. Only the one in Mara was significant for players, both because Sister Margaret there is an early quest giver and because the area around the church was the primary meeting place for players in the whole city, because it offers a variety of services and Richland is protected from attack by the minions of the machines.

The New Paradigm argues that religion evolved from magic, as specific compensators consolidated into general ones over a long period of history, motivated by the need of professionalizing clergy to avoid disconfirmation of their value to parishioners and by the growth of formal religious organizations. But if magic works, there may be no need for religion. Magical skills are specialized, and they are mechanical in the sense that a very specific set of steps is required to achieve a specific result. Typically in role-playing gameworlds, one must do something to gain skill, often conceptualized as training but requiring paying a specific price to an NPC vendor of the skill. One may also require raw materials, especially when the magic is conceptualized as *alchemy*, a form of chemistry that follows its own set of principles. In *The Matrix Online*, the resources are conceptualized as segments of computer code, and indeed programmers in the real world tend to reuse code from other sources when doing their work, including hackers if their project requires complex efforts.

All of the examples considered in this book illustrate a principle that is most obvious in the case of *The Matrix Online*: The program actually manages two levels of reality, almost as if it were two programs operating in synch. As mentioned in the previous chapter, these are often referred to as the *display model* and the *world model*. The first depicts what the user sees, moment to moment, on the computer screen. The second governs how the virtual objects interact. The user may see the ornate wall of a church, perhaps with a stained-glass window and a statue of a saint in a statuary niche. That is the display model, which handles the challenge of portraying the wall from different distances and perspectives, and even under changing lighting conditions. However, the display model does not prevent the avatar from walking through the wall; that is the task of the world model. Typically the world model is simpler, in the case of an ornate wall being nothing more than a flat plane beyond which the avatar cannot go. It may include actions, such as receiving a blessing from the statue of the saint by praying while standing in proximity to it, or opening a door in the wall.

This dual nature of the virtual world has implications for magic. Casting a magic spell typically causes flashes of light in an animation that looks supernatural, but what happens below the surface of the program may not differ much from an action that is not magical. A mage in *World of Warcraft* may hurl a ball of fire, while a hunter shoots an arrow, the first appearing supernatural and the latter natural, but the effect on the enemy may be identical. The display models differ, but the world models are the same. In *Lord of the Rings Online*, Rumilisoun could hurl balls of fire, but they are conceptualized in the game's narrative as hot coals rather than a magic spell, in accordance with the antimagic ideology of Tolkien's mythos.

The best games that incorporate magic develop very complex conceptual and quasi-social structures to house it, providing much of the scaffolding for the story of the game. The MMO-like solo-player game *Elder Scrolls IV: Oblivion* is an ideal example because it offers a logical classification of six schools of magic, listed in table 7.1.[18] Avatars have eight attributes that determine their abilities in complex ways, and that can be altered by magic, potions, disease, and progress up the levels of experience. For example, the attribute called *luck* affects the outcome of everything the avatar attempts to do, whereas *strength* determines how much the avatar can carry, resistance to fatigue, and power in physical melee combat. Three other attributes contribute to performance of magic and increase gradually as spells of the associated type are used. *Willpower* resists fatigue, as strength does, but most crucially it increases the speed at which the avatar regenerates spent *magicka*, the fuel that powers spells and is called *mana* in many other games. *Intelligence* increases the maximum supply of magicka the avatar can have. Each school has its *guildhall* headquarters in a different town, and an unspecialized local branch of the Mage's Guild can be found in a seventh town, Bruma.

My *Oblivion* avatar, Barbara, joined the Mage's Guild, in order to experiment with all of these specialized forms of magic. Each local branch of the guild sells spell abilities, in exchange for gold, and offers quests. Completing a particular quest for the head of the branch will cause that leader to send a positive recommendation to the Council of Mages, and recommendations from all seven branches gave Barbara admission to the Arcane University just outside Imperial City, where she could learn advanced skills.

The recommendation quests tended to focus on social tensions within the guild, and upon the particular form of magic practiced by the given guildhall. At Cheydinhal, the local leader, Falcar, asked Barbara to retrieve the magical Ring of Burden, which had fallen into the well. To accomplish this, Barbara was given an alteration spell that allowed her to breathe underwater and that increased the amount of weight she could carry. This proved crucial to her success, and in the water she discovered the corpse of Vidkun, an associate mage who had drowned seeking the ring because its magic altered gravity and made it weigh as much as an entire suit of armor.

Table 7.1 Schools of Magic in *Elder Scrolls IV: Oblivion*

School	Result of Spells	Attribute	Guildhall
Alteration	breathe under or walk on water, open locks, shield from physical and magical damage, and alter encumbrance	Willpower	Cheydinhal
Conjuration	summon otherworldly creatures, summon magical weapons and armor, and reduce an undead creature's willingness to fight	Intelligence	Chorrol
Destruction	inflict magical fire, frost, and shock damage, and reduce resistances to magic attacks	Willpower	Skingrad
Illusion	charm, conceal, create light, silence, paralyze, command or affect morale or aggressiveness	Personality	Bravil
Mysticism	absorb, reflect, and dispel magic, move objects, sense life, and bind souls	Intelligence	Leyawiin
Restoration	restore, fortify, or absorb physical and magical attributes, cure disease, and resist magical attacks	Willpower	Anvil

As soon as she had entered the university, Barbara was given a quest whose completion awarded her a magic staff. She had a choice among three kinds of staff—destruction, illusion, or mysticism—and among three spells for each type. She selected a destruction staff that hurled balls of fire, which was one of her favorite spells, because the chief value of the staff was to allow her to continue to fight even after her magicka was exhausted. The choice was not really crucial, because at that point she was rich enough to buy a variety of staves in stores, using cash obtained by selling the equipment looted from vanquished enemies to armor merchants. Thus, the mage's staff she earned upon matriculation at the university was chiefly of sentimental value, a detail that reminds us that other institutions of society compete with religion to perform various functions. For some people, massage in a commercial parlor may relax them as much as prayer in a church, and a magical staff bought in a store functions the same as one awarded after completing a quest for the Mage's Guild.

While the guild holds a monopoly on its six forms of magic, an avatar can gain magical abilities of two other kinds, one more scientific and the other more religious: alchemy and shrines. To begin the study of alchemy in *Oblivion*, Barbara needed only to buy a novice's mortar-and-pestle set from an alchemy store, at a cost of forty-four gold pieces out of the two thousand she had at that point, and collect ingredients for her first concoctions. At the same store, she bought mandrake root and elf cup cap, two herbs with which she could make a potion that would cure disease. Her second creation was a Detect Life potion that would allow her to find a living being within twenty-three feet, even if it were invisible. She picked up one of the two ingredients, rat meat, at the alchemy store, but could have obtained it more cheaply by killing rats. The second ingredient, a bread loaf, was not for sale, but was readily available for free at the dinner table in any branch of the Mage's Guild. Barbara did not go far in her studies of alchemy, because her advancing skills as a mage gave her spells which accomplished the same things at no cost. For example, to get the recommendation from Jeanne Frasoric, head of the Bruma guildhall, she had to find a missing mage. By using a life-detecting spell, she easily found him, standing right in plain view but invisible, and the challenge was forcing him to admit that he and the others in the guildhall were playing pranks on Jeanne Frasoric because they felt she was incompetent at magic.

Like alchemy, religion in *Oblivion* is more valuable for avatars who are not mages. For example, one may get healed of wounds and disease by praying at the main altar in any one of eight chapels, one in each town. A skilled mage like Barbara needed neither potions nor altars, but simply healed herself with the appropriate spell. Nonetheless, the complex religion of this world provided a nice mythological background. The inscription on a heavy commemorative coin included in the collector's edition of the game reads, "The empire is law—the law is sacred—praise be Akatosh and all the Divines." Akatosh is one of nine gods, the others being Talos, Kynareth, Zenithar, Stendarr, Mara, Dibella, Arkay, and Julianos. Barbara felt an especial affinity to the last of these deities, and often spoke this prayer: "Come to me, Julianos, for without you, my wit is weak to sort the wheat from the chaff, and my eyes should neither know the true from the false, nor sense from folly, nor justice from prejudice and interest."[19]

Elder Scrolls IV: Oblivion suggests that if magical power actually existed, yet required specialized skills and resources to operate, then elaborate bureaucracies comparable to religious denominations would arise. Yet they might not resemble the Roman Catholic Church, depending upon the nature of the skills and resources, and the broader social organization of the virtual world. The structure of the Mage's Guild, mapping onto both a typology of forms of magic and a geography of towns and social groups, is one plausible alternative.

Spells and Skills

Avatars in gameworlds have skills, each represented by a number in the database server, which develop through experience and training, as illustrated by voodoo progress in *Pirates of the Caribbean Online* and Jedi progress in *Star Wars: The Old Republic*. Based on a series of popular comedy-adventure movies, which in turn were based on an amusement park ride, the fantastic virtual Caribbean inhabited by pirates cannot be expected to offer accurate social-science lessons, yet one of the most bizarre scenes in the films is based on a real event and connects reality to magic. Jack Sparrow, an erratic and self-centered pirate, is the center of the story, and he appears as a quest giver in the MMO, always sitting at a corner table in the Faithful Bride, a tavern in Tortuga. His first appearance in the second movie, *Pirates of the Caribbean: Dead Man's Chest*, shows him with outlandish facial makeup playing the role of a witch doctor for a primitive tribe. As noted in chapter 4, a real pirate named Lionel Wafer actually had such an adventure and wrote about it in his 1699 autobiography, providing enough ethnographic detail that his story is widely considered accurate.[20] Thus, when I set out to study magic in *Pirates of the Caribbean Online*, I named my research avatar Lionel Wafer.

As Lionel gained experience, his "notoriety" increased, conferring new abilities step by step and proving his worthiness as a pirate. When his notoriety reached 5, he was summoned to Tia Dalma on the Pantano River in Cuba. Her own notoriety was much greater than his, as explained on the game's website: "This mysterious mystic loathes the presence of the Royal Navy and the East India Trading Company in the Caribbean. They do nothing but stir up trouble at a time when her beloved islands are already plagued with evil. She has devoted her powers to driving them away and, to that end, will help any Pirate who fights them by giving lessons in the arts of Voodoo. Tia Dalma resides deep within the swamps of Cuba."[21]

Lionel had always fancied he would make a good magician, so he was flattered when she promised to teach him "the way of the dark arts." His first course required him to collect the ingredients for an elementary voodoo doll, which he could use as a weapon. He needed three buckets of pitch from sinking three East India ships, and three bundles of straw from sending three Navy ships to the bottom. Remarkably, the net result of dooming six ship crews was only the ability to form straw into the shape of a doll, with the pitch added to hold the shape. To give life to the doll, she instructed him to collect blood from ten stone crabs, six giant scorpions, and ten swamp alligators. Then to complete the magic, he collected bone dust from ten undead bandits and six undead pirates.

Later, when he reached notoriety 7, Tia Dalma taught him his first secrets of teleportation, which required constructing a teleport totem and giving Dalma some things she needed for her own work: twenty swamp alligator teeth, sixteen bayou alligator tails, and three leaves from giant flytrap plants. In order to bind the totem to Tortuga, allowing him to travel there without need of a ship, he had to find an artifact in a chest buried on that island.

At notoriety 12, he gained a teleport totem for Port Royal from Lucinda, a Gypsy, in the form of a medal that had belonged to the first man in the British Navy to set foot on the island. He obtained the totem to teleport to Cuba from Tia Dalma herself, at notoriety 14, by obtaining twenty alligator scales and three giant flytrap roots, though not the ones available in her own swamp, but rather those on Tortuga. Achieving notoriety 23 allowed him to earn the last teleport skill from Romany Bev, a senior Gypsy on a volcanic island named Padres del Fuego. First, she asked him to defeat fourteen undead slashers, fourteen undead grenadiers, and four undead Gypsies, who have the same powers as Lionel when he wields a voodoo doll. After this slaughter, she gave him the Eye of Nabai, which would allow him to visit her island whenever he wanted.

Of the nine Gypsies to be found on four of the islands, Lionel came to believe that Romany Bev was closest to Tia Dalma, and for one week he was constantly teleporting back to her to help defend Padres del Fuego against attacks by Jolly Roger's undead forces. Romany Bev even helped Lionel make a batch of voodoo rum for a crewmember named Gunner, which required him to loot a barrel of cursed dark sugar, two barrels of dread bitters, and cursed barnacles, sinking four ships in the process, plus eight fleas taken from the bodies of undead grenadiers, twelve scorpion stingers, and eight teeth from undead Spanish pirates.

When a valuable relic was stolen from the shack where Tia Dalma dwelled, she sent Lionel to Romany Bev to confirm suspicions about the culprit's identity. She agreed that Jolly Roger was behind it. The relic held part of the spirit of someone dear to Tia Dalma, and Lionel not only helped her retrieve it but assisted in a vain attempt to liberate the spirit shard from it. In return, she gave him a voodoo doll in the form of a pirate. Later, Lionel gathered some items that would help Tia Dalma complete the exorcism, and vanquished four of Jolly Roger's lieutenants in revenge: General Bloodless in Murky Hollow at Port Royal, General Hex in the Misty Mire on Tortuga, General Sandspine in the Rat's Nest on Tortuga, and General Darkhart in the catacombs on Padres del Fuego. His reward was a taboo doll for his collection, which is catalogued in table 7.2. The numbers in parentheses after the dolls' names are: (A) the attack power the doll possesses and (L) the experience level an avatar must have to use it.[22]

Lionel first interacted with Tia Dalma's Gypsy sisters at notoriety 7, when he bought a voodoo cutlass from Angel O'Bonney on Port Royal. It cost 480 gold pieces, while at that point he had only 559, and its resale value was a meager twenty-four gold pieces. Yet it seemed worth the price, because the cutlass was enchanted with a voodoo hex that would heal some of his lost health, even during battle, by waving it in the air. Gypsies also sell five kinds of potion which an adventurer may drink during combat to restore health, in increasing order of health points: tonic (costing three gold coins), remedy (six coins), holy water (nine coins), elixir (fifteen coins), and miracle water (thirty coins). Voodoo dolls in Lionel's collection provide a range of magical abilities, including some help in team battles. Red Fury increases the strength of friendly pirates; Spirit Mend heals all targets without splitting the healing, and Hex Guard protects other pirates from voodoo attacks.

As he was completing his education in the varieties and uses of voodoo dolls, Lionel reached level 30 in general experience, which made him ready to learn about another magical weapon, the voodoo staff. Tia Dalma explained they could be much more powerful than dolls, and she assigned him a number of tasks to prepare him to use this power properly: "To be usin' the staff, you must be strong of heart. And I only know one way to test the strength of a heart. This be a test against the elements... earth, air, fire... and the sea herself." This required defeating forty-two of various kinds of undead, after which he needed to collect the materials from which a voodoo staff could be constructed: branches from demonic tree men and shrunken heads from storm reaper ships. To give the staff power, he defeated many of the enemies shared by Tia Dalma and himself: assassins of the East Asia Trading Company, Dragoons of the British Navy, and raiders among the bravest of the undead, then defeated four dozen of Jolly Roger's minions on the aptly named Isla Tormenta. The final challenge to gain the voodoo

Table 7.2 Wafer's Collection of Voodoo Dolls in *Pirates of the Caribbean Online*

Purchased from Romany Bev	Acquired in Various Ways
Grudger Doll (A = 25, L = 17), a dark doll shaped like a tough pirate, Red Fury	Hex Reflector Doll (A = 25, L = 15), reflects all voodoo magic back to the caster, Voodoo Reflect
Vengeful Doll (A = 32, L = 22), a grim doll that increases the battle fury in others, Red Fury	Warding Doll (A = 22, L = 12), auto-resists one voodoo attack, Hex Ward
Wrath Doll (A = 38, L = 27), a doll shaped like an infamous pirate, Red Fury	Mind Control Doll (A = 32, L = 18), this might make the enemy stop attacking you, Not in the Face!
Restoration Doll (A = 19, L = 15), a doll filled with good voodoo power, Spirit Mend	Sight Binder Doll (A = 28, L = 18), attunes targets from a distance, Evil Eye
Renewal Doll (A = 25, L = 20), a festive doll that glows with good voodoo magic, Spirit Mend	Doll of Cleansing (A = 20, L = 16), removes all negative status effects, Cleanse
Life Doll (A = 31, L = 25), a powerful voodoo doll with mighty healing powers, Spirit Mend	Hero Doll (A = 10, L = 7), heals health over time, Regeneration
Enchanted Doll (A = 18, L = 13), enchanted with strong hexes to ward off evil, Hex Guard	Oriental Doll (A = 24, L = 14), protects other pirates from ranged attacks, Wind Guard
Magic Doll (A = 24, L = 18), a rare doll that pulses with voodoo magic, Hex Guard	Pirate Doll (A = 6, L = 15), bind to the spirits of the Caribbean with this rare doll, increases the damage of the weapon
Mysterious Doll (A = 29, L = 23), a mysterious voodoo doll with powerful protection spells on it, Hex Guard	Taboo Doll (A = 8, L = 20); many pirates fear the power and unknowns of this legendary doll; increases the damage of the weapon

staff was to sink three of Jolly Roger's own Black Harbinger ships, which at levels 35 and 36 were more formidable than Lionel's own frigate, the *Crimson Rose*, and he needed to use all the tactical wile in his possession to defeat them.

His first attempts to use his voodoo staff were awkward, because he did not at first understand how to activate the voodoo power. He smashed some crabs on the head with it, battering them slowly into insensibility, before he realized the proper method. Concentrating his mind on the staff and ignoring the enemy attacks, he drew his arm back as the staff filled with power, then released it, and fire leapt forward, blasting the enemy. After a few experiments, he recognized the power of the staff, but found his collection of voodoo dolls much more interesting. Tia Dalma explained to Lionel that the voodoo power they commanded did not really belong to them: "Power be in the knowin'... knowin' the earth... and knowin' the creatures that be livin' there." She told him that she had once owned a collection of wood and stone carvings symbolizing the diversity of animals: alligator, cockroach, crow, fly, monkey, jaguar, rock crab, scorpion, shark, snake, vampire bat, wasp, and wolf. Two others represented sentient plants, the flytrap and the enchanted tree stump. She gave him permission to collect these sculptures, which were strewn across the Caribbean in the possession of enemies of nature, and would increase his wisdom about the magical qualities of nature.

In the third *Pirates of the Caribbean* movie, we learn that Tia Dalma is not in fact a woman but the avatar of the sea goddess Calypso who captivated Odysseus and lived with him on a distant island. After a long sojourn, according to Homer, Hermes was sent to release Odysseus from her spell: "Calypso there, the glorious goddess, saw him as he came, and knew him; for the ever-living gods are to each other known, though one may dwell far from the rest."[23] Yet none of the mortals in the movies recognized who Tia Dalma really was, and they might have given a different meaning to the word *calypso*, a style of folk music that originated in the Caribbean, as did the voodoo that she practices.

There are no gods in the *Star Wars* mythos, which chapter 4 noted has affinities with Zen Buddhism. Magical powers are based on the Force, which may simply be one of the ordinary forces of nature, but one that a very few individuals can control through their minds, perhaps because their biological inheritance includes a large number of nanoscale symbiotic organisms in their cells, called midi-chlorians. Individuals who are force sensitive need rigorous spiritual training, both to be able to control the Force and to avoid using it for evil, selfish purposes. However, in both *Star Wars Galaxies* and *Star Wars: The Old Republic*, Jedi get precious little spiritual instruction after their first few levels of play. In *Galaxies*, most new powers come as a matter of course, when the avatar gains enough experience to reach one or another especially rewarding levels of general progress. As in *Pirates of the Caribbean*, Jedi in *The Old Republic* simply buy new powers from a trainer, once their experience has risen a sufficient amount.

In the backstory, Jedi do learn a quasi-Buddhist ideology, however, and the bonus book included in the collector's edition of *The Old Republic* provides its general principles. They are not required to control the Force, only to avoid emotional entanglements that would motivate the user to apply Force magic to selfish purposes:

> There is no emotion; there is peace.
> There is no ignorance; there is knowledge.
> There is no passion; there is serenity.
> There is no chaos; there is harmony.
> There is no death; there is The Force.[24]

An avatar can reject these principles and still control the Force. This possibility provides much of the interesting detail in the Jedi quests, which are embedded in much more complex stories than is the case for most other MMOs. In particular, a rival group of Force sensitives, called the Sith, have a different code. As imparted inside the gameworld by Sith Lord Spindrall to Bester, my Sith inquisitor avatar, this code reads:

> Peace is a lie, there is only passion.
> Through passion, I gain strength.
> Through strength, power.
> Through power, victory.
> Through victory, my chains are broken.

I chose the name Bester, not only because the avatar begins his life as a slave and must *best* the aristocrats to become fully free, but because Alfred Bester was the first science fiction writer to win the prestigious Hugo Award for best novel in 1953. As noted in chapter 4, his two most influential works were both novels about paranormal powers like those associated with the Force—telepathy in *The Demolished Man* and teleportation in *The Stars My Destination*.[25] Conscious of the fact that *Star Wars* was derived from the *Flash Gordon* mythos, which in turn was derived from the Mars novels of Edgar Rice Burroughs, I patterned my Jedi knight after Burroughs.[26] In particular, John Carter, the main hero of his Mars novels, had a degree of aristocratic detachment, because he was an Earthman who had married a Martian princess and thus was living in an environment very different from his home world. In *Gods of Mars*, he found himself opposing the traditional Martian religion, which was fundamentally a fraud.[27] As in the case of

Lionel Wafer, a European adventuring in the Caribbean, he was certainly not devoid of passion. Burroughs the Jedi possessed a very powerful ethical code, something Wafer lacked, to provide discipline over magic.

Alchemy, Chemistry, Cryptobiology

Alchemy is widely considered to be a primitive form of chemistry in which false magical ideas are mixed with some accurate knowledge of the behavior of physical substances. However, scholars of the occult have long noted that several fundamental concepts of alchemy spring from the alchemists' desire to transform their own spiritual natures, rather than from the mundane desire to control soulless matter.[28] Turning lead into gold can be a metaphor for turning an ordinary person into a magician, a sinner into a saint, or a child into an adult. So-called primitive tribes typically have initiation rituals inflicted upon adolescents that may involve mutilations like circumcision, and a social process of cutting the child off from his mother as well.[29] Graduation rituals in school are a pale reflection of this ancient tradition.

Many gameworlds treat alchemy mechanically, as a technology that follows rigid laws for the combination and transformation of substances—merely different laws from the ones that govern chemistry. In *EverQuest II* the procedures for doing alchemy differ not at all from those for practicing other crafting professions. Given that Cleora had the opportunity to try out all nine major crafting skills in *EverQuest II* before settling on the sage profession, she was able to determine that they are structurally identical with each other, merely differing in the symbolisms attached to exactly the same technical processes. This fact illustrates again the parallel between magic and technology, and the fact that supernatural images in gameworlds merely cloak rigid technical realities with an aesthetic symbolism.

Before she could do any crafting, Cleora needed to acquire the resources. While questing across Norrath, she found a very large number of spots where she could gather different kinds, such as wood from fallen tree limbs and minerals from deposit outcroppings. Players put quantities of these resources up for sale, which could be bought for the virtual money that Cleora accumulated, in the form of copper, silver, gold, and platinum coins. A few cheap but essential resources, such as coal and incense, could be bought from nonplayer characters called *vendors*, usually standing very near the facilities required to do the actual crafting. Trainer NPCs provided the early levels of training, but above the early stages Cleora needed to buy instruction books through the centralized sales system which had been picked up by other avatars during their questing.

The most convenient place to do crafting was right outside her home in New Hallas, because she had access to resource storage in her home, other storage in the local bank, and a full set of required facilities just a few steps from her door. To work as a sage, Cleora needed to stand at a desk which had writing materials on it, three candles which lit when she worked, a crystal ball that flashed, and other equipment. From a long list that grew as she learned new spells, she would select a project, check whether she had all the necessary materials, and start the process. She would wave a quill pen in the air, and another quill pen would hover over a levitating scroll and an inkwell, doing the actual scribing, as mystic symbols materialized in the air and flowed into a nearby tome on a lectern.

Table 7.3 lists a half dozen of the many spell scrolls Cleora could create, starting with three versions of Karana's Hold. Spells in *EverQuest II* can have as many as six tiers: apprentice, journeyman, adept, expert, master, and grandmaster. As Cleora worked, she would gain levels of crafting experience, which allowed her to learn and successfully craft ever more potent spells. Notice that each spell requires very specific material resources, yet the result is a virtual scroll on which the spell is written. Cleora was a member of the conjuror class, so only the last of the spells in the table was suitable for her own use. She could give or sell the others to members of the appropriate classes—Fury, Wizard, and Templar for the spells in table 7.3—but making any of them increased her skill and thus provided benefit even if the spell were never used.

During the production process, something often goes wrong, and one of three icons appears with a phrase naming the problem. The avatar must immediately click one of six icons in response, two of which are the same as the one marking the problem. An icon showing an open book must be responded to with either *incantation* or *spellbinding*; an icon of a hand writing must be responded to with either *scripting* or *notation*, and an icon of obscure symbols must be responded to with either *calligraphy* or *lettering*. The two responses in each pair differ on whether they increase or decrease durability, the rate of progress, or the probability of success making the item. The system is exactly the same for jeweler and alchemist, the two other specializations for scholars. Among a jeweler's six responses to problems are two that connote mere technical proficiency: *round cut* and *faceting*. But the other four have mystical qualities: sixth sense, mind over matter, center of spirit, and focus of spirit. Yet responses are coded only in terms of whether they are correct or incorrect, not whether they are natural or supernatural. An alchemist works at a chemistry table, and its responses actually sound scientific: exothermic, endothermic, synthesis, reactions, analyze, and experiment.

Maxrohn, my high-level Human priest in *World of Warcraft*, was an alchemist. He could have selected any other profession, but alchemy seemed suited to his

Table 7.3 Examples of Spells Crafted by Cleora in *EverQuest II*

Product	Level	Materials	User	Effect (Simplified)
Karana's Hold (Journeyman)	7	1 rough malachite, 3 roots, 3 severed elm, 2 basic incense	Fury	roots enemy in place for 12.6 seconds (less effective if enemy is level 36+)
Karana's Hold (Expert)	7	1 rough lapis lazuli, 3 roots, 3 severed elm, 2 basic incense	Fury	same as Journeyman, but harder for the enemy to resist
Karana's Hold II (Journeyman)	21	1 rough agate, 3 belladonna root, 3 severed ash, 3 sparkling incense	Fury	roots enemy in place for 17.5 seconds (less good if enemy is level 50+)
Ro's Blade II (Journeyman)	25	1 gold cluster, 3 belladonna root, 3 severed ash, 3 sparkling incense	Wizard	augments the weapon of an ally in a group, inflicting 15–18 heat damage every second
Divine Strike III (Journeyman)	25	1 rough agate, 3 belladonna root, 3 severed ash, 3 sparkling incense	Templar	does 349–396 divine damage to target (210–257 damage if target is undead)
Conjuror's Pact II (Journeyman)	28	1 gold cluster, 3 belladonna root, 3 severed ash, 3 sparkling incense	Conjuror	augments a summoned minion (pet) to reduce an enemy's elemental and magic resistance, lasting until canceled

role as an explorer of supernatural phenomena. Each avatar can have two primary professions, and given an alchemist's need for herbs, he selected herbalism to complement it. The *World of Warcraft* wiki reports:

> The alchemist mixes herbs found by Herbalism and reagents in order to concoct elixirs, potions, oils, flasks and cauldrons with a variety of effects. A player can create healing, invisibility, elemental resistance and mana potions; oils to coat weapons; and much more. Alchemy is useful to all character classes. Melee fighters can use alchemy to create buff and healing potions. Spell casting classes can use alchemy to create mana potions and related buffs. You can create potions for yourself, sell them to others, or give them to your party members and friends. Alchemists are well loved when they hand out potions.[30]

At around skill level 375, Maxrohn gained the ability to transmute one alchemical element into another. To do this he needed special training, and had to collect ingredients from which to manufacture a Philosopher's Stone,[31] which became his transmutation tool. Transmutation follows fixed laws. For example, earth can be turned into water, water into air, air into fire, and fire into earth. These four classic elements from European alchemy are not the only elements that exist. The crucial fluid for powering magical effects in *World of Warcraft* is mana, and it is convertible to and from fire. To get some of the ingredients, Maxrohn often went hunting in the more difficult zones of Outland, the shattered fragment of a planet separate from Azeroth, the main planet of this gameworld. There he would find high-level animated creatures representing earth, air, fire, and water, personified representations of how this planet was disintegrating into its fundamental components.

The eponymous rifts in *Rift* represent the four main elements of European alchemy, plus two others: life and death. Each rift is a passageway to a different plane of existence where one element predominates, and through which horrible creatures based on that element invade other planes. But it is also the case that every player's avatar relates especially to one of the six elements, depending upon the race to which the avatar belongs. Table 7.4 lists these correspondences, including the name of the evil Blood Storm god associated with the given element. An avatar's racial affinity to a particular element confers a degree of resistance to its effects, rather than implying any positive affiliation with the deity. Note that this connects alchemy to the fundamental nature of the avatar as a virtual person, a hint of the sophisticated scholarly theory of alchemy.

Gameworlds naturally vary in their systems of magic, either because of their designers' attempts to differentiate them from existing games or as an expression

Table 7.4 The Six Elements of *Rift*

Plane	Race	Faction	Resistance	Blood Storm God
Earth	Ethian	Defiant	Desert Dweller's Birthright	Laethys
Air	Bahmi	Defiant	Shalastir Heritage	Crucia
Fire	Kelari	Defiant	Legacy of the Fire Islands	Maelforge
Water	Dwarf	Guardian	Miracle of Hammerknell	Akylios
Life	High Elf	Guardian	Grace of the Forest	Greenscale
Death	Mathosian	Guardian	Legacy of the Shade	Regulos

of their cultural origins. Given that it was based on Chinese culture, *Perfect World* employs the traditional Chinese system of elements: earth, water, fire, wood, and metal. This five-element system evolved during the Warring States period two millennia ago, in connection with astrology and comparable attempts to predict the future or decide on the proper course of action in politics and military planning, as well as in the private lives of individuals.[32] My avatar, Deorumira, had a secondary avatar called a *genie*. Looking like a small fairy or sprite, this cute creature flew around her head and helped deal with enemies. It had its own ladder of experience, which it climbed by gaining affinity points. Whenever it gained some, I would open part of the interface and spend them on increasing the genie's affinity to one of the five elements of alchemy.[33]

When *God and Heroes* launched, it did not contain a crafting system, so neither of my avatars could become alchemists. However, many nonplayer characters had this power, and many quests involved bringing them the materials necessary for making a folk medicine or an object possessing supernatural powers. Given the unusually close relationship between each avatar and a particular god, it is especially interesting to look at the magical quality of some of the special powers conferred by the god upon the avatar, once the avatar has accomplished a particular deity quest. A couple were passive traits that slightly improved the player's statistics, but most were spells that cost *favor* when they were cast. Favor was a magical substance that could be attained only from the avatar's deity, and Aspera obtained hers from Trevia.

Siphon Life was available at level 1 and instantly stole between 121 and 241 units of health from an enemy, at a cost of 60 favor units and not being repeatable for 180 seconds. At level 10, Plague Drop became available, inflicting between 76 and 142 points of damage on an enemy at a cost of 50 favor points, with a "cooldown" of 300 seconds. Especially dramatic was Summon Empusa, which could be acquired at level 20, cost 80 favor, and had a cooldown of 1,800 seconds. Empusa was a hideous woman with flames for hair who would attack nearby enemies and could be the difference between victory and defeat in desperate situations. Unfortunately, she herself decided which enemies to attack, given that she was represented as an autonomous personality rather than a physical force that could be controlled perfectly. Thus she sometimes attacked enemies standing some distance away and not involved in the battle, thus increasing the number of opponents and resulting in defeat rather than victory.

These Trevia examples reveal clearly something that can be discerned with difficulty in all the fantasy games. While alchemy is like chemistry, chemistry connects to biology, and many kinds of magic are what we might call *cryptobiology*. Stealing health, infecting an enemy with a disease, and summoning a supernatural minion—even the fire that Empusa breathes—all involve biological metaphors. In many of the games, eating food restores health, yet cooking food so it may be eaten in *World of Warcraft* is comparable to alchemy. Alchemy and cryptobiology connect to another rigorous science, namely economics.

At level 25 in *Gods and Heroes*, Aspera could acquire a magical economic ability called Gratiae of Trevia, creating a magic coin at a cost of 320 favor and with a cooldown of 3,600 seconds. That was one hour of actual game time, so a player who wanted to create several of these coins had to find many other things to do while passing the 3,600 seconds after each one. One way to obtain favor was to advance to a new level of experience, which filled the supply; each death emptied it. Another way was to purchase special oblation materials from a vendor, or loot them from an occasional enemy, or gain them as a quest reward. An example would be pieces of sacrificial bread. Every twenty minutes or so, the avatar would perform an oblation, with a gesture like pouring wine on the ground, which would cause favor to increase very, very slowly until it was time for the next oblation.

Aspera found she could purchase favor directly for cash money from Pericles, who stood on the steps of the Temple of Trevia in Rome. At level 30, she needed to buy 320 favor units to fill her favor container, and Pericles would sell three different quantities: small (40 favor at a cost of 1 gold aureus and 73 silver denarii), medium (80 favor for 3 gold aurei and 32 silver denarii), and large (160 favor for 8 gold aurei and 62 silver denarii). Unfortunately, some favor seemed to get lost in the process, so she always needed to purchase two large and one medium, to make each Gratia. Two of these expensive coins were required in the deity quest that became available at level 30.

This quest was exceedingly important and correspondingly difficult. The religious leadership of Rome sensed great danger, even as their city was rising toward its historic glory. The Pontifex Maximus explained to Aspera that the rulers of the city had once failed to take advantage of the opportunity to know the entire future. As reported by the Christian writer Lactantius around the year AD 300, the Cumaean Sibyl had once

> brought nine books to the king Tarquinius Priscus, and asked for them three hundred philippics, and that the king refused so great a price, and derided the madness of the woman; that she, in the sight of the king, burnt three of the books, and demanded the same price for those which were left; that Tarquinius much more considered the woman to be mad; and that when she again, having burnt three other books, persisted in asking the same price, the king was moved, and bought the remaining books for the three hundred pieces of gold.[34]

Now Aspera was sent far into the wilderness to find that immortal Sibyl, named Deiphobe in *Gods and Heroes*, a name taken from Virgil's *Aeneid* but that may refer to a priestess of the Sibyl rather than the Sibyl herself.

Aspera found Deiphobe living in a cave set up a little like a tiny temple, and willing to help recover some lost prophesies by resurrecting the spirit of an ancient seer named Agorthetes. Taking action to resurrect the dead in gameworlds requires magic of the kind we call cryptobiology, but the result is a magical form of information technology. Deiphobe explained further: "It has been my blessing and curse to converse with the spirits of the dead, as Aeneas knew when I accompanied him into Hades. The wisdom of the dead is more valuable than diamonds or gold, but the cost is sometimes as dear."

The initial cost for Aspera was questing to three different remote locations, first to dig up the skull of Agorthetes from a pile of sand in Glareosus Ridge in the Abellinum region. Next she retrieved two golden eyes by killing Cyclops enemies in Arges Gorge, and the essence of ten Inferni from the Dead March caverns in distant Desertum Hollow. The last was quite difficult, because the Inferni were individually very difficult to defeat, and were in pairs accompanied by a warrior. Aspera succeeded only by using all her wiles and magic. For example, she found she could attack one of the enemies while hiding around a corner where the enemy's companions could not see her, and she once sacrificed Empusa to save her own life. After one of the teams of enemies had been destroyed, its members would automatically resurrect, but each only a set time after its death. Because each had taken so long to kill, they resurrected alone in sequence, thus being much easier to kill the second and third times.

Only after Aspera had brought the magical ingredients to Deiphobe did she learn she also needed two Gratia magical coins, but she had none, which required her to trek back to Rome, buy favor from Pericles, and wait an hour between creating the coins, walking up and down the steps of the temple and fretting. The coins were needed to place over the golden eyes, after they had been inserted in the skull, part of the Roman ritual of placing pennies on the eyes of a corpse to pay Charon for conveying the deceased across the river Styx to Hades. Unfortunately, when Aspera attempted to complete the ritual, all hell broke loose.

On the player forums for *Gods and Heroes*, several people admitted they had been unable to complete this quest, and Aspera was among them, although at least two players said they had been able to complete it. As with an earlier quest that required collecting stolen relics and returning them to the tomb of King Latinus, the quest appeared to be bugged, because a key nonplayer character was absent or invisible. That is, the character may have existed in the world model, but not in the display model. In this case it was Agorthetes, who appeared briefly as a giant, and then seemed to attack Aspera invisibly, but in a way that did not permit her to fight back. In addition, a few difficult demons had appeared, little online advice existed about what was supposed to happen in the quest, and it seemed rather difficult for a player to complete at level 30. While the game seemed designed for a cap of level 40, 30 was the maximum when Aspera struggled. After she failed, she returned to Rome in hopes that all she needed to do was create two more Gratiae. Back in Deiphobe's cavern she discovered this was not the case, and she would need to start back at the beginning, retrieving the skull and other materials.

As frustrating as this experience was, it taught a lesson about the limits of magic. Someday, Aspera believed, the level cap in *Gods and Heroes* could be raised to 40, and the bug in the quest would be repaired. In principle, she could have tried again right away as a member of a group, but there were two problems with that plan. First, while Aspera did have experience doing group quests, the research methodology used in this book generally required solo play, because I needed extra time to document what was happening, and thus was a poor partner for players who were not gathering data for a book. For example, during my 194 hours running Andivius and Aspera, I took about nine thousand screenshot pictures, which always caused delays. Second, given the relatively low population of the Mars server, and the fact that having minions biased the game toward solo play for everyone, it was hard to find partners for quests. The head of the SPQR tribe was among those who gave up on this quest, after three failed attempts. True, this level 30 deity quest was the same for followers of all eight deities, so they could combine as they could not for low-level deity quests. It hardly seemed worthwhile to complete a terribly costly quest that rewarded the avatar with a magic spell of dubious utility, especially when the avatar had already explored all of ancient Rome's territory and had completed most quests, over four hundred of them by Aspera alone. It seemed time to surrender Aspera to the ravages of virtual time and cancel my account in what was admittedly a fascinating but finite game.

Conclusion

The spell is cast. The pun here may not be immediately obvious, and it does not concern spelling in the sense that mages in the Ritual Magick tradition spell magic as *magick*. Rather, the operative word is *cast*, which refers to the cast of characters in a drama. Magic in gameworlds is not what Frazer meant by the term, but rather a set of images that define roles like priest and alchemist differently in concept from others in the cast of characters, yet based on the same invisible mechanics inside the computer program. When Aspera passed away, she was cast into Hades, and the dizzy spell of questing excitement I had experienced with her ended.

There are two reasons why gameworlds cannot incorporate real magic, in which mere wishing makes reality change. First of all, in any consistent world, even those with exotic natural laws, there is no room for the supernatural. A Pagan god might be possible, but only because many Pagan traditions consider deities to be merely more powerful versions of mortals, operating under their own constraints. A world without rigid constraints would quickly unravel into a blooming, buzzing confusion. Second, a world in which natural laws can be violated is an unjust world. That is, a real magician is a criminal who violates the rights of others who are not magicians. Yet, for the sake of rich fantasies, many gameworlds pretend to be magical, in the same manner as a stage magician pretends that prestidigitation is marvelous. Given that great technical skill deserves our admiration, perhaps both game magic and stage magic are indeed marvels.

8 MORALITY

In traditional societies, religion sanctifies the particular system of morality endorsed by the culture. Jesus and Moses delivered new commandments from God to their followers, and two or three millennia later these rules still play important roles in defining ethical behavior. There is every reason to doubt that fictional religions in a gameworld really influence the average player, but they do form an important part of the background against which players make decisions, and moral issues abound in the backstories and quest rationales. In particular, competing factions of avatars are often associated with competing fictitious religious traditions. Thus, we cannot expect criminology theories to apply well to gameworlds, nor can we assume that avatars are capable of faith. Yet insights can be gained from examining the moral implications of fictitious creeds.

There are two main sociological approaches to research on how religion may support morality. The first conceptualizes morality in terms of the values believed to guide an individual's actions, and the function religion performs inculcating and supporting these values. The second approach focuses more on social control over deviant behavior, primarily operating through interpersonal interactions between individuals, and the ways in which religion may reinforce factors through which this control has its influence. The first is often described as a variety of *macrosociology*, the collection of perspectives that examine whole societies as units. The second is often called *microsociology*, the study of interactions between individuals and within small groups.

Values can be defined as the most general principles that guide social action.[1] They are shared definitions of abstract goals that should be achieved, and traditionally it was believed the values are internalized during childhood by individuals who are well socialized, or not internalized by individuals who become first juvenile delinquents and then adult criminals. However, religion has always held out the hope that faith, prayer, and divine intervention can produce moral regeneration, saving a person from sin. Looking back on the vast literature written from this perspective, I believe it is useful to discern three primary variants, each expressing a core set of ideas that might be integrated with the others, but to some degree standing alone. These can be called functionalist, cognitive consistency, and group identity theories.

Functionalism is a school of thought that conceptualizes society as a structure composed of institutions, held together by a shared set of values. Religion is the institution that both sanctifies the other institutions, such as the government and the military, and promulgates a moral system that sustains the unity of all the institutions. Over the centuries, the institutional structure of the society has evolved in response to various problems, challenges, and events. It has adjusted to maximize the harmony between institutions and the stability of the social system. From this perspective, religion is most effective if it is based on very ancient traditions, allowing some of the other institutions to change more rapidly in adjusting to current conditions. This is a very conservative theory of the role of religion, and thus it supports the traditional social class structure, but it is not right-wing in the militaristic sense of the term, because it says little about the proper relationships with other societies. This theory may not apply with much force to the behavior of player-operated avatars, yet it seems to have been built into the fictional societies of many of the virtual cities and races in gameworlds.[2]

Cognitive consistency theory connects the culture with the mental processes of individuals, assuming that values and major tenets of belief are primary, because more specific norms and opinions are logically derived from them. Much of the early social-science literature in this area focused on the social psychology of what it called *cognitive dissonance*, the tendency of people to respond vigorously to eliminate any contradictions that arise in their thinking.[3] More recent theories of both religion and of cognition, in contrast, suggest that human cognition works from the bottom up, beginning with a very large number of separate memories, concepts, and learned behaviors, only with great difficulty assembling them into larger structures. In artificial intelligence, this assembly process is called *chunking*, and takes place most readily only on a very low level of tiny details.[4] In terms of the New Paradigm, specific compensators exist long before general compensators do, and values—which are a kind of very general compensator—may be difficult if not impossible to assemble out of the smaller components that dominate human thinking. However, religion provides the supernatural semblance of cognitive consistency, even when it is not in fact possible to develop a general perspective about life on the basis of empirical observation or practical experimentation. The most obvious place to look for this theory in gameworlds is in the consistency of design that is expressed in the mythology and programmed into the constraints that limit avatar behavior—for example, whether the system allows one player to loot the virtual possessions of an enemy after killing an opponent's avatar, which logically ought to be possible but is prevented in many games.

Group identity is implicated in conflict between groups, when religion becomes a battle cry or waving banner, distinguishing one's own group from the enemy. In his exceedingly influential book *The Social Sources of Denomination-alism*, H. Richard Niebuhr noted that the religious denominations of immigrants resist assimilation, and may even become more different to preserve their identities, even as their members are assimilating in every other way.[5] Morality, at the extreme in group identity, becomes the proper rule for behavior in interacting with allies, and enemies do not deserve ethical consideration. Of the three dimensions of values theory, this is the one most applicable to gameworlds. However, the norms are often built into the computer program—for example, making it impossible for one *World of Warcraft* Orc to attack another, while an Orc can attack a Night Elf whenever the rules for the virtual locale permit player-versus-player combat. Orcs revere shamans rather than priests, because their culture is in a prereligious tribal stage of development, whereas the long-civilized Night Elves worship the moon goddess Elune. For players, these religious niceties may not be very significant, but they do symbolize the social identities of Orcs and Night Elves, and play significant roles in the lores of the two virtual cultures.

In a classic study of juvenile delinquency, Travis Hirschi summarized the competing criminological theories of his day: strain theory, control theory, and subcultural deviance theory.[6] All three of these concern dynamics that take place at the level of single individuals, in interaction with other individuals, and thus are microsociology. Hirschi's study sought data to decide which one of these theories was correct. However, from today's perspective, all three of them apply in varying degrees under different conditions, and all three connect with the three macrosociological theories.

Strain theory argues that some people are forced to commit deviant acts because they lack the opportunity to achieve the culture's goals by conforming to established rules of behavior.[7] A society extols the virtues of wealth and prestige, but some people are poor and downtrodden. Therefore they steal to get money, and engage in gang violence to gain status in their neighborhoods. Strain theory connects to functionalist theories of value, because the goals people seek are the values of the society, and yet a system that functions well overall will function poorly for some individuals. As Robert K. Merton long ago explained, the individual has several choices when following the norms of society fails to serve the values. One option is crime, which he defines as seeking the values but rejecting the norms.[8] Religion can offer the status of membership in a mutual-admiration society, thereby reducing the strains that produce criminal behavior. Gameworlds can play a comparable function for players, according subjective status within the gang that is their *World of Warcraft* guild.

Control theory holds that people are more likely to commit deviant acts if their ties to society are weak, especially their attachments to the people closest to them in their social network. This perspective emphasizes not the social influence that operates through social bonds but the bonds themselves. Hirschi himself was a proponent of this theory. Much of the earlier research used the term *social disorganization*, noting that crime rates are high in chaotic parts of modern cities, where many people lack social bonds.[9] Whereas strain theory derived the high crime rates among poor populations from their frustrations, control theory blamed their lack of stable social relationships. Religious organizations and movements actively recruit people to membership, thereby giving them social bonds, thus reducing deviance quite apart from any norms or values the religion may promulgate.[10] In the context of gameworlds, control theory predicts that members of guilds or other stable groups of players will be less likely to engage in hostile behavior than solo players.

Subcultural deviance theory argued that the root cause of deviance is social influence from other people who are already deviant. Through interaction, people are influenced to conform to the norms of their immediate social group, and many kinds of deviant subculture exist, including religious cults and criminal gangs. A classic formulation of this perspective, the differential association theory of Edwin Sutherland, focused on the communications people receive from each other, arguing that people become deviant if the preponderance of messages they receive endorse deviant behavior.[11] From a modern perspective, Sutherland's conception is an information theory. Applied to religion, it would give a central role to the norms and values communicated through church sermons, sacred scriptures, and informal communications with congregations. Applied to gameworlds, it suggests that each guild or avatar faction is a distinctive subculture, following its own norms, which often may be in conflict with the norms of other groups.

In practice, these various theories may cooperate, as well as compete, and the same can be true for religious factions within a society. An often-quoted passage from *The History of the Decline and Fall of the Roman Empire* by Edward Gibbon nicely makes this point: "The policy of the emperors and the senate, as far as it concerned religion, was happily seconded by the reflections of the enlightened, and by the habits of the superstitious, part of their subjects. The various modes of worship which prevailed in the Roman world were all considered by the people as equally true; by the philosopher as equally false; and by the magistrate as equally useful. And thus toleration produced not only mutual indulgence, but even religious concord."[12] As philosophers, we may agree that religious beliefs are false yet valuable. But as social scientists the question becomes valuable for whom, under what circumstances, and with what degree of confidence based on empirical research. We must also consider situations when a rift appears in society, separating two or more of the groups from each other, modulating religious harmony into dissonance.

An Ethical Rift

Perhaps the most sophisticated moral conflict depicted by a gameworld in 2011 was *Rift*, which launched on March 1 of that year. Both physical reality and moral consensus are disintegrating in a world named Telara, along cultural lines that are exceedingly well developed. Twenty years ago, Telara was attacked by the Blood Storm, a coalition of highly specialized gods led by Regulos, deity of death. Many of the races of Telara unified in opposition to this invasion, and called upon their indigenous gods for aid in this conflict. Regulos desired to destroy Telara, but other members of the Blood Storm had their own agendas. Crucia, goddess of air, vented her ire against the High Elves of Telara, but feuded with her nominal ally Laethys, goddess of earth, and, indeed, with Regulos. The diverse peoples of Telara united in defense of their world, and sought help from the Vigil, the five gods who created Telara: Bahralt, Mariel-Taun, Tavril, Thedeor, and Thontic. Dissention among the Blood Storm and unity among the peoples and gods of Telara led to the defeat of the invasion, the death of Regulos, and the creation of a supernatural barrier called the Ward to protect the world.

However, death for the god of death merely means transformation and temporary weakness. At this point, rifts have begun to appear, both physical ones in the Ward that allow demons to invade from the six alien planes of existence represented by the six gods of the Blood Storm, and social rifts that have shredded the old alliance. Most significantly, two factions have developed among the Telarans, each blaming the other for the current danger and each representing a different response to the crisis. The Guardians are religiously devout and seek to reestablish communion with their gods, who mysteriously seem to have withdrawn from the world. The Defiants resent the aloofness of the good gods and have turned to advanced technology as a secular alternative. These factions had evolved before the original invasion, but apparently consolidated more fully during and after the conflict. The player enters Telara from passage through death, to become an Ascended warrior of one or the other faction. To explore this rift-ridden world, I ran two avatars: Mildryth in the religious Guardian faction all the way to the initial maximum level 50 of experience, and Eilliam in the antitheistic Defiant faction up to level 25, beginning immediately after the March 1 launch.

Mildryth, a female High Elf cleric, had died twenty years before, fighting heroically against the Blood Storm. Resurrected by supernatural methods belonging to the Guardians, she was effectively pulled across two decades of time, leaping a rift of nonexistence to a new existence. After she had become oriented and carried out a few low-level missions against minor horrors that had been unleashed by the chaos around the rifts, an NPC leader named Catelyn Silera explained:

> Though we had a grudging peace with the Defiants after Regulos was defeated, his return and the continual invasion of the planes have given our differing world views mortal consequences. While we Guardians restore the power of the Vigil to strengthen the Ward that protects Telara from Regulos and the Blood Storm, the Defiants attempt to save Telara with profane technologies. If they prevail, the Vigil will be weakened and the Blood Storm will devour us all. We Guardians will fight to our deaths to make sure the Defiants do not allow the dragons to destroy Telara.

As Mildryth came from the religious past to join the Guardians, Eilliam came from the scientific future to join the Defiants. He also was a hero who had perished in the original war, resurrected by naturalistic technologies the Defiant engineers had frantically developed to match the supernatural powers of the Guardians. Unlike Mildryth, who was a cleric, he was a mage, conceptualizing magic as technology rather than religion. He arrived back on Telara on the very last day of its existence, long after Mildryth had arrived, because the second war was lost despite her heroic efforts. On that day he helped complete the Failsafe, a time machine that sent him back to the same day as Mildryth's resurrection, in order to change history, if possible, and prevent the death of his world. However, there was a profound rift between their factions, and renewed cooperation may have been impossible. As a Defiant NPC named Tasim Saza explained:

> Guardians—bah! They could be helping us gain the power to defeat Regulos and the rest of the Blood Storm. Instead, they work against us on behalf of their failed gods. There will be a reckoning after we've slain Regulos, if not before. They are like children who were once burned, and now cry whenever they see a flame. After the fall of Port Scion, the Guardians were completely unwilling to consider using sourcestone technology again, though such power is necessary to overcome the Blood Storm. All power is dangerous, which is why we must learn to master it. By knowing how to use our eldritch machines correctly, we can minimize the danger, while gaining the strength to protect Telara.

Mildryth and Eilliam began their new lives only a short distance apart, yet profoundly separated. She entered at the southern point of Silverwood, and he at the northern point of Freemarch, near the two ends of a great bridge that had spanned the gulf just east of Port Scion. But the central section of the bridge had been destroyed, so this severed arch was no longer a path between their territories. Each of them was given a mission to use extraordinary power to pull a leader of the opposite faction across this geographic rift and kill him. But they themselves could not leap across. In the frantic chaos of the constantly erupting rifts, no thought was given to making peace between Guardians and Defiants, uniting again against the Blood Storm.

This dire situation suggests not two but four moralities. The culture of the Guardians represented a religious morality, whereas the culture of the Defiants represented a secular one. They were comparable but opposed, because both wanted to save their world, yet they promoted incompatible means to accomplish this. Two concepts from anthropology describe this situation, cultural relativism and functional equivalence. *Cultural relativism* holds that each culture's distinctive moral system is right for it, and none is better than any other. Among the famous anthropologists who argued this position was Franz Boas, whose many students were extremely influential on twentieth-century American cultural anthropology.[13] In its pure form, cultural relativism suggests that cultural differences are historical accidents, rather than being rooted in race, psychology, or even the level of technological development of the society. Boas argued that a given cultural feature found in two societies could have had a very different origin in each of them, yet, once established in each culture, could be resistant to change. The key ideological implication of cultural relativism is that the powerful colonial societies that dominated the world during the lifetime of Boas and his students did not possess superior cultures, nor did the dominated societies possess inferior ones. In modern terms, extreme cultural relativism seems to hold that human societies are the path-dependent results of random events, thus undercutting any claims that one or another is morally superior.

Functional equivalence is a step beyond cultural relativism, arguing that different norms in different societies serve the same function but in alternative ways. Bronislaw Malinowski was famous for arguing this theory, using examples from the inhabitants of the Trobriand Islands in the Pacific, whom he had studied extensively.[14] The favorite example for college students is the differing norms for teenagers among Europeans versus Trobrianders. Teenagers in Europe and the societies culturally derived from it were traditionally forbidden to have sex with each other, but it was perfectly fine for them to share a meal together. Among Trobrianders, sex during the teenage years was perfectly fine, but young people were forbidden to share meals together, and had to eat at their own homes. Students laugh about this example, and fantasize about the *bukumatula* houses where Trobriand teenagers were allowed to sleep together. Some of my women students at the University of Washington, after hearing about these exotic customs, put a sign saying "bukumatula" over the entrance to their dormitory, a private joke since most people seeing the sign would not know what the word meant. However, Malinowski's point was quite serious. In each society, an important aspect of married life was forbidden to unmarried couples, thus protecting the institution of marriage. Two very different norms served the same value.

The third morality in *Rift* was the lost coalition between Guardians and Defiants, which somehow fitted their two moralities together into a larger system, without dissolving either. In political circles, *multiculturalism* has long been hotly debated. Should a society be a "melting pot" in which immigrants must assimilate, thereby abandoning their original culture? Or, more subtly, which aspects of their original culture can they preserve, while adopting the essential institutions of the wider society? This is a classic issue in the sociology of religion, as introduced by Niebuhr in 1929. Once German immigrants to America stop speaking German, should they also stop being Lutherans?

A striking real-world example was the wave of enthusiasm around the year 1892 in the New York City Mission Society for converting Jewish immigrants to Christianity. The mission society was not a particular evangelical group but a center of interdenominational Protestant social work. A rabbi's son named Hermann Warszawiak appointed himself the society's tool for converting fellow Jews. Every Saturday for several months, Warszawiak addressed large groups of Jewish men in the Society's DeWitt Memorial Church, displaying considerable powers of oratory.[15] On Wednesdays, Warszawiak held a discussion meeting for Jews. Members of the audience would write challenging questions on numbered cards, and Warszawiak would answer them. Why do Christians not keep the commandments of Moses? How could Jesus be the Messiah when the prophesies said that war would cease upon the Messiah's appearance? How could God have a son? Why does Jesus crucified on the cross call out to God, instead of calling for his Father—indeed, if Jesus is God, why does he call out at all? This might lead to a discussion of the Trinity, about which Warszawiak had written a pamphlet. Years later, Kenneth D. Miller, president of the Mission Society from 1939 to 1952, called Warszawiak's mission to the Jews "neither wise nor effective."[16]

The women's branch of the society set up a sewing school for Jewish girls. The existing sewing school was held on Saturday, but to avoid the Jewish Sabbath another was established on Wednesdays, enrolling a total of ninety-eight children "thus opening up to us for missionary visitation, 74 Hebrew families."[17] The only religious aspect was recitation of the Lord's Prayer. The training began with stitching simple straight lines, progressing through overhanding, darning, patching, buttonholes, hemstitching, and making clothing for dolls. Graduates could immediately get jobs with dressmakers. The head of the women's branch commented, "The Jewish girls acquired the stitches more rapidly than our Gentile children.

The characteristics of the race, ambition to excel, and perseverance in what they undertake, came out prominently and their patience in mastering difficult work was surprising."[18] In both cases, the Christians and Jews demonstrated great interest in each other and respect for each other, but essentially no conversions were accomplished. The Jewish immigrants became Jewish Americans, thankful for the help that Christian Americans had given them and ready to contribute to American progress themselves, but not becoming Christians. Thus, when Blood Elves joined the Horde that had been organized around the Orcs in *World of Warcraft*, they remained true to their own culture, rather than becoming Orcs.

The fourth morality in *Rift* is the value system of the Blood Storm, which seems just as precarious as the temporary alliance between Guardians and Defiants. The core value of the Telarans is defensive, preserving their world. The core value of the Blood Storm is aggressive, seizing a world that did not belong to them. Each of the six deities in the Storm had his or her own purposes for the world, and Regulos was the only one for whom its complete destruction was the primary goal. However, death was the net effect of the unraveling of both coalitions, at the same time that the actions of the players are dedicated to experiencing an interesting life in this rift-afflicted world.

Angels and Devils

Given that MMOs and the solo-player games described here involve a tremendous amount of fighting, each game must find a rationale for the conflict and an ethical schema that allows the player to feel good about killing. Here in addition to *Rift* we consider six very different examples: *Faxion*, *Aion*, *Chronicles of Narnia*, *Constantine*, *Fallen Earth*, and *Star Wars: The Old Republic*.

The challenge of defining good and evil in the context of a competitive social system is well illustrated by *Faxion*, a small gameworld that I explored before it was finished, and that was shut down less than four months after its official launch. *Faxion* is an example of what I call an online *arena* game. In gamer lingo, an arena is a battlefield in an MMO where players compete directly with each other, often killing each other, with relatively little focus on battling nonplayer characters, or on quest chains based on complex story lines. That is, the emphasis is on player-versus-player (PvP) action, rather than player-versus-environment (PvE) action. This means that the system is a zero-sum game, in which winners entail losers. In a PvE game, the losers can be nonplayer characters, and thus all the players can be winners. Many popular games are mixtures, giving players the choice whether to emphasize PvP or PvE. *Faxion* is mostly PvP, and the somewhat limited PvE action supports the much more important PvP action. It is not easy to produce a backstory to make an arena game very interesting, and *Faxion* seems to have succeeded at this by drawing upon a very traditional structure of moral conflict: the battle between Heaven and Hell over the Seven Deadly Sins in an afterlife called Limbo.

I ran one avatar up to level 25, visiting all of the areas of *Faxion* except Hell, in February 2011, when the game was unfinished and during a closed beta test. Thus, the nondisclosure agreement for beta testers prevents me from saying much about the experience of playing the game before commercial release, and *Faxion* has already been shut down so I cannot explore its public version. However, I am sure the developers will not mind me commenting that the concept and design of *Faxion* are extremely interesting, and here I can draw upon public reports about the game. The game's FAQ page described the moral conception of *Faxion*:

> Faxion Online takes place in the realms of Limbo where time and space do not exist. It is here where players start their journey in the afterlife. All religions through time can be found, and their followers are sprinkled amongst the population. The Capital City of Limbo is Purgatory, and it's a place that does not judge nor hold anyone in higher regard than another. It simply serves the residents and their needs as they find their way for their own retribution. In addition to the city, the Seven Deadly Sins have manifested themselves into physical locations, each represented with its own theme. With each manifestation of the Sin have come the people that represent it. From the Gluttonous who tend the farmlands, to the Prideful Atlans building their Tower into the skies, players will have the opportunity to meet and face off against many indigenous people and creatures that represent the afterlife, limbo and the sins.[19]

Notice the phrase "does not judge" and use of the word "retribution" rather than "redemption." *Faxion* takes place in an afterlife that begins with a Christian conception but adds other religions and functions beyond good and evil. Indeed, *Faxion* is pronounced *faction*. Each avatar belongs to one of two factions in the afterlife, the angels of Heaven or the devils of Hell. However, as the web page describing the classes of avatars notes, there may be no real difference between good and evil: "Ah, the classic struggle. Light versus Dark. Good versus Evil. Heaven versus Hell. Most people know where they stand the moment the conflict is mentioned. But maybe the choice ain't so simple!"[20] While different in appearance and symbolism, the two factions are mirror images of each other, with no actual difference in game function or morality. Each faction has the three standard classes of avatar. Among the angels, a tank is called a *crusader*, a healer is a *guardian*, and a mage-type DPS avatar is a *diviner*. Among the minions of Hell, the names are *reaver*, *zealot*, and *occultist*. My avatar was an angelic diviner named

Constance who very much loved earning her wings and visiting Heaven. Yet had she been an occultist, the experience would not have been very different, and I am sure Hell is a very nice place to visit.

A zone is devoted to each of the Seven Deadly Sins: wrath, greed, sloth, pride, lust, envy, and gluttony. Beau Hindman, a blogger on the *Massively* game news website, described the last of these zones: "One particularly disgusting area that was themed after hunger and greed was filled with beautiful orchards and ripening fruit at the front of the zone. In the middle section sat large wooden buildings that hosted massive, slimy creatures who ate everything in sight. In the rear of the zone was the true playground—a massive trash pile filled with (I'm guessing) stinking, rotting mounds of food and refuse."[21] This zone is the Fields of Hunger, representing gluttony. A different zone, Avarice Canyon, represents greed.

One of the roots of MMOs in the gaming family tree is arcade shooting galleries. Much of the action in PvE consists of killing nonplayer enemies and looting their dead bodies. Thus, one can imagine the moral dilemma that would be faced by a real angel required to kill innocent people in Avarice Canyon, in order to get the garnets, amber, lapis lazuli, emeralds, and gold they are carrying. Clearly such an angel would need to hold in abeyance the commandment "Thou shalt not steal." Also obtained from the corpses of NPCs are zone-specific *offerings* which increase the standing of one's faction in the particular zone.

At any given moment, some of the zones are contested or belong to one faction or the other, and outside the valley immediately surrounding Purgatory City, members of one faction may attack and kill members of the other. One way a single player can do this is often called *ganking*. One hides near a group of NPCs and waits for a lower-level member of the other faction to arrive and get nearly to the end of a battle with an NPC. At this moment the opponent is vulnerable because the NPC has caused a good deal of damage. The player leaps out of the shadows and slaughters the opponent, with no thought of mercy. Yes, my innocent, angelic character was ganked in *Faxion*, but angels were encouraged to gank just as much as devils were.

In April 2011, the Faxion website reported the discovery of an ancient artifact, which a picture showed as a pair of ancient tablets, both carrying the angel-with-a-halo symbol used by the heavenly forces.[22] Inscribed on them were the "10 Commandments of PvP":

1. I am thy pwner, thy god of pvp
2. Thou shalt slay thy neighbor
3. Thou shalt not wait for provocation
4. Thou shalt target the healers before any other

5. Thou shalt not be forced to queue for a kill
6. Honor thy guild and group
7. Thou shalt covet thy neighbors phat lewts
8. Thou shalt not crai more n00b
9. Thou shalt teabag thy kill
10. Thou shall take screenshots or, forsooth, it did not happen

Some of the terminology in this radically different version requires translation.

To *pwn* (pone) other players is to defeat them utterly, and *pvp* of course refers to player-versus-player combat. *Phat lewts* (fat loots) means good returns from stealing. *Crai* is a poker term—check-raise all-in—and *n00b* (noob or newb) refers to a new player, with whom one should not take chances but exploit to the hilt. *Teabagging* is the blander of two gamer terms for sexually desecrating the corpse of a defeated adversary, by placing one's avatar over it and repeatedly crouching and standing. The other term is *corpse-humping*. I especially followed the last commandment, because taking screenshots (pictures off the computer screen) was my main method of research data collection.

Aion similarly has two factions, the Elyos and the Asmodians. These are the English names for factions in a Korean game, so we cannot conclude that the original idea was to have the Elyos represent the Elohim from the Bible, nor that the Asmodians are ruled by Asmodeus, the king of demons in Jewish lore. The *Aion* wiki says of the Elyos: "Their environment is filled with light and growth and because of this, the Elyos have been shaped into having a more lively, vibrant, 'lighter' appearances. They are considered the more beautiful of the two races. Some of the Elyos also have feathered wings, giving them an angel-like appearance."[23] Of the Asmodians, the wiki says: "They live in a darker, more dangerous environment than the Elyos and have thus been shaped into having a more demonic appearance."[24] Early levels of experience advancement focus on environment-oriented quests, often killing NPCs, but after about level 20 or 25, the focus shifts heavily to player-versus-player combat between the two factions.

I ran one avatar up to level 25 in *Aion*, named Junellen and representing my paternal grandmother, June Ellen Wheeler Bainbridge, who was a gentle and nice person. Gameworlds present a challenge for ancestor veneration avatars when the venerated person was in fact very nonviolent. At very early levels, Junellen was able to advance largely by picking wildflowers, and she did not mind battling nonplayer characters until she reached the point when she gained her angelic wings, learned how to fly, and was expected to switch to PvP combat. She refused to "kill" other real people, even in a game, so I was forced to end my exploration of *Aion* at that point. When I abandon an avatar, I like to leave it at a symbolic virtual place. A humorous but challenging *Aion* quest involves being teleported by a student who is only just learning how to send avatars through space to a designated location. The student failed, accidentally sending Junellen deep into Asmodian territory, where today she still stands on a high ledge, overlooking an Asmodian stronghold and pondering how humans could possibly be so cruel as to kill each other.

Throughout essentially all the MMOs, interaction with nonplayer characters is given moral significance. Of course, the NPCs cannot suffer or rejoice, but interacting with them can serve either as a morally instructive parable or as a training routine in game theory where service to another being can be directly rewarding. Much of the time, a player is well advised to attack any attackable NPC from which wealth can be looted, whether or not it is an enemy. Thus, in this sense the game usually teaches immorality. Even when a player cooperates with an NPC, such as a quest giver, the motivation is personal gain rather than benevolence. But sometimes the moral situation is more complex.

A rather subtle example comes on a seashore called Thontic Shallows in *Rift*, where a number of sickly dwarf NPCs are crouched in prayer, hoping for a cure to their malady. Mildryth cured six of them by giving them sacred reeds harvested from the nearby water, on a quest called "A Holy Remedy." This was not done out of altruism, but because the reward for completing the quest was 3,690 experience points, seventeen gold coins, and twenty-nine silver coins. It was not easy, because the water and some of the nearby land was infested with nasty crabs called *shallowcap scuttlers*. At the time, Mildryth was at level 33 of experience, while the crabs were level 35. With exercise of her skills, she could defeat them, but at considerable cost in time. However, she found that if she stood very near one of the dwarfs, he would stand up and assist in the fight, greatly reducing the time needed to kill a crab. Each time she killed one, she gained 436 experience points, plus often looting something valuable from the corpse, sometimes even seventy-five silver coins, using her butchering skill to gain a heavy hide, after which she was immediately ready to kill another.

Exploitable situations like this often possess a degree of complexity, caused by the way the situation fits into the wider context of rules and resources. If Mildryth stood between two of the sickly dwarves, both of them would attack the crab, and she would lose the opportunity to gain experience and loot the corpse. This was true because of the rules used in *Rift* to determine who owns a kill. Some MMOs give credit for a kill to the first avatar who attacked the NPC, but *Rift* apparently does so in terms of which avatar did the most damage to it, and two dwarves counted as one for this algorithm, together doing more damage per second that Mildryth could. She positioned herself beside the dwarf at the west end of the shore, who was far from the nearest other dwarf, where she could fire bombard meteorites at several crabs in the area, sometimes having to walk a few steps away from the dwarf to get within range, then quickly backing up to battle the crab next to her tireless dwarven helper, with whom she advanced an entire level of experience.

Chronicles of Narnia: The Lion, the Witch, and the Wardrobe encourages cooperation, despite the fact that it is nominally a solo-player game. The four playable characters are children whose virtues must be combined to achieve success: Peter (strong, natural leader), Susan (mature, patient), Edmund (athletic, desires to succeed), and Lucy (adventurous spirit, empathy, desires to do what is right). For example, at one point, three of the children must hang onto an ogre while Susan carefully shoots arrows into it. The player must switch from child to child, playing as them in turn and sometimes combining two, holding hands or with one on the shoulders of the other. If played on a game system having two controllers, such as PlayStation 2, on which I completed it, a second player may join in, either for the whole game or for any desired parts of it, operating one of the avatar children cooperating with another avatar child operated by the other player.

This game was based on the first of a series of Christian allegory novels by C. S. Lewis and produced in connection with a Disney movie.[25] The lion Aslan represents Jesus Christ, but this is not obvious to somebody playing the game. He appears only in *cut scenes*—unplayed scenes duplicating some action from the movie—as a Christ figure who dies sacrificially to be reborn. Although Aslan is not explicitly connected to Christ, the fact that a player cannot interact with Aslan provides a certain sacred distance. As in many games for children, failure to master a challenge does not lead to the death of the character played by the user. Instead, the player is simply sent back to the beginning of the challenge.

Given that electronic games depend upon advanced technologies, it is worth noting that C. S. Lewis and his friend J. R. R. Tolkien were critics of technology who wrote medieval fantasies based on Anglican or Roman Catholic religious values, and may have wished to turn the clock back to supposedly more innocent days of yore. When he began the Narnia novels, Lewis was already famous for an epistolary novel, *The Screwtape Letters*, in which agents of the devil plot how to steal the soul of a Christian, written in a somewhat light and ironic tone.[26] For fantasy readers, he was especially well known for a trilogy of technophobic, Christian science fiction novels. The premise is that Earth alone of all the planets experienced the Fall and requires salvation. The first of the trilogy, *Out of the Silent Planet*, takes place on Mars, and *Perelandra* takes place on Venus, each of which has some qualities of the Garden of Eden. *That Hideous Strength* is set on Earth, the "silent planet" that had fallen from God's grace and must be quarantined so the other planets will not be contaminated. This concluding novel describes an epic struggle between the scientific forces of evil embodied in a research institute whose acronym is N.I.C.E. and a few humanistic forces of good symbolized by the character of Ransom, a Christ figure, and the spells of Britain's traditional magician, Merlin.[27]

Chronicles of Narnia may be a Christian allegory, but most of our examples are either unrelated to Christianity or, like *Faxion*, reverse one or more of its values. In the solo-player game called *Constantine*, the very first thing a player must do is go to Hell. Based on a movie and graphic novel, the story concerns John Constantine, a faithless soldier in the war between Heaven and Hell, at a time when infernal demons have broken a truce and begun invading Earth. Many of his weapons have biblical origins: a pistol that fires stones from the road to Damascus, a machine gun shooting nails used to crucify martyrs, holy water grenades, a bomb called the Shroud of Moses, and, finally, the spearhead that slew Jesus. Constantine's mission requires him to shuttle back and forth between terrestrial Los Angeles and Hell's devastated version of the city, where infernal explosions hurl melting cars and buses through the sulfuric air. At the end, Constantine must fight against both the angel Gabriel and Mammon, the son of Satan. Then he discovers that God had engineered the demonic invasion to strengthen religious belief, which only reinforces his view that God is really no better than Satan.

Fallen Earth shares with *Constantine* the premise that the world is going to hell, but without any of the Christian symbolism. A virus plague, emerging from India or Pakistan, has destroyed civilization, and the game concerns small groups of survivors living around the Grand Canyon in Arizona. As the game manual explains, "The later stages of it caused some sort of muscle contractions that looked like dancing, which reminded someone of a multi-armed Hindu god, and so it got named the Shiva Virus."[28] Where a few gameworlds have three factions, and most have only two, *Fallen Earth* has fully six, each responding in a different way to the catastrophe, and having different relations with the others. The Children of the Apocalypse seek conquest, whereas the Enforcers emphasize law and order. The Techs seek salvation through scientific research and engineering development; the Travelers are businessmen; and the Vistas are environmentalists. The Lightbearers are the nearest to a religious cult, following a leader with the Hindu religious name Shakti:

> The Lightbearers' mission to restore health and safety to humanity gathers many to their banner. Doctors have brought their knowledge of the healing arts and the tattered remains of the Hippocratic Oath to the group. Martial artists who have chosen to use their abilities to help and protect others have become the group's warriors and defenders. Spiritual students have put a worthy philosophy into practice through the good works of Shakti's followers. Those mutated by the dreaded Shiva Virus have found guidance and training with the Lightbearers.[29]

Star Wars: The Old Republic involves a war between a republic and an empire, each with its own moral code, just as the original *Star Wars* movies do. However, the game is set about 3,500 years earlier in galactic history, and it adds two ways of exploring good and evil within each of the factions, rather than assuming that the Galactic Republic is good and the Sith Empire is evil. Each avatar belongs to one of these main factions, and cannot defect to the other one. But within each faction, the player can choose how to complete many of the missions, gaining points on either the Light Side or the Dark Side of the Force, which confer the ability to use different resources as the game progresses. These choice points are presented as major moral decisions, but they do not affect faction membership, because each faction is presented as a precarious alliance of groups with competing interests. In addition, a primary avatar will develop a positive or negative reputation with its secondary avatars, based on such things as how polite the primary is in dealing with third parties as well as with the secondaries. Thus, the moral structure of *The Old Republic* consists of three dichotomies, of varying degrees of importance, two of which evaluate the avatar's behavior in a series of many small steps.

Two Modes of Piety

Many of the gameworlds considered here are mythologized versions of the European Middle Ages, and the Asian games seem to draw equally strongly on feudal periods in the histories of their own nations. Aside from *Dark Age of Camelot*, the one that most realistically represents medieval Europe is *The Sims Medieval*, the most recent example of the long-running Sims series.[30] Launched in 2000, this exceedingly popular family of games is practically its own distinctive genre, having elements of both real-time strategy and role-playing games, but also rather like a dollhouse with simulated inhabitants called Sims who possess simple artificial intelligence and are guided by the player to go about somewhat realistic daily lives. A version similar to an MMO, *The Sims Online*, existed from 2002 until 2008. *The Sims Medieval* differs from the others in having a number of quests that form the basis of the action, each one possessing many steps and comparable to a movie in which the player must follow the script rather closely.

As in an RTS game, the player does not experience the world through a single avatar, but there are featured characters called *heroes* who can play the central role in several quests, including two priests but also the monarch of the area and a bard, blacksmith, knight, merchant, physician, spy, and wizard. As noted in the first chapter of this book, RTS games are often called god games, and in this case the player is actually treated as God by the heroes and other characters, and called the Watcher. While the computer interface allows the player to see any part of the world from any desired distance, the view is always from some distance and from above. While the player cannot act within the world, the player can instruct the hero where to go and which of many choices to take.

At the beginning of time, the Watcher rejoiced to see life evolving in the world, but took no role in its development, until people arrived and began behaving stupidly. Selecting a few of the more gifted humans as his instruments, he began providing them with bits of guidance, which took the form not only of practical rules, such as might be required to cook a bowl of vegetable soup, but also of moral codes. Under a new monarch, civilization arose, with many institutions, each headed by a leader under the authority of the monarch. Two branches of the same religion competed with each other, the Jacobans and the Peterans, each named after a mysterious founder, Jacob and Peter. The game's wiki describes their very different styles:

> Jacobans are followers of the Jacoban branch of the in-game religion. They believe in a god known as the Watcher, who created them, watches them, and guides them. However, they believe that the Watcher is vengeful and merciless and thus must be feared and appeased by submitting to a strict moral code, lest It decide to punish them. Accordingly, Jacoban priests work to drive fear and obedience into the hearts of worshipers by making intense sermons, putting up dire proclamations, and shaming Sims into absolving their sins. The Gothic style of Jacoban cathedrals and the heavily-dyed and adorned clothing the clergy wears is notably awe-inspiring and expensive-looking. It's very likely most donations to the church only serve to fund further luxuries and lavish living.[31]
>
> Unlike Jacobans, Peterans believe the Watcher is kind, loving, and ultimately wants Sims to be happy. With that in mind, Peteran priests try to emulate the Watcher's nature by being compassionate and spreading happiness to as many people as possible. Their sermons are often humorous and informal, with impromptu public evangelizing being common. Peterans are notably very cerebral and contemplative, with every monastery keeping archives of books. Peterans also seem to practice a form of mysticism, often praying for answers, studying the Watcher for insight, and writing "with the Watcher" to pen new religious texts. Peterans appear more humble than Jacobans; the clergy wear simple robes and live in plainly styled and modestly decorated monasteries.[32]

Table 8.1 compares the two priests, based on information taken from the in-game encyclopedia and the text displayed by the game when running both heroes. The Peteran priest is humble and benevolent; his first quest as

Table 8.1 The Two Competing Types of Priest in *The Sims Medieval*

	Jacoban Priest	Peteran Priest
Architecture	Cathedral	Monastery
Description on p. 1 of in-game lesson for the Hero	Jacoban Priests tend to possess great material wealth and conduct their business of religion vigorously and with force (if necessary). Sims must live their lives according to a strict moral code lest punishment be delivered!	Peteran Priests are ascetics devoted to their faith. They preach compassion and understanding, and try to encourage others to live their lives according to The Watcher's principles.
Special Abilities	Absolve Sims, Post Proclamations, Reflect on the Watcher, Bestow Watcher's Touch, Bestow Watcher's Blessing	Evangelize, Pray, Bestow Watcher's Favor, Study Watcher, Write with the Watcher
Well Water Action	Consecrate	Bless
Sermons Generate	Fear	Popularity
Sermon Options	Calm: Sermonize with serenity. The Watcher is merciful to His flock . . . most of the time. Intense: Sermonize in a fierce and fervid tone. Repent, for the hour of The Watcher is at hand!	Casual, humorous, somber, or insightful (after praying to the Watcher or having achieved a high level of experience)

I experienced him was to employ the Watcher's guidance to find a lost child. In the context of a sociological discussion of morality, the behavior of the Jacoban priest is far more interesting, so we shall get to know him through three quests he undertook. Clearly, he represents an established church in league with the monarch, who may provide moral guidance for the society but also exploits his parishioners for economic gain. This is the double game played by many real religions.

The Jacoban cathedral was large and imposing, but the only portions where the priest takes actions are the main hall and his private apartment. The latter has a pulpit and pews and is the site for most interactions with other Sims, although some take place in the courtyard outside the main entrance. Every day, the Jacoban priest was required to complete two responsibilities for the cathedral, selected by the computer from a long list. These included absolving Sims of their sins, giving a sermon, converting two Sims to the Jacoban faith, discussing the Watcher with two Jacobans, bestowing the blessing of the Watcher on someone, posting a proclamation, and paying taxes that went to the monarch. Aside from a tiny anteroom suited only for performing his private religious devotions, his apartment contains a bed, a table with two chairs, a fireplace for heat and cooking, and a chamber pot instead of modern bathroom. Indeed, the only bathtub in the town seems to belong to the monarch. All interior spaces are lit by candles, in the cathedral as well as elsewhere.

The Jacoban's first quest was "The Witch Is Back," subtitled "The Watcher Laughs in the Face of Magic." It began when the Jacoban needed to perform holy rites at the local cemetery, so the Watcher would not forget the souls of those Sims who had passed away. Discovering that an unholy woman was using magic to desecrate the cemetery, the Jacoban rushed to the monarch to warn him. Remembering that the Jacoban had recently given a sermon against witchcraft, the monarch surmised that this was just a ploy to increase the influence of the church, and failed to take action. After performing some of the priestly duties, the Jacoban went to bed for the night, but had a nightmare in which he was captured by unspeakable horrors. In dreams and at many other points in life, Sims are given binary choices, in this case to run or to confront the horrors. The Jacoban chose to defy the monsters, and won a temporary enhancement to his game abilities, called the Victorious buff. This experience in a dream encouraged him to confront the witch in real life.

At the town square he accused the woman, but she responded scornfully, "Your precious 'Watcher' cannot help you defeat me, little man. Your faith is just talk! Mine provides me with true power—more power than you can imagine!" He returned to the cathedral to seek aid from the Watcher, but he found the witch was there, taunting him and saying she planned to drain all life from the town before moving on to destroy the next one. Clearly his role as a Jacoban priest was no longer a confidence game, in which he extracted wealth from the populace by instilling unnecessary fear. Now the threat was real, and he had to defend his flock against it. The first step was to gain some divine protection by conducting sessions with individual believers, absolving them of their sins, and the second was to give a fiery sermon to the multitude. He then built his own spiritual defenses by reflecting upon the Watcher for two hours, a devotional exercise in which he gazed upward in the direction of the Watcher, with his hands raised in supplication.

Confident in his righteous anger, he rushed to the forest, where the witch was hiding, and demanded that she leave the area. Suddenly, he found that he was paralyzed, and the witch's magic was draining the life out of him. In desperation he called out to Jacob, the founder of his faith, to lead him to safety deeper in the forest, where the church owned some property, but he became lost and stumbled back to the cathedral, near death. He was famished, so he ate a bowl of gruel; his energy was exhausted, so he tried to sleep, but nightmares attacked him.

Drawing upon his last vestiges of faith, he resolved to regain his health and then return to the forest to complete the quest. However, falling behind in accomplishment of a quest drains energy and reduces morale, and his personal fatal flaw was a tendency to become morose anyway. Each day he was supposed to complete two responsibilities for the church, but, constantly exhausted, he was unable to succeed. With the passage of time he weakened, falling ever further behind in his quest to stop the witch, and losing reputation as well as health day by day. The ultimate disgrace came when he was thrown into the stocks, on display amid public scorn for failing in his duties. With his final ounce of spirit, he resolved to end it all, and staggered to the Judgment Pit where people are executed by being thrown to the beast that dwells deep within. This huge serpent tossed his helpless body against the walls of the abyss, but remarkably not causing his death. Instead, he found himself utterly exhausted but still alive, having unintentionally completed a brief quest called "The Leap of Faith," giving him an even better relationship with the Watcher. Returning to the cathedral, he acknowledged his failure by formally abandoning the witch quest.

Subdued but not chastened, the Jacoban regained his health, sleeping peacefully and eating his gruel, devoting all his slowly growing energies to performance of his priestly duties. Then another threat came to town, in the form of a *cultural faire* that extolled the vices of secularism. With dedication rather than confidence, he took on another quest, "Cultural Crusades." He had two choices, either to learn about the new culture and incorporate elements of it into his church or to engage in hostile actions that would smash secularists. True to his morose nature, he chose hostility. Guided by a church handbook called *The Jacoban Anti-Culture Manifesto*, he laid his plans. He first did a reconnaissance of the fair, where he spiked the well with Jacoban faith, and then mailed out an anti-culture proclamation.

Seeing that people were wearing gaudy and indecent clothing, he paid a tailor to make somber uniforms and forced four Sims to wear them. He then went to the monarch, stressing the unity of church and state and gaining authority to have the seller of liquor placed in the stocks. A particularly distressful aspect of the new secular culture was technological innovation, such as eyeglasses that might help sinners see pornography and clocks that might help lazy parishioners limit their hours of prayer. As a symbolic gesture, he seized a pair of eyeglasses and an hourglass, placed them in the chamber pot in his bedroom, and urinated on them, thereby desecrating them.

The climax of his quest was a fiery sermon he gave in the cathedral. Afterwards, he asked five of the secularists why they had attended. Their friendly answers perplexed him, but he concluded that he must have vanquished their nonreligious tendencies, and proclaimed victory in his quest. The possibility did not enter his mind that they had come to his cathedral to express pity for a man whose folly was so profound he did not even understand he was a fool. In his own mind, the ethical principle revealed by this quest was: "Destroy all that is in your way, and the path to salvation shall reveal itself."

His last quest was a pilgrimage to the distant birthplace of Jacob, founder of the church. The monarch offered to pay most of the costs, if the Jacoban could raise one hundred simoles, the currency used in the realm. He got ten from Bryce, the chief architect, but failed to get any from Rupert, Earl of Smortlee, and just a few coins from Aris the Moneylender. A recent convert provided the last money needed, but it seems likely that all the others who had contributed really just wanted to get rid of this troublesome priest. After all, for its spiritual needs, the town could turn to the rather more pleasant and less greedy Peteran priest. Needing a ritual article of clothing for the pilgrimage, the Jacoban ventured to his church's secret vault in the forest, relieved to see that the witch was not there, but was lightly injured by a bear on the way back.

At the cathedral he performed religious duties and instructed his assistant Sybald so he could take care of the cathedral during the absence of its priest. He got a traveling bag and stowed it on the ship that would transport him. Lastly, he went to the market in the village and bought the ingredients required to make a large bowl of vegetable soup for the voyage: a cabbage, a mushroom, an onion, and a turnip. With this soup in his inventory, he strode confidently to the ship, which quickly set sail. He has not been seen since.

Hellfire

The widespread belief that religion enforces morality in the "real" world may be false. In other words, the belief that religion helps humans be good may be just another religious compensator. Being able to trust other people is a fundamental goal for every mentally healthy person, because we rely upon friends and family members to help us, to fulfill obligations to us, and to avoid cheating us. Yet humans are far less trustworthy than we would wish, so we seek ways of controlling their behavior. We can imagine many ways in which religion might accomplish this, but among them is the *surveillance* theory that gods can watch our behavior even when no other human being is watching, and punish us supernaturally, either by inflicting misfortune upon us in this life or sending us to hell after this life is finished.

The classic work that identified issues to be resolved concerning the influence of religion on behavior focused not on crime but on suicide, and was published in 1897 by the French sociologist Émile Durkheim.[33] He was not the first to write analytically on this topic, and most of his statistics had earlier been published by Adolf Wagner and Henry Morselli, who had noticed that suicide rates were much higher in some Protestant regions of Europe than in Catholic regions.[34] Durkheim assumed without mentioning that Protestants did not differ from Catholics in their relationships with God, so a higher suicide rate was not divine punishment. Indeed, Durkheim was himself neither Protestant nor Catholic, although writing in a Catholic country, and he seems not to have had personal religious beliefs. Like Laplace, quoted at the beginning of chapter 3, he had no need of the hypothesis of God to explain the difference in suicide rates.

Durkheim's suicide theory had elements of functionalism and control theory. In his later work, he argued that God was the personification of society, functioning as a support for its institutions, but in *Suicide* he focused on how the individual fitted into society and thus was controlled by it. In particular, he said that suicide might result from either or both of two kinds of social disorganization: (1) *egoism*, the breakdown of intimate social relationships, and (2) *anomie*, the breakdown of norms and values. Protestant society was less unified than Catholic society, so it suffered from egoism, and later writers drew from Durkheim's work a second lesson, that weakness of religion of whatever denomination could cause anomie and thus suicide and many other kinds of dysfunctional behavior.

As a whole Durkheim's work raises a very serious question: Is religion good but false? In terms of the surveillance idea: belief that God is watching will make a person behave properly, even though God does not exist. Decades after Durkheim wrote, his theories ran into serious difficulty. Working with my collaborator Rodney Stark, criminologist Travis Hirschi examined the relationship between faith and virtue in a marvelous, massive dataset he had assembled on California high school students. In the journal *Social Problems*, Hirschi and Stark published "Hellfire and Delinquency," reporting there was no connection.[35] Teenagers who were religious were every bit as likely to commit delinquent acts as their irreligious peers.

Over the following years, studies by other researchers performed in various geographic areas gave conflicting results. Stark then returned to the topic, using a nationwide dataset, and discovered what I call the *Stark effect*.[36] In regions of the country where religion is relatively weak among the population, such as California, the religiousness of an individual person does not matter. But in areas where religion is strong, it does. The Durkheimian interpretation would be that religion reinforces society's morality when society is unified around religion, but faith loses this power in the absence of the social supports provided when most people are religious. There is a less favorable interpretation, however. Perhaps in religious areas, where most people attend church, being irreligious is just a form of deviant behavior, which correlates with other forms of deviant behavior.

Some of my own research, done both in collaboration with Stark and afterward, returned to the question of whether religion prevents suicide. Using data on church membership and suicide rates for states and cities in the first two-thirds of the twentieth century, we found no differences in the prevalence of suicide between Protestant and Catholic areas. Independently, Whitney Pope argued that Durkheim had misinterpreted European data, and the Protestant-Catholic differences there were not real.[37] But Stark and I did find much higher suicide rates in areas of the United States where church membership was low in the period 1906–1936.[38] This could have been the spurious result of the fact that high rates of geographic migration correlate positively with suicide and negatively with church membership,[39] but controlling for migration statistically did not erase the apparent power of religion to deter suicide.

Unfortunately, the story does not stop here. I returned again to the topic with data from the end of the twentieth century, finding two things.[40] First, the negative correlation between church membership and suicide was much weaker than in earlier historical data. Second, religion's apparent effect could easily be wiped out by controlling for migration. One interpretation is that during the twentieth century, secularization eroded a real power that religion had possessed. Another interpretation is that the collection of statistics became more objective over the course of the century, because in early decades many suicides that took place in religious communities were not recorded as suicides, because of religious repugnance at self-murderers. I simply do not know. But one further conclusion is that gameworlds may not be unrealistic in this respect. Faith may not deter deviance within them, but it may lack that power outside them as well. The best way to consider the ramifications of this perspective is to consider the popular game-world most closely connected to a real-world suicide.

Gameworlds vary in terms of how much moral guidance the gods provide to humans, but the deities in *Age of Conan* are extremely unfriendly, and thus represent the ultimate in divine estrangement. In this, they are true not only to the psychotic visions of suicidal Robert E. Howard, the author of the original Conan stories, but also to the experience of ancient peoples, for whom the forces of nature were as frequently harsh enemies as benevolent friends. Conan lived in the Hyborian Age, after Atlantis had sunk but before recorded history, when three main societies were spiraling toward war: Aquilonia (Rome), Stygia (Egypt), and Cimmeria (the Celts).[41] My main avatar in *Age of Conan* was Orastes, the priest of Mitra in Aquilonian society described in chapter 5, and I used three other avatars to gain cross-cultural perspective on the main religions in this virtual world. Boadicea was a shaman among the Cimmerians, who revere the stern god Crom. Atlantea was a priestess of Set, and Eridanos was a necromancer, both among the Stygians. Each of the three cultures of this imagined ancient world has its own personality, expressed through their gods as well as the nonplayer characters: Cimmerians like Conan are stoic but passionate, Stygians are sadistic but clever, and Aquilonians are rational and businesslike.

In preindustrial societies, features of the natural world are often explained through legends telling the story of a human being, whether named and prominent or anonymous. Belesa, priestess of Mitra, told Orastes that a medicinal herb called bloodroot originated from the corpse of a man exiled from the city of Tortage for stealing dog meat who was torn to shreds by wild beasts. In ancient cultures, great ideas are personified as gods. With some justice, it can be said that Christ is mercy personified, so this principle may still apply. Yet mercy is unknown in the religions of the Hyborian Age. From Sharak of Stygia, their first mentor, both Atlantea and Eridanos received a cynical blessing: "Gods go with you, so they may see you take your inevitable beating."

The nearest thing to a theological debate in the Conan stories came when Belit, queen of the Black Coast and Conan's lover, asked him if he feared the gods. He replied, "Some gods are strong to harm, others, to aid; at least so say their priests. Mitra of the Hyborians must be a strong god, because his people have builded their cities over the world. But even the Hyborians fear Set." When asked about his own gods, he explained:

> Their chief is Crom. He dwells on a great mountain. What use to call on him? Little he cares if men live or die. Better to be silent than to call his attention to you; he will send you dooms, not fortune! He is grim and

loveless, but at birth he breathes power to strive and slay into a man's soul. What else shall men ask of the gods? . . . There is no hope here or hereafter in the cult of my people. . . . In this world men struggle and suffer vainly, finding pleasure only in the bright madness of battle; dying, their souls enter a gray misty realm of clouds and icy winds, to wander cheerlessly throughout eternity. . . . I have known many gods. He who denies them is as blind as he who trusts them too deeply. . . . Let teachers and priests and philosophers brood over questions of reality and illusion. I know this: if life is illusion, then I am no less an illusion, and being thus, the illusion is real to me. I live, I burn with life, I love, I slay, and am content.[42]

In another story, Howard explained, "It was useless to call on Crom, because he was a gloomy, savage god, and he hated weaklings. But he gave a man courage at birth, and the will and might to kill his enemies, which, in the Cimmerian's mind, was all any god should be expected to do."[43] One of the epithets spoken by a character in *Age of Conan* is "Crom's spit!" Cimmerians believe meteorites are rocks thrown by Crom when he is angry, and they tell legends about when Crom battled his rival, Ymir, as the two hurled mountains at each other. After an earthquake, a guard comments, "I wonder if Crom is testing us." Fennella, a brave young huntress, relies upon "the strength of Crom flowing in my veins." An older woman, Kyna, complains, "Time has leached the strength of Crom from my bones." A broken man named Laoric, who has lost both his wife and his left arm, barely surviving in the icy northern mountains, complains, "We are nothing to Crom! There is no hope in this life or the next."

Mitra seems to represent civilization—not very loving but at least helpful through establishing laws that protect society. Those who place their faith in Mitra may greet someone by exclaiming, "The light welcomes you!" They respond to good news by saying, "Thank Mitra!" Their response to bad news may be, "Blessed Mitra, I pray it is not true." Priests of Mitra seem sincere and call themselves "humble servants." Persus, an acolyte of Mitra and a healer, blesses Orastes, saying "Mitra protect you against the Nemedians." Archpriest Zyras laments the war between Aquilonia and the Nemedians, because both worship Mitra. As if to resolve the logical contradiction through faith, he says, "The good god protects us all." Thus, the benevolence of Mitra is precarious, especially when challenged by Set.

Set represents death. Like Crom, he is described as "father of all," but he is the Great Serpent who demands blood sacrifice. Sharva of Khemi exclaims, "Blood for the snake god!" When Atlantea tells Osithma that his friend Khakhtes has been eaten by a gigantic serpent, he praises Set in joy, seeing his friend's sacrifice as an important part of Set's plan for the world. Set speaks to Naboth, an addled wizard standing alone in a wasteland, telling him that time is nothing but sand in an hourglass. Intending to transform ordinary snakes into serpent guardians, Naboth told Atlantea to bring him cobra eyes and scorpion pincers, and is confused when these magically powerful objects kill the snakes instead. Undeterred, he commands her to bring him the blood of a sacred serpent. Atlantea objects that killing a sacred serpent is a crime, and he merely urges her to hurry to a merchant who sells the blood, before the priests seize him and torture him to death.

In Howard's stories, Set's disciples seek great power from black magic, regardless of the cost. At the climax of a great battle, Tsotha exclaims, "Oh, Set! ... grant us victory and I swear I will offer up to thee five hundred virgins of Shamar, writhing in their blood!"[44] Elsewhere, Howard offered a quatrain in devotion to the Serpent God:

> Under the caverned pyramids great Set coils asleep;
> Among the shadows of the tombs his dusky people creep.
> I speak the Word from the hidden gulfs that never knew the sun
> Send me a servant for my hate, oh scaled and shining One![45]

Given that Crom does not answer prayers, except with rage, the Cimmerians practice no religious rites, and shamans like Boadicea have no status as clergy. In contrast, the Vanir invaders, who have ravaged the countryside near Conarch Village, are very superstitious and work themselves into a religious frenzy before every battle, in a rite they perform at a huge war totem statue they have dragged into Conall's Valley. Boadicea sneaked into the Vanir camp and destroyed the totem. This act of sacrilege drew down no supernatural retribution, thus planting the seeds of doubt in some Vanir minds, and discouraging their next attack on the village.

Despite all the pretty words about Mitra, he is a jealous god. In a square called the Traitor's Common in the Aquilonian capital, Tarantia, Orastes met Novatus, an acolyte of Mitra, who sought to prevent an advocate of Set from speaking in public. Years ago, the Traitor's Common had been the site where corpses of criminals had been hung to rot, as a warning to other potential traitors. Conan had ended that grisly practice, and it had become a meeting place for discontented people. The advocate of Set contemptuously dismisses the way Mitra priests mislead the feeble citizenry, saying: "Set is synonymous with power, because Set grants power to those who are willing to take it."

Orastes replies, "Set demands human sacrifice in return for this 'power.' Nothing is worth that price." The advocate of Set replies that the priests of Mitra extort money from farmers and merchants, cozy up to aristocrats, and are nothing better than whores.

When Orastes says Mitra helps suffering people, the advocate of Set points to all the starving people who are not helped at all, and the victims of petty bandits who find no justice. He suggests that history shows no evidence that Mitra has really blessed Aquilonia: "Ah yes, the so-called flower of civilization. Yet three thousand years ago, on this very spot, a civilization existed that made Aquilonia seem a dirt-choked hovel, Acheron, whose beauty and power leave echoes that still exist today. Weep, people of Tarantia, for what was lost when Acheron fell." In the end, Orastes lost the debate, prompting further doubts about his own faith.

Later, Adeonus, a priest of Mitra, tried to put the rising conflict in a religious context: "People suffer, but Mitra is watching. Weighing our deeds and actions in these moments of despair." This is the question of theodicy, the existence of evil in a world ruled by a good god. Perhaps evil is a test, or a form of spiritual training, but this makes sense only if Mitra offers salvation after the test has been passed, and it is not clear that he does.

One tiny piece of evidence comes when Adeonus asked Orastes to deliver medical supplies, an act of charity. Then Orastes showed Adeonus the Mirror of Mitra, which a woman named Lordana had asked him to find. She was once a rich lady, but misfortune turned her into an impoverished widow begging on the streets of Tarantia. She believed that her luck resulted from this cursed mirror, which thieves ultimately had taken from her, but Adeonus explained this was not true. Priests of Mitra spread many false rumors about the curses possessed by their church's relics, in order to discourage people from stealing them. Adeonus expresses regret about the torment this superstition caused Lordana, and we may speculate that the mirror really represented her vanity, yet the fact remains that the priests of Mitra spread false beliefs to their own benefit.

Conclusion

Moral is morale writ small. That is, many theories consider morality to be the expression of social solidarity, and people behave ethically only because they are optimistic that their own group is trustworthy. One of the classic concepts from the philosophy of ethics is the *social contract*, an implicit agreement of the members of a group to work toward collective benefit, and thus to help rather than harm each other.[46] This is very different from religious theories of morality, which begin with the idea that humans are born with an obligation to God to behave according to the commandments of the religion. A social contract is a voluntary agreement made between people, rather than ordained by the deity. People who sit down to play a card game agree it is improper to have an ace up one's sleeve, but it is physically possible for one of them to cheat in this way.

Online gameworlds, in contrast, rely upon the godlike computer program to enforce the rules. In the exception that proves this rule, *Pirates of the Caribbean Online* allows players to collect extra cards they can use for cheating at poker or blackjack, but the statistical possibility of being caught and fined means this is merely a refinement in the rigid game rules.

The lesson most gameworlds teach is that morality should be limited to members of one's own faction, and avatars are expected to suspend moral thinking when dealing with nonplayer characters and avatars belonging to a different faction. This is an extension of what social scientists call *amoral familialism*, limiting one's moral behavior to members of one's own family, and treating everybody outside the family according to strategies based entirely on the interests of the family, sometimes cooperating but often shamelessly exploiting outsiders.[47] *World of Warcraft* is very explicit in providing the background for this, and a character named Tirion Fordring was forced to decide between blood and honor in a story by a chief creator of this gameworld.[48] The world called Azeroth contains too many competing groups for the resources available, and past wars have degraded the environment still further. Each group has no choice but to form alliances with a few others on the basis of pure expediency, and then to steal the resources of every other group. Whatever hopes religion may offer, false or true, the material Earth we ourselves inhabit may be evolving into a condition like *World of Warcraft—Azeroth* contains all the letters of the names of Earth and Oz—and so a grim game begins.

9 CULTS

Among the most interesting and misunderstood religious phenomena in the real world are cults. In fact, this term is quite ambiguous as to meaning, and many scholars prefer to use the phrase *new religious movement*. This terminological shift is unsatisfactory for two reasons. First of all, many of the groups commonly called cults are really not new at all, such as the various New Jerusalem groups called Swedenborgians after their founder, Emanuel Swedenborg, who died way back in 1772.[1] Second, at least three kinds of new religious movements are not called cults. Perhaps most important here are *sects*, which are splinter groups that break away from more established denominations and profess intensified versions of a traditional faith. There are also *symbiotic movements* within established denominations that do not lead to a rupture, such as the various orders of the Roman Catholic Church or lay organizations such as Opus Dei. Also, there exist a few *church movements* that break away from existing groups but aim to become more liberal, rather than more conservative as in the case of sects.[2] Here we must simplify, focusing on cults, but with a little attention to sects, and illuminating the vast diversity of movements that have been given these labels.

Although pure coincidences, it is worth noting that both *cult* and *sect* are "four-letter words," which is a synonym for obscenity. These are terms of disparagement as well as description, often applied by journalists in lurid depictions of scandals in small religious groups involving sexual exploitation or violence. In the social science of religion, they are often described as *deviant* groups, which for many people means *evil* or *sick*. Yet for social scientists, *deviance* means simply divergence from the statistical norm, *norm* meaning merely average, not good.

To be sure, the classical sociological theory called *functionalism* argued that the established churches represented the core of the society, working for the benefit of the entire population, and expressing myths that were essential for the healthy functioning of the society as a harmonious whole. A variant of this theory was the Marxist interpretation—that the churches functioned for the benefit of the ruling elite, rather than the majority.[3] Both of these theories start with the assumption that humanity is organized into a few huge societies or classes, and that religion represents unity. The opposite seems more likely to be true: *society* is a crude abstraction, and human social life is primarily based in small groups and local networks connecting individuals, where dynamism rather than stability reigns.[4] From this perspective, there is nothing strange or pathological about religions that are also based in small groups, and that may differ tremendously from each other, innovating rapidly over time.

Decades ago I wrote, "Cult is culture writ small."[5] From Plato to Hobbes, many writers have described the state as an individual man writ large, a view inspired by monarchies and monotheisms, yet I saw merit in reversing the analysis and viewing small-scale phenomena as reflections of large-scale realities.[6] Similarly, a game is society writ small. Within many gameworlds there exist a very large number of bands of enemy NPCs, often limited to a small area in the virtual geography, and they are often depicted as religious cults.

When I first stated the principle that cults are cultures, I was studying a family of new religious movements that were historically connected to each other: Scientology, the Process Church of the Final Judgement, Rosicrucianism, the Order of the Golden Dawn, General Semantics, and Psychoanalysis. Indeed, even this brief list indicates that the borders of religion become unclear, once we move far away from mainstream Christian denominations. For a social scientist, one of the great values of studying cults is that they exhibit many of the features and dynamics of whole societies, yet are small enough to be observed by a single researcher, and go through their evolutions far more rapidly. As with geneticists studying fruit flies rather than elephants, it can be a great advantage to study small and rapidly changing social organizations.

In my field ethnography of the Process, which had about two hundred members, I was able to observe and informally interview essentially all the members, and the group went through two major transformations during the five years I was in contact.[7] The Children of God (studied later and not part of the same family of groups) was about fifty times larger, so I augmented observations with a questionnaire administered to more than a thousand members, but it too changed rapidly during the study.[8] It should be noted that for most of human existence, people lived in hunter-gatherer bands or early agricultural tribes of comparable sizes, exhibiting similar volatility, and it was then that religion emerged as a distinct dimension of culture.

One of the greatest challenges for social scientists is that all of the field's names for fundamental concepts are ultimately refined versions of terms that already exist in ordinary language, and may have etymological histories going back centuries or even millennia. Cult is not merely "culture writ small," but also "cultivation writ small," and this fact immediately reminds us of *agricultur*e, which is in fact where the word sprouted up. In classical Latin, *cultus* is the past participle of *colere*, meaning to till the soil or to farm. It has a bewildering set of possible metaphoric meanings: a laboring, labor, care, cultivation, culture; style, care, way of life, cultivation, civilization, refinement, luxury; an honoring, reverence, adoration, veneration; attire, dress, or garb.[9] When Christians refer to the "cult of the virgin," they do not mean something strange, but rather the conventional practice of veneration of the Virgin Mary. A religious cult, in modern terminology, cultivates a distinctive practice of veneration based in a new way of life, perhaps even having unique clothing. In our book *A Theory of Religion*, Rodney Stark and I defined key terms thus:[10]

> Def.56 A *church* is a conventional religious organization.
>
> Def.57 A *sect movement* is a deviant religious organization with traditional beliefs and practices.
>
> Def.58 A *cult movement* is a deviant religious organization with novel beliefs and practices.
>
> Def.59 *Deviance* is departure from the norms of a culture in such a way as to incur the imposition of extraordinary costs from those who maintain the culture.

This is a very conventional set of definitions, but they all depend upon the existence of a conventional culture based in a unified society. To members of the wider culture, cults appear pathological. Thus, journalists and others who declaim about cults but understand them only poorly tend to present a simple conceptual model that disparages more than it describes: cults are small groups of brainwashed followers, under the psychological dominance of a wicked charismatic leader. To be sure, most cults do center on an individual leader, although a few are led by couples or small groups of leaders. In addition, the concept of charisma is indeed used in sociology, but a common theory of it holds that charismatic leaders express the existing dissatisfactions of followers more than they actually change the followers' minds.[11]

Innovation typically is accomplished by individuals, but in interaction with others. The membership tends to be strongly focused on creating a distinctive culture, and this may look like brainwashing to outsiders, especially as any strong culture tends to submerge the individual into the collectivity. That is one reason why many of the most intense examples, including both the Process and the Children of God, were communal. Of one such extreme cult it was said: "And all that believed were together, and had all things common ... and the multitude of them that believed were of one heart and of one soul: neither said any of them that ought of the things which he possessed was his own; but they had all things common." That particular radical cult was early Christianity, as described in Acts 2:44 and 4:32.

Real experts on cults, the scholars and scientists who have studied them closely, know very well that members generally have not been brainwashed. One piece of solid evidence is the fact that very large proportions of the recruits to new cults drop out after a few weeks or months, and real commitment comes only after years, when the individual has constructed a life within the cult that cannot easily be abandoned.[12] From the standpoint of members, involvement in a cult is a very dynamic process. The most comprehensive classic model of cult recruitment makes this abundantly clear. Developed by John Lofland and Rodney Stark to explain how people were converted to membership in Sun Myung Moon's Unification Church ("Moonies") early in its history, the Lofland-Stark model incorporated many of the main ideas introduced at the beginning of the previous chapter. It describes a series of steps a person must go through in order to join a small, radical religious movement:

> For conversion it is necessary that a person:
> 1. experience enduring, acutely felt tensions;
> 2. within a religious problem-solving perspective;
> 3. which lead to defining himself as a religious seeker;
> 4. encountering the cult at a turning point in his life;
> 5. wherein an affective bond to adherents is formed (or preexists);
> 6. where extra-cult attachments are low or neutralized;
> 7. and where, to become a "deployable agent," exposure to intensive interaction is accomplished.[13]

Note that this model describes a person who already experiences a difficult situation in life but, as is made clear in step 3, is taking action to find a solution to problems, rather than being passively brainwashed by a cult leader. A religious seeker has consciously undertaken a quest for meaning, more serious than the quests in gameworlds but similar in nature. The first step in the model, tensions, means that the recruits already feel greatly dissatisfied with life. Here, Lofland and Stark had *strain theory* in mind, the possibility that the wider society fails to give the recruits the opportunities they need to achieve a good life, either as society defines it or as they personally do. The second step, problem-solving perspective, suggests that people have alternative theories about what is wrong with their lives and how they can fix it. Other perspectives include the psychotherapeutic perspective (get professional help to transform yourself) and the political perspective (band together to transform society). In fantasy MMOs, the religious problem-solving perspective is especially plausible, because supernatural powers really do exist inside the gameworlds, whereas they do not exist in the "real world."

Step 4, the turning point of the model, suggests that a person is most likely to join a cult when other lines of action have come to an end, such as finishing school, getting a divorce, or being fired from a job. Turning points also involve a temporary weakness in social relationships, triggering the dynamic described in steps 5, 6, and 7. A loss of prior social bonds introduces *control theory*, the theory that people are most likely to deviate when the social relationships that enforce conformity are weak. Developing bonds with members of a cult, and interacting intensely with members, introduces *subcultural deviance theory*, the idea that deviant behavior constitutes conformity to the norms of a deviant group.

What happens to the Lofland-Stark theory if the wider culture disintegrates, in a process of *anomie* and *social disorganization*? On the one hand, far more people are likely to suffer tensions, but also less tension is required to motivate a person to join a cult. If the wider culture is strong and stable, only people experiencing very high levels of tension will abandon conformity and endure the social costs of deviance. But if the society breaks down, the barrier to joining drops. This point was made over eighty years ago by Frederick Thrasher, who carried out a study of gangs in Chicago and concluded that they arise in neighborhoods experiencing high levels of social disorganization.[14] This illustrates a general principle: when large-scale social structures break down, small-scale structures will arise spontaneously to take their place. Indeed, the full sweep of human history is a chaotic struggle to build ever bigger societies, beginning with the tiny hunter-gatherer band of perhaps forty individuals, the size of a small cult.

This line of analysis precisely describes the situation in the most popular fantasy gameworlds. In both *EverQuest II* and *World of Warcraft*, the disintegration of society is so extreme that it has led to disintegration of some of the physical territory of the gameworld. In both *EverQuest II* and *Rift*, the good gods have become separated from the world, reflecting and aggravating the disintegration of society. In both *World of Warcraft* and *Warhammer Online*, the Elves have split into two opposed factions, and have allied themselves with other races in two opposed factions, probably as a temporary expediency. For the game designers, such backstories not only add drama but provide a plausible explanation for why there are so many independent groups of enemy NPCs in the world. Some of those, like the gurgling Murlocs in *World of Warcraft*, are defined as separate species, but a standard explanation for separate groups of human NPCs is that they are members of religious cults.

This brings the theoretical analysis back to the macrosociological theories: functionalism, cognitive consistency, and group identity. It is very realistic to give small groups of NPCs a distinctive religious identity as a cult. Doing so explains their separation from society, their exotic practices, and the justification for slaughtering them on behalf of a precarious player-operated faction that seeks to reestablish conformity and unify society. While many of the gameworld cults may not be realistic in their details, including the common feature that they practice empirically effective forms of magic, there is something both realistic and frightening about them. If, as many people believe, our own world is fragmenting rapidly, then we can expect it to become progressively more like *World of Warcraft*.

The Scarlet Crusade

Among the most interesting and fully developed radical religious movements among gameworld nonplayer characters, the Scarlet Crusade in *World of Warcraft* is arguably a sect rather than a cult, but it illustrates the full range of tensions that exist within religion, and between religion and secular society. I explored it when the level cap was 80 using four avatars: Catullus (level 80 Blood Elf priest), Maxrohn (level 75 Human priest), Incognita (level 20 Undead priest), and Annihila (level 70 Undead death knight). This mixture of priests and Undead provided the best possible perspective, given the nature of the Crusade, as described on WoW's main wiki:

> The Scarlet Crusade is a religious organization dedicated to the eradication of the undead. They are a major adversary of the Forsaken, and several quests in Tirisfal Glades involve attacks on Scarlet Crusade troops, leaders, and strongholds. The Scarlet Crusade maintains several bastions throughout the former lands of Lordaeron, namely the Scarlet Monastery, Hearthglen, Tyr's Hand, the fortified cathedral of Stratholme, and several smaller camps and watchtowers spread throughout the area. It is also the only hierarchy left of the Kingdom of Lordaeron after its destruction by the Scourge. After the attack on the Scarlet Enclave, the Scarlet Crusade renamed itself to the Scarlet Onslaught and operates in Northrend.[15]

Lordaeron was the capital of the Human Empire, until it was destroyed in the Third War, when biological weapons infected all animal life, killed many people, and transformed a few semisurvivors into rotting, zombie-like Undead. Indeed, the invader was the Lich King, the ruler of armies of reanimated corpses. A faction of his army broke away, became the Forsaken, and established their headquarters in the sewers under the ruins of Lordaeron. Incognita was a member of these Forsaken, who began her existence in Tirisfal Glades. The Lich King's commander in the destruction was a former Human aristocrat named Arthas who had been transformed into the most powerful of the Lich King's death knights. Annihila was a human who died in the war and then was recruited to become a death knight in service to the Lich King, at one point even bowing before him in total submission.[16] The surviving Humans gained allies and became the Alliance, to which Maxrohn belongs.

Despite frequently being of Human origins, the Undead joined the opposing Horde faction, to which Blood Elves like Catullus also belong, competing against the Alliance for dominance over the planet Azeroth. I believe both Incognita and Annihila were originally humans, although some members of the Forsaken seem to be former Elves. Their deaths rotted away most of their memories, including their knowledge of the Human language. Forsaken speak a crude language called Gutterspeak, but have also learned the language of the Orcs, who are the core of the Horde, and whose attack against the Humans began the great wars.

My first encounter with the Scarlet Crusade was when Incognita was forced to battle against them in Tirisfal Glades beginning on March 17, 2007. Interestingly, her first interaction was on a quest called "The Scarlet Crusade" that has subsequently been removed from WoW, as the developers labored to improve the story line. Executor Arren in Deathknell Chapel, a village church that is rotting nearly as badly as the bone-exposing flesh of the Forsaken, told Incognita: "My scouts have reported that a detachment of the Scarlet Crusade is setting up a camp southeast of here. The Scarlet Crusade is a despicable organization that hunts us, and they will not rest until every undead—Lich King's Scourge or no—is destroyed. We must strike first! Be careful, their unholy zeal makes them dangerous adversaries."

As she battled converts of the cult, they would shout at her in the Human language, but the portion of her brain that knew that tongue had perished, so she did not understand. Had she still been fluent in her original language, she would have known they were shouting: "The Scarlet Crusade shall smite the wicked and drive evil from these lands!" "You carry the taint of the Scourge. Prepare to enter the twisting nether." "There is no escape for you. The crusade shall destroy all who carry the Scourge's taint." "The light condemns all who harbor evil. Now you will die!"[17]

One part of the crusade's philosophy recoils against anything that is neither dead nor alive. Many traditional cultures and religions are very strict about maintaining clear boundaries between categories—for example, not mixing certain foods that can be eaten separately.[18] As *WoWWiki* explains, "The Twisting Nether is a formless place of magic and illusion. It is indistinct and chaotic, with no size or shape."[19] Thus it is the proper hell for beings who themselves embody chaos, and whose bodies are constantly rotting.

The reference to "light" is key. The Human religion in *World of Warcraft* focuses on the Holy Light, a secularized religious concept that is central to their culture. Every Human avatar, like Maxrohn, enters the world just outside North-shire Abbey, a local religious center complete with stained-glass windows, a library of sacred books, and a bell tower. After completing just a few local quests, a priest like him is sent to nearby Stormwind City to receive training in the Cathedral of Light. It is possible that in ancient days the Light was considered a god, but in modern Human religion the Light possesses neither will nor personality, but represents an abstract ethical system. In orthodox Human theology, the Light is a system of principles a person can follow to make moral judgments, but the Light itself cannot condemn anyone. Yet converts to the Scarlet Crusade apparently personify the Light, saying that "the light condemns." This pattern is common for sects in the modern real world. A mainstream denomination becomes highly secularized, the supernatural elements draining from its doctrines, so a sect restores the former supernaturalism and returns to the archaic view that gods are supernatural persons having will and emotion, rather than abstractions.

Situated not far from the ruins of Lordaeron stands the Scarlet Monastery, traditional headquarters of the Scarlet Crusade. Originally dedicated to the Holy Light, it became the site of a religious schism during the calamity at the end of the Third War, gathering all those priests and paladins who swore that all members of the Scourge, including the Forsaken, were implacable enemies of life and must be slain. This complex of religious architecture consists of four areas: graveyard, library, armory, and cathedral. Both Catullus and Maxrohn penetrated deep into the monastery to learn its secrets. One they would not have noticed, because both were ignorant of real-world religious symbolism, was the implication of the Crusade's symbol. The word *crusade*, of course, comes from a word for cross. The cult's symbol, displayed everywhere in yellow on red banners, is a Celtic cross lacking the cross arms, which are assumed to be the parts of the cross to which the arms of Jesus Christ were nailed. This would be a perfect new symbol of highly secularized denominations in the real world: a Christian cross from which Christ has been removed.

Catullus entered when he had reached only level 37, on October 26, 2007, and thus was not powerful enough to go alone. Therefore, he went as part of a party of five fellow Horde members, led by Schibilia, an Undead warrior. The others were Zuggzugg, an Orc warrior; Dolmagas, another Orc warrior; and Maior, a Blood Elf rogue. As the only healer in the party, Catullus was expected to assist the others, yet his main research goal was to copy some of the rare books in the library. In the Hall of Champions, the inner sanctum of the armory, they defeated Herod, the Scarlet Champion, who shouted "Blades of light!" as he died. Next, they fought their way through the chapel gardens into the cathedral, where they killed most of the Crusade's top leadership, but Catullus could not convince this bloodthirsty party to enter the library.

Two days later, he was fortunate to join a party that was headed toward the library, led by a Blood Elf named Levolta, including two other Blood Elves, Xeek and Zansa, plus an Orc named Lucifroner. The others tolerated the erratic behavior of Catullus, who was frantically using his priestly power to save his teammates' lives one minute and the next minute frantically copying pages of a library book. After accomplishing their mission to assassinate Crusade leaders and get the Scarlet Keys required to enter other parts of the Monastery, the other team members logged off, but Catullus ran back to the Athenaeum to copy more books.

He was able to add these historical volumes to his collection: *The Scourge of Lordaeron, Beyond the Dark Portal, Archimonde's Return and the Flight to Kalimdor, The War of the Ancients, The World Tree and the Emerald Dream, Arathor and the Troll Wars, War of the Spider,* and *Aftermath of the Second War. The Scourge of Lordaeron* told of the corruption of Arthas, who began the Third War as a noble prince of the Human Empire. Seeking magical power to defeat the Lich King, he embarked on a quest to obtain the cursed runeblade Frostmourne. "Though the sword did grant him unfathomable power, it also stole his soul and transformed him into the greatest of the Lich King's death knights. With his soul cast aside and his sanity shattered, Arthas led the Scourge against his own kingdom. Ultimately, Arthas murdered his own father, King Terenas, and crushed Lordaeron under the Lich King's iron heel."

Over three months later, when he had ascended to level 68 of general experience, Catullus joined a party to enter the high-level Crusade redoubt Stratholme. In retrospect, he concluded that the word *redoubt* was the correct term, because the experience caused him to doubt the morality of the missions he completed, and to doubt his own doubts. Indeed, dominance over Stratholme is in doubt, because the territory of this ruined city is hotly contested between the Scarlet Crusade and the Scourge, so the team was forced to fight both sides in order to penetrate to the archive that was the goal for Catullus. This time, the team consisted of only four members, and the other three were all fellow Blood Elves of the Alea Iacta Est guild: Rilei, Celeres, and Nerelia.

One goal for Catullus was simply to retrieve from the archive in Stratholme a family portrait belonging to Tirion Fordring, the tragic character from "Of Blood and Honor," whom we mentioned earlier.[20] The title of the quest, "Of Love and Family," plays off the title of Chris Metzen's novella. The picture shows Fordring standing before a calm sea, flanked by his wife and their son when he was still a boy. Catullus actually had an opportunity to meet Fordring back then—but paradoxically a week after retrieving the portrait—because the Caverns of Time transported him to an earlier year and to the town of Southshore, where Fordring was planning strategy for the war that had not yet ruined the Human Empire.

The instructions for the quest say, "Inside the Scarlet Bastion is a painting of great personal value to Highlord Tirion Fordring. Search for a painting of our twin moons. Chip away at the paint until you uncover the master work, 'Of Love and Family.' May the Light guide your actions, and please handle the painting with the utmost care." The picture of the two moons of Azeroth actually looks like a picture of the planet Jupiter, with one of its moons in the foreground. The metaphor suggests that behind any fascination we may have with sciences like astronomy lies our commitment to other human beings, beginning with our own family. One source of doubt for Catullus was that in order to satisfy Fordring's nostalgia for his lost wife and son, he was forced to send many Undead of the Scourge back to their graves, and to kill many members of the Scarlet Crusade.

His second mission, "The Archivist," required him to murder Archivist Galford of the Scarlet Crusade and burn the archive. This mission was given to Catullus by Duke Nicholas Zverenhoff at Light's Hope Chapel in the Eastern Plaguelands: "Anything taken to an extreme is hazardous to our world, Catullus. Take for example, the Scarlet Crusade. Do you believe that their blind zealotry serves a greater good? How many innocents have they destroyed in the name of the Light? Blasphemers, one and all! One in particular interests me, though; the Archivist Galford of Stratholme: A man that watches over the Crusade's most valued documents. Destroy him and burn down his archives! Should you succeed, return to me and be rewarded." While Zverenhoff offers a rationale, he also offers material rewards, so one motivation for Catullus was simply to advance his personal wealth and level of experience by killing an academic and destroying books. Where, in this calculation, was any consideration for Galford's sincerity or the inestimable historical value of the archive? This conundrum was a second source of doubt for Catullus.

To obtain a very different perspective, Maxrohn visited the Scarlet Monastery after he had reached level 70 in experience, far above the levels of the defenders. He could crush them instantly, at no danger to himself, but they recognized their helplessness and did not attack him. He admired the elegant architecture of their many cloisters, the Gallery of Treasures, the Athenaeum, and the Cathedral. He admired the amazingly extensive library where Catullus had copied only a small fraction of the books lined up on endless shelves. But his deepest impression was of the Chamber of Atonement connected to the Forlorn Cloister and Honor's Tomb in the graveyard. This was a torture chamber, where Undead prisoners were stretched on the rack. A Scarlet Torturer screamed at his victim: "You will talk eventually. You might as well spill it now. Confess and we shall set you free." Of course, by "free" the torturer meant "dead." Interrogator Vishas yelled, "Tell me . . . tell me everything! Naughty secrets! I'll rip the secrets from your flesh!" The Scarlet Torturer was only level 30, so Maxrohn destroyed him with a single spell. Vishas was an elite enemy, far more resistant to damage, but at level 32 he lasted only a few seconds longer, before reaching the destination he intended for all Undead: death.

Annihila's perspective was more nuanced. Given the decay her memory had suffered, it was hard to be certain about anything, but she tended to think she was twice undead. She had probably been a Human like Incognita, probably a paladin who combined the qualities of priest and warrior. Then she was rendered half dead by the plague, recruited to the Scourge, and then broke away from it as one of the Forsaken. But then the Lich King captured her again, and corrupted her into being one of his death knight minions. During his attack on the Eastern Plaguelands, she was ordered to kill a former friend from before her deaths. At first she refused, but after much soul searching—that is, searching for any shred of soul left within her—she complied.

Then, at Light's Hope Chapel, she was liberated from the Scourge. Though nominally a member of the Horde, as all Undead are, she felt drawn to her Human origins. Finding no solution for her tormented state of alienation from other Undead and Humans, she fled to Outland, that crumbling fragment of the planet Draenor, far distant from Azeroth. When both Horde and Alliance counterattacked against the Lich King, and invaded the Northrend continent on Azeroth where he had established his citadels, she refused to join. Returning to Azeroth would mean going home, but just as the Undead had no real life, she had no home. Deep in her solitude she laughed: "The only salvation for me would be to join the Scarlet Crusade and destroy myself!"

Origins of Cults

In chapter 5, introducing the role of priests, I based part of the argument on the models of cult formation Stark and I had written about decades ago.[21] Fictional cults in gameworlds naturally draw upon the related popular notions that cult leaders are crazy, frauds, or adept at organizing small groups that engage in collective exploration in new supernatural directions. Many of the small NPC cults in gameworlds are not described in any detail, but a few have extensive backstories. Often, one's avatar comes across a cult that holds a small territory, with a leader, practicing some obscure ritual, and perhaps organized around an attempt to harness arcane magical powers, but how the cult arose remains a mystery. In some cases, we can infer the cult's history with some confidence. The Cult of the Magus in *Warhammer Online* is a good example.

This is a small cult, occupying two levels of the foothills near the Valley of the Damned in the High Pass region of the Human territories, where the Empire battles the Norsemen across stern, snow-clad desolation. Aside from a few tents and campfires, they possess little except their fanaticism. Their goal appears to be to conduct rituals or cast spells in order to extract unnatural energies through a swirling portal to a different plane of existence called the Empyrean. From time to time, one of their Magi Orators shouts a few words of their doctrines:

> Life is change. Rather than live blindly and pretend this fact does not exist we embrace it and it drives our purpose.
>
> We are all but pieces in the grand game. Each one of us a plot thread used to weave the eternal story. We must see and accept this and we will be rewarded for our service.
>
> The foolish men of the south follow a mortal man and call him a god! They know not of the gods and we shall bring this knowledge to them at the end of a sword.

This last quotation seems like something that a real ancient Norseman might have shouted, referring to Jesus Christ when he spoke of a mortal man called a god. Yet the god in question was Sigmar, the deity revered by the southern Empire. Remarkably, this fantasy god has his own *Wikipedia* page, which begins by explaining:

> Sigmar Heldenhammer is a fictional deity in the Warhammer Fantasy setting. He is the patron deity of The Empire. Before he became a god, Sigmar was a man, albeit an exceptional, perhaps even superhuman one. The young chieftain of the Unberogens who lived 2,500 years before the present day of the Warhammer universe, he united the barbarian human tribes into what would become the mightiest human nation—the Empire. His sign is a twin-tailed comet or a war hammer. Sigmar appears to be inspired by a series of heroes from myth, fantasy literature, especially Robert E. Howard's Conan the Cimmerian, as well as historical figures, particularly Charlemagne and Charles Martel. An image of a hammer-wielding barbarian appeared on early versions of Warhammer Fantasy Battle fighting Orcs and Goblins.[22]

The leader of the Cult of the Magus, Hredric Blackheart, is an extremely powerful mage, far too sturdy for my avatar, Williamwheeler, to defeat in solo combat, and we know little about his background. Yet it is probably correct to infer that he and his cult have come from the Temple of Change, which is immediately northeast of their camp and plays a key role in an epic quest series called "Cleansing an Empire." Williamwheeler was a Knight of the Blazing Sun, thus defending the Empire against the Norse invaders and sworn to Sigmar. Repeatedly, he was able to force his way into the temple, and became familiar with its features. A vast structure consisting of one immense room, the rear of which is dominated by a stairway-framed compass rose of arrows on which advanced mages stand at set points, managing something like a network of ley lines. The main area is used by mages to train zealot followers, who quake visibly, either from excess of emotion or the effect of magical spells. My avatar's quest tome explained, "This temple swells with a power the Northmen pray to as the Raven God. Within its walls both the willing and the weak of heart become forever changed. It has the power to both create and uncreate: the power of change."

Followers of Sigmar regularly call the followers of the Raven God a cult, because they define their own faith as the standard against which to judge all the others. We do not know the details of the relationship between the Cult of the Magus and the Temple of Change, but the names and the situation suggest that Blackheart had led a group of zealots out of the temple to form his cult, taking their quest for magical power one step further into deviance. As in the case of the Scarlet Crusade, we might want to use the word *sect* rather than *cult*, yet in fact all cults that have been studied closely have been found to have originated in an earlier new religious movement. The founder of a new religious group in the real world has almost invariably served an apprenticeship in an earlier group.[23] The difference between sect and cult is that the leaders of the latter bring fewer members with them from the old group, and in connection with that fact are able to innovate more radically. The example I studied most closely was the Process Church of the Final Judgment, whose founders had served their apprenticeship inside Scientology.[24] Before founding his own cult, Jesus served his apprenticeship in the already established cult of John the Baptist.

The relationships between the Cult of the Magus and the Temple of Change suggest that more attention should be given to the relations between cults, rather than treating each one as a separate episode of religious deviance. The shining examples are the cults connected with separate gods of the Blood Storm in *Rift*, most extensively studied by my main avatar, Mildryth, in the high-level Shimmersand zone of Telara. There the Guardian government maintained a penitentiary called the Flatyard for incarceration of members of five of the six cults listed in table 9.1. The descriptions come from *Telarapedia*, the main *Rift* wiki.[25] Collectively they are called Dragon Cults, because each deity is represented by a dragon, but each also represents one of the elements of alchemy and seeks to invade Telara through a particular kind of rift by means of demons associated with that element. The cults originated from the rift dividing the six deities of the Blood Storm, and through the efforts of a leading person on Telara who believed that the war could be settled through an alliance with one of these deities, necessitated by the fact that the five traditional deities of Telara had chosen to absent themselves from the struggle.

Table 9.1 The Dragon Cults of *Rift*

Cult	Deity	Element	Description
The Abyssal	Akylios	water	"Mostly composed of evil mages and priests who seek out the dead rituals of sacrifice, summon forth demons, and cast horrific rituals."
Storm Legion	Crucia	air	"Essentially a hive mind due to the influence of Crucia, and those who have served in the cult for the longest periods of time are an embodiment of her will."
The Endless Court	Regulos	death	"From nihilistic madmen who believe Telara should receive the gift of tranquil death, to mortals so hungry for power they would rule over the undead, Regulos's followers are the worst of the worst."
House Aelfwar	Greenscale	life	"Mostly composed of a breakaway faction of High Elves under the leadership of Prince Hylas, who seek to destroy civilization and remake the world as a primordial jungle."
The Wanton	Maelforge	fire	"Pyromaniacs who only wish to set things on fire and watch them burn; as Maelforge is the embodiment of chaos, so are his followers."
The Golden Maw	Laethys	earth	"Members of the cult are greedy and prize wealth and resources, for those who are touched by Laethys are overcome with greed."

The first of the six listed in the table is the least well organized of them, an instance of what is called a *general movement* in sociology.[26] It lacks a formal structure and leadership, and it is the one not represented in the Flatyard, perhaps because it has no leaders worth arresting. Water is fluid, but air is even more diffuse, and the entire atmosphere is one unitary entity, so the cult of the air dragon most closely fits the popular image of a cult that sucks out the individuality of a member. The Endless Court is the most extreme of the cults, and Mildryth later battled them in the highest level, Stillmoor, where they sought to welcome their death god at a vast crater called the Eye of Regulos. In the low-level Silverwood zone, Mildryth had received a vision of Prince Hylas idealistically proclaiming that life was the one principle that should be followed, an accentuation of the Guardian distrust of magical technology, with the implication that civilization should be abandoned in favor of living in harmony with nature. He seemed not to realize that many forms of life are harmful, from disease-causing germs to cancer cells. Whereas members of the Wanton wish to destroy everything, members of the Golden Maw wish to possess everything.

It was the Golden Maw that focused Mildryth's attention, after she had completed some quests around the perimeter of the Flatyard and had entered it disguised as a prisoner. Mildryth's first challenge was to develop a reputation among the other prisoners, so she began by accepting an assignment from Slither, who occupied a central role in the inmate social network. First she defeated another "new blood" in hand-to-hand combat, then stole a box of "sigaras" (presumably cigars) from one inmate and gave some to three of the gang leaders, then insulted the leader of the Storm Legion gang and assassinated him with a shiv. All these tasks were but a series of tests, showing that Mildryth had the guts to be valuable, set up by the one cult that had not been involved in any of them, the Golden Maw. This earned her a meeting with Hazeed, the leader of the Golden Maw, who had set up a secret headquarters under the prison, entirely unbeknownst to the other four cults. He gave her one last test, to kill three members of each of those competing gangs.

Now Mildryth learned what was really going on. As if in ultimate defiance of the Guardians, Hazeed was using the prison as a staging point for a massive effort to open an unstoppable rift, so Laethys could enter Telara and conquer it on behalf of earthly greed. There was even a secret tunnel under the Flatyard, through which any members of the Golden Maw could have escaped had they wished to do so, and which was being used for shipping the necessary resources. Following advice from the Guardian leadership, she sabotaged Hazeed's effort, and confronted him in his hidden lair, when she demolished his rift machine. Finally, at the Golden Summit, far south of the Flatyard, she confronted Hazeed again at the very moment he was about to open a rift for Laethys. Earth enemies attacked her, including spiders, scorpions, and stone golems, but eventually she prevailed, and both the rift and the Golden Maw became closed chapters in the history of the Blood Storm war.

There is something remarkably appealing about the *Rift* conception, which itself is a distillation of many previous games and works of fantastic literature. Unlike in the real world, almost everything that happens has meaning, in terms of a set of concepts arranged in a logical structure. This is reminiscent of the macrosociological theories, such as structuralism in anthropology, and especially of functionalism in its most sophisticated version, called *structural functionalism*. A structure of five concepts, not unlike gamegods, was presented in the 1951 book *Toward a General Theory of Action*, familiarly called "the bible" of this intellectual movement and edited by its leaders, Talcott Parsons and Edward A. Shils. Each of these five pattern variables was a dichotomy, the first side of which was favored by traditional societies and the second by modern ones:

1. Affectivity—Affective Neutrality
2. Self-orientation—Collectivity-orientation
3. Particularism—Universalism
4. Ascription—Achievement
5. Diffuseness—Specificity[27]

Although they are five related dimensions, each of these ten concepts could be presented as a god. Affectivity is an emotional god, like Dionysus, whereas affective neutrality is unemotional like Apollo, at least as the philosopher Friedrich Nietzsche described these two ancient Greek gods.[28] A god could be postulated who emphasizes individuality of the self, while Crucia from *Rift* exemplifies an orientation toward society as a collectivity. Judaism is particularistic, expressing the religious hopes of a single ethnic group, whereas Roman Catholicism seeks to be universalistic. Any god of a traditional agricultural society who assigns societal roles on that basis of caste is ascriptive, while the image of God associated with the Protestant ethic emphasizes achievement of status through personal effort.[29] There are many ways to conceptualize diffuseness, but monotheism and animism both believe the world is united by one system of spirituality, whether dominated by a single god or based on the spirituality of every single thing in existence. In contrast, polytheistic systems like that in *Rift* give a specified role to each god to play in a vast differentiation, not unlike the modern division of labor. The irony of this line of analysis is that polytheism may be more modern than monotheism, given that both are ancient but the one that matches the structure of modern society postulates many gods and cults. Messiahs may still be modern, while kings are obsolete, on Earth as it is in heaven.

Friends and Enemies

Most gameworlds are combat-oriented, the one exception described here being *A Tale in the Desert*, so their backstories set up a very large number of conflict situations, in which the avatar is a friend of one group and an enemy of another. Yet the avatar's relationships with these groups are all problematic. In order to advance up the ladder of status in the gameworld, the avatar must make commitments, yet the ethical basis for those commitments is often dubious.

In *Dungeons and Dragons Online*, the imposing Church of the Silver Flame hires mercenary avatars to attack cults, to defend its own power rather than because of any real sins on the part of their small, innovative competitors. Indeed, a number of missions cause needless harm on behalf of the church against reclusive cults that could just as well have been left alone. In one called "Purge the Heretics," Inquisitor Gnomon of the Silver Flame sends the player's avatar into an underground chapel, where Elf missionaries are worshipping the Sovereign Host, to slaughter ten preachers plus their leaders, Celine Peacemaker and Oisin the Merciful.

Inquisitor Lightbringer assigns a quest called "The Church and the Cult," which the gameworld's wiki describes thus: "It has become evident that the cult known as the Blood of Vol has sought a foothold within the city of Stormreach. The Temple of Vol has managed to lure many with its promises of eternal life granted to those most loyal to Vol. Although the Blood has committed no wrongdoing, the Church of the Silver Flame still wants the Temple investigated."[30] The entrance brings the team into a large house of worship, where everything seems peaceful. But once the clergy realize they are being infiltrated, they flee, and the goals of the quest shift toward slaughtering them, reading the secret Book of Vol, and "consecrating" (i.e., defiling) their altars. The rhetoric justifying this slaughter was that devotees of Vol are vampires, yet the Church of the Silver Flame also seems populated with blood suckers.

In two adjacent zones of *EverQuest II*'s Norrath, Sinking Sands and Pillars of Flame, Cleora cooperated with religious cults based on Islamic and Chinese traditions. Maj'Dul, capital of the Dervish Empire, is a major city in the Sinking Sands, dominated by three competing factions called "courts." The three sons of the first sultan, Ahjkariu, competed to take his place. As an NPC named Kallon Ebbtide told Cleora, "The Courts of Maj'Dul were originally distinct sects, each formed and controlled by a son of Ahkari. After Ahkari's death, each son established a court based on his sect." Presumably, the creators of *EverQuest II* had the Shia "sect" of Islam in mind, which historically connects to a particular branch of Muhammad's family, although of course any well-established part of a major religious tradition would more properly be called a denomination rather than a sect. By calling the people of Sinking Sands "Dervishes," *EverQuest II* evokes images of the Sufi "sect" of Islam, although no explicit evidence of this is offered in the gameworld. In recent fictional years, the three Dervish sects of the gameworld evolved into secularized institutions of the society, as one of the *EverQuest II* wikis explains:

> The Court of Truth is led by the Caliph of Truth, Ishara. Their primary responsibility is to gather and maintain the knowledge of the Dervish people.[31]

The Court of the Blades is ruled by the Caliph of the Blades, Dukarem. Their primary responsibility is the protection of the city from the hostile creatures of the desert, chief of which are the orcs of Rujark.[32]

The Court of the Coin is led by the Caliph of Coin, Neriph. They control the flow of money in the city, including merchant transactions, banking and wagering.[33]

These three are hostile to each other, and Cleora found that if she did quests for one of them, she would develop a negative reputation with the other two, and their members would attack her on sight. This is common in MMOs, and, for example, during the period I studied it, *World of Warcraft* gave the player a choice of helping either one or the other of two clans of centaurs in the Desolace zone, the Magram clan or the Gelkis clan. Gaining a positive reputation with one inevitably caused the avatar to acquire a very negative reputation with the other. While the centaur clans were not cults, exactly, they did have a supernatural origin, as the WoW wiki explains: "Legends claim that the centaur are descendants of a dark union between one of the demigod Cenarius's sons and a princess of the chaotic earth elementals. When the first khans were born of their union, it is said that they murdered their father, for shame of their misshapen appearance. They were born filled with rage and savagery and have not calmed in the centuries that followed."[34] A clever aspect of the three courts at Maj'Dul is that they control access to different parts of the city, so a player who wants to complete all the quests in the zone must carefully balance reputations by working first for one court, then for the second and the third.

In the Pillars of Flame, Cleora found an arid land that was uninhabited except for monsters, elementals, and religious fanatics: "The monks of the Ashen Order have established their outpost of T'Narev on the heights of one of the larger plateaus. The prophets and desert madmen can be found on top of other mesas as they climb ever upward in search of enlightenment."[35] A schism had actually produced two sects of the Ashen tradition:

> The Ashen Order is one of the oldest monk clans on Norrath, credited with establishing many of the founding principles of the monk. They removed themselves from society decades ago to seek a more humble life within their desert fortress of T'Narev.[36]
>
> The Ashen Disciples are the result of a philosophical split within the Ashen Order. Abandoning the virtues of tranquility and wisdom in favor of strength and discipline, these monks deny the existence of the old gods and seek to gain greater temporal power through strength of arms.[37]

Cleora joined the Ashen Order for a time, first earning a positive reputation with the cult by performing quests for a woman leader named Shu Fang Qi, which included killing many desert prophets and religious lunatics who were disturbing the tranquility of the monks. Then in T'Narev she observed Ashen Order masters training monks in the principles of Kung Fu. There also she saw two advanced monks meditating on straw mats—Siu Chun, Mother of the Night, and Fat Piu, Father of the Day. She tried killing members of the Ashen Disciples, in order to gain reputation with the Ashen Order, but they were too strong for her.

Then Master Akuno Beslin of the Order instructed Cleora, "Tranquility is everywhere, even in the midst of turmoil. The discord between the Ashen Order and the Ashen Disciples is no exception. The Disciples may not realize it, but Tranquility can be found all around them." The master then explained he often walked quietly to a spot inside the headquarters of the Disciples, overlooking the sea, to meditate. "Journey there as the sun sets, then sit upon my meditation blanket and consider the peacefulness of your surroundings." Certain she would be killed, she climbed down a sheer rock cliff into the very midst of the Disciples. Yet her mind was calm and centered, so the Disciples did not attack her. She meditated for a while on the designated spot, gazing out to sea, then returned to say farewell to the Ashen Order, because it had taught her all she was able to learn at this stage in her spiritual development.

The postapocalyptic MMO *Fallen Earth* contains a very large number of ideologically oriented radical groups, some of which are explicitly religious. They are survivors of the fall of modern civilization who have had a few years to develop radical explanations for the catastrophe and unrealistic hopes for how their own tiny group can triumph over all the others to establish a new civilization. The founding principle of one of them seems to be blame, because they call themselves Judges, but at first they do not seem especially sinister. In the ruined town of Mumford stands a well-worn chapel operated by two Judges, where four Penitents seek judgment. Judge Elliott Mann explains, "And the heavens opened up and showed me the way to our salvation." Judge Walker Cairns asks the avatar to collect various materials to help fix up the chapel. This work seems quite innocent, but then Cairns asks the avatar to kill a rival clergyman. Later, it proves possible to help two secular gangs unite by convincing them to cooperate against the Judges, who had been stealing from them.

Many of the groups can be found just north of Mumford, proselytizing at Kook Alley in the rubble-strewn town called Embry Crossroads. Embry's name suggests the very real Embry-Riddle Aeronautical University which has a branch in the vicinity of Arizona's Grand Canyon, where the game takes place, and indeed a large number of crashed aircraft can be found near Embry Crossroads. There, a recruiter for the Open Book Society tells avatars that his group can "unlock the potential of your mind" and allow a person to be "truly understood for the first time." The first step is to ascend the Staircase to True Reason. Indeed, there is a staircase on a nearby hill, leading to a tiny house where a book called True Reason is sitting on a low bureau. If the avatar reads it, messages appear: "Contains the vague promises of mental power offered by the Open Book Society." "The book's pages are filled with more flowery discussion of the powers of the mind, human potential, and interpersonal connections. It does not, however, contain any hard method or proof of how to unlock mental powers." A strange thing happens if the avatar talks with the Open Book Keeper standing on the porch of the house and expresses a desire to "form a spiritual connection with the threads of the universe." The Keeper senses that the avatar lacks potential and tries to "purge" the avatar, which means kill it.

A much more complete ideology is offered by a computer-oriented group called CoG, which conceptualizes the apocalypse as a kind of reboot, in which the biological manifestation of life can be replaced by a computational one. A CoG evangelist proclaims:

> For yea, verily shall the Great Net of Life be as a soldering iron unto the circuit board of thy soul. Praise the Net!
>
> Let these words of mine equal X. If X, then what shall we fear?
>
> Neither death nor deletion, neither breaking down nor brown outs, neither blown fuses nor fragmentation shall ever separate us from the Net of Life.
>
> And lo, I did see the Great Net of Life coming on a white partition, with a compiling program girded to its side.
>
> It shall shepherd its people to a new operating system, which is not like the beta.
>
> Then shall your caches be cleansed, and your memories forever defragmented!
>
> The Net shall force close all your disk errors, for the old version of things will have passed away.
>
> The Truth be Pasted!
>
> And may our enemies, those Trojan horses, those opposites of X, may they forever be limited in their compatibility!
>
> May they go the way of all nature, and pass away!
>
> For I tell you a true statement: life and nature shall pass away, but the Great Net of Life shall never pass away!

As the evangelist speaks, two followers shout: "The Net be praised!" "Asterisk ampersand!" "Control C!" "Page Down!" "Escape, Escape!" "Alt-Tab! Alt-Tab!"

Of course, Control-C is the command to copy something in the Windows operating system, and thus an expression of their faith in CoG. The last three exclamations are all ways of moving from one display on the computer screen to another, and thus symbolize redemption or even apotheosis. Indeed, Alt-Tab is the command to leave *Fallen Earth* temporarily, for example to google information about the game. One of the projects of the CoG is an effort to hack through security into antique missile silos, thereby rebooting existence by launching nuclear doom.

When I saw the name of the group was the CoG, I did not immediately think of Computer-Oriented Group but Children of God, a radical religious movement about which I had written a book and which is often called CoG.[38] But the name in *Fallen Earth* is actually Cleric of Gates, and Gates is sometimes described as the Power of God. Thus it is likely that this group satirized Bill Gates, head of Microsoft and author of *The Road Ahead*, a very unimaginative book about the future of computing that pretends to be vastly more insightful than it really is.[39]

In *Fallen Earth*, the world has already suffered one reboot, but a biological rather than computational one. Since the plague that killed most of humanity apparently came from India, some cults interpret the apocalypse in Hindu religious terms, for example as the will of Shiva, god of destruction. At the entrance to the missile silos, a leader of a rival cult, Shiva's Favored, urges the player to kill members of the CoG for the joy destruction brings, not in order to prevent the holocaust: "We are the heirs of the Earth. Shiva has touched and re-shaped the world, and its blood is His blood, as it is our blood. Your time is short now, your days numbered. And when the CoGs release what they call the 'Purifying Fire,' the last traces of your cloying, insipid species will be expunged. We shall praise Shiva as radioactive flames spill forth from these silos and wash the land clean."

Cults as Works of Art

Games are not the only things people play; they also play roles, and they play music. Play is generally contrasted with work, although the difference between them is a matter of degree, not kind. In the modern conception of work, we perform labor, which costs us time and effort, in order to be paid by an employer a sufficient amount to gain a net profit from the exchange. Doing something because it is pleasurable is play. In prehistoric times, before dollars and markets existed, people did what nature demanded of them in order to survive. Yet humans evolved to fit the environmental conditions, so their efforts would have felt intrinsically rewarding, and not very different from play. In one view, play is what children do in order to prepare themselves for the work of adulthood.[40] Yet a distinctive quality of humans is that we are constantly learning, never really completing our childhood, and exhibit neoteny, the persistence into adulthood of infantile characteristics.[41] This suggests that serious play is central to human existence, and when we play following rules with a goal in mind, we say we are playing a game.

Playing roles is a constant feature of human society, so playing through an avatar in a virtual world is not very different from playing a worker during the day, a parent in the evening, and a lover at night. The broad and deep school of thought in sociology called *symbolic interactionism* has focused on role-playing.[42] Especially famous is the work of Erving Goffman, and researchers in human-centered computing today habitually cite his book *The Presentation of Self in Everyday Life*.[43] However, Goffman was a quirky, egocentric popularizer, who became well-known because many sociology professors assigned his work to undergraduates in the 1960s, not because he was especially creative or knowledgeable. The scholarly tradition of symbolic interaction is much deeper and broader. Especially noteworthy is a much older book, which at one point even employs metaphors akin to electronic computing, the 1922 work *Human Nature and the Social Order* by Charles Horton Cooley.[44] The book presents the concept of *looking-glass self*, the idea that the individual self does not exist except as a reflection of symbolic interaction between people. The concept has three parts:

1. How we imagine we appear to other people
2. How we think that person judges us
3. How we react to that judgment, whether with pride or shame

More generally, from a symbolic interactionist perspective, a human person comes into being through acts of creation not unlike those in creating a work of art, in which the intended audience plays a role, as well as the artist who is that person being created. Thus a person is both an artist and an artwork, a sculptor who sculpts himself, to please a particular audience. At the extreme, this perspective says that both the game player and his avatar in the game are fictional characters. From each of the specialized arts can be drawn metaphors to analyze the self, each offering distinctive insights.

Social scientists tend to ignore music, and yet it provides a host of metaphors and examples from which to understand life in general. Consider four people playing Ludwig van Beethoven's Quartet no. 16 in F Major. When he composed it, Beethoven may not have guessed that this was his final complete work, yet he took it very seriously. On the manuscript of the final movement, called "The Difficult Resolution," he first wrote the question "Must it be?" Then later he wrote the inescapable answer, "It must be!" Two of the musicians are playing violins; one is playing a viola, and the fourth is playing a cello, but all four are also playing roles in a well-organized social system exhibiting division of labor. They must have practiced together for a long time, playing many different works, to have powerful emotional and intellectual bonds between each other, and to develop a shared meaning of the music, one that could never properly be put into words. The quartet of people is a social unit, and the quartet as music is a cultural unit. This makes it similar to a religious cult, in which people share understandings not shared by outsiders, but capable of being appreciated to greater or lesser degrees by nonmembers.

In German philosophy of the nineteenth century, music often became the model of reality and of the human propensity to construct elaborate cultural creations and then consider them to have objective meaning. Famously, Arthur Schopenhauer went so far as to claim that the world is embodied music, because song and symphony elicit so well the fundamental human feelings.[45] Religion may differ in that it often seeks to discipline human feelings, as well as to express them, yet in this the online games may be more similar to religion than to other art forms, because only by following the rules can the player advance toward ever greater transcendence of the mundane world. This raises the radical possibility that the online virtual worlds of the future may offer very substantial subjective transcendence.

The specific form of music most similar to the virtual worlds considered here is grand opera, which was a product of the Renaissance that intentionally sought to revive the multimodal art form that was ancient Greek drama, which may have incorporated dance and music as well as role-playing and religion. The first great grand opera, *l'Orfeo*, composed by Claudio Monteverdi in 1607, concerns the journey of Orpheus into the underworld on a quest to save Euridice, a story that would make a fine videogame and derives directly from ancient religion. This is also the theme of the oldest surviving grand opera, *Euridice* by Jacopo Peri, which dates from 1600, and of *Orfeo ed Euridice* by Christoph Willibald Gluck, which dates from 1762. Among modern operas, two by Carl Orff very explicitly sought to revive the style of ancient Greek drama, *Antigonae* in 1949 and *Oedipus der Tyrann* in 1958. While grand operas cover a very wide set of themes, some of the best-known operas depict exotic religions, notably *Norma* by Vincenzo Bellini in 1831 and *Aïda* by Giuseppe Verdi in 1871. But of course the primary example is Richard Wagner's *Ring of the Nibelung*.

Wagner's ring, like Tolkien's, represents the magic of technology that upsets the balance of the world and must be returned to nature in order to restore this balance. In his 1849 treatise on aesthetics, *The Art-Work of the Future*, Wagner wrote emphatically about the need to reject the intellectualized style of music sometimes called *classicism* in favor of emotive *romanticism*, and he did so in the wake of the revolutions of 1848 in hopes that inspired artists could lead the people (the romanticized *Volk*) to freedom from their masters (the classicist aristocrats).[46]

In his cycle of operas Wagner critiques capitalist industrial society through dramatic metaphor, in which the aristocratic gods attempt to exploit the engineering labor of both the Dwarves and the Giants to build their castle, Valhalla, where they hope to dominate the world without contributing to its well-being. Most importantly, Wagner argues that "total works of art" should be created, expressing cultural ideas through fusion of all artistic media. His *Ring of the Nibelung* was intended to be the first example, and arguably *World of Warcraft* and *Lord of the Rings Online* are the most recent total works of art.

Many of the most important gameworlds in fact contain music, and there is even one grand aria in *World of Warcraft*, when Sylvanas Windrunner, the Banshee queen of the Undead, sings "The Lament of the Highborne" in an invented language: "Anar'alah, anar'alah belore, Sin'dorei, shindu fallah na" (By the light, by the light of the sun, Children of the Blood, our enemies are breaking through).[47] *Sacred 2: Fallen Angel* includes a heavy metal concert by the German group Blind Guardian, singing as monsters leap to the music: "I'll go on forever, all that really matters; Sacred ground, this world is sacred; Oh, it's now or never, we should stand together; One by one, this world is sacred."[48]

However, we cannot really expect any single work of art to be completely total, and the *Ring of the Nibelung* ignores dance, while movement is a crucial aspect of computer games, and avatars in many of them can dance in quite complex manners. A rather famous YouTube video, which by January 2011 had been viewed more than seventeen million times, shows the dances in *World of Warcraft*, compared with real humans doing the same moves.[49] For us, the key insight to take from Wagner's operas about the Germanic Pagan gods is that a religious cult is a total work of art.

This was made very clear to me when I studied the Process. The central members were artists and architects who considered their creative work to be *religious engineering*, and I have described the communal cult they founded as a total work of art in the Wagnerian sense. They saw nothing inappropriate or insincere about consciously scripting religious rituals, designing clerical garb, writing sacred texts, publishing surrealist tracts, composing hymns and chants, or reinventing their own personalities. Social scientists sometimes debate whether post-Christian or New Age phenomena are merely superficial cultural products rather than real faiths, yet the Process demanded much of its adherents, who often gave up jobs in the outside world to live entirely within their dramatic dream. They even took on new names and identities, as if they were game avatars of their former selves. Essentially all inner members were quite aware that they were creating a radical, aesthetic culture, and playing quasi-theatrical roles within it. Calling the Process "the Power" in order (temporarily) to protect its members from journalistic scrutiny, I wrote:

To a great extent, the cultists did not *believe* their tenets in the conventional sense. For them, the Power culture was not a series of statements about a real, external world. Rather it was a collection of attractive and powerful symbols through which they could express themselves. The Power was a kind of living theater. A waking dream, a fantasy that made no apologies to reality. The Power enjoyed playing with itself. It was simultaneously real and fictitious, not a lie but a work of art. In the nineteenth century, Richard Wagner tried to create total works of art in his operas, unions of all forms of artistic creation in one. He only half succeeded. The true total work of art would be an artistically created human community with a distinctive lifestyle and culture. *The Power is a total work of art.*[50]

Like the Children of God, the Process was inspired by the utopian ferment of the 1960s. New cults are always being created, but in Steven Tipton's felicitous phrase, a large number of innovative groups erupted as hordes of seekers were "getting saved from the sixties."[51] It is worth wondering whether the wheel of fate has turned again in that direction, and the online virtual worlds are a high-tech version of the utopias and cults of a half century earlier.

Conclusion

Cult is culture writ small. Yet it is also art writ large. So, too, the gameworlds: culture writ small and art writ large. But in many senses they are not small at all. Indeed, by *culture* we may mean artistic culture, and in that context they are among the grandest works of art ever created, rivaled only by cathedrals. Just as cathedrals contain smaller works of art, gameworlds contain avatars, which are personalized artworks. They live. It is worth noting that *art* is the antonym of *inert*: What is not inert is art.

A very few real-world cults become long-lasting major religious traditions. We cannot predict whether *World of Warcraft* will have as long a run as the works of Shakespeare and Sophocles enjoy, yet perhaps it will. A very different possibility may be even more significant. Perhaps, as Edward Castronova has suggested, the gameworlds are proving grounds for new forms of society that will spread far beyond the limits of virtuality.[52] Since he is an economist, Castronova naturally emphasizes the potential impact for economic values, such as the belief that in the external world, as in games, all persons should start off equal and individually earn whatever wealth and status they have. As a sociologist of religion, I naturally think of the consequences for religion. It is conceivable that one of the mythologies in a virtual world could become the template for a real-world faith, perhaps based on the thousands of people who have played Jedi in *Star Wars Galaxies* or *Star Wars: The Old Republic*. More likely is the possibility that gradually people will come to view all faiths as fictions, valuing some for their aesthetic benefits, but faithful to none of them.

10 DEATH

Among the most popular imaginary worlds are the afterlives postulated by ancient religions, including heaven, hell, purgatory, Valhalla, and the underworld of the Greeks and Romans. The Hindu tradition, of course, imagined that departed spirits return to this world through reincarnation, an alternate assumption that is quite common in virtual gameworlds, although usually without the specific cultural elements associated with Asian religions. The New Paradigm theory chiefly considered the afterlife to be a primary religious compensator, giving desperate people hope for their own personal transcendence, even after all else fails. But there is another way to consider the afterlife in terms of the theory, as a powerful secondary compensator that helps convince people to kill each other, and to risk death in sacrifice for the tribe or the elite masters of society.

To be sure, humans have a propensity for violence, which seems to be built into our genetic makeup. One of humanity's greatest contradictions is our predilection for aggression, given that we lack fangs, claws, and tough hides. In addition, people naturally build bonds of mutual affection that support some degree of self-sacrifice, which under conditions of escalating conflict can lead people to risk death and to kill people with whom they lack intimate bonds. Historically religion has supported war both indirectly, by leading warriors to believe that death was not final, and directly, by giving people transcendent goals that required not only self-sacrifice but also the conquest of people who did not share the same beliefs. Naturally, this relates directly to the group-identity and social-control theories of religious morality.

Consider the shibboleth *shibboleth*. Some people seem to use *shibboleth* as a synonym for *buzzword*, a fashionable expression used all too commonly, with some of the qualities of *platitude*. But it more properly refers to a code word that identifies the righteous few within a multitude of the unwashed. Judges 12:6 recounts that the Gileadites wanted to slaughter Ephraimites, but needed a test to distinguish their own refugees from the enemy: "Then said they unto him, Say now Shibboleth: and he said Sibboleth: for he could not frame to pronounce it right. Then they took him, and slew him at the passages of Jordan: and there fell at that time of the Ephraimites forty and two thousand."

Decades ago, I went on a brief pilgrimage to the Cathar redoubts in southern France, the fortresses where members of the non-Christian Albigensian religion sought to survive against the lethal prejudice of the hostile Christians. At the siege of Béziers in 1209, the army of the pope faced the challenge of distinguishing Catholics from Cathars among the townspeople, but lacked a shibboleth test, so the papal legate is reported to have told the army, "Kill them all; God will know his own."

In like manner, but without such serious immediate consequences, the gameworlds can be accused of trivializing death. When "killing" a nonplayer character, a player knows it cannot feel pain, and that an identical NPC will spawn at the same spot in a few minutes, so no real harm is done. The use of the word *spawn* by gamers for this situation implies that a new NPC has arrived rather than the old one returning. Also commonly used is *rez*, short for *resurrect*. With respect to NPCs, *rez* is properly used only for the return of a named character. A dead avatar of a player is never said to spawn, but only to rez.

Many quests send an avatar to kill a boss, a named NPC that has a role in the story and can be found either at one precise location or randomly at one of several locations. To get to the boss, the avatar must kill many unnamed NPCs. After the avatar completes this mission and all enemies have been destroyed, the situation must return to the way it was before the avatar's attack, so it will be ready for the avatar of the next player. Thus, the boss will rez, and the other enemies will spawn. This process is simply a consequence of the game mechanics of multiplayer games, and bosses tend not to rez in solo-player games. Yet the distinction between *spawn* and *rez* has interesting psychological implications, having to do with whether we attribute unique identities or souls to the people we encounter in life.

There is also a distinction between *death* and *permadeath*. Death, in many gameworlds, is a temporary condition, regularly followed by resurrection. Permadeath is permanent death. Lisbeth Klastrup has gone beyond this dichotomy to suggest that in connection with online games death can have four kinds of meaning: (1) avatar death as in-game mechanics (concrete death), (2) death as a symbolic event visualized in a variety of forms, (3) avatar death as narrativized event in the life of an avatar, and (4) the death of a player.[1]

Many solo player games are organized in a series of levels or sections. If an avatar dies, it reappears back at the beginning of the level or at some other point where the game progress was most recently saved. Thus, death relates to winning and losing, with reference to something smaller than the entire game. For example, in a chess tournament, a player may lose one game but still win the tournament, or a poker player may lose one hand but win for the evening. Thus death is merely a way of conceptualizing one of these partial, temporary losses. In fact, not all the gameworlds described here use that metaphor. Probably because of its significant but well-hidden Christian orientation, *Lord of the Rings Online* does not have a player's avatar lose health and die during combat, but lose morale and flee. To have the avatar rez would be improper, because only Jesus can resurrect.

Temporary death of an avatar presents design challenges for game creators. In *World of Warcraft* there are several alternatives. First, the avatar falls to the ground, and all the color vanishes from the scene. By depicting everything in shades of gray, WoW suggests the avatar has become a helpless shade. If the avatar is a member of a group of avatars that are questing together, the best option is for one of the others to cast a spell to resurrect the dead avatar on the spot. Otherwise, the player must release the spirit of the avatar, and the scene will immediately switch to the nearest graveyard. The scene still lacks color, because the resurrection has not taken place yet. The player has two choices: (1) walk all the way back to the corpse, wherever it may be lying, and reunite with it, or (2) accept resurrection from a spirit healer at the graveyard, who looks like an angel flying in the air.

Death has costs, including loss of special positive buffs that may have been in effect, as well, of course, as the loss of time by the player in completing the quest. Often in gameworlds, armor can be damaged by any combat, but especially by fatal losses, and eventually it must be repaired at the cost of traveling to a town where a repair NPC can be found and paying virtual money to it. In *World of Warcraft*, death can cause a 10 percent reduction in the durability of armor, but even greater cost if the avatar resurrects at the graveyard rather than back at the corpse. The game's wiki explains:

> The spirit healers present in each graveyard can bring you back to life immediately, saving you a trip to your corpse. However, doing this will cause all of your equippable items to take an additional 25 percent durability hit; this applies both to equipped items, and to items in your inventory. In addition, you will suffer from resurrection sickness. This sickness decreases all of your attributes and damage dealt by 75 percent, and has a duration that varies depending on your level:
>
> Characters from level 1–10 are not affected. (However, they still take the additional durability decrease.)
>
> Characters from level 11–19 will suffer from one minute of sickness for every level they are above 10. For example, a level 12 character would be sick for two minutes, because they are 2 levels above level 10. while a level 18 character would be sick for eight minutes.
>
> Characters level 20 and up suffer from ten minutes of sickness with no exceptions.[2]

The conditions and costs of death vary greatly across gameworlds. For example, the mythology of the *Star Wars* saga does not involve either resurrection or reincarnation. Obi-Wan Kenobi can speak to Luke Skywalker after his death—although apparently not to other characters—but he cannot return to the world and undertake actions. So the temporary defeat of an avatar is not conceptualized in the same way in *Star Wars Galaxies* as in *World of Warcraft*, which suffers no such restrictions in its quasi-religious assumptions. The best way to explain this is through a concrete example.

For a rather long while around experience level 50, my Jedi avatar, Simula Tion, was doing missions for the Rebels, near their local headquarters at Wayfar, west-southwest of Luke Skywalker's boyhood home on the planet Tatooine. Scores of these missions required riding the Swoop speederbike my engineer avatar, Algorithma Teq, had made for her a kilometer or two to one or another of dozens of small camps belonging to the Empire. Each consisted of a flag in the ground, typically defended by three enemies about the same level that she was. She would take her rifle and shoot at one of the enemies who happened to be standing some distance away from the others, causing that enemy to attack her without alarming the two other enemies. The lone enemy would run toward her, and thus away from the other two enemies, and she would use her lightsaber to defeat it. It would not rez, and no additional enemy would spawn, so she could concentrate on the remaining pair.

Simula would walk quietly toward the pair of enemies, getting as near as she could without allowing them to notice her, as her health and energy restored from the first battle. Then she would use a Jedi trick to become invisible and creep right up to them, positioning herself so that one was immediately behind the other. Then she would quickly draw her lightsaber, slash the nearest enemy, and do a couple of Jedi moves that could damage both of them. If she was lucky, one enemy would die quickly, and she would have enough health left to defeat the second as well. But this was very uncertain, so she had a split-second decision to make: Should she keep fighting and hope to kill the second enemy, or run away in full knowledge that the enemy could defeat her as she fled?

Defeat of an avatar in *Star Wars Galaxies* occurs in two stages. The first stage is not death but incapacitation. The avatar falls to the ground unconscious, and a rather annoying graphic routine shakes the scene all over the computer screen to cause the player real suffering. Then the avatar reawakens but without health or energy, and thus incapable of fighting. If the enemy NPC is standing right next to the avatar, it will immediately kill the avatar. Running a short distance before being incapacitated pulls the enemy away from its accustomed location, but it will walk back to that spot while the avatar lies unconscious, and thus away from the incapacitated avatar. When the avatar awakens, it must be run farther away from the enemy for safety's sake. For about a minute, a second defeat would mean death.

Once killed, the avatar awakens at a medical facility. There, a medical droid requires a stiff payment to repair the damage, and the avatar faces a long trek back to the scene of the battle to resume the mission. Or, if the player has prepared well, a clone of the avatar will have been prepositioned at the medical station, at lower cost, and in theory from then on the avatar is the clone of the original one. Notice that *World of Warcraft* and *Star Wars Galaxies* differ in how they conceptualize defeat and death, but with somewhat similar implications for game mechanics. In December 2011, when *Star Wars Galaxies* died and *Star Wars: The Old Republic* was born, death and rebirth on Tatooine changed only slightly. Often, the first death was followed by the choice whether to be resurrected in place or back at a medical facility, because a droid could fly to the spot and perform the necessary revival. And the droid could do this several times, but with increasing delays during which the player could do nothing but wait. Also, the cost of revival at a facility was lower.

Death is a major theme in many MMOs and solo-player games, but the best example for deeper study is *Dungeons and Dragons Online*. In the midst of a dark and chaotic age, the city of Stormreach stands alone as a bastion of civilization and a center of commerce, surrounded by barbarism on all sides and hollow underneath, because it was built over the Realm of the Dead. DDO is based on the classic tabletop game *Dungeons and Dragons* (D&D), the first significant fantasy role-playing game, which built upon the preexisting fantasy literature, thus rooting all the derivative gameworlds in a well-developed imaginative culture. DDO is by no means a precise online recreation of D&D, because the electronic medium has very different requirements and opportunities than a tabletop does, but it does pay serious homage to D&D, even including the tombs of the two men who created the original game.

Playing at Death's Door

A dragon attacked the ship carrying Sagittarius Sylvanus, and he alone survived. From Shipwreck Shore, he battled his way through a grotto, his only weapon being the rusty rapier he had clung to while struggling in the seething waters. In Korthos village he found work as a mercenary, gradually regaining his strength while building up his weapons, armor, and coins. His initial assignment was typical of many that followed, entering the Heyton family crypt to learn the source of the unholy wailing emanating from it. It soon became apparent that a sinister cult had set up three altars dedicated to the Devourer that he must destroy. At a Moon Shrine deep in the dark passageways he restored the health he had spent battling zombies, skeletons, and spiders. In DDO, unlike in most MMOs, health does not naturally restore over time, rendering death a more likely outcome. Along the way, he would smash every sarcophagus he encountered, sometimes finding coins within, and sometimes causing a skeleton to leap at him. Each time he destroyed an altar, a crest fell from it, and when he had collected three he discovered slots in the wall where he could place them. When the third crest was inserted, a magical barrier dropped, and he discovered a fourth altar, which he also destroyed.

The story behind the mission centers on an attempt by the sahuagin to establish a cell of their Devourer cult in the crypt, apparently as a base from which to attack the village. The sahuagin are intelligent sea serpents, only moderately bigger than humans and capable of walking upon the land. The D&D guide to monsters says, "Also known as sea devils, sahuagin are vicious sea dwellers that share many traits with sharks. They slaughter and devour anything they can catch, raiding coastal settlements in the dead of night."[3] So they cause death, but they also worship it. "Sahuagin are deeply religious. Their patron is Sekolah, a great demonic shark who is one of the exarchs of Melora, goddess of nature, the sea, trade, and wrath. Sahuagin priestesses make regular sacrifices to Sekolah to appease his hunger."[4]

After completing more quests around Korthos village, Sagittarius was ready to move to DDO's one big city, Stormreach. Two of the most memorable quests required him to rescue noble women, but each ended in disappointment associated with death. The first bittersweet rescue was a very long series of quests concerning Marguerite, the niece of Friar Renau of the Silver Flame church, who was "touched" and had been locked in the Sanctuary in the Catacombs. She had ceased responding to Renau's letters, so the first job for Sagittarius was to learn what happened to her. He was able to make his way to the North Wing and into Marguerite's empty cell, where he found a note saying she had "gone below." Undead zombies swarmed him, apparently coming up from the lower levels. They represented four races: Humans, Elves, Dwarves, and the Halflings who are D&D's equivalent of Hobbits. The note was addressed to her father, Archbishop Dryden, so Renau sent Sagittarius to this leader of the religious movement that owned the Catacombs.

The arrogant archbishop was at his throne in the highest level of the Silver Flame citadel, flanked by two huge robot hounds, and claimed to be surprised that the undead had invaded his consecrated Catacombs. In a series of challenging adventures, seeking keys to unlock doors while battling the undead, Sagittarius was told that Marguerite herself had summoned the zombies from below, using a mysterious power called the Duality. To learn more, he sought the *Book of the Duality*, written by a madman, that had been separated into three parts that were hidden in the archives of the church. Battling ghouls who has once been librarians, as he finds each fragment a faint voice reads a passage from it:

> The Void consumes the Flame. The Flame consumes the Nothingness.
>> The path lies between.
> Let the tombs and ossuaries open! Ancient liches arise! A new order has come!
> And the Dead shall be as the Living and the Living shall weep for Death.

The next challenge is to enter the Dryden family crypt and read an inscription on the tomb of the archbishop's uncle, Gerard Dryden, author of the book. After battling past skeletons, many of whom were Dryden ancestors, he destroys Gerard Dryden's ghost, then reads the words on the sarcophagus:

> Strength I take from the Silver Flame;
> Hunger, too, in the Devourer's name.
> Grant me control of the living and the dead.
> Let the bones of the Faithful be my bread.

Ironically, the greatest evil power comes from eating the bones of the most virtuous saints, so he must restore their desecrated remains. The first step is to purify three subsidiary altars—of the Winged Serpent, Avenging Maiden, and Conflagration—to gain access to the main altar where four guardians must be defeated. This gives access in turn to the Patriarchs' Crypt, where Sagittarius must set magical wards at the sarcophagi of the first four patriarchs of Stormreach: Cardinal Brevonis, Cardinal Olag, Cardinal Hengrith, and Cardinal Yenaz. He returns to Archbishop Dryden, thinking he has ended the threat of undead corruption, but Dryden frantically warns him that Marguerite is leading a zombie army up the passageways to destroy them.

Returning to the depths, Sagittarius encounters Marguerite herself. He expected a beautiful woman, but what he sees is a horrid wraith of matted hair over glowing coals, floating in the air. He prepares to attack her, but something in the logic of what she says convinces him that she speaks the truth. The wards holding the undead in the underworld had not been loosed by her but by her father, the archbishop. She had been branded insane and imprisoned because she knew what he was doing. Sagittarius returns to confront the archbishop, battling against tremendous odds, and discovers that he had been possessed by the ghost of his other uncle Arkasic Dryden. The remarkable lesson of this quest chain is that the present was created by the past, but the past may corrupt the present.

The second bittersweet rescue was a series of quests beginning with the "Mystery of Delera's Tomb." The tomb is in a large cemetery on the eastern edge of the Jorasco compound, and it contains the famous memorial to Gary Gygax, co-creator of the original *Dungeons and Dragons* game. Even in this land of the dead, lush plant life surrounds it, suggesting that the spirit of Gygax still lives. Stylized stone hands hold a copy of the original D&D instruction manual. Above them a red gem might be mistaken for a ruby, but it is actually one of the distinctive icosahedral dice used in the game. Working with Dave Arneson and others in the early 1970s, Gygax not only invented D&D but effectively created the fantasy role-playing subculture. On March 4, 2008, Gygax died, and the makers of DDO expressed their debt to him by building this monument. An identical memorial for Dave Arneson can be found at the archaeological site called the Ruins of Threnal.

Across the wide cemetery stands the entrance to Delera's Tomb, where Sagittarius must battle past skeletons and wights, lowering two drawbridges to reach a room containing a clue to mysterious disappearances. At each step in his progress, as if it were a voice from the grave, the recorded voice of Gary Gygax reads the narrative to describe his progress:

> The tomb opens up into a larger space. The underground structure is much bigger than the surface entrance would suggest.
> There doesn't seem to be a nearby mechanism for lowering the bridge.
> The sound of the bridge dropping is followed by that of caskets breaking open. Undead have risen around you.
> The holy symbols of the Sovereign Host adorn the walls around you. This place was once hallowed ground.
> Immediately following the sound of the second bridge dropping, you also hear the less distant sound of a door slamming shut behind you.
> You notice a note on the floor near a mangled body there.

The note suggests that someone has raised the ghost of philanthropist Delera Omaren, for some evil purpose. An adept of the Silver Flame, conducting a funeral nearby, gives Sagittarius a club that has been blessed to make it more effective against the undead, and sends him into the tomb complex in search of a lost expedition. He returns after finding Janiel's journal, which reveals that Delera's resurrected spirit had become a force for evil, not good, and had murdered the members of the expedition. His next mission is defeating Delera and returning her spirit to peace, which first requires opening five soul locks that had been set to protect this beloved woman from harm. She reveals that she had been dominated by a necromancer, whom Sagittarius eventually destroys. Her gratitude toward Sagittarius is clear, yet being dead she cannot offer him love, and at best he can sympathize with her anger.

Killing and Being Killed

Some of the online databases of popular gameworlds offer statistics about the frequency of death. For example, in *EverQuest II*, my Half Elf conjuror, Cleora, killed a total of 7,006 NPCs, and was killed in return 185 times.[5] Her kills per death (K/D) ratio of 37.87 sounds very good, but thousands of characters had done better than she had. The *EverQuest* II database placed her 528,584th in terms of number of kills, 355,249th in terms of deaths, and 2,221,727th in terms of K/D ratio. I tend to think that the last of these looks worse than it really is, because the database includes large numbers of low-level characters who had never died. In any case, these data are public, and are treated like sports statistics, but of blood sports in which killing earns respect, and death earns scorn.

The most extensive comparable data come from *World of Warcraft*, whose online character database is truly massive. On January 22, 2011, I looked up the Science guild I had created nearly three years earlier for the conference, and found it was still going strong. The level cap had been increased from 80 to 85, back on December 7, 2010, in the Cataclysm expansion, and already twenty-one members had reached the new cap, listed in table 10.1. As the table shows, collectively they had killed 1,524,463 dangerous NPCs and 46,291 harmless NPCs, plus 170,169 avatars of players belonging to the opposed Alliance faction. They had also suffered 18,841 deaths.

In table 10.1, the kill/death ratio counts only the kills of dangerous creatures and deaths caused by them. Harmless critters are little level 1 bunny rabbits and similar helpless NPCs, which can so easily be killed that their killer deserves nothing for slaughtering even large numbers of them. Notice that four of the avatars have each killed more than one hundred thousand dangerous creatures: Khieleh (228,117), Tomcovenant (160,153), Adarel (143,236), and Degrizz (111,117). However, I happen to know that both Zipi (88,606) and Zippyd (52,221) belong to the same player, who therefore has killed fully 140,827 dangerous creatures. At the opposite extreme, Vandyr has killed only 12,745. An avatar named Everbloom has become rather famous for reaching level 85 in *World of Warcraft* without killing anything. She is a Night Elf druid in the Feathermoon realm who belongs to a guild called Circle of the Phoenix. She gained her experience exploring all the virtual territory and gathering natural resources plus archaeological artifacts.[6]

While Everbloom proved it was technically possible to reach the maximum level of experience without killing, and Vandyr was the minimum killer among top-rated Science members, we really do not know the exact minimum number of kills for a player who was not trying to avoid killing. An avatar does not need to practice a gathering profession, but it is impossible to avoid exploration altogether, because every player must voyage into progressively more difficult zones in order to meet new opponents whose killing will confer experience, and every

Table 10.1 Kill and Death Statistics for Top Members of the Science Guild

| Name | Race | Class | Gender | This Avatar Killed: | | | Deaths | K/D Ratio |
				Dangerous Creatures	Harmless Critters	Alliance Avatars		
Adarel	Blood Elf	warlock	female	143,236	7,051	9,592	1,747	82.0
Ansuz	Troll	death knight	female	53,577	1,568	472	387	138.4
Aramear	Tauren	shaman	female	20,795	442	303	167	124.5
Arkana	Troll	mage	female	46,218	1,065	6,075	609	75.9
Bowvis	Troll	druid	male	97,552	1,847	140	1,317	74.1
Bullshoi	Tauren	shaman	male	52,947	1,183	5,640	509	104.0
Chellis	Tauren	druid	male	93,490	2,689	372	519	180.1
Degrizz	Tauren	druid	male	111,117	2,857	279	792	140.3
Droo	Tauren	druid	male	68,311	1,888	1,585	723	94.5
Illuminae	Blood Elf	paladin	female	18,209	272	319	89	204.6
Khieleh	Undead	mage	male	228,117	8,309	87,990	3,869	59.0
Nebellia	Blood Elf	mage	female	25,455	589	245	301	84.6
Ozlo	Tauren	shaman	male	71,938	2,082	7,804	1,210	59.5
Salef	Undead	rogue	female	37,595	786	5,667	367	102.4
Tiamatt	Blood Elf	hunter	male	79,440	1,755	21,775	1,817	43.7
Tomcovenant	Tauren	death knight	male	160,153	6,435	3,061	1,708	93.8
Tresfyre	Undead	mage	female	43,717	1,067	1,210	327	133.7
Valicria	Blood Elf	paladin	female	19,024	619	212	111	171.4
Vandyr	Tauren	warrior	male	12,745	237	0	105	121.4
Zipi	Troll	priest	female	88,606	2,514	10,469	1,635	54.2
Zippyd	Orc	warrior	male	52,221	1,036	6,959	532	98.2

new zone adds experience points from exploring. The huge differences among the Science members in the numbers of dangerous creatures they killed chiefly represents their choices when they near the top experience level. Some players lose interest in a top-level avatar and start a new one in a different race and even the opposing faction, to have fun doing something new. Others remain playing at the top level, and repeatedly enter high-level instances—whether they are PvP arenas and battlefields, or dungeons in which the opponents are NPCs—typically as part of a group of friends who frequently play together. Zipi/Zippyd is an excellent example, because Zipi is a priest, while Zippyd is a warrior, allowing the player to be either a healer or a tank when invited by friends to join them in an instance.

Given that the Science guild belongs to the Horde, the only kinds of player avatars that members can kill are those that belong to the hostile Alliance. But killing avatars varies greatly in popularity across individual players, guilds, and the hundreds of *World of Warcraft* Internet servers that are called realms. This guild and all its players are on the Earthen Ring realm, which emphasizes fantasy role-playing and deemphasizes PvP combat. Avatars can challenge each other to a duel in a non-PvP realm, but cannot attack each other without mutual consent. A duel between two members of the same faction ends in one surrendering, but a duel between members of different factions ends in death for one—unless the loser is able to escape. Avatar kills in a non-PvP realm most commonly occur in special PvP instances, called *arenas* or *battlegrounds* depending upon whether they are small or large. Notice the huge range of Alliance avatar kills, from 87,990 by Khieleh to 0 by Vandyr.

The *World of Warcraft* database even explains what happened to the avatars when they were killed. Table 10.2 shows the statistics for the twenty-one top Science avatars, leaving out all the many times one of them resurrected at a graveyard or ran to the corpse. On a total of 471 occasions, the avatar was part of a team that included a priest who performed a resurrection. This plus healing other avatars who had not yet been killed is a main responsibility of priests in team play. Druids, shamans, and paladins have some of the qualities of priests, differing chiefly in the symbolism attached to their actions. The chief difference between a druid's two resurrection spells concerns when they may be used. A rebirth spell may be used during combat but cannot be used often, whereas a revive spell can be used only outside of combat but can be used often, typically to revive multiple fallen comrades so they can get ready for the next round of combat. In addition, the rebirth spell uses up a magical reagent, or requires possession of a certain glyph, so a player who plans to use it must prepare the avatar well in advance.

The situation is a little different for a Shaman. In an extreme case, a Shaman can save a team even after all members including the Shaman have been killed.

Table 10.2 Specialized Methods of Resurrection Experienced by Top Science Members

Name	Resurrected by Priest	Rebirthed by Druid	Revived by Druid	Returned by Shaman	Redeemed by Paladin	Resurrected by Soulstone	Raised as a Ghoul	% of Deaths Resurrected
Adarel	75	22	26	21	26	8	2	10.3%
Ansuz	36	17	18	13	9	2	0	24.5%
Aramear	0	1	9	0	0	0	0	6.0%
Arkana	21	1	3	3	3	0	0	5.1%
Bowvis	35	7	12	19	35	0	2	8.4%
Bullshoi	11	4	2	3	6	1	1	5.5%
Chellis	23	13	17	20	33	14	2	23.5%
Degrizz	24	27	26	27	39	0	3	18.4%
Droo	38	1	2	50	23	3	0	16.2%
Illuminae	0	3	0	5	0	0	0	9.0%
Khieleh	63	26	45	40	30	0	1	5.3%
Nebellia	11	8	14	6	14	0	0	17.6%
Ozlo	6	11	31	1	12	1	0	5.1%
Salef	2	2	0	0	2	0	0	1.6%
Tiamatt	0	0	4	0	6	0	1	0.6%
Tomcovenant	101	35	68	90	89	0	12	23.1%
Tresfyre	9	9	10	8	7	0	0	13.1%
Valieria	3	1	5	2	4	5	0	18.0%
Vandyr	0	0	1	1	0	0	0	1.9%
Zipi	7	9	18	12	18	24	1	5.4%
Zippyd	6	2	2	3	2	1	0	3.0%
TOTAL	471	199	313	324	358	59	25	9.3%

First Shamans reincarnate themselves, then resurrect the others, a maneuver that can be performed only rarely. Paladins are a hybrid class, originally being warrior priests but also having the ability to perform other roles. A Paladin can perform a redemption spell on dead comrades, restoring them to life, at the cost of much of the magical mana substance, and this can be done only outside of combat. Soulstones are gathered from dying enemies by Warlocks, and can be used for resurrection as well, in a complex set of ways. I have never had the pleasure of being raised from death as a ghoul, but an advanced death knight avatar can do this, as much as one might prefer other means of resurrection.

The final column in Table 10.2 reports what fraction of the avatar's deaths were followed by all forms of resurrection listed, the remainder having been accomplished by the spirit at a graveyard or by running from a graveyard to one's corpse. The avatars with relatively high percentages clearly engage in team activities more of the time. The great diversity of methods of resurrection reflects the gameworld's strategy to keep players paying their monthly subscription fees for a long time. The diversity of classes of avatars encourages players to run multiple avatars, each of them for hundreds of hours, and different kinds of healers require different explanations for their healing abilities. The net result is a complex mythology about the supernatural with distinct stories for civilized priests, nature-oriented druids, and tribal shamans. This is a form of magical multiculturalism that accomplishes some of the same diversification functions as polytheism.

Costs and Benefits of Being Dead

Death in nearly all gameworlds described here has three main characteristics: it is temporary, costly, and couched within the distinctive mythos that makes one game different from another. For example, in *Dark Age of Camelot*, a somewhat Pagan concept sets the terms within which a player manages the costs, which all boil down to lost time, not only the period of the temporary death during which game progress cannot be achieved but also the potential loss of progress already achieved through the investment of time.

During life, characters may perform a ritual at a bindstone, where they will resurrect if they are killed. As they voyage across the world, for the sake of convenience they will perform this ritual at the local bindstone. An NPC named Mordren explained this to my main avatar, Glastonbury, as they stood before a ten-foot-tall stone carved with the image of a dragon and some runes. This particular stone fell to earth immediately after King Arthur's death, but others stand in most towns. Beside the stone was Brother Jeremiah, a healer, who can restore the resurrected character's constitution, at the cost of a few virtual coins, each of which had been earned by investing play time.

However, death costs the character valuable experience, which healers cannot restore. When Glastonbury died, he could regain lost experience by returning to the scene of his demise, where he would find his own tombstone marked with his name, which any passerby could read. Thus it was embarrassing as well as costly in experience to leave the tombstone. Kneeling in prayer at it, which could be dangerous if it were near enemies, as was often the case, would restore experience and erase shame.

One quest undertaken by Glastonbury, "Willing Sacrifice," connects resurrection directly to Christianity. Brother Codeth asks the good friar if he attends church regularly, a habit that is good for the soul. When Glastonbury answers that he does, Codeth praises his faithfulness and urges him to gather a group of friends, one of whom is willing to give his life, because the complex series of actions required to complete the quest includes the death of one member of the party.

Thus, it is possible for death to accomplish a goal, as well as to carry costs. Many quests in many games require the avatar either to reach a certain point deep within a dangerous area or to get to a heavily defended point and grab a virtual item. On occasion, it is just too costly to kill all the enemies there, so players confident in their understanding of the situation may rush in and achieve the goal, in full knowledge they will be killed before they can escape. Like the DAOC quest "Willing Sacrifice," some quests in other games require temporary death.

Nicholas Farepoynt, hero of the highly linear solo-player game *Daemonica*, repeatedly enters a half-dead state in which he can interrogate corpses in order to solve a series of murders. His story takes place in a small English village around the year 1350. Some time earlier he had fallen in love with a woman named Clarise, who was Beast Hunter and recruited him to her grim profession. During one of her voyages into death, she loses her grip on life, and he is left to confront unimaginable horrors entirely alone. In a world where demons abound and justice is rare, Beast Hunters roam in search of murderers, whom they torture to death. Often, the only source of information about their crimes is the corpse of the victim, but in the first case the corpse had already been cremated and thus was not available for interrogation. The local doctor explained to Farepoynt why the village was beset by horrors: "Sins, dear Sir. Everything that happens is God's will. Rotten plants, choking mist, animals behaving strangely. All this for our sins. What could be worse than God's punishment? There's no point in defending ourselves, we will all pay in the end."

The first corpse is that of the young undertaker of the town, who was executed for murdering the woman, yet who was innocent and lost his life in the mayor's rush to judgment. Farepoynt drugs a guard so he can steal the corpse from the gallows and take it to the basement of his small house, where he hangs it before preparing a flask of soulgreep. He had collected the herbs required to concoct this potion in the woods around the village: one devil's luck and two units each of gwynlock, watersleep, and tear of stone. In his diary, he later described the effect of drinking soulgreep: "My sight blurred and painful cramps were going through my body with stronger and stronger intensity. Then they ceased. And at this very moment, when my body was actually dying and one of the demons was already by my side waiting to tear out my soul and carry it to the realm of oblivion, I started to cry in the language of the creation, in Daemonica."

At the depths of his trance, Farepoynt is transported to the central room in the Temple of Sacrifices, where doorways are separated by artwork depicting murder by five means: strangulation, a weapon, fire, water, and poison. For each corpse he must interrogate, he enters the door beside the correct form of death and must answer a question about the case at each of three altars. The corpse of the undertaker then answers Farepoynt's questions, in return for a promise to cremate him on a funeral pyre ready for that purpose east of town. That general area also includes a cemetery and a monastery that play roles in the series of mysteries.

Daemonica reminds us of a very important fact of history: prior to the development of modern science, people possessed very limited means to learn the meaning of events, and they surmised that the dead had valuable knowledge that could be reclaimed through psychic mediums or other semi-supernatural methods. If science today is nearing a point of stagnation, especially in those sciences closest to human life, then ancient alternatives such as communication with ghosts may acquire renewed plausibility.

Death was a constant companion for Greenwix, my avatar in *Forsaken World*. A vampire belonging to the Kindred, she awakened after decades of dreamless slumber in her crypt. She immediately received a revelation, appropriate for the Virgo astrological sign operative at that moment: "The veiled face of the Goddess is stricken with great sorrow." Her own sign, however, was Libra, presenting a fine balance between life and death. She prayed a prayer of birth that moved the gods to bless her, and she prayed again every few minutes, sometimes receiving additional blessings. Her first gift from the gods was a blood drinker's tunic, which increased her defense by 23 points, and her store of mana by 95. Her first quest giver, Humar the Castellan of the Sanguine Circle, reminded her, "Even those who dwell in shadow have reason to fear the night."

As Greenwix explored a relatively small portion of *Forsaken World* on her way to level 25 of experience, she often drank blood from enemies to hasten their deaths, even as she used other skills and various weapons to kill them. Remarkably, given that she was a vampire, her primary weapon was a cross. *Forsaken World* is a Chinese game, but intentionally created for the international market, and so it draws on a good deal of European mythology, including Dracula-related notions of vampires. However, a cross is generally used to defeat a vampire in the movies, rather than by a vampire to defeat others. Greenwix's first cross weapon was a neophyte's crux, which bestowed an additional 114 points of health on her, as well as doing 87–100 points of damage to enemies each time she used it. The cross was huge, nearly as big as she was, and she wore it on her back, right-side up, presumably implying she was not a follower of Satan. Many of her early quests required visiting a graveyard, and her entire war-ravaged world is at death's door. Yet her Kindred race came into being through a magical attempt to overcome death:

> The beautiful demi-goddess Shylia, and the noble human Herghevid were the perfect couple in every way. Time however, worked against them. While Herghevid began to age, his ensuing death could not be accepted by Shylia. Therefore she sought a method to keep them together forever, and she found it with the "Mythic Embrace." Shylia performed the Mythic Embrace by pouring her blood, which contained the essence of life, into Herghevid's body, thereby giving him everlasting life. Their offspring were the first of the Kindred race.[7]

Dungeons and Dragons Online provides the most complete model of how death can be both costly and profitable. One region, called the Necropolis, contains a vast number of tombs, each of which is a dungeon associated with a quest. This is the ancient burial ground of Stormreach, so it contains the residue of many hopes and fears from the past. A sense of foreboding hovers in the air, although there really is no evidence that the dead are about to escape from their tombs and ravage the living city. Rather, in each quest Sagittarius is required to invade a tomb and typically put to death one or another monstrous being.

Players who were attempting to play for free did not have access to the Necropolis, whereas monthly-fee-paying "VIP" subscribers could enter at no additional cost. To explore the economic system of DDO, I ran Sagittarius through what is called a *premium account* in which I had to use points bought for dollars to buy adventure packs such as the one for Demon Sands, which cost $5.95. The Necropolis is the biggest of these, sold in four increasingly more advanced parts for $1.75, $2.45, $2.45, and $5.95. Given that completing all the quests takes scores of hours, the total of $12.60 is comparable to a one-month subscription and thus quite reasonable. The first three of these adventure packs involve tombs in the Lower Necropolis, and the fourth was added subsequently in a different instance called the Upper Necropolis.

A particular challenge for Sagittarius was that my research method required him to do all the quests solo, as I took thousands of screenshots and collected other data. DDO is designed for team play, however, and the designers provided a costly alternative for solo players. In the Market, an avatar can hire one NPC mercenary, called a *hireling*, paying virtual gold. But it is also possible to hire five of these secondary avatars using points, which can be bought inside the game for real dollars. Except when special sales are in effect, the lowest cost to buy a point is one US cent, when buying five thousand of them for $49.99. Most of the dungeons cannot be completed solo, and the main reward comes at the moment of completion, so there is good reason for players to team up. The only way to complete most missions solo is by the use of hirelings. Suppose a middle-ranked solo avatar nears the conclusion of a dungeon that will award many experience points and virtual coins, but dies. Without leaving the dungeon, the player can enter the DDO store, buy a magic cake to restore the avatar to life, and hire five mercenaries for the final battle, for just under five dollars.

Quests in the first three Necropolis adventure packs are organized as three books in *The Litany of the Dead*. Book 1 combined four parallel missions followed by a capstone, all based on the metaphor of blood: "Tomb of the Burning Heart," "Tomb of the Crimson Heart," "Tomb of the Immortal Heart," "Tomb of the Sanguine Heart," and "The Bloody Crypt." These dungeons tended to follow the standard computer game design of battling past many minor enemies, perhaps encountering secondary bosses, then battling the main boss of the dungeon at the end. For example, the DDO wiki describes the goal of the last of these: "Loremistress Jinna tasked you with the destruction of an ancient alchemist named Salasso. She warned you that his power is great and unless his heart is found and destroyed, he is truly immortal."[8] Reaching Salasso requires entering chambers and opening locks associated with each of the four tombs explored in the earlier quests.

Book 2 of *The Litany of the Dead* is oriented toward the metaphor of shadow, which can mean both the ambiguous realm between life and death and a world of illusion where some features of ordinary reality do not hold. It has the same structure as Book 1: "Tomb of the Shadow Guard," "Tomb of the Shadow King," "Tomb of the Shadow Knight," "Tomb of the Shadow Lord," and "The Shadow Crypt." The last of these is "a twisted game of darkness and shadow. North becomes South, East becomes West, nothing is as it seems."[9] The corridors that connect rooms of the Shadow Crypt do not adhere to conventional geometry, but go from door to door at random, making it very difficult to complete tasks in their proper order.

Book 3 concerns curses: "Tomb of the Blighted," "Tomb of the Forbidden," "Tomb of the Tormented," and "Tomb of the Unhallowed," culminating in "The Cursed Crypt." The curse in the first tomb is pollution of the environment. A fountain near the entrance provides vials of blessed water which can be used to open root barriers, opening a pathway to cleanse ten urns of blight and the fountains feeding three corrupted waterfalls that are preventing the team from entering the chamber where they must kill the mummy guardian. The Tomb of the Forbidden is cold, inhabited by ice monsters, and cursed by mysteries that freeze the warm blood of living creatures. In the four cardinal directions of the Tomb of the Unhallowed, four guardians must be summoned from another plane of existence called Dolurrh, then destroyed before their leader Amahte can be returned to the Realm of the Dead.

Sagittarius never reached the Cursed Crypt, because he was unable to complete the Tomb of the Tormented, a truly tormenting challenge. It consists of three main areas, each of which has a grating for a floor through which can be seen gigantic rats gnawing on corpses. The challenge is to get one rat from each area to crawl through a maze to the corpse of Akhom. Only when three are chewing on him does he awaken and become vulnerable to attack. The only way to guide the rats through the mazes is to drop chunks of rotten flesh to them through a series of openings in the floor. The source of the flesh is rotten corpses that become animated, which makes it possible to hack chunks of meat off them. They fall writhing on the floor, but become animated again after a few minutes. The three mazes are increasingly difficult, with doors and dangers that block or kill the rats.

While the Upper Necropolis contains the Black Mausoleum, most of the action takes place in a wilderness area called the Orchard of the Macabre, rather than in tombs. There lies the Desecrated Temple of Vol, into which a quest sent Sagittarius to battle vampires and find the high priest, hoping to enlist the aid of the followers of Vol against the Black Abbott, who had sealed them in the temple centuries before, and now loomed over the Necropolis from his Mausoleum. He had been one of the priests of the Lady Vol, before betraying her and beginning his evil march to become a god.

Sagittarius entered the temple in the company of his favorite NPC cleric, the Elf woman Fayden Maeleth. She is a follower of the Undying Court, and as he was examining the locks that prevented them from entering, she explained her faith to him: "Existence is a spiritual journey requiring far longer than a single lifetime. Only the Undying can ever truly learn what great wonders lie at its end." That insight eased the urgency of their mission, so they discussed many things, including the ancient faith that had built the temple. Sagittarius had often battled its believers, and heard them castigated as vampires, yet he had never seen them harm anyone who had left them in peace. He and Fayden decided they would remain in the temple and learn ancient wisdom from the Cult of Vol.

Memorials

This chapter noted that there are memorials for Gary Gygax and Dave Arneson, the creators of the original *Dungeons and Dragons* tabletop game, in *Dungeons and Dragons Online*. Chapter 6 began with a description of the Shrine of the Fallen Warrior in *World of Warcraft*, a memorial to an artist who died tragically young. *World of Warcraft* also contains the best-known living memorial in a game-world, Caylee Dak. The main WoW wiki explains: "Caylee Dak is a level 70 elite quest ender located in the Aldor Rise in Shattrath City. She was named after a 28 year old player named Dak Krause who died of leukemia on August 22, 2007. He was born March 10, 1979. The NPC model itself is an exact replica of 'Caylee,' Mr. Krause's character, bearing the same model and gear, as well as the same pet, Dusky, by his side."[10] Caylee Dak is the goal of a quest given to members of the Alliance in the garden at Stormwind Keep, by a little NPC girl named Alicia. She asks the player's avatar to deliver a poem to Caylee, because she herself is too young to visit Outland, where the huntress is adventuring. Caylee responds to the poem by bowing and giving a blessing. The poem is a slightly edited version of a popular verse written by Mary Elizabeth Frye, which expresses a pantheist view of death transcendence.[11] It begins:

> Do not stand at my grave and weep,
> I am not there, I do not sleep.
> I am in a thousand winds that blow,
> across Northrend's bright and shining snow.

Battleground Europe is remarkable for its virtual funerals. Also titled *World War II Online*, this gameworld was released in 2001 by Cornered Rat Software and constantly improved over the following years, showing remarkable endurance despite a somewhat small audience. It lacks predefined quests belonging to a fantasy story line, and a player cannot make any progress without directly battling against other players. All the avatars are male military personnel, who at any given moment are on either the Axis (German) or Allied (French and British) side, along the entire western front in the year 1940, and the action consists of campaigns lasting several weeks in which each side tries to capture territory belonging to the other. By general agreement, the political context of the actual Second World War is not discussed, and nothing related to the Nazis is depicted in this gameworld. What is depicted, with admirable detail and accuracy, is the weaponry. From each soldier's combat knife, up through rifles and machine guns, including artillery, tanks, and even a diversity of aircraft, players may experience the military technology of the era, almost as if they had gone back in a time machine to see the hardware in action with their own eyes. Many of the qualities a player might expect to find in an MMO are missing, yet their absence is more than made up for by the museum quality of the depiction of the artifacts of a particular time and place in the past.

War is about death. The avatars in the gameworld come back to life immediately, but not so the players who die in "real life." It is noteworthy that Cornered Rat adds the names of deceased players to a memorial in each virtual city, which as of September 5, 2010, totaled fifty-four of them.[12] One YouTube video begins, "Notre Dame Cathedral, Verdun, August 9th, 2003. In loving memory of Thomas 'Sdshill' Holt: We mourn the loss of a friend we all felt we knew so well. We will never forget you." Dozens of soldiers march into a church, then kneel down. A few moments later they march across the countryside, firing their guns into the air by way of salute for their fallen comrade, and then engage in playful acts of mayhem as Sdshill might have enjoyed were he still alive. The video ends with the poem "High Flight" by John Gillespie Magee, Jr., who actually died in World War II, which contains the familiar words quoted by President Reagan when he responded to the *Challenger* disaster: "I have slipped the surly bonds of Earth." With 45,023 views by September 9, 2012, this was one of the most seen *Battleground Europe* videos on YouTube.[13]

The person who posted the video, Wwiiolvideo, offered this comment: "This is a unique aspect of the online game Battleground Europe/WWIIOnline— when beloved players die in Real Life, players remember them with an online funeral service." Later, on a blog, he responded to a question about how he learned of the death:

> Generally speaking you have to know the family one way or another, likely fellow squad members. Sometimes a brother or son plays and they tell us. CRS is told, they officially check to see if it happened, and put the player's name on a monument (assuming the family does not object). In our case he had not been heard from in months so our squad leader contacted the family and found out he was gone. SDShill was a prominent member of a part of the WWIIOL forums known as Offtopic, or OT. He always had a gentle quip or a twist to throw onto a conversation that made everybody smile and sometimes think. It was why he was so beloved. So when it came to his funeral, rather then some stately activity like a gunline or a parade, it was decided to do wacky crazy stuff that he would enjoy, seeing his game compatriots goofing off. Really, perfect for him.[14]

The most famous gameworld funeral was held in *World of Warcraft* in 2006, on the Illidan Internet server, which was a PvP version of the gameworld that permitted members of one faction to attack members of the other, outside the low-level zones where players learn how to operate their avatars. Using the name Yanoa, a player posted a notice on a realm-related forum:

> On Tuesday of February 28th Illidan lost not only a good mage, but a good person. For those who knew her, Fayejin was one of the nicest people you could ever meet. On Tuesday she suffered from a stroke and passed away later that night. I'm making this post basically to inform everyone that might have knew her. Also tomorrow, at 5:30 server time March, 4th. We will have an in game memorial for her so that her friends can pay their respects. We will be having it at the Frostfire Hot Springs in Winterspring, because she loved to fish in the game (she liked the sound of the water, it was calming for her) and she loved snow. If you would like to come show your respects please do. Thanks everyone.[15]

The gameworld's wiki explained what happened next:

> One of the Horde guilds faced a devastating blow. An officer from this guild passed away in real life and, out of respect, the Horde posted on the Illidan forums that they would be holding an in game funeral for her at her favorite spot in the game, the hot springs of Winterspring. Being on the Illidan realm forums, Alliance also had access to view the thread. A guild called Serenity Now secretly organized a funeral crashing, to be video taped and shown across the world. Led by Azshira, all of Serenity Now stormed through the Timbermaw Cave into Winterspring, and fought with approximately 100 Horde who had showed up for the funeral service.[16]

The video was uploaded to YouTube on March 19, 2006, with the title "Serenity Now bombs a World of Warcraft funeral." By July 30, 2011, it had been viewed 5,079,285 times and 42,577 comments had been posted on its YouTube page.[17] Of those who rated the video, 17,327 liked it and 3,481 disliked it. A few who wrote comments were horrified at the desecration of the funeral. For example, one wrote that "raiding a memorial service is wrong. This was more for her parents than anything to show them she had a lot of support. They went to that area because the girl loved snow and loved fishing in that area. If you looked at the forum post you would see that they asked people not to attack their service." Others felt that the raid was entirely appropriate, because it was in harmony with the theme of *World of Warcraft*, and the deceased would have enjoyed the great furor. As of August 18, 2011, the Serenity Now guild was still alive, and still receiving complaints from players who disapproved of the attack.[18] The video is eight minutes long, which means that viewers could have played it for a total of as much as forty million minutes, which is almost exactly the life expectancy of a human being. Thus an entire human life was devoted to this memorial for a game player.

Worlds die as well. Prior to their destruction, I did my best to explore *Tabula Rasa* and *The Matrix Online*, documenting them as best I could through thousands of screenshots, and then publishing about them.[19] I did the research reported here on *Star Wars Galaxies* beginning at the end of 2008, and when I learned in mid-2011 that it was being shut down in a few months, I resumed research there and will report results in a subsequent publication. However, if people want to understand what these games were like, they can watch hundreds and even thousands of amateur YouTube videos taken within them, including pictures of special events or personal experiences in the last moments of their lives.

A very lonely world death is depicted in a *Tabula Rasa* video posted by iRacer-Matt, which begins with his avatar standing on a bridge before the entrance of a futuristic fortress, firing his gun at Thrax infantry, massed below. The location seems to be Foreas Base in the Corcordia Divide region of the planet Foreas. I know the place well, but I verified by checking my map of that area—a map of a place that no longer exists, if it ever did exist. iRacerMatt runs north through the force field that seals the entrance of the fortress against enemies, and chats with the avatar of another player, before climbing to the top of an inside wall, a place my avatar had stood many times because it provides an excellent view of the entire fort. A message flashes on the screen: "You have been disconnected from the server."[20]

Endtime videos by both Plukh and Thenesmaster begin in a PvP arena called C.E.L.L.A.R. (Coalition of Enlistees Likely Looking for Aggressive Retaliation), where a dozen players are battling each other in anticipation of doom.[21] This arena could be reached from multiple locations, so it was a logical meeting place for avatars who wished to share their deaths with others. CommanderGrog, who was one of the players using the German-language interface, posted a marvelous high-definition action video of groups of human avatars retaking a portion of New York City from the extraterrestrial invaders, before returning to a distant planet for the end of their entire universe.[22]

The hosting company did give *Tabula Rasa* a dignified death, allowing top-level avatars to return briefly to Earth and attack a stronghold of the Neph invaders. The location of this stronghold was Madison Square Park, and the introductory screen showed enough of Manhattan to reveal that prior to the Neph invasion Americans had completed restoration of the World Trade Center site over a decade after its high-tech terrorist destruction, but now the Freedom Tower stood over an entirely ruined city. A video posted by KevSniper shows the last second of the Manhattan battle, quoting the final transmission from Tabula Rasa: "As we return to Earth, our battle comes to an end. Thank you to all the fans who have supported us for the last few years! We hope you have enjoyed your journey through the galaxy and that the next worlds you visit will be filled with excitement and fun."[23]

Many videos of the final moments of *The Matrix Online* are set at the same virtual location, Mara Central. The one posted by blokenamedbob shows his avatar running past the huge church, ignoring it as *The Matrix* tended to ignore traditional Christianity, and rushing toward the monument that is the focal point for the neighborhood.[24] Called the Hypercube, it is a tall, red assembly of large squares, rather like picture frames. A hypercube, or tesseract, is a four-dimensional cube, conventionally depicted in three dimensions as one cube inside another, with their corresponding corners connected by lines. But this hypercube seems to be a monument to disintegration, and has no such logical structure. In May 2008, over a year before the end, the popular gamer blogsite MMORPG.com posted a screenshot of the top of this monument taken by Fickey, covered with perhaps as many as twenty bodies of dead avatars, with the church in the background, appropriately showing its messy trash containers.[25] What are dead bodies but just a form of garbage? In the video by blokenamedbob, about a hundred avatars assembled around the monument, and several began jumping up on one or another of its ledges, where they soon slump lifeless.

Like blokenamedbob, tsusai ended life in the Matrix near the Mara church, and, notably, both had open the part of the interface showing the names of all their buddies who were online at the moment.[26] Tsusai tussled with other avatars near the telephone booth where avatars always congregated at Mara, because it was a teleport point to everywhere else in this virtual city and was in an area entirely safe from the sinister Machines. Then she walked around the church, through the flock of pigeons always found beside it, neglecting to enter for prayer, and it is worth noting that the group tsusai belonged to was named the Devil's Advocates. Her life ended a few moments later at a local nightclub, where she and dozens of other avatars danced into oblivion. M1ke212's video is very brief, showing about two dozen avatars standing between the church and the monument, as a siren-like noise indicates that the lethal signal has been sent from the Internet server, and all fall dead.[27] S0NICShadow's video does take an avatar into the church, but only to have a fistfight with other avatars, before climbing the monument.[28]

Thundr's video shows a dozen avatars standing on a ledge of the monument, above dozens more on the pavement between the monument and the church. As they share the experience of doom, part of the soundtrack of the last *Matrix* movie plays in the background. It is the climactic song, called "Neodammerung"—a play on the main character's name, Neo, and the German term *Götterdämmerung*, meaning the twilight of the gods. A chorus sings words in Sanskrit, which purportedly translate into English as:

> From delusion lead me to truth
> From darkness lead me to light
> From death lead me to immortality.
>
> He who knows both knowledge and action,
> with action overcomes death and with
> knowledge reaches immortality.[29]

There is much to ponder here. Nobody connected to *The Matrix* seems to take Christianity seriously, although a few think Neo is the messiah. If so, he is a Buddhist or Hindu messiah. Avatars congregate around the Hypercube monument both because it was the landmark of the neighborhood where players always congregated and also because it represents the mathematical nature of reality in a computer-generated gameworld. For the neo-Buddhist perspective of *The Matrix*, in which the real world is every bit as much an illusion as the gameworlds, it is possible to imagine a technological substitute for religion.

First of all, a public digital library would need to be established, reviving *Tabula Rasa*, *The Matrix Online*, *Star Wars Galaxies*, and several others, and offering them free to everyone, just as public libraries do with books. There would be technical challenges, in part because the different worlds use different software systems, and legal or financial ones, because the companies that own the intellectual property for these worlds do not want them competing with their current products. Then it would be possible to resurrect deceased players in them via avatars, such as Caylee Dak. Either human volunteers would operate the memorial avatar, emulating the real person to the extent that they could, or an artificial intelligence agent could be constructed on the basis of detailed data about how the deceased person had played that avatar. The feasibility and desirability of this plan are topics for discussion at another time, but it suggests a possible reconceptualization in future decades that may consider religion to be wholly irrelevant to death.

Conclusion

The die is cast. In this chapter, this famous phrase might seem a bad pun: to *die* as a member of the role-playing *cast* of characters in a drama. But we should remember who said these marvelous words, and in what context. Julius Caesar spoke them when he took his army across the Rubicon River, thereby making him an enemy of the Roman government, a decision that would lead either to his death or to the death of the Republic. We do not know exactly which game of chance he had in mind, but dice like those used today did exist in ancient Rome, and Caesar was clearly analyzing the most momentous historical moment of his civilization as a move in a game. In the gameworlds described in this book, death similarly is but one move in a wider game.

Upon hearing of the death of a politician renowned for his gaming tactics, Talleyrand is supposed to have said, "I wonder what he meant by that." Or, in a different telling of the story, it was said about Talleyrand himself. What death means has been a central motivation for religions since the beginnings of time, and gameworlds seem fascinated by it. For avatars, it is usually just a temporary setback, and for undead avatars and NPCs it is the defining characteristic of their lives. However, games die, too, and it is not inconceivable that a nuclear war or asteroid impact would kill our world as well. This possibility, however remote, raises the question of whether all of human life is but one random roll of cosmic dice.

11 QUESTS

Religion is a quest for meaning, and gameworlds mirror this fact by being assemblies of quests. With the possible exception of some of the more philosophical branches of Buddhism, religions assert that human life and the wider universe both have meaning, and indeed share the same meaning. The most familiar way in which religion does this is to assert that God gives the universe purpose, by establishing a plan or a set of laws, or simply by creating the universe as an act of will. If many gods exist, then the universe has multiple purposes, often at variance with each other, because each god provides meaning in one or another sector of reality. However, if no gods exist, then the universe itself lacks meaning. We may, if we struggle mightily, invest meaning in the universe, acting as the feeblest of gods ourselves, just as we may invest meaning in a gameworld.

Physicists, astronomers, and cosmologists are very far from having a unified theory of everything, but it is possible to discern two competing perspectives, which have much in common and seek to explain the same facts, but which differ on one essential point. The most widely held view, currently associated with so-called string theory, asserts that there is only one rigorous mathematical description of the universe, and the universe logically must follow that pattern.[1] In terms of practical research and grand theorizing, the challenge is how to explain the precise quantitative relationships between the forces of nature and other parameters that can be observed empirically. Perhaps, once the full truth is known, it will be possible to derive the features of the universe logically from one undeniable set of axioms, as number theory seeks to prove facts about the distribution of prime numbers on the basis of inescapable definitions of number.

The second perspective is sometimes called the *anthropic principle*, because it gives intelligent observers such as human beings a key epistemological role to play. This theory employs logic, but asserts it is not central to the mystery of existence. An infinite variety of universes is logically possible having an unlimited diversity of parameters and mathematical relationships between them. However, only in one particular universe would human beings exactly like ourselves evolve and come to ask why the "laws of nature" were so conducive to their existence. Here, because it connects well to both religion and games, I will draw on my own work on the anthropic principle, originally communicated in a talk given at the annual meetings of the American Sociological Association, New York City, August 20, 1996. It was subsequently presented to participants at two meetings: Shared Future: The Prospects of Revolution (Asian Forum Japan, Tokyo, Japan, September 2–6, 1996) and Nonlinear Dynamics in the Behavioral and Social Sciences (National Research Council, Washington, DC, November 15–16, 1996), then published as a book chapter in 1997.[2]

Humans have long wondered why the world is conducive to human life, but at some point in history somebody first articulated the question in a logical manner, considering alternative hypotheses rather than operating within a traditional religious faith. It seems possible this occurred in ancient Greece, so I call that hypothetical moment in time the *omicron point*, after one of the letters in the middle of the Greek alphabet, dividing the first half of human intellectual history from the second half. The Catholic priest and scientist Pierre Teilhard de Chardin liked to speak of the goal for humanity—perhaps identical with God—as the *omega point*.[3] From the standpoint of an English-speaker, omicron (little "o") and omega (big "o") are essentially the same letter, merely holding very different positions in the alphabet and in the words where they convey meaning. It is worth remembering that the "one iota of difference" of this expression is the Greek letter "i," a difference that led to thousands of deaths. Homoousians and homoiousians of early Christian history slaughtered each other over this iota, because the homoousians believed that Christ was the same as God, whereas the homoiousians believed he was only similar. Now, we can quip, a similar bloody battle looms between anthropists who prefer omicron and monotheists who prefer omega.

Thales of Miletus, who may have predicted the solar eclipse on May 28, 585 BC, is widely regarded as the first great Greek scientist-philosopher-mathematician, so it is conceivable that he or others of the Ionian school first privately asked the pivotal question, which would place the omicron point about 2,600 years ago.[4] Two centuries later, *The Laws* by Plato asked, "How do we know the Gods exist? Why, to begin with, think of the earth, and sun, and planets, and everything! And the wonderful and beautiful order of the seasons with its distinctions of years and months!"[5] This is the *argument from design*, which seeks to derive God's existence from the regularity of the universe, but in most formulations chiefly from the fact that nature is conducive for human existence.

One could argue that the pivotal question was not well and fully asked until the anthropic answer had also been formulated, which would place the omicron point near the middle of the twentieth century. Apparently some classical Greek philosophers—such as Empedocles, Anaxagoras, and Democritus—possessed ideas that potentially could lead to the anthropic insight. Their concepts of atoms, biological evolution by competition, mechanistic causation of physical processes, and a universe governed by the conjunction of "nature and chance" presage modern thought but do not quite achieve it.[6] Early in the twentieth century, biochemist and sociologist Lawrence Henderson published *The Fitness of the Environment* (1913) and *The Order of Nature* (1917), offering a detailed chemical analysis to support the view that the properties of hydrogen, oxygen, carbon, and other elements are so improbably well suited for the evolution of life that no mere "mechanism" can be responsible, and the universe shows the hand of "teleology," or God.[7] But this update of the argument from design came just when physicists were beginning to raise very serious questions about the nature of atoms, and astronomers were recognizing that the universe was vastly larger than anyone had previously imagined.

There are eight or nine planets in the solar system, give or take Pluto, but only one of them is capable of supporting intelligent life. As of January 15, 2012, the online *Extrasolar Planets Encyclopaedia* reported that the existence of 725 planets had been confirmed outside the solar system, yet at best only a half dozen of them had orbits that might put them in the temperature range where life could evolve.[8] However, this is not a random sample, because it is easier to detect extrasolar planets that are either large or unusually close to their stars, or both. We have no idea what a proper random sample of planets would tell us, but given all the mass locked in stars and other objects, the amount of the mass in the universe consisting of biological molecules is an absolutely infinitesimal fraction of the total. Thus, we are an exceedingly rare event, even before considering the possibility of other regions of reality where Henderson's criteria are not met.

In a 1986 book presenting the anthropic principle, John D. Barrow and Frank J. Tipler note that if the characteristics of certain isotopes of beryllium, carbon, and oxygen were quantitatively only slightly different than they are, the stars would not have produced sufficient carbon, upon which life depends.[9] If the gravitational constant were slightly different from its actual value, all stars would have been red dwarfs incapable of warming planets sufficiently for life, or they would all have been blue and too short-lasting for life to evolve.[10] Apparently, life depends upon an exceedingly improbable concatenation of coincidences in the magnitudes of various physical constants.[11]

Improbabilities can be countered by large numbers of cases. Physical constants appear to be uniform throughout the observed universe, but cosmologists have proposed a number of models in which the constants of nature would vary, although over larger scales than we can currently observe. In 1981, Allan Guth proposed that the universe could contain fully 10^{83} separate regions that are causally disconnected.[12] Each region is a volume of space small enough that light could have crossed it since it came into existence, and thus that region shares a uniform set of physical constants or laws of nature. Two causally disconnected regions would have always been sufficiently separated that light from one never had time to reach the other, and their physical constants are different. This large number of separate domains increases the chance that one of them will have physical constants conducive to the evolution of life. Guth's particular theory postulates that this multiplicity of disconnected regions arose during an early inflationary period of the existence of the cosmos, when expansion after the "Big Bang" was unusually rapid. Since Guth wrote, other models have been proposed, including the idea that universes give birth to many additional Big Bangs within them, producing daughter universes that have some but not all of the same properties, allowing evolution by natural selection to occur on the level of entire universes.[13]

However, recent evidence that the rate of expansion of the universe may actually be increasing raises questions about all theories that assume the rate is slowing from an earlier very rapid rate. Furthermore, the traditional, popular theory of probability may be naive in conceptualizing chance as random selection of one case from a collection of varied cases. There is an alternative mathematical and philosophical conception called *Bayesian probability* after an early proponent of it, Thomas Bayes (1702–1761).[14] It starts from the perspective of a human being who seeks to make predictions, but who lacks complete knowledge. Thus it does not necessarily assume that a probability distribution somehow exists outside the human mind, in the real world. Rather, it treats the notion that chance selects among alternatives merely as a convenience in making calculations, not a description of how the universe functions.

Whatever the fundamental mechanisms, the anthropic principle notes that at one time and place—perhaps only one, and perhaps others do not really exist—conditions were propitious for the evolution of intelligent life. Cultural evolution leads to the omicron point. As a metaphor, we can say that the purpose of the universe is to get to the moment when one person asks—with full consciousness of the meaning of the question—what the purpose of the universe is. The religious answer is: to serve God's will. The anthropic answer is: to ask the question. Human life is a quest for meaning. *Quest is question writ small.*

Social scientists almost never consider the lessons of cosmology, yet a remarkable insight relevant to gameworlds leaps up if we make that connection. Just as there are no physical laws other than those that lead to the omicron point, there are no laws of human social behavior other than those needed to produce the particular society that first asks the question. It happens that my chief mentor in Harvard graduate school, sociologist George Homans, believed there were no undiscovered social laws, and thus doubted that forms of society much different from the past were possible.[15] If the society that achieved omicron really was ancient Greece, then any social evolution beyond warring city-states is unstable. Lo and behold! That is the kind of society depicted in *World of Warcraft* and many other fantasy gameworlds. Perhaps the coming Dark Age, after the fall of our civilization, will be a return to normality.

Is the universe real? This question connects directly to whether gameworlds are real. Both are real, if humans invest them with meaning.[16] To be sure, if we fail to eat, we starve to death and can no longer play games. If we fail to build families and reproduce biologically, then society dies, and there will be no more games. Yet much of "real world" society goes far beyond survival and reproduction, so it could be said that computer games and virtual worlds are segments of the large portion of our culture that is not really real, but significant nonetheless.

At the same time that elements of the modern anthropic principle were being developed, many scientists considered whether any external force was required to bring the universe into existence. If the net sum of all forces in the universe— positive versus negative—is zero, no work is required to bring it into existence. Within that universe, the law of conservation of mass and energy may hold.[17] Some postulate that the cosmos is a chaotic ensemble of universes, varying without limit along all relevant dimensions, but if they are separate from each other in the sense that light from one cannot reach another, then they do not individually exist in any objective sense.[18] Each is real only to its intelligent inhabitants, if any exist within it.

Gameworlds are not very different. Avatars cannot travel from one to another. They become psychologically real to people who dwell within them. The player, of course, can travel from one to another, but cannot transfer goal-directed accomplishments across the boundaries between realities. The creators of the gameworlds are like gods. Indeed, in the *World of Warcraft* mythos the planet Azeroth was created by Titans, who represent the game developers. Many of the most successful gameworlds have a complete backstory that confers overall meaning, as well as meaningful stories in all the quests. We speak of "playing a game," with the implication that play differs from work in that it lack goals. Yet the gameworlds are complex systems of goals.

One of the most admired books about computer development, *The Soul of a New Machine* by Tracy Kidder, offers a concept that links goals to play in the context of information technology.[19] It is a study of how a team of people at the Data General Corporation developed a new minicomputer that was completed in 1980. The company was in furious competition with others, and the work schedule the team was forced to follow was nearly suicidal. However, their level of motivation and energy was extremely high, despite the fact they could not expect any success they achieved to be permanent, as their competitors would already be working furiously to develop the next generation of computers. Kidder explained that their intense activity was *playing pinball*. In an arcade game like pinball, the reward for winning is being able to play the next game.

The question becomes: Who determines the goals? In gamer language: Who is the quest giver? Comparison of two gameworlds can illustrate the possible answers: *Pirates of the Burning Sea* and *Tabula Rasa*. In the New Paradigm of the sociology of religion, human action is goal-directed, operating through time from the past to the future. Thus it is apt that the first of these two gameworlds is set in the past, the second in the future, and that both frame challenges we face today. Coincidentally, the maximum experience level in both MMOs was 50, so I took an avatar all the way to that level to make sure I gained all the information needed to understand the full meaning of a life in those environments. Both contain many references to religion, yet unlike most other games considered here, nothing supernatural ever happens in either of them. Religion is a motivating force that has implications for the material world experienced by humans, and people may invest secular institutions such as science with some of their religious hopes. But there is no direct evidence that gods exist in either of these virtual worlds.

Questing in the Past

Consuelo Seoane voyaged to the Caribbean in 1720, as an early career officer of the Spanish navy, in *Pirates of the Burning Sea*.[20] His primary sense of purpose came from his duty to Spain and King Philip IV, as filtered through the naval bureaucracy and delivered to him in the form of direct orders. As captain of a military vessel he had considerable freedom to chart his own course, however, especially in the context of a sea contested by the British and French, as well as by bands of pirates operating from remote islands like the Bahamas. For example, from time to time the waters near one or another port became the scene of chaotic battles, without benefit of declaration of war, and there was always the possibility he would encounter a hostile enemy who gave him no options beyond fight or surrender. Con personally disliked chaos, preferring any conflict to be legally sanctioned, so he sought well-defined missions that could give clear meaning to his life. At times, when he had free time, he might accept a task for a civilian, but at first he made no attempt to create a personal life for himself.

Con was neither more nor less religious than the typical Spanish officer, and he left matters of the spirit to the priests and missionaries. As a Spaniard, he held a particular animosity toward the British, which was only increased by the fact that their monarch was a Protestant, while his was a Catholic. If the truth must be known, he experienced some discomfort with the fact that church and state were two largely separate systems of authority that combined in the person of the king but sometimes contradicted each other. He tried not to think about the fact that Pope Clement XI was an Italian, whose original name, Albani, came from the fact his family had originated in Albania. Should not the pope of Spain be a Spaniard? Indeed, was there not a contradiction in the fact that the detested French had the same pope as his own nation did? He did not take much solace from the fact they all were Christians, nor did he initially ponder the fact that much of the world was not Christian, such as the many Islamic nations.

The first action he experienced was defending an outpost, aptly named Diablo Shore, against pirates, first with his sword and then with a ship. As the battle ended successfully, he was horrified to see that the commander of the fort, Captain Tristan Dragón, was mortally wounded. Con offered to seek a priest who could perform last rites, but Dragón exclaimed, "No! There is no time. God will have to accept me as I am, for I must tell you of the map." Dragón gave Con a mysterious map, told him to go to Vera Cruz to seek its significance, then expired. In so doing, he gave Con a quest series having to do with the international competition for the resources of the burning sea, and thus giving Con's life both direction and significance.

In *Pirates of the Burning Sea*, the Spanish hold three separated territories: Cuba, Venezuela, and Mexico, including the seaport named Vera Cruz, or "true cross," by Hernán Cortés when he discovered the place on Good Friday in 1519. As soon as he landed there, Con acquired a set of additional quests that would establish him in the local society: helping the harbormaster with local defense, meeting the town magistrate, strengthening his seamanship with a naval trainer, visiting the auction house to start building up a bank account, and speaking with the town crier to learn about a host of other opportunities. In the tavern he asked Silvestre Salvador, one of Dragón's former shipmates, about the map. The man explained that Dragón had sailed to a distant trading post, where he bought the map for a great price: "The captain never told us exactly what our mission was. In fact, he was quite secretive about it." This left Con very uncertain what if any mission he was on concerning the map, so he accepted many short-term quests from the magistrate and other quest givers, to build his experience and resources, to be ready for whatever might come next.

Some quests are simple and straightforward, and end quickly. For example, at experience level 16, Con met Father Padillo, the priest of Campeche in the Yucatán, who was worried about the souls of some swamp dwellers who were behaving like maniacs. Rumors said they were "the spawn of the Devil himself," but the priest suspected this was just a superstition. As Con left to investigate, Padillo said, "Bless you, my child, Go with God, and let Him be the light that guides you back home." After discovering that these demons were just violent psychotics, and after being forced to kill a few of them in sword fights, Con did indeed return safely, without any visible light beaming from above to illuminate his path. While happy to hear there was nothing magical about the swamp people, the priest was not quite ready to abandon the Devil theory: "The Devil, like Our Lord, works in mysterious ways; just because you saw no horns or tails does not mean this was not the Devil's work. Yet I suspected it would be something like this. There are so many lost souls in the New World, and the evil one enjoys toying with them." Despite its swift conclusion, this quest suggests that multiple meanings may be attached to any human behavior. A quack doctor, Bernardino Patudo, suggested that the insane behavior of the maniacs was the result of mercury poisoning from a medicine Patudo had prescribed for many of the swamp dwellers.

Other quests are extended explorations in order to uncover new quests and to learn the wider meaning of a long-term mission—what is often called a *quest arc* or a *story arc*. Perhaps indiscreetly, Con asked several people about the mysterious map, and a rich man named Rafael Alvarez recognized its strange symbols as the secret language of the Knights Templar: "After Pope Clement V disbanded the Templars, their riches were claimed by the avaricious Kings of Europe. However, some believe that their greatest wealth was hidden away, never to be seen again." Alvarez then became Con's advisor, as Con undertook quests to learn more about the map. Being an honest man himself, and being accustomed to respecting aristocrats, Con did not at first suspect that Alvarez was manipulating him. Only at their dénouement did Con learn that the treasure map led to something far more valuable than gold, and that there was writing in a second language on it. Alvarez exclaimed: "It is Arabic, fool. I wish you luck finding anyone in the Caribbean who knows it, besides me. Unless you happen to meet a Barbary Pirate five thousand miles off course!" Search for the meaning of the map continues through several more quests, as the junction of Templar hieroglyphics with Arabic letters suggests, with esoteric religious significance. The goal was not gold but the Philosopher's Stone, not because it really could work magic, but because the quest givers believed it could.

A second major quest arc began with strange rumors that corsairs of unknown origins were attacking merchant ships. The meaning of *corsair* is open to debate, depending upon the political theory one happens to hold. To some, they were pirates, pure and simple, criminals who had no right to attack their innocent victims. A different theory says they were *privateers*, not pirates, a legalistic distinction because privateers hold letters of marque and reprisal from a recognized nation, allowing them to attack ships belonging to a hostile nation. At this point in history, European seafaring nations were in a constant state of quasi-war, sometimes erupting into open hostilities but also conducted covertly and through agents like the privateers. Con discovered that the particular corsairs in his case were the North African privateers called Barbary pirates, thus Muslim ships preying upon Christian ships. To be sure, the Barbary pirates were a very real and significant part of world history for centuries, but the Caribbean was rather beyond their usual area of action. Given his knowledge of Spanish history, Con was very aware of the Moorish occupation of Spain centuries before, and identified with the Crusaders in the interminable conflict between Christendom and Islam. Then his attitude changed when he actually met some of these Barbary Corsairs.

At experience level 27 he seized the Corsair flagship and met Rihana, niece of the Corsair leader, Ibrahim. Despite the fact that she was a Muslim, and her skin was much darker than his, she was the most beautiful woman he had ever seen. His intuition correctly told him that she was intelligent and possessed a remarkable personality. At this turning point, *Pirates of the Burning Sea* actually gave Con a choice concerning which one of six North Africans to love. Three of them were women: Aliah, Malika, and Rihana. Three of them were men: Abdul-Hakim, Rashid, and Tariq. Not infrequently, complex quests in sophisticated games allow the player to complete a mission in different ways, with more or less difference in the outcome. Here the choice partly concerns gender, between three female and three male potential lovers. Of course, the NPCs do not have either XX or XY chromosome pairs, and the gameworld provides no option to produce children. The NPCs are just pixels on the screen, lines of codes in the computer program, and a few bytes of data concerning a small number of variables. Like most other popular MMOs, *Pirates of the Burning Sea* has no gender bias, so both avatars and NPCs who are Spanish naval officers may be either male or female. This is historically inaccurate, of course, but equally hospitable to players of either gender, and it sets the stage for relations between avatars and NPCs that would have been considered unconventional in the year 1720.

One choice that was not given to Con was to fall in love with a Christian. Whatever his or her gender, Con's beloved would be Muslim. Suddenly, when he fell for Rihana, Con's duty to the king of Spain was balanced by love for an enemy of Spain. Now, within the constraints set by fate, he would begin to assign himself personal quests, which over time might bring him and Rihana together. When humans adopt new life goals, they also adopt new conceptions of life, and new perspectives produce new motives. The creators of this historical gameworld were quite aware that the Barbary pirates were not active in the Caribbean, but they used this inaccuracy to give the player a new insight: the Barbary pirates were not pirates. Uncle Ibrahim was not a crude buccaneer but an educated ambassador of Dey Muhammad ben Hassan of Algiers, on a special mission but also seeking more civilized relations with the European powers in their colonization of the New World.

Con saw Rihana again when he had reached level 43, inside a cave that was the headquarters of a group of Barbary Corsairs at Grand Turk Island, believed by some to be the first part of the Americas discovered by Columbus. He began doing quests for the Corsairs, while also seeking the Philosopher's Stone, thereby blending the map quest arc with the Barbary quest arc. At level 45 he married Rihana and they set up a splendid home inside the elegantly refitted hull of a ship. For a while he continued to undertake quests, building up considerable wealth, a sterling reputation, and a fleet of ships owned by him personally rather than by the Spanish Navy. Finally, at level 50 he retired to live in comfort with Rihana. Uncle Ibrahim gave them a splendid North African yacht, an Arcadia model Mastercraft Xebec that Con named the *Rihana*, capable of a speed of 16 knots, when they vacationed far across the Burning Sea.

At a high level of organization, *Pirates of the Burning Sea* is a historical novel in three chapters, personalized to fit the nation and name of the avatar, and placed in a rather accurate historical setting.[21] The early levels are "Chapter One: Captain Seoane and the Map Of Destiny!" Meeting Rihana and the circumstances around this fateful encounter are "Chapter Two: Captain Seoane and the Pirates of Barbary!" The advanced levels, when Con interacts repeatedly with Rihana and other Algerians, are "Chapter Three: Captain Seoane and the House of Solomon!" At the end, Con gains Rihana for himself, and gives the Philosopher's Stone to Spain, thus satisfying his personal desires as well as his societal duty. Along the way, he completes a very large number of lesser quests, many of them unrelated to others but some connected into short arcs, all in some way reflecting the geographic and historical environment, including relations between social groups such as the competing colonial nations. Thus, *Pirates of the Burning Sea* illustrates beautifully how quests give significance to life by serving a range of human motives and by fitting together into a larger structure of meaning. Religion is part of each of the cultures, and many of the quests concern esoteric religious groups, but nothing supernatural exists in this world. Consideration of Spain's history after 1720 indicates that possession of the Philosopher's Stone was of no value to this sinking nation.

Questing in the Future

Tabula Rasa takes place on two distant planets, about four hundred years after the action of *Pirates of the Burning Sea*. A similarity is that in both the avatar is exploring new territory during an age of discovery, but a big difference is that the humans in *Tabula Rasa* are not seeking their fortunes but fleeing an invasion that seized their home planet, Earth. Thus the starting point for any success achieved by an avatar is a monumental defeat suffered by the avatar's entire species. There is a connection to religion, because the invaders were the Bane army, a collection of aliens enslaved in earlier wars, commanded by the Neph, who were the Nephilim mentioned twice in the Hebrew Bible, rendered as giants in the King James Version:

> There were giants in the earth in those days; and also after that, when the sons of God came in unto the daughters of men, and they bare children to them, the same became mighty men which were of old, men of renown. (Genesis 6:4)
>
> And there we saw the giants, the sons of Anak, which come of the giants: and we were in our own sight as grasshoppers, and so we were in their sight. (Numbers 13:33)

In *Tabula Rasa*, the mysterious Neph are not giants, nor are they supernatural in origin. Rather, they are a faction of an ancient and technologically advanced extraterrestrial civilization, in conflict with the opposing faction, the Eloh. This name comes from *elohim*, a Hebrew word for God or gods, but again in *Tabula Rasa* it refers to ancient extraterrestrials, so advanced that they would seem like gods to primitive humans. Here, the game adopts a major twentieth-century myth, which can be traced back centuries in European thinking to the works of Emmanuel Swedenborg or even earlier, that conflates gods with extraterrestrials. The popular books of Erich von Däniken, starting with *Chariots of the Gods*, argued that ancient peoples mistook extraterrestrial visitors for gods, especially when they gave humanity new knowledge in an effort to raise the cultural level of our species.[22] The flying-saucer craze suggested that aliens might be visiting our planet even today, and could possibly be encouraged to help a few of us advance to higher levels of intellectual and spiritual advancement. A number of groups arose, often described as religious cults but also oriented toward the mythologies of science, that considered extraterrestrials to be ascended masters who could teach much to individual Earthlings who happened to be especially sensitive to spiritual nuances and not constrained by faith in conventional religion.

Tabula Rasa ignores all the cultic connotations of flying saucers, and postulates that an ancient galactic civilization actually exists, whose scientific knowledge is so far beyond our own as to seem supernatural. The famous Third Law proposed by science-fiction writer Arthur C. Clarke states: "Any sufficiently advanced technology is indistinguishable from magic."[23] The Eloh have placed fragments of their scientific knowledge in shrines across the universe, and the chief story arc for an avatar is finding those shrines, learning how to use the knowledge to gain ever more advanced technological powers, and eventually be ready to defeat the Neph and liberate the Earth.

Each of the Eloh shrines is in a remote location and contains a Logos symbol, a hieroglyph that communicates one truth that had been discovered by the Eloh, comparable in some ways to a symbol representing a chemical element, which can be combined with others to produce more complex structures of knowledge and thus power. These Logos symbols are collected in the avatar's *tabula*, or tablet, and *tabula rasa* is a Latin expression referring to a clean slate on which wisdom can be written. Essentially every well-designed gameworld begins with a tutorial, a relatively nondemanding part of the world in which a new player learns how to handle the computer interface and the most basic rules for avatar behavior. On the level of ideas, well beyond gameplay, *Tabula Rasa* was educational, the equivalent of a philosophy college.

William Bridgebain awoke to find himself in a small military enclave on the planet Foreas, lacking specialist training and rather thoroughly disoriented. Presumably, he had been an ordinary citizen back on Earth, who was lucky to escape during the Neph cataclysm, and now had no choice but to take up arms against the vastly more powerful enemy. Since I crafted his character to reflect that of my grandfather, who was a surgeon and medical researcher in New York City, I naturally imagined his goals were to increase his medical knowledge and defeat the Bane army so he could return home. This meant I planned one aspect of his future life at the very beginning, setting my own goal for him in his advancement from level 1 to 50 of experience, gaining specific professional skills.

MMOs differ greatly in how specialization is handled, but *Tabula Rasa*'s system was unique. Every character began as a *recruit* in the army of the Allied Free Sentients, and at level 5 had a choice between becoming a soldier and seeking a life of action or a *specialist* who would gain technological skills. William Bridgebain became a specialist, and then at level 15 had to decide between becoming a *sapper*, who would deal with machinery of war, or a *biotechnician*. He became a biotechnician, and at level 30 decided to become an *exobiologist* rather than a *medic*, in keeping with my grandfather's scientific pretensions rather than his medical practice. Each recruit receives information about these alternatives in *Welcome to the AFS: Allied Free Sentients Official Field Manual*, which explains: "Exobiologists expand their biotech foundation into a new field of study. Rather than mastering group-support abilities, these troops turn enemies against themselves. No other AFS troops have as many methods for creating allies at their disposal; exobiologists can summon assistants, create allies from enemy corpses, and even tactically clone themselves."[24]

The really novel feature of the system is that at every decision point, the player could save a clone, who then could serve as a second avatar taking the other career path. I had planned to create an engineer as my second avatar, which was one of the level 30 options after taking the sapper path at level 15. Engineers can create traps to snare enemies, automatic turrets that fire guns, and enhancements to the armor of fellow AFS soldiers. However, the technology I really wanted to explore was robotics, which could add a variety of semiautonomous artificially intelligent warriors to the battlefield. I was prevented from exploring this alternative technological course by the termination of the gameworld, described in the previous chapter and reported from Bridgebain's perspective at the end of this section.

At level 3, after completing brief military missions, Bridgebain was informed that he was a receptive, having the potential to gain Logos Information that could give him powers other soldiers lacked, and was ordered to find his way past Bane adversaries to Luna Cave for his first contact with Eloh. Most soldiers in the AFS are not receptives, because they are NPCs, lacking the capability for insight that real humans possess, and every player was a receptive. In the cave, an Eloh spoke to him, but it was neither a biological organism nor a god, but a technology-generated hologram. His first Logos, which immediately went in his tabula, was a hieroglyphic of a lightning bolt, representing power.

Each of the two planets in *Tabula Rasa* had multiple continents and zones within them. In the starter zone on Foreas, called Wilderness, Bridgebain ultimately found eighteen Logos symbols: *area, around, attack, chaos, damage, enemy, enhance, feeling, future, heal, here, mind, movement, power, projectile, self, time,* and *trap.* When he started, the *future* Logos was very much in his future, and he did not gain it until level 40, after he had collected many others on both planets. Some shrines were deep in caverns and secured behind locked gates that not could be opened unless his tabula already carried certain other symbols. For example, to get *here* he needed already to have *mind* and *power,* the two logical prerequisites for opening a locked door for which concepts were the key. When he wanted his clone to join him, he needed four Logos symbols that spelled a sentence: "*I friend summon here.*" But to unlock the portal to the shrine that gave him *summon,* he needed already to have *friend, star, life, enlighten,* and *here.*

Tabula Rasa offered many quests beyond the main Logos arc, some of them fitting together into lesser arcs having their own meaning, but as is true for other high-quality games, they share the quality of exploration. Once a set of quests in one location has been completed, the game needs to send the player on to a new area, and the typical mechanism is a *delivery quest.* In these, the avatar takes something from a quest giver in one place and brings it to a quest receiver in another place, or does a round-trip from a quest giver to an area where a resource can be obtained, ending by delivering it back to the quest giver. Within an area, the player needs to become familiar with the terrain and the challenges that lie within it, which often means learning how to battle a new kind of enemy and how to find paths around physical barriers.

Some medium-quality games send the avatar back into the same dangerous territory two, three, or more times, with a different goal each time. This saves the game maker the effort of creating many new environments, but it also gives the player the satisfying experience of returning to an area after having learned about it, thus enjoying the benefit of what had been learned the previous time. *Tabula Rasa* did not use that repetitious strategy much, because its emphasis was on learning new things, including many philosophical insights about human existence.

There are many ways to interpret the conflict between the Eloh and the Neph, but one of the most fruitful concerns the need for technological progress to be accompanied by the development of wisdom. A student should learn not merely to gain power but to become transformed. The Neph use their incomplete knowledge of the Logos to achieve short-sighted, selfish goals. Perhaps the last thing the Eloh learned, in their own grand quest to comprehend the universe, was that it is wrong to give information to creatures who have not yet achieved the wisdom to integrate that information into an ethical system. Thus, there are two reasons why the Logos shrines are strewn across multiple planets, primarily in remote locations.

First, there is *gameplay*. Complex games are costly, and many MMOs require subscription payments as well as the original purchase of the game, so they must provide players with hundreds of hours of action. Ascending up a series of experience levels and skill ladders takes time, most of which is spent completing minor missions and traveling across a wide landscaped blocked by enemies who must be gradually destroyed. Games that have serious story arcs insert secondary quest arcs and unrelated activities to slow down completion of the main story. Thus, the wide distances separating most Eloh shrines are a strategy of gameplay design, which both delays the conclusion and provides a connective structure to hold together all the miscellaneous activities that are not parts of the story arc. To get to a remote Eloh shrine requires an avatar to have achieved a high enough level of general experience to be able to defeat the enemies that stand as barriers across the route to the shrine. Bridgebain could not gain the very last Logos until he had reached the level cap at 50. Since narratives of meaningful human action always tell stories of surmounting barriers to achieve goals, this game design strategy feels quite satisfying to players.

Second, there is *education*. Having more of a message than most games, *Tabula Rasa* needed many opportunities to teach lessons. Quite apart from their function as repositories for Logos elements, the two planets, Foreas and Arieki, were lessons in themselves. Foreas was rather earthlike, with lush plant growth and many animals, some of which were not especially dangerous. Arieki was far more alien, barren, and intersected by lava flows. Thus, Foreas was green, Arieki was red, and together they were a sermon about preservation of Earth's environment. Each of the two planets, in turn, was home to two other intelligent groups with which members of the AFS could interact.

The two groups on Foreas, the Foreans and the Cormans, were both friendly to the avatars who interacted with them, and both themselves were refugees. The Foreans had come to Foreas, and named it after themselves, after their unchecked use of technology had destroyed the environment of their home world. Now they had renounced technological progress, had become extremely religious, and sought to live in harmony with nature. At the end of one quest, they even decided to destroy the historical records of their home world, so no one could use the information contained in them to make the same mistakes again. The Cormans are idealists from Earth who left before the Neph attack, disgusted with Earth governments and seeking to chart their own destiny. Disparaged by NPC members of the AFS army as "treehuggers" and living in geodesic domes, they seem like hippies yet are scientifically quite advanced. Thus they primarily represent the possibility of future-oriented utopianism among humans, whatever particular ideology it might incorporate in the lives of members.

The two groups on Arieki, the Brann and the Atta, are less friendly and challenge conventional wisdom even more deeply. Arieki was used by the Brann civilization as a prison planet, but when the Neph's Bane army destroyed their home world, the convicts escaped from their cells. They have built a very rudimentary society rather like a set of competing Mafia families, lacking much sense of justice and seeking knowledge only for petty self-interest, rather than as a step toward wisdom. The Atta, in contrast, are the natives of Arieki and possess a perfectly functioning hive society, fully adapted to the natural environment and hostile only because all of the invading alien groups represent threats to their society. Unwilling to cooperate or even communicate with the AFS, the Atta attacked Bridgebain whenever he entered their territory on a quest. He could hardly blame them.

The ultimate insight achieved by playing *Tabula Rasa*, and the most alarming, is that humanity really is not currently ready for its wisdom. Surrounding any MMO is a larger, more cutthroat game, in which it battles against other games for commercial success. Often, a game is created by a small company, but then published by a large company, comparable to the way a book is written by an author and then distributed through a publisher. If a solo-player game is not very successful commercially, it will continue to be sold so long as any customers are available, and the copies that have been sold will continue to function for as long as machines exist on which to play it. An MMO, however, needs some company to maintain the Internet server that connects the players to each other and maintains a secure database. Often, very interesting MMOs and nongame virtual worlds have been shut down because their publishers found them unprofitable or the publishers wanted to move on to promote new products. That, sadly, is what happened to *Tabula Rasa*.

Richard Garriott, the genius behind *Tabula Rasa*, was in outer space when doom began. Really! William Bridgebain was with him. Honest! During the first decade of the twenty-first century seven men paid millions of dollars each to fly to the International Space Station, and Richard Garriott was one of them. He took with him a memory device containing the data defining all the *Tabula Rasa* avatars, and William Bridgebain was among them. His twelve-day flight began with the launch of Soyuz TMA-13, and ended with the landing of Soyuz TMA-12, in mid-October 2008. While in orbit, he broadcast a sentence written in the Logos language from *Tabula Rasa*, which translated into English said: "Earth is the cradle of humanity, but a person cannot stay in a cradle forever." This is a famous proverb by the Russian spaceflight pioneer Konstantin Tsiolkovsky, but it did not resolve the question of how far from the cradle humanity has crawled.

While Garriott was in outer space, the large Korean company that hosted *Tabula Rasa* decided to pull the plug, so it could promote a new fantasy game, *Aion*, it was about to launch. I have advocated the creation of a public digital library to preserve culturally valuable virtual worlds, but little progress in this direction has been achieved.[25] I did put a DVD of my thousands of screenshots and portions of the now lost *Tabula Rasa* wiki in Henry Lowood's archive at Stanford University, and included were 216 screenshots documenting the Logos language. Every trash novel ever published exists somewhere, and could easily be scanned to make a file that could be shared at low cost with everybody over the Internet. But, lacking a revolution in preservation of virtual worlds, no one will ever again visit Foreas and Arieki, on a quest for adventure or for wisdom.

When it was announced that *Tabula Rasa* would close down, one small area was added back on Earth, Manhattan's Madison Square Park and the adjacent subway station. That park is only a very short walk from Gramercy Park, where my grandfather had his medical office and condominium, and halfway between is the New York City Mission Society where his mother had directed the women's branch of social workers and urban missionaries in the 1890s. William Bridgebain tried as hard as he could to complete his final quest and return home, but he failed, and soon afterward his world ended.

A Hierarchy of Goals

Gameworlds differ in the degree to which they offer large-scale contexts of meaning for the action. Solo-player games tend to be rather linear, with a set route from beginning to end, and a refreshing sense of accomplishment at the finale, when often the highest-level boss enemy must be killed. MMOs, in contrast, seek to hold the player even after achieving the highest-level of experience, and they tend to use three strategies for doing this. First, in varying degrees they work hard to get the player to join a guild or other long-lasting social group, often increasing the pressures to join teams as the avatar climbs the ladder of experience, hoping that friendship ties will keep the player in the game. Second, they offer two or more different races of character, each of which starts out in a different area of virtual geography and has different quests to do, in hopes the player will want to start over from the beginning and complete what amounts to a second variant of the game's larger quest sequence. Third, commercially successful games tend to add over time a variety of dungeons, instances, arenas, and battlegrounds for high-level avatars, each constituting a mini-game or fresh quest sequence that offers excitement and status other than the main ladder of experience, which the avatar has already maxed out.

In addition to experience, all successful MMOs offer several additional ladders of status advancement, such as reputations with various NPC groups, skills in various crafting professions, and in some cases special status points for defeating other players in PvP combat. Usually, ascent up these status ladders can be achieved without doing quests beyond the initial ones associated with training, by *grinding*, which can be defined as the mindless killing of monsters or performing other routine tasks, in the absence of any wider meaning. Players often comment that grinding is an uninteresting chore, and high-quality games invariably build meaning into the action by scripting quests around rich stories.

This section of the chapter will illustrate how individual quests can be chained together into quest arcs or large-scale missions, thereby connecting each battle with a monster and trek across territory with deeper meaning. First, a sixteen-step quest arc from the American game *Warhammer Online* will show how short quests can be connected to each other, and rooted in the lore that gives meaning to the gameworld. Second, one of the solo-player games in the Japanese *Legend of Zelda* series will show how quests can be woven together to form the fabric of a game. Finally, the Chinese game *Perfect World* will illustrate the ambiguity of meaning in the universe that humans inhabit.

My first *Warhammer* avatar, Williamwheeler, was a Human who completed the early levels of experience in the border territories of the decaying empire where his people were defending themselves against northern barbarian invaders. Then he visited the exotic but allied High Elves, completing one of the *traveling quests* that encourage a player to explore new territories by rewarding an avatar for simply going to a distant location. After performing miscellaneous quests in the Shadowlands zone and becoming minimally acquainted with the High Elves, he was ready to understand the first stage of the quest series called "Echoes from the

Past." A High Elf officer named Argolis Wildhelm, who serves as the contact person for several quests, explained how the current war was rooted in Elven history.

The ancient Elven civilization had split into two factions, the High Elves who joined the Order alliance and the Dark Elves who joined the Destruction alliance. In the vast world war then in progress, much local action was meaningless or accidental, but the Dark Elf enemy seemed to be especially interested in the nearby ruins of Mirelen, almost as if it held a secret of supreme importance for the wider struggle. The quest series begins with an attempt to gain a clue about what the motives of the Destruction forces might be. Thus the "Echoes from the Past" quest arc was largely a progressive revelation of a deep secret, not only conferring experience and material rewards on the avatar but also uncovering more of the meaning of the conflict. Here are the arc's sixteen steps:

1. The avatar enters Mirelen and slays a Uthorin Loreseeker to gain a clue about what lore he is seeking. A weathered parchment is found, then taken to a High Elf historian, Scholar Riana.
2. They scrutinize the parchment and see the sigil of Saruthil, a symbol that identifies a famous exiled sage. This sends the avatar to an artifact in Mirelen being defended by members of the Shining Guard against minions of the Dark Elves.
3. The avatar finds a wooden ark containing ancient scrolls and takes them to Argolis Wildhelm.
4. Fragments of the crucial scroll are missing, which must have been stolen by Dark Elves. The avatar tracks down, kills, and retrieves scroll fragments from three enemy leaders: Korolir Blackbolt, Risathyn Pa'al, and Urdaen Gloombrow.
5. The avatar delivers the complete scrolls to Scholar Riana.
6. Riana explains that Saruthil's last prophecy was so horrible that he broke its words into fragments, hiding them in various ways. The avatar must fight past enemies to find a keystone having an invisible inscription.
7. Riana and the avatar use the Dragon Tome to decipher the Prophecy of Saruthil, which is depicted by a sudden flash of light.
8. To complete their understanding of the prophecy, the avatar must leave the lands of the Elves and voyage across the ocean to Osland in Human territory.
9. Based on a local rumor, the avatar looks for a clue about Saruthil at Lissariel's Glade.
10. The avatar follows magical hints to Nagarythe Ward.
11. Deep in a forbidden cave, the avatar must open a magical barrier by setting the appropriate colors for four orbs: Orb of Asur, Orb of Cadaith, Orb of Menlui, and Orb of Shyish.

12. The barrier was protecting a wooden chest containing a scroll, written by Saruthil and predicting doom in war, that also reveals the location of Saruthil's exile. The avatar must now find Saruthil.

13. Saruthil is suspicious of the avatar, and his suspicions deepen when Uthorin warriors suddenly appear, having followed the avatar and now ready to assassinate Saruthil. However, the avatar defeats two waves of assassins and gain's Saruthil's trust.

14. Saruthil says he will soon attend a Council of Sages to prepare for the great struggle, but he warns that a lesser but still dire threat looms, sending the avatar back into Elven territory, to an outpost at the Wellsprings of Ellyrion, to warn the Shining Guard.

15. Deep in a cavern in the southern mountains, the avatar finds clear evidence of the hidden threat.

16. The avatar must kill a boss NPC, demon Laeth'r Snarlwhip, who is using the caverns as a staging point for his goblin minions.

Several of these steps require killing enemies. For example, three of the Dark Elves happen to be standing around the keystone in step 6, unaware that it is important but prepared to kill any ally of the High Elves who nears them. Killing an enemy adds to the avatar's experience, and in many cases the corpse can be looted for gold or goods, just as in grinding but with a sense that the kill has positive meaning in terms of the gameworld's lore. Most of the quests require travel, whether local or long-distance, and trekking across virtual territories is one of the main time-killing activities in virtual worlds. However, here the travel produces knowledge, represented by the scrolls but also expressed through increasing familiarity with the landscape, which can be useful for other quests that are not related to this arc. The final boss ends this quest arc, but not the wider story embodied by Saruthil, who interacts later on with high-level avatars on the Isle of the Dead, where the fate of the world will be decided.

The first step in this quest arc was recommended for avatars that had reached at least level 9 of general experience, and the final step was recommended for those level 18 or above, and indeed Williamwheeler had to perform many other smaller missions to become strong enough for the last step of "Echoes from the Past" and did not finish until level 20. Many of these were lore-centered missions that resonated in some way with the main quest arc.

For example, Scholar Riana assigned him a four-step arc called "Thirst for Knowledge." First, he traced glyphs from an ancient well, then saw the name Laurilion the Fair among the few runes still legible. Riana told him a little of the tale of this ancient archmage, a beautiful woman whose situation had become dire. "In her grief she called upon Isha, begging the goddess for intercession. Into that cry she poured her soul; shame she surrendered, rage and fear, making of her prayer a vessel containing the last of her hope, laced with power." Like the parting of the Red Sea for Moses, a path opened up that seemed to lead to freedom, but hope became despair when she saw that the vast sea ahead offered no escape. "She uttered a lament of such power that the words were burned upon the rock with the force of her anguish." In the end, the words must not be known, because their grief is so powerful they drive anyone who learns them insane.

The manner in which small quests can fit into a narrative that encompasses the entire world is perhaps best illustrated by a solo-player game. *The Legend of Zelda: Ocarina of Time* is one of the most highly regarded videogames of all time, and when it was released in 1998, it marked a watershed in many ways. The fifth in the Zelda series, it was the first to offer a three-dimensional environment, but it was remarkable in the current context both because it was based on a religious premise and because it was the prototype for quest design in many later games. The sacred premise of the virtual world called Hyrule was presented as narrative over a cut scene at the beginning:

> Before time began, before spirits and life existed . . .
> Three golden goddesses descended upon the chaos that was Hyrule . . .
> Din, the goddess of power . . .
> Nayru, the goddess of wisdom . . .
> Farore, the goddess of courage . . .
> Din . . .
> With her strong flaming arms, she cultivated the land and created the
>   red earth.
> Nayru . . .
> Poured her wisdom onto the earth and gave the spirit of law to the world.
> Farore . . .
> With her rich soul, produced all life forms who would uphold the law.
> The three great goddesses, their labors completed, departed for the
>   heavens.
> And golden sacred triangles remained at the point where the goddesses
>   left the world.
> Since then, the sacred triangles have become the basis of our world's
>   providence.
> And the resting place of the triangles has become the Sacred Realm.

Note that the three goddesses represent characteristics that a person may exhibit or even achieve: power, wisdom, and courage. The hero of the Zelda stories is a boy named Link, associated with the color green and starting this game as an unappreciated lad living among other children in the Kokiri Forest. All the other children have guardian fairies who fly around them, but not Link. His great unspoken quest is to gain respect by growing into a powerful, wise, and courageous man who saves the world from destruction and injustice.

The people of the forest worship the Great Deku Tree, and it is this tree who safeguards their realm and tells the story of the goddesses. A powerful warlock named Ganondorf curses the Great Deku Tree, and this arboreal father figure sends a special fairy to bring Link to his aid. Link accepts the mission to protect the forest, but after completing several quests successfully, and killing the first area's enemy boss, Gohma, Link is shocked when the tree dies. The Great Deku Tree had known that it was doomed and enlisted Link in order to prepare him for the much more demanding quests to come.

The early hours of the game, up to the death of the tree, all served as a tutorial for new players, teaching them how to use the interface, how to complete various moves and actions, and how to navigate the environment. Link acquired a magic sword during this training period, and took giant steps toward becoming an adult. Indeed, one test of increasing maturity was the ability to endure the death of the tree, understanding the deeper context in which it had lived, and expanding Link's consciousness to a much wider world.

Link learns that Princess Zelda's archenemy, Ganondorf, seeks the sacred triangles for himself, because when combined into the Triforce they allow the user to satisfy wishes, even evil ones. In dying, the Great Deku Tree gives Link a magical emerald. His childhood will be complete if he can obtain two additional magic gems, a ruby and a sapphire, each of which requires defeating a boss enemy in an enclosed area after completing a series of preparatory quests. Along the way, Link acquires an ocarina and learns to play various melodies on it, including Sun's song, which changes night into day and day into night. He gains the ocarina of time, which allows him to get the Master Sword in the Temple of Time, thereby achieving adulthood, and to switch between stages of his life, becoming at will either child or adult. As earlier he had collected three gems, now he needs to undertake groups of quests to gain light, forest, fire, water, shadow, and spirit medallions. Only after he has all of them is he ready to use the Master Sword to battle Ganondorf.

In MMOs and many recent solo-player games, an avatar gains increased maximum health (hit points), allowing the avatar to survive battles with ever more powerful enemies, with each additional level of experience. In *Ocarina of Time*, the avatar gains hearts by completing important quests or by finding a fragment of a heart in an odd location along the way while doing other quests. Thus, there are really two very different lines of quests leading to each boss and each artifact, one explicitly part of that chapter of the story and the other involving collecting the hearts needed to be able to battle that boss. Along the way, the avatar collects not only gems that can be used to purchase virtual items but also special equipment, such as ocarinas, swords, and shields, and completing some side quests confers useful but nonessential abilities.

The ultimate goal of *Ocarina of Time* is defense of the Triforce against Ganondorf, and near the end each of its three components is held by a different character. Ganondorf holds Power, while Link has Courage, and his friend Princess Zelda has Wisdom. Two major stages of the gameworld require Link to collect three gems and six medallions, each involving a subgame that can take several hours to complete. Thus, just as the Triforce is a triangle composed of triangles, the gameworld is an assembly of major components in sets of three. It is difficult to think of a more precise model of how the structure of subtasks, missions, and areas of virtual geography can be combined according to a conceptual scheme to make a world in which action is meaningful.

Most of the games described here have a primary series of levels of accomplishment and potency, often called *experience*, which can be conceptualized as the major quest arc, whatever side quests there also may be. Each of the avatar types in *Star Wars: The Old Republic* is expected to complete a very explicit, long series of quests, which amount to the plot of a distinctive novel written about that character. *Lineage II: Goddess of Destruction* has organized progress in a "Path to Awakening," even obtaining trademark protection for this phrase. The game's website proclaims: "Advanced progression toward your destiny awaits! On your journey to awakening, you will be guided along a clear path of attainable goals and rewards for achieving those goals."[26] This path involves quests that function like rites of passage at experience levels 20, 40, and 76, each involving a transformation of the avatar's class. An extensive anthropological literature exists about advancement trials and rituals of initiation, with an emphasis on puberty and formal coming to adulthood, but also including status transformations in religious hierarchies.[27]

Many MMOs have multiple ladders of status, some relatively secondary and varying in their degree of separateness. For example, a priest in *World of Warcraft* may also be an alchemist, an herbalist, and a fisher, advancing separately up each of these four ladders, although it is best to keep all of them at comparable levels. Levels of experience are sometimes arranged in groups that are given evocative names, and an excellent example is in *Perfect World International*, which combines levels into categories of spiritual cultivation. At experience level 9, one can do race-appropriate quests to become a spiritual adept and gain new powers. Thereafter, every ten levels another quest grants additional spiritual cultivation and powers: "Aware of Principle," "Aware of Harmony," "Aware of Discord," "Aware of Coalescence," "Transcendent," "Enlightened One," and "Aware of Vacuity." This last stage beyond enlightenment could hardly be more different than, for example, the Christian notions of salvation or sainthood, but it matches schools of Buddhism that take detachment to the logical conclusion of immersion in virtual worlds: realization that the real world is not real. The higher groups of levels contain subgroups, and the final quest series obtained at level 79 is saturated with elements of Asian religion:

15. Talk to the Celestial Elder at the City of Buddha
16. Talk to the Dreamweaver Elder
17. Kill Ru Ci the Confucian Templar southwest of Dreamweaver Port
18. Return to the Celestial Elder
19. Kill the Brigand Transient in the Hallucinatory Trench
20. Search the Ocean Pillar in the Hallucinatory Trench
21. Return to the Celestial Elder[28]

However, this is not the end. The protoexistentialist philosopher Friedrich Nietzsche advised that we go beyond good and evil.[29] In *Perfect World*, what lies beyond good and evil is good or evil and nothingness. The fully enlightened one, who has realized vacuity, returns to a normal life, but with a choiceless choice between good and evil, becoming either a sage or a demon, serene in either case.

Conclusion

Quest is question writ small. All life is a quest for answers, first of all about how to obtain food and other requirements of survival, and next to find satisfaction for social desires required by the tremendously demanding facts of human reproduction and child rearing. Yet if survival is assured, at least until death at old age, human questing does not cease. Many aspects of human society are compensatory, providing subjective status for those who lack it in the wider context. While some games require quick reaction time, the primary measures of progress are social status with respect to, and from, other players, plus knowledge. The experience of an avatar is preserved as information inside the computer database, but the experience of the player is preserved in memory, from such small details as which direction to turn after entering a castle, to the best strategy for luring individual enemies away from a group so they can be slaughtered one at a time, to a plan of which zone in the virtual cosmos to enter next. Especially when the mythos of a gameworld provides wider meanings that connect to the realities of human existence, questing can be an entirely satisfying way of advancing real wisdom.

When a quest is finished, a tenacious player accepts a new quest. The crucial decision point arrives when a player's curiosity about a gameworld has been largely satisfied by hundreds of hours of questing, and the player becomes a quest giver—deciding to create a new avatar and enter a new gameworld. Popular religions assert that a second life exists beyond this one, and perhaps more beyond that. A Valkyrie carried a dying hero from the battlefield to Valhalla to fight again for the gods. But Valhalla is destined to fall, and perhaps a second-order Valkyrie will then come to take the hero to a third game. When angels die in the Christian heaven, where do they go? Perhaps they dance on the head of a pin. At the current moment in history, gameworlds are giving us a new perspective on the human quest, one that combines the arts and simulates most aspects of real life. Their fundamental answers are optimistic: When this quest is done, there will be another. When this game is done, there will be another. When this life is done . . .

THE GAMEWORLDS

Age of Conan. This is a high-quality MMO released in 2008 by the experienced Norwegian game company Funcom. Based on Robert E. Howard's stories about a mythical ancient era in human history, this is fundamentally a psychohistory that considers individual human personalities to be the pivotal factors in shaping events. Conan, the barbarian king who conquered a variant of the Roman Empire, is the larger-than-life personality about whom the stories revolved, but he plays only a minor role in this gameworld. Casting a long shadow over the stories is the personality of Howard, raising key questions about the psychiatry of fantasy. The central figure in *Age of Conan* is the player's avatar, who struggles to regain lost memories, and the psychologies of non-player characters are also paramount. *Age of Conan* draws heavily upon Howard's rather sophisticated and adult-oriented literature, but not upon the popular but crude Conan movies. Three very different cultures are in contact, but currently at peace, so that an avatar who belongs to one can safely visit the others. Aquilonia is similar to Rome, Stygia to Egypt, and the Cimmerians to the Celtic tribes. Quests often have an occult flavor, and many fictional religions are depicted, centrally those of the three cultures.

Aion. Created by the South Korean game company NCSoft, this high-quality fantasy gameworld launched late in 2008 in its home country, then spread around the world in the autumn of 2009. Early levels introduce the player to the mythology and serve as a tutorial for the many complex features through player-versus-environment quests. At level 10 the player gains the ability to fly, but uses that talent only sparingly for a while as other environment-oriented quests complete the player's education. At level 25, the emphasis shifts to player-versus-player combat between two factions, the somewhat angelic Elyos and the rather sinister Asmodians, in a PvP zone called the Abyss, although PvE quests also exist at higher levels. Each faction possesses a rather majestic city, Sanctum for the Elyos and Pandaemonium for the Asmodians. As with other Asian games that have been adapted for an international audience, without a very intensive study it is difficult to know how much of the mythology and terminology are original, versus being transformed during translation, and how much the game is based on native Asian culture rather than being an Asian expression of world culture.

Battleground Europe. Also titled *World War II Online*, this massively multiplayer online military simulation was released in 2001 by Cornered Rat Software and constantly improved over the following years, showing remarkable endurance despite a somewhat small audience. It lacks predefined quests belonging to a fantasy story line, and a player cannot make any progress without directly battling against other players. All the avatars are male military personnel, who at any given moment are on either the Axis (German) or Allied (French and British) side, although it is possible to defect to the other side, with a fifteen-minute pause to prevent defectors from taking advantage of knowledge about the momentary configuration of the battlefield. The setting is the entire western front in the year 1940, and the action consists of campaigns lasting several weeks in which each side tries to capture territory belonging to the other. By general agreement, the political context of the actual Second World War is not discussed, and nothing related to the Nazis is depicted in this gameworld. What is depicted, with admirable detail and accuracy, is the weaponry. From each soldier's combat knife, up through rifles and machine guns, including artillery, tanks, and even a diversity of aircraft, players may experience the military technology of the era, almost as if they had gone back in a time machine to see the hardware in action with their own eyes.

Chronicles of Narnia: The Lion, the Witch, and the Wardrobe. Released in 2005 for the major videogame systems, this game was developed by a British company named Traveler's Tales and published by Buena Vista Games. Although ultimately based on the 1950 C. S. Lewis novel, it was most closely connected to the 2005 Disney movie, which downplayed the Christian allegory of the book. On videogame systems possessing two controllers, it can be played either solo or duo. Either way, the game follows the set adventures of four children, often combining in pairs and occasionally the entire quartet. Narnia is a mythical kingdom, which the children magically visit from their home in London, during World War II. Adults cannot visit Narnia, and the children do not realize that the magic lion is actually Jesus Christ. So the whole mythos represents both childhood fantasy of individual people and the childhood stage in cultural development that was followed by Christian maturity.

Constantine. This 2005 solo game distributed by Warner Brothers Interactive was based on the movie of the same year and title, and both were based on the DC supernatural horror comic *Hellblazer.* Demons have begun to enter the world from Hell, and hero John Constantine is part of an effort first to exorcize them, then to find the source of the invasion and block it. Especially notable are the scenes that take place in hell, which is depicted as a modern city engulfed by flames, including melting automobiles floating in the dark red air.

Da Vinci Code. Released by the Collective and 2K Games in 2006, simultaneously with the film version of Dan Brown's novel, this game is somewhat different from both, chiefly because it added many low-level enemies who needed to be defeated in complex hand-to-hand combat, and added many new puzzles to be solved. A solo game, it primarily takes the viewpoint of the novel's hero, Robert Langdon, but occasionally is played through the heroine, Sophie Neveu. The depiction of four real churches is a distinctive feature of the game.

Daemonica. A solo-player game for the PC dating from 2006, this is a visually and computationally simple game organized around complex puzzles. The focus is almost entirely on solving a connected series of murder mysteries, partly by collecting clues and other resources necessary for the investigation, and partly by talking repeatedly with a relatively small cast of nonplayer characters. Reviews generally criticized *Daemonica* for being dull and slow-paced, yet it is quite interesting as a representative of mystery solving in a highly constrained environment. The connection to religion is not only that the tiny village where the action takes place has a monastery but that the protagonist must undergo trances that transport him to a hidden temple in order to interrogate corpses to solve their murders.

Dark Age of Camelot. Launched in 2001 by Mythic Entertainment, this pioneering massively multiplayer gameworld depicts competition among three great realms in the Dark Ages of northwest Europe: Albion (England), Hibernia (Ireland), and Midgard (Scandinavia). Among MMOs, this early example innovated in realm-versus-realm combat. An avatar trains in a newbie zone of one realm, then levels up and learns the mythos of that realm in mid-level zones, before joining other high-level avatars in battlegrounds and instances, fighting against the other two realms in extremely complex wars involving fortresses, siege engines, and long-lasting guild alliances. Over the years, a number of additional levels and dungeons were added, so *Dark Age of Camelot* has remained a very attractive world, despite its declining popularity in the face of ever stiffer competition. The religions of the three cultures remain somewhat in the background, although there is a good deal of attractive religious architecture, and the main quest lines relate to the actual quasi-religious folklore of the three cultures.

Dungeons and Dragons Online. Based on the classic tabletop game *Dungeons and Dragons*, this MMO was developed by Turbine Entertainment Software and launched in 2006. It is a rather faithful adaptation of D&D to the multiplayer online environment and pays homage to its origins, even respectfully including tombs of the two deceased creators of D&D, and the recorded voice of one of them. The geographic center of the gameworld is Stormreach, a city containing many feudal familiars and factions, but emphasizing groups of players who enter "dungeons" to battle against evil nonplayer characters. The city is surrounded and undermined by a very large number of these instanced dungeons, and many of the quests concern zombies and the resurrection of the undead. Two of the largest additions to the city, together constituting the largest set of dungeons, are called the Necropolis and consist of tombs, each of which presents its own puzzles and challenges. To balance its emphasis on cooperative group play with a way that solo players could handle the dungeons, *Dungeons and Dragons Online* developed a system of mercenaries, multiple semiautonomous secondary avatars who could be hired to take the place of real player teammates when none were available.

Elder Scrolls IV: Oblivion. Released by Bethesda Softworks and 2K Games in 2006, this vast solo-player game is indistinguishable from a major MMO, except for the fact that it lacks avatars of other players. Boasting a major city and many small towns separated by wild terrain, it possesses extremely complex systems of nonplayer characters and a complex backstory that focuses on attempts by a fanatical cult to open gates to a demon-infested plane of existence called Oblivion. As the number in the name implies, this is the fourth in a series of games that together have created an extraordinarily rich fantasy world.

EverQuest II. The original *EverQuest* was created by an American subsidiary of Sony and released early in 1999 by Sony Online Entertainment. In 2004, *EverQuest II* employed far more advanced graphics, incorporated a range of improvements, and rebuilt the virtual world called Norrath. This pair of gameworlds constituted major steps in the development of the genre and in the consolidation of a widely shared collection of traditional mythic elements, such as elves, orcs, goblins, and ogres. Norrath clearly is not our own world, but it mirrors a key concept from real history. When the Roman Empire fell, a Dark Age covered the western half of its territory, setting the basis for the medieval society that followed the Dark Age hundreds of years later. A dark age also occurred between *EverQuest* and *EverQuest II*, when the gods abandoned Norrath and parts of its physical geography were shattered.

Fallen Earth is a postapocalyptic MMO created by independent game developers named at the time Reloaded Productions, launched in 2009 and currently operated by GamersFirst using a mixed free-to-play and subscription system. It depicts conflict between numerous small gangs and cults in a chaotic corner of the United States, some years after the fall of civilization. FE is set in and around the Grand Canyon in Arizona, including simplified versions of many real locations, such as the town of Kingman and the nearby state prison. While stressing violence in much of the gameplay, including many quests that require the player to kill many nonplayer characters, *Fallen Earth* has some of the qualities of a nongame virtual world because it places emphasis on scavenging resources from the environment with which to craft many needed tools, weapons, foods, and medicines. For example, ammunition for the early-level rifles must be made from outcroppings of copper found here and there across the landscape, and many other important materials are found in garbage piles, wrecked vehicles, and even long-dead corpses.

Faxion. This 2011 MMO was developed by Ignition Entertainment, originally a British company but now owned by United Television, an Indian conglomerate. Emphasizing player-versus-player combat, it primarily takes place in regions representing the seven deadly sins, where angels battle devils, but also has regions representing heaven, hell, and purgatory. Quests seem primarily designed to train the player, to give the avatar resources and abilities, preparing for the PvP combat that is the heart of *Faxion*—which is pronounced *faction.*

Final Fantasy XI. As the name implies, this is the eleventh in a long-running series of fantasy adventure games, and it was produced by a Japanese company called Square (later Square Enix) in 2002 locally, and in 2003 for the world audience. Until the release of *Final Fantasy XIV* in 2010, it was the only MMO in the series, the others being solo-player games. *Final Fantasy XI* is unusual in that it can be played not only on a personal computer but also on a PlayStation 2 or an Xbox 360, allowing users with these very different systems to interact with each other online. It was also distinctive in attempting to unite players from different continents, speaking different languages, on the same team, incorporating an elaborate phrase-translation dictionary for four languages: Japanese, English, French, and German. From a hierarchical menu, a player selects one of these phrases, and then each member of that player's team sees the equivalent phrase in their own language.

Forsaken World. Launched late in 2010, this MMO by the Chinese game company Perfect World Entertainment is oriented toward the international market, and thus is not based on Chinese culture but on European concepts, such as vampires, elves, and dwarves. As with other Asian games, however, the religious culture is not in any way connected to the Judeo-Christian-Islamic tradition. Nor is it based on western Paganism, although it does incorporate the widely used concept reminiscent of Norse traditions that the original deities failed after creating the world, and everything has been going downhill ever since.

God of War. This 2005 solo-player PlayStation 2 videogame is a saga in which the Spartan warrior Kratos seeks vengeance against Ares, god of war. With the half-hearted assistance of the other gods, Kratos goes through a series of adventures, all related to ancient Greek mythology, gaining magical power step by step until he himself is almost a god, ready to face Ares in personal combat. This popular and much-praised game excels in two quite separate yet reinforcing ways. First, the game play from moment to moment is visually exciting, stretching the player's abilities, yet smooth and comfortable in execution. Second, the narrative makes good sense, despite its bizarre premise, because it deftly draws upon many familiar elements of ancient civilization. The integration of these virtues was a remarkable achievement by the game designers.

Gods and Heroes: Rome Rising. Released in 2011 by Heatwave Interactive, this MMO is set in and around ancient Rome, with the action taking place about 247 BC. Thus it is unusual among MMOs, if not quite unique, in having a historical setting, rather than presenting a fantasy gameworld. Each avatar forms a relationship with a particular classical deity, each of which possesses a temple in Rome. *Gods and Heroes* does include some fantasy elements, and attempts to present Rome as a cultural idea rather than to duplicate it exactly. The virtual city itself is very impressive, although of necessity smaller than the actual metropolis, which at its height may have held a million inhabitants, and more reminiscent of Rome as it was in the early imperial period than the middle of the republic. However, many details ring true, such as quests connecting two of the real men named Publius Decius Mus (grandfather and grandson), and an area of an early zone where salt for food preservation is produced.

GodStoria: The Bible Online. This 2010 browser game was created by FIAA (Fascination, Innovation, Authentic Amusement), the German branch of a small international game effort. Although incorporating Christian symbolism, it depicts portions of the ancient Middle East at the time when Hebrew history begins in the Old Testament. It is an economy-focused strategy game, in which neither construction of buildings nor conduct of battles are depicted in any detail, yet it is an interesting illustration of the abstractions and resource flows that take place beneath the surface of more visually exciting games.

Guild Wars Trilogy. Originally developed by ArenaNet in the United States, and published by NCSoft in Korea, this high-quality fantasy MMO was issued in three equal parts: *Prophecies* in 2005, *Factions* early in 2006, and *Nightfall* late in 2006. Often described as episodic, because it was issued in parts that could be played separately, *Guild Wars* uses an unusual economic model, requiring the user to buy each of the three parts—or later all three bundled together as *Trilogy*—but charging nothing for the right to play online. With an emphasis on group play, this gameworld is heavily instanced, so that each team will have most geographic areas to itself, and other teams will experience other versions of the same area. This allows more emphasis on telling complex stories, incorporating nonplayer characters in many small dramas, and the mythology is very rich. Given the emphasis on group play, much effort has been invested making the game suitable for solo players through providing many kinds of secondary avatars that take the place of other players.

Legend of Zelda: Ocarina of Time. This 1998 Nintendo game was the fifth in the Zelda series and the first to offer a three-dimensional environment. Originally written for the Nintendo 64 game console, it was ported over to the GameCube, which means it can be played on the more recent Wii, with which all GameCube games are compatible, and a version for the Nintendo 3DS was released in 2011. Among the most highly acclaimed and influential games, it had many of the features of later online role-playing games. It has a well-deserved reputation for being difficult, because its sequencing of quests was halfway between the older and newer traditions. At any given point, the player usually has several choices where to go next and which intermediate goal to accomplish; however, there were a few obligatory battles like fighting the boss at the end of a level in older games, preventing the player from progressing until that boss is defeated. Some bosses required a high level of skill and cannot be defeated simply by doing other tasks first to build up strength. MMOs, in contrast, provide multiple routes to success, while old-style games were entirely linear. *Ocarina of Time* segments an otherwise nonlinear play space with bottlenecks.

Lineage II: Goddess of Destruction is the current Westernized version of a 2003 fantasy MMO published by the Korean company NCSoft. It is often cited as an example of how Asian player preferences for MMOs differ significantly from those of players in Europe or North America. In particular, there is an emphasis on *grinding*, killing large numbers of nonplayer enemies, some quests requiring killing as many as two hundred of them. Western players often criticize Asian games like *Lineage II* for having weaker mythologies and story lines, but this point is debatable because Western critics may simply fail to appreciate much symbolism that would be obvious to Asian players. In the

Lineage mythology, prior to modern times gods and giants battled against each other for control, leaving the world in a chaotic condition with many magical forces at work, and inhabited by six races: Humans, Elves, Dark Elves, Orcs, Dwarves, and mysterious Kamael, who are living combat weapons who worship the goddess Nornil.

Lord of the Rings Online. Developed by Turbine Entertainment Software and launched in 2007, this high-quality MMO is a faithful depiction of Middle Earth from J. R. R. Tolkien's novels. Set halfway through the history Tolkien described, LOTRO actually includes key characters from the books in some of the quests, and others take place in specific locations where important scenes took place in the books. True to Tolkien's ethical principles, LOTRO limits combat between players to special circumstances in which their inner demons are temporarily released, and the emphasis is on the creation of a fellowship for good, uniting the Hobbits, Humans, Elves, and Dwarves. Also in accordance with Tolkien's principles, magic exists but its use by players is discouraged. Both individually and in groups, players own virtual houses, and the gameplay encourages crafting of virtual goods and archaeological exploration of Middle Earth.

The Matrix Online. Originally created by Monolith, then hosted by Sony Online Entertainment, this MMO existed from 2004 until 2009. It represents the virtual city depicted in the trilogy of movies that began in 1999 with *The Matrix*, inhabited by ordinary people who imagine the city is real, renegade computer programs pretending to be people, and the avatars of the players who know very well the city is a mirage. In this vast city there are a very few churches, and a small number of quests connected to them, but the chief relevance for religion is precisely how unimportant it is in a world where immortality and magic are mere technological affordances. For example, in a fantasy gameworld the hurling of a bolt of lightning is typically depicted as a magical spell, whereas in *The Matrix Online* it is depicted as a routine in a computer program—which of course is what it actually is, regardless of how the particular game conceptualizes it.

Perfect World. Launched in China in 2005 by Beijing Perfect World, this MMO was adapted for the international market in 2008 and is often described as the chief Chinese competitor to *World of Warcraft*. The cultural setting remains traditional Chinese, including virtual architecture, clothing, and concepts pertaining to magic and religion. For example, one long quest series begins by talking with a Taoist master and involves a long process of "spiritual cultivation." The international version is free to play, but as an avatar ascends the experience levels, it becomes progressively more desirable to purchase virtual enhancements in an online shop.

Pirates of the Burning Sea. Created by Flying Lab Software and hosted by Sony, this 2008 MMO depicts the Caribbean Sea in the year 1720. Despite the unavoidable adjustments for the online gaming environment, PotBS is remarkably sensitive to historical accuracy—for example, assigning the names of many real historical personages, including obscure ones, to the NPCs. With fair accuracy, the Caribbean is depicted as the locus of a kind of "cold war" between Britain, France, Spain, and the actual "pirates" who held a few of the islands. The diversity of sailing ships appears accurate, and their behavior in various winds and currents are not unlike those in the real world, given some simplifications for the nonmariners who command them. Many cultural elements, from music to medicine, are also depicted with a degree of authenticity, relating to the century, if not the precise year, in which this MMO takes place.

Pirates of the Caribbean Online. Released in 2007 by the Disney Interactive Media Group, this MMO is based on Disney's *Pirates of the Caribbean* films, which in turn were based on an amusement park attraction at Disneyland and three other Disney theme parks. Several of the quest givers are major characters from the movies. With very limited areas of virtual land and highly simplified sailing methods, this game seems designed for children, yet it contains content that may be unsuited for young people, including many animated corpses and quests that require overt card-game gambling. However, as is the case for the movies, a good deal of actual history and culture is hidden beneath the crude fantasy veneer, and the group defense battles against the minions of Jolly Roger are both complex and lots of fun.

Rift. This 2011 fantasy MMO from Trion Worlds is an extremely high-quality distillation of ideas from many other games, packaged in a well-conceived world with rich and consistent backstory. Reviewers often say they would have given their highest ratings had it not been so eclectic, but the rift concept takes spontaneous group play to a new level, and thus *Rift* is innovative as well as imitative. Two factions compete: the Guardians, who are religious and oriented toward the past, versus the Defiant, who are technological and oriented toward the future. Each has a different response to the challenge that faces their world, the constant eruption of rifts opening a door to one or another of six alien planes of existence, through which demons invade. A high-quality mapping interface alerts players when a rift opens in their vicinity, and encourages them to team up to defeat the demons and close the rift.

Rome: Total War. Released in 2004, this is one of a series of high-quality solo-player strategy games created by the British company the Creative Assembly. There are two main ways of approaching the game. First, one may play through a predefined series of battles punctuated with peacetime episodes of resource-building over the three centuries ending with the death of Augustus and the completion of the transition from Roman Republic to Roman Empire. Second, one may repeatedly play a large number of specific historical battles, chosen ad libitum, some of them outside this time frame, altering the initial conditions as well as real-time tactics during repeated runs. Like many of the best strategy games, *Rome: Total War* has qualities of a realistic computer simulation of real history. Amateurs have been encouraged to create variants of the battles and graphics, and the most impressive "mod" of this game is *Europa Barbarorum* (Europe of the Barbarians) which sought to increase the historical accuracy of a game that already was fairly accurate.

Runes of Magic. The one gameworld in this set created in Taiwan, it was launched in 2009 by Runewaker Entertainment under the new model in which games are free to play but valuable virtual items can be bought in an online shop. Adapted for the Western market by the German firm Frogster Interactive, the game has a style and content that are highly eclectic. The backstory begins when the god Ayvenas creates the world Taborea, as if he were writing a book, which starts in balance but gradually becomes increasingly chaotic and escapes from the control of Ayvenas. Lacking direct control from a deity, some inhabitants of Taborea sought magical powers in order to become gods themselves. Others sought a better course, creating the Eye of Wisdom and establishing the basis for a high civilization. Two races, Elves and Humans, struggle to find their own distinctive meanings in a diverse world.

Sacred 2: Fallen Angel. This 2008 solo-player game from the German company Ascaron Entertainment was designed very much like an MMO, with a vast territory and six character types, but lacking other players. There are two alternative paths, Light and Shadow, and four of the character types are able to choose either, while the Seraphim are committed to Light, and the Inquisitors are committed to Shadow. As in MMOs with a strong story, there are many core campaign quests, but these are outnumbered by optional side quests, giving *Sacred 2* the nonlinear quality of most MMOs.

Sims Medieval is a 2011 solo role-playing game, set in a slightly fantasized medieval European village. It is an extension of the long-lasting and very popular *Sims* games, which are like real-world environments and traditionally lacked combat and did not emphasize story-based quests but the conduct of everyday life. *Sims Medieval* was something of a departure from this tradition, because of its reliance on quests like those in a fantasy MMO. Perhaps because of their sensitivity to social interaction between people possessing different personalities, and their typical lack of violent combat, Sims games are often considered to be girls' games. An MMO, or dollhouse-like virtual world, called *Sims Online* existed from 2003 until 2008. One can only speculate whether an MMO based on *Sims Medieval*, including some optional violence but not emphasizing it, might be successful in the current MMO market.

Spore is a single-player game, loosely based on biological and cultural evolution, released by Maxis and Electronic Arts in 2008. The player starts with a single-cell organism and gradually shapes it through five stages, each of which has a different game design: cell, creature, tribal, civilization, and space. *Spore* has some of the qualities of a construction set, real-time strategy game, and role-playing avatar game. While not a multiplayer game, *Spore* allows users to upload their creature designs for other people to try, as well as videos of game episodes.

Star Trek Deep Space Nine: The Fallen is a solo-player game for personal computers released in 2000, based on the *Deep Space Nine* series of the *Star Trek* television franchise, which aired from 1993 until 1999. Much of the action involves fighting one's way through mazes, using technology like phasers and tricorders that were depicted in the TV series, but complexity was added by the fact that one can run through the game three times, experiencing the events from the different perspectives of three stock characters. The background is the vicinity, history, and religion of the planet Bajor, all tied into the rest of the *Star Trek* mythos by the Deep Space Nine space station operated by the United Federation of Planets in cooperation with the Bajorans, who had not yet joined the Federation.

Star Trek Online was developed by Cryptic Studios, launched early in 2010, and depicts the year 2409 in the *Star Trek* universe, at which point the galaxy has degenerated into multisided episodic warfare. While many criticisms have been leveled against this MMO, it has many very attractive features and displays a good deal of creativity on the part of the designers, including the Foundry system, which has allowed players to create something approaching two thousand missions of their own, many of high quality. Over its first year of existence, STO offered several moderate expansions, adding three new major quest arcs with the associated new virtual environments, but in the second year little was added, perhaps, as online commentators speculate, because the game was experiencing financial difficulties. When STO was purchased by the Chinese company Perfect World, very substantial effort was invested in converting the game to a mixed economic model including "free-to-play," with the opportunity to purchase many luxuries, and a complex multicurrency system for integrating "freemium" customers with those paying for traditional subscriptions.

Star Wars Episode III: Revenge of the Sith. This 2005 game, produced by the Collective and Ubisoft, is based on the film of the same name and was released in the same month. In addition to two-player combat aspects, it is primarily a solo-player game in which the player switches off between the two main characters of the film, Obi-Wan Kenobi and Anakin Skywalker, running one or the other in the appropriate scenes. Like the movie, the game ends with combat between these two characters, which has religious significance, because both are leaders of the Jedi cult, and moral significance, because they follow the Light Side and Dark Side of the Force, respectively.

Star Wars Galaxies. Hosted by Sony Online Entertainment from 2003 through 2011, SWG depicts eleven planets from the *Star Wars* universe, including Tatooine from the original 1977 film and Naboo from the 1999 prequel, *The Phantom Menace*. Several of the locations from the movies are depicted, and at times the player gets to interact with one of the characters, although not usually the main ones—except for Han Solo, Chewbacca, and C-3PO. Darth Vader and Luke Skywalker do make cameo appearances, but more often the familiar characters seen are secondary ones like Jabba and Watto. Set immediately after the destruction of the first Death Star in the original movie, and thus after the deaths of Amidala and Obi-Wan Kenobi, SWG imagines widespread but low-level conflict between the new Galactic Empire and the Rebel Alliance, but most of the quests involve local, peripheral conflicts. Much of the emphasis is on living on virtual worlds in a galaxy far, far away, not only giving players crafting professions but also even allowing them to be cantina entertainers.

Star Wars: The Old Republic is set in the *Star Wars* fictional universe roughly 3,500 years before the period depicted in the movies, but under very similar social, cultural, and technological conditions. Launched late in 2011, it was developed by BioWare, as an MMO extension of a successful 2003 solo-player game *Star Wars: Knights of the Old Republic*. Both emphasize elaborate predetermined story lines but with numerous choices for the player, and SWTOR is to some degree like a motion picture punctuated by episodes of game combat. Many planetary environments are often smaller than those in *Star*

Wars Galaxies but visually complex. Given how new SWTOR is, comparison with other MMOs must be tentative, but in its first manifestation it constrained the player far more than the others described here, yet offered much more fully scripted dramatic scenes.

Tabula Rasa. This short-lived but intellectually remarkable MMO was launched late in 2007 by Destination Games and NCSoft, and closed early in 2009. The premise is that only a few years in the future the Earth was invaded by a vicious extraterrestrial army called the Bane, but a few humans were able to escape to the planets Foreas and Arieki, where they formed alliances with the indigenous civilizations against the invaders. In addition to exploring these alien worlds and battling the Bane, the avatar must collect Logos symbols from widely dispersed and often hidden shrines, where they were left by an ancient civilization called the Eloh. Assembled into sentences, these Logos elements are like scientific theories or engineering designs, which give the user advanced powers.

A Tale in the Desert. Created and distributed by a small company named eGenesis, *A Tale in the Desert* is set in ancient Egypt and involves cooperative efforts to construct Egyptian society, rather than combat either between players or against nonplayer characters. ATITD goes through eighteen-month *tellings*, at the end of which the game ends, progress is erased, and the game begins again. Research for this book was conducted in Telling 4. Although ATITD has the specific levels of advancement of a competitive game, it has many of the qualities of a nongame virtual world. Many of the missions involve more-or-less authentic ancient Egyptian culture, prominently including the religion.

Warhammer Online. Developed by Mythic Entertainment in 2006, this MMO is inspired by a series of earlier Warhammer games dating back as far as 1983, and emulated Mythic's earlier *Dark Age of Camelot* in emphasizing realm-versus-realm combat. An avatar belongs to one of six nations, grouped in two factions, and, after completing two starter zones to gain experience, adventures across many regions where members of the opposing faction are often encountered. This gameworld has many battlefields and a whole series of mechanisms for assembling avatars quickly into teams. Many PvE quests have powerful religious or magical content that involves unearthing ancient secrets, performing rites at shrines, and undertaking espionage to discover the supernatural schemes of the opposing faction.

World of Warcraft. Released in 2004 by Blizzard Entertainment, WoW became the dominant MMO of the first decade of the twenty-first century, drawing upon the experience of prior experiments in this field, and influencing everything that came afterward. This was actually the fourth in a series of games, beginning with *Warcraft: Orcs and Humans*, a two-person strategy game dating from 1994, so WoW was based on a mature mythology. A world called Azeroth had been inhabited by multiple intelligent races, notably Elves and Humans, that possessed high civilizations. But the Elves had split into two factions, and the Humans had been attacked by primitive Orc invaders from another world, leading eventually to the alignment of two major factions, the Alliance and the Horde, each consisting of a half dozen races. Some were tribal and possessed shamans, while others were more civilized and possessed priests, although the most technologically advanced races tended to ignore religion altogether.

NOTES

CHAPTER I

1. Michael Lummis and Ed Kern, *World of Warcraft: Master Guide* (New York: BradyGames, 2006); Lummis and Kern, *World of Warcraft: The Burning Crusade* (New York: Brady Games, 2007); William Sims Bainbridge, *The Warcraft Civilization: Social Science in a Virtual World* (Cambridge, MA: MIT Press, 2010).
2. Robert Wuthnow, "The Contemporary Convergence of Art and Religion," in *The Oxford Handbook of the Sociology of Religion*, ed. Peter B. Clarke (Oxford: Oxford University Press, 2009), 360–74.
3. Samuel Taylor Coleridge, *Biographia Literaria* (New York: Kirk & Merein, 1817).
4. Alfred Tennyson, *Poems* (Boston: Ticknor, Reed, & Fields, 1854), 1:225.
5. E. E. Evans-Pritchard, *Witchcraft, Oracles, and Magic among the Azande* (New York: Oxford University Press, 1937); Anthony F. C. Wallace, "Revitalization Movements," *American Anthropologist* 58 (1956): 264–81; Anthony F. C. Wallace, "The Institutionalization of Cathartic and Control Strategies in Iroquois Religions Psychotherapy," in *Culture and Mental Health*, ed. Marvin K. Opler (New York: Macmillan, 1959), 63–96; Robert B. Edgerton, "Conceptions of Psychosis in Four East African Societies," *American Anthropologist* 68 (1966): 408–24; Julian Silverman, "Shamans and Acute Schizophrenia," *American Anthropologist* 69 (1967): 21–31; I. M. Lewis, *Ecstatic Religion* (Baltimore: Pelican, 1971); T. M. Luhrmann, *Persuasions of the Witch's Craft* (Cambridge, MA: Harvard University Press: 1989); Harvey Whitehouse and Luther H. Martin, eds., *Theorizing Religions Past: Archaeology, History, and Cognition* (Walnut Creek, CA: Altamira, 2004).
6. Christina Larner, *Witchcraft and Religion: The Politics of Popular Belief* (New York: Blackwell, 1984).
7. T. S. Eliot, *Four Quartets* (Orlando, FL: Harcourt, 1971), 59.
8. Wayne Grudem, "A Brief Summary of Concerns about the TNIV," *Journal for Biblical Manhood and Womanhood* 7, no. 2 (2002): 6–8; the TNIV is available online: http://www.biblegateway.com/versions/Todays-New-International-Version-TNIV-Bible/.
9. David S. J. Hodgson, Bryan Stratton, and Michael Knight, *Spore: Official Game Guide* (Roseville, CA: Prima, 2008), 119.

10. John Bohannon, "Flunking Spore," *Science*, October 24, 2008, 531; John Bohannon, T. Ryan Gregory, Niles Eldredge, and William Sims Bainbridge, "Spore: Assessment of the Science in an Evolution-Oriented Game," in *Online Worlds: Convergence of the Real and the Virtual*, ed. William Sims Bainbridge (London: Springer, 2010), 71–86.

11. John H. Holland, *Adaptation in Natural and Artificial Systems* (Ann Arbor: University of Michigan Press, 1975).

12. William Sims Bainbridge, *Sociology Laboratory* (Belmont, CA: Wadsworth, 1987); Bainbridge, *Instructor's Manual for Sociology Laboratory* (Belmont, CA: Wadsworth, 1987).

13. Bruce Damer, *Avatars* (Berkeley, CA: Peachpit, 1998); William Sims Bainbridge "Avatars and Virtual Immortality," *The Futurist* 45, no. 2 (2011): 32–33.

14. Leigh Achterbosch, Robyn Pierce, and Gregory Simmons, "Massively Multiplayer Online Role-Playing Games: The Past, Present, and Future," *Computers in Entertainment* 5, no. 4 (2007); William Sims Bainbridge, *Online Multiplayer Games* (San Rafael, CA: Morgan & Claypool, 2010).

15. Josephine S. Gottsdanker and E. Anne Pidgeon, "Current Reading Tastes of Young Adults," *Journal of Higher Education* 40, no. 5 (1969): 381–85.

16. J. R. R. Tolkien, *The Fellowship of the Ring* (New York: Ballantine, 1982), x.

17. Humphrey Carpenter, *J. R. R. Tolkien: A Biography* (Boston: Houghton Mifflin, 1977).

18. Émile Durkheim, *Elementary Forms of the Religious Life: A Study in Religious Sociology*, trans. Joseph Ward Swain (London: Allen & Unwin, 1915); Durkheim, *Suicide: A Study in Sociology*, trans. John A. Spaulding and George Simpson (New York: Free Press, 1951).

19. Robert Worth Frank, Jr., "The Art of Reading Medieval Personification-Allegory," *ELH* 20, no. 4 (1953): 237–50.

20. Eric Mylonas, *Dark Age of Camelot: Epic Edition* (Roseville, CA: Prima Games, 2005).

21. Snorri Sturluson, *The Prose Edda*, trans. Arthur Gilchrist Brodeur (New York: Oxford University Press, 1916).

22. http://support.darkageofcamelot.com/kb/article.php?id=042; no longer active.

23. William Sims Bainbridge, *Online Multiplayer Games* (San Rafael, CA: Morgan & Claypool, 2010), 16.

24. Nicolas Ducheneaut, Nick Yee, Eric Nickell, and Robert J. Moore, "Building an MMO with Mass Appeal: A Look at Gameplay in World of Warcraft," *Games and Culture* 1 (2006): 281–317; William Sims Bainbridge, "The Scientific Research Potential of Virtual Worlds," *Science*, July 27, 2007, 472–76; Bainbridge, *The Warcraft Civilization: Social Science in a Virtual World* (Cambridge, MA: MIT Press, 2010); Bainbridge, "When Virtual Worlds Expand," in *Online Worlds*, ed. William Sims Bainbridge (Guildford, UK: Springer, 2010), 237–52; Katherine Bessiere, Fleming Seay, and Sara Kiesler, "The Ideal Elf: Identity Exploration in World of Warcraft," *CyberPsychology and Behavior* 10 (2007): 530–35; Hilde G. Corneliussen and Jill Walker Rettberg, eds., *Digital Culture, Play, and Identity: A World of Warcraft Reader* (Cambridge, MA: MIT Press, 2008); Bonnie A. Nardi, *My Life as a Night Elf Priest: An Anthropological Account of World of Warcraft* (Ann Arbor: University of Michigan Press, 2010).

25. Chris Metzen, "Of Blood and Honor," in *Warcraft Archive*, by Richard A. Knaack, Christie Golden, Jeff Grubb, and Chris Metzen (New York: Pocket Books, 2002), 545–613.

26. R. S. Warner, "Work in Progress toward a New Paradigm for the Sociological Study of Religion in the United States," *American Journal of Sociology* 98 (1993): 1044–93; Ted G. Jelen, ed., *Sacred Markets, Sacred Canopies* (Lanham, MD: Rowman & Littlefield, 2002).

27. Rodney Stark and William Sims Bainbridge, "Towards a Theory of Religion: Religious Commitment," *Journal for the Scientific Study of Religion* 19 (1980): 114–28; Stark and Bainbridge, *A Theory of Religion* (New York: Lang, 1987).

28. John von Neumann and Oskar Morgenstern, *Theory of Games and Economic Behavior* (Princeton, NJ: Princeton University Press, 1944); Johan Huizinga, *Homo Ludens: A Study of the Play-Element in Culture* (London: Routledge & Kegan Paul, 1949); Erving Goffman, *The Presentation of Self in Everyday Life* (Edinburgh: University of Edinburgh, Social Sciences Research Centre, 1956); Eric Berne, *Games People Play: The Psychology of Human Relationships* (New York: Grove, 1964); Alvin W. Gouldner, *Enter Plato* (New York: Basic Books, 1965); George Caspar Homans, *Social Behavior: Its Elementary Forms* (New York: Harcourt, Brace, 1974).

29. William Sims Bainbridge, *Sociology Laboratory* (Belmont, CA: Wadsworth, 1987); "Neural Network Models of Religious Belief," *Sociological Perspectives* 38 (1995): 483–95; *God from the Machine: Artificial Intelligence Models of Religious Cognition* (Walnut Grove, CA: AltaMira, 2006).

30. Rodney Stark and William Sims Bainbridge, *A Theory of Religion* (New York: Lang, 1987), 36–39.

31. Laurence Iannaccone and William Sims Bainbridge, "Economics of Religion," in *The Routledge Companion to the Study of Religion*, ed. John Hinnells (London: Routledge, 2010), 461–75.

32. Pascal Boyer, *Religion Explained: The Evolutionary Origins of Religious Thought* (New York: Basic Books, 2001); Scott Atran, *In Gods We Trust* (New York: Oxford University Press, 2002); Justin L. Barrett, *Why Would Anyone Believe in God?* (Walnut Creek, CA: Altamira, 2004).

33. H. Porter Abbott, "Unnarratable Knowledge: The Difficulty of Understanding Evolution by Natural Selection," in *Narrative Theory and the Cognitive Sciences*, ed. David Herman (Stanford, CA: Center for the Study of Language and Information, 2003), 143–62; Abbott, *The Cambridge Introduction to Narrative* (New York: Cambridge University Press, 2008).

34. Harvey Whitehouse, *Modes of Religiosity: A Cognitive Theory of Religious Transmission* (Walnut Creek, CA: Altamira, 2004).

35. Talcott Parsons, "Evolutionary Universals in Society," *American Sociological Review* 29 (1964): 339–57.

36. Pitirim A. Sorokin, *Social and Cultural Dynamics*, 4 vols. (New York: American Book Company, 1937–1941).

37. Pitirim A. Sorokin, *Fads and Foibles in Modern Sociology and Related Sciences* (Chicago: Regnery, 1956).

38. Oswald Spengler, *The Decline of the West*, trans. Charles Francis Atkinson, 2 vols. (New York: A. A. Knopf, 1926–1928).

39. Richard S. Westfall, *Science and Religion in Seventeenth-Century England* (New Haven, CT: Yale University Press, 1958); Robert K. Merton, *Science, Technology and Society in Seventeenth-Century England* (New York: Harper & Row, 1970).

40. William Sims Bainbridge, "Artificial Intelligence," in *Leadership in Science and Technology*, ed. William Sims Bainbridge (Thousand Oaks, CA: SAGE), 464–71.

41. William Sims Bainbridge, *Satan's Power: A Deviant Psychotherapy Cult* (Berkeley: University of California Press, 1978); *The Endtime Family: Children of God* (Albany: State University of New York Press, 2002).

CHAPTER 2

1. http://guide2games.org/.
2. Zack, "The Elder Scrolls IV: Oblivion," Guide 2 Games, http://guide2games.org/2008-reviews/487/the-elder-scrolls-iv-oblivion/.
3. Ben, "Guild Wars: Prophecies," Guide 2 Games, http://guide2games.org/2009-reviews/1869/guild-wars-prophecies/.
4. SeriousGamer, "The Legend of Zelda: Ocarina of Time," Guide 2 Games, http://guide-2games.org/2009-reviews/3045/the-legend-of-zelda-ocarina-of-time/.
5. SeriousGamer, "The Sims Medieval," Guide 2 Games, http://guide2games.org/2011-reviews/6567/the-sims-medieval/.
6. Kevin Darlington, "World of Warcraft," Guide 2 Games, http://guide2games.org/2008-reviews/76/world-of-warcraft/.
7. William Sims Bainbridge and Rodney Stark, "Sectarian Tension," *Review of Religious Research* 22 (1980): 105–24.
8. http://sda.berkeley.edu/cgi-bin/hsda?harcsda+gss10.
9. James C. Witte, Lisa M. Amoroso, and Philip E. N. Howard, "Research Methodology: Method and Representation in Internet-Based Survey Tools," *Social Science Computer Review* 18 (2000): 179–95.
10. E. E. Evans-Pritchard, *Witchcraft, Oracles, and Magic among the Azande* (Oxford: Clarendon, 1937); Evans-Pritchard, *Nuer Religion* (Oxford: Clarendon, 1956).
11. Available online at http://coburn.senate.gov/public/index.cfm?a=Files.Serve&File_id=774a6cca-18fa-4619-987b-a15eb44e7f18.
12. Bonnie A. Nardi, *My Life as a Night Elf Priest: An Anthropological Account of World of Warcraft* (Ann Arbor: University of Michigan Press, 2010).
13. Bonnie Nardi, "Creative Collaboration in an Online Game," NSF Award Abstract #0829952, http://nsf.gov/awardsearch/showAward.do?AwardNumber=0829952.
14. Walt Scacchi, Bonnie Nardi, Richard Taylor, Gloria Mark, and Cristina Lopes, "Decentralized Virtual Activities and Technologies: A Socio-Technical Approach," NSF Award Abstract #0808783, http://nsf.gov/awardsearch/showAward.do?AwardNumber=0808783.
15. Yong Ming Kow and Bonnie Nardi, "Culture and Creativity: World of Warcraft Modding in China and the US," in *Online Worlds: Convergence of the Real and the Virtual*, ed. William Sims Bainbridge (London: Springer, 2010), 21–42.
16. William Sims Bainbridge, "When Virtual Worlds Expand," in *Online Worlds: Convergence of the Real and the Virtual*, ed. William Sims Bainbridge (London: Springer, 2010), 237–52.
17. Walt Scacchi, "Game-Based Virtual Worlds as Decentralized Virtual Activity Systems," in *Online Worlds: Convergence of the Real and the Virtual*, ed. William Sims Bainbridge (London: Springer, 2010), 225–36.
18. Available online at http://coburn.senate.gov/public/index.cfm?a=Files.Serve&File_id=a7e82141-1a9e-4eec-b160-6a8e62427efb.
19. Anita Hamilton, "Can Gaming Slow Mental Decline in the Elderly?" *Time*, July 11, 2009, http://www.time.com/time/health/article/0,8599,1909852,00.html.
20. Anne McLaughlin and Jason Allaire, "Collaborative Research: Improving Older Adult Cognition: The Unexamined Role of Games and Social Computing Environments," NSF Award Abstract #0905127, http://nsf.gov/awardsearch/showAward.do?AwardNumber=0905127;

Maribeth Coleman, "Improving Older Adult Cognition: The Unexamined Role of Games and Social Computing Environments," NSF Award Abstract #0904855, http://nsf.gov/awardsearch/showAward.do?AwardNumber=0904855.

21. Jonathan Chait, "Issa Targets the Scourge of Silly-Sounding Research," *New Republic Online*, February 16, 2011, http://www.tnr.com/blog/jonathan-chait/83606/issa-targets-the-scourge-silly-sounding-research.

22. YouCut, http://majorityleader.gov/YouCut/.

23. Dan Vergano, "How Some Politicians Stumble on Science," *USA Today*, December 5, 2010; http://www.usatoday.com/tech/science/columnist/vergano/2010-12-05-politics-science_N.htm.

24. Doug James, Steve Marschner, and Kavita Bala, "Sound Rendering for Physically Based Simulation," NSF Award Abstract #0905506, http://nsf.gov/awardsearch/showAward.do?AwardNumber=0905506.

25. Max Weber, *The Protestant Ethic and the Spirit of Capitalism* (London: Allen & Unwin, 1930).

26. Tom Coburn, *The National Science Foundation: Under the Microscope*, report available online, http://www.coburn.senate.gov/public/index.cfm?a=Files.serve&File_id=2dccf06d-65fe-4087-b58d-b43ff68987fa, p. 38.

27. William Sims Bainbridge and Wilma Alice Bainbridge, "Electronic Game Research Methodologies: Studying Religious Implications," *Review of Religious Research* 49, no. 1 (2007): 35–53.

28. http://dmitriwilliams.com/research.html.

29. Searle Huh and Dmitri Williams, "Dude Looks Like a Lady: Gender Swapping in an Online Game," in *Online Worlds: Convergence of the Real and the Virtual*, ed. William Sims Bainbridge (London: Springer, 2010), 161–74.

30. Celia Pearce and Artemesia, "The Diasporic Game Community: Trans-Ludic Cultures and Latitudinal Research Across Multiple Games and Virtual Worlds," in *Online Worlds: Convergence of the Real and the Virtual*, ed. William Sims Bainbridge (London: Springer, 2010), 43–56; Jeremy N. Bailenson and Kathryn Y. Segovia, "Virtual Doppelgangers: Psychological Effects of Avatars Who Ignore Their Owners," in *Online Worlds: Convergence of the Real and the Virtual*, ed. William Sims Bainbridge (London: Springer, 2010), 175–86.

31. Nicole Ellison and Clifford Lampe, "The Role of Social Network Sites in Facilitating Collaborative Processes," NSF Award Abstract #0916019, http://www.nsf.gov/awardsearch/showAward.do?AwardNumber=0916019.

32. Nicole B. Ellison, Charles Steinfield, and Cliff Lampe, "Connection Strategies: Social Capital Implications of Facebook-enabled Communication Practices," *New Media and Society* 13 (2011): 873–92.

33. Bonnie Nardi, Nicole Ellison, and Cliff Lampe, "Understanding Science: Context for Senator Tom Coburn's 'Under the Microscope' Report," *Interactions* 18, no. 6 (2011): 32–35.

34. Arlene de Strulle and Joseph Psotka, "Educational Games and Virtual Reality," in *Leadership in Science and Technology*, ed. William Sims Bainbridge (Thousand Oaks, CA: SAGE, 2011), 830.

35. Rodney Brown, "MassDiGI Unlocks $500K Achievement from Commerce Dept.," *Mass High Tech*, September 27, 2011, http://www.masshightech.com/stories/2011/09/26/daily11-MassDiGIunlocks-500K-achievement-from-Commerce-Dept.html.

36. Frank Cifaldi, "The Strong Receives Over $100K Grant for Video Game Preservation," *Gamasutra*, May 26, 2011, http://www.gamasutra.com/view/news/34866/The_Strong_Receives_Over_100K_Grant_For_Video_Game_Preservation.php.

37. "Virtual Sprouts: Web-based Gardening Games to Teach Nutrition and Combat Obesity," SEPA Grant 1 R25 RR032159-01, http://www.ncrrsepa.org/grants/virtual-sprouts-web-based-gardening-games-teach-nutrition-and-combat-obesity.

38. Available online at http://www.whitehouse.gov/sites/default/files/microsites/ostp/pcast-nitrd-report-2010.pdf.

39. Ross S. Kraemer, William Cassidy, and Susan L. Schwartz, *Religions of Star Trek* (Boulder, CO: Westview, 2003).

40. Jennifer E. Porter and Darcee L. McLaren, *Star Trek and Sacred Ground* (Albany: State University of New York Press, 1999), 3.

41. *Memory Alpha*, "Christianity," http://en.memory-alpha.org/wiki/Christianity.

42. John de Lancie and Peter David, *I, Q* (New York: Pocket Books, 1999).

43. *Memory Alpha*, "In the Hands of the Prophets (episode)," http://en.memory-alpha.org/wiki/In_the_Hands_of_the_Prophets_%28episode%29.

44. *Memory Alpha*, "Star Trek: Deep Space Nine—The Fallen," http://en.memory-alpha.org/wiki/The_Fallen.

45. *Memory Beta*, "The Fallen (game)," http://memory-beta.wikia.com/wiki/The_Fallen_%28game%29.

46. *Memory Beta*, "Obanak Keelen," http://memory-beta.wikia.com/wiki/Obanak_Keelen.

47. Judith Reeves-Stevens and Garfield Reeves-Stevens, *Star Trek: Prime Directive* (New York: Pocket Books, 1990).

48. *Memory Alpha*, "Klingon," http://en.memory-alpha.org/wiki/Klingon.

49. *Memory Alpha*, "Rules of Acquisition," http://en.memory-alpha.org/wiki/Rules_of_Acquisition.

50. See Émile Durkheim, *The Elementary Forms of the Religious Life* (London: Allen & Unwin, 1915), and Max Weber, *The Protestant Ethic and the Spirit of Capitalism* (London: Allen & Unwin, 1930).

51. Joseph Conrad, *Heart of Darkness* (New York: New American Library, 1950).

CHAPTER 3

1. Cassius Jackson Keyser, *The New Infinite and the Old Theology* (New Haven, CT: Yale University Press, 1915), 28.

2. *EQ2i*, "Zones by Level," http://eq2.wikia.com/wiki/Zones_By_Level.

3. *EQ2i*, "Druid Rings," http://eq2.wikia.com/wiki/Druid_Rings.

4. William Sims Bainbridge and Rodney Stark, "Scientology: To Be Perfectly Clear," *Sociological Analysis* 41 (1980): 128–36; William Sims Bainbridge, "Science and Religion: The Case of Scientology," in *The Future of New Religious Movements*, ed. David G. Bromley and Phillip E. Hammond (Macon, GA: Mercer University Press, 1987), 59–79; Bainbridge, "The Cultural Context of Scientology," in *Scientology*, ed. James R. Lewis (New York: Oxford University Press, 2009), 35–51.

5. William Sims Bainbridge, *Satan's Power* (Berkeley: University of California Press, 1978); Bainbridge, "Social Construction from Within," in *The Satanism Scare*, ed. James T. Richardson, Joel Best, and David Bromley (New York: Aldine de Gruyter, 1991), 297–310.

6. Alvin W. Gouldner, *The Coming Crisis of Western Sociology* (New York: Basic Books, 1970).

7. William Folwell Bainbridge, *Around the World Tour of Christian Missions* (New York: Blackall, 1882); *Along the Lines at the Front: A General Survey of Baptist Home and Foreign Missions* (Philadelphia: American Baptist Publication Society, 1882); Lucy Seaman Bainbridge, *Round the World Letters* (Boston: Lothrop, 1882), *Jewels from the Orient* (New York: Fleming H. Revell, 1920); *Yesterdays* (New York: Fleming H. Revell, 1924).

8. Providence, Rhode Island, death records, vol. 12, p. 153.

9. William Folwell Bainbridge, *Around the World Tour of Christian Missions* (New York: Blackall, 1882), 343.

10. Lucy Seaman Bainbridge, "Mrs. Dana's Christmas Day," undated newspaper clipping, ca. early 1870s.

11. William Folwell Bainbridge, *Self-Giving: A Story of Christian Missions* (Boston: Lothrop, 1883), 36.

12. *EQ2i*, "Brell Serilis," http://eq2.wikia.com/wiki/Brell_Serilis.

13. *Zam*, "Brell Serilis," http://eq2.zam.com/wiki/brell_serilis.

14. *EQ2i*, "The Trial of Clay," http://eq2.wikia.com/wiki/The_Trial_of_Clay.

15. As of January 2011, the only way to rise above level 80 was to subscribe to *EverQuest II* for an entire year.

16. *EQ2i*, "The Trial of Bronze," http://eq2.wikia.com/wiki/The_Trial_of_Bronze.

17. William Sims Bainbridge, *Satan's Power* (Berkeley: University of California Press, 1978), 181.

18. Friedrich Nietzsche, *Die fröhliche Wissenschaft* (1882), chap. 341, available online at http://www.textlog.de/21554.html.

19. *EQ2i*, "Gods," http://eq2.wikia.com/wiki/Gods.

20. *SacredWiki*, "Kybele, Goddess of Nature," http://www.sacredwiki.org/index.php5/Sacred_2:Book_1_-_Kybele%2C_Goddess_of_Nature.

21. James Lovelock, *Gaia: A New Look at Life on Earth* (New York: Oxford University Press, 1979).

22. Alfred Tennyson, *In Memoriam* (London: Edward Moxon, 1851), v; the labyrinth phrase is on p. 146.

23. See Edward Lucas White, *Andivius Hedulio: Adventures of a Roman Nobleman in the Days of the Empire* (New York: E. P. Dutton, 1921).

24. The lifting of the nondisclosure agreement was announced on the *Gods and Heroes* web site: http://godsandheroes.com/gods-heroes-lifting-the-nda/.

25. *Gods and Heroes*, "Scout," http://godsandheroes.wikia.com/wiki/Scout; *Gods and Heroes*, "Nomad," http://godsandheroes.wikia.com/wiki/Nomad.

26. Ninian Smart, *The Religious Experience of Mankind* (New York: Scribner, 1969).

27. James O'Donnell, "The Demise of Paganism," *Traditio* 35 (1977): 45–88.

28. Rodney Stark, *The Rise of Christianity* (Princeton, NJ: Princeton University Press, 1996); Stark, *The Victory of Reason: How Christianity Led to Freedom, Capitalism, and Western Success* (New York: Random House, 2005).

29. Rodney Stark and William Sims Bainbridge, *A Theory of Religion* (New York: Lang, 1987).

30. Jérôme Carcopino, *Daily Life in Ancient Rome* (New Haven, CT: Yale University Press, 1940), 121–22.

31. "Dark Elf," *Lineage II* website, http://www.lineage2.com/en/game/races-and-classes/dark-elf.php.

32. William Sims Bainbridge, *The Warcraft Civilization: Social Science in a Virtual World* (Cambridge, MA: MIT Press, 2010).

33. Eric Mylonas and Robert Howarth, *Dark Age of Camelot Epic Edition* (Roseville, CA: Prima Games, 2005), 213.

34. Howard Grossman, Gerald Guess, Zane Seraphim, and Troy Silver, *God of War: Official Game Guide* (Roseville, CA: Prima Games, 2005).

CHAPTER 4

1. Allen Newell, *Unified Theories of Cognition* (Cambridge, MA: Harvard University Press, 1990).

2. Alan Turing, "Computing Machinery and Intelligence," *Mind* 59 (1950): 433–60; William Sims Bainbridge, "Artificial Intelligence," in *Leadership in Science and Technology: A Reference Handbook*, ed. William Sims Bainbridge (Thousand Oaks, CA: SAGE, 2011), 2: 464–71.

3. Tracy Kidder, *The Soul of a New Machine* (Boston: Little, Brown, 1981).

4. William Sims Bainbridge, *Sociology Laboratory* (Belmont, CA: Wadsworth, 1987); Bainbridge, "Minimum Intelligent Neural Device: A Tool for Social Simulation," *Mathematical Sociology* 20 (1995): 179–92; Bainbridge, "Neural Network Models of Religious Belief," *Sociological Perspectives* 38 (1995): 483–95; Bainbridge, *God from the Machine: Artificial Intelligence Models of Religious Cognition* (Walnut Grove, CA: AltaMira, 2006).

5. David E. Rumelhart and James L. McClelland, *Parallel Distributed Processing* (Cambridge, MA: MIT Press, 1986).

6. Marvin Minsky, *The Society of Mind* (New York: Simon & Schuster, 1988).

7. William Sims Bainbridge, "Religious Insanity in America: The Official Nineteenth-Century Theory," *Sociological Analysis* 45 (1984): 223–40.

8. Paul Bloom, *Descartes' Baby: How the Science of Child Development Explains What Makes Us Human* (New York: Basic Books, 2004); Bloom, "The Duel between Body and Soul," *New York Times*, September 10, 2004.

9. Michael S. Gazzaniga, "The Split Brain Revisited," in "The Hidden Mind," ed. John Rennie, special issue, *Scientific American*, 2002, 26–31; D. J. Turk, T. F. Heatherton, W. M. Kelley, M. G. Funnell, M. S. Gazzaniga, and C. N. Macrae. "Mike or Me? Self-recognition in a Split-brain Patient," *Nature Neuroscience* 5 (2002): 841–42.

10. S. Zeki, "The Disunity of Consciousness," *Trends in Cognitive Sciences* 7 (2007): 214–18.

11. George A. Miller, "The Magical Number Seven, Plus or Minus Two: Some Limits on Our Capacity for Processing Information," *Psychological Review* 63 (1956): 81–97.

12. Pascal Boyer, *Religion Explained: The Evolutionary Origins of Religious Thought* (New York: Basic Books, 2001); Scott Atran, *In Gods We Trust: The Evolutionary Landscape of Religion* (Oxford: Oxford University Press, 2002).

13. Ioan M. Lewis, *Ecstatic Religion: An Anthropological Study of Spirit Possession and Shamanism* (Harmondsworth, UK: Penguin, 1971); Lewis, "The Social Roots and Meaning of Trance and Possession," in *The Oxford Handbook of the Sociology of Religion*, ed. Peter B. Clarke (Oxford: Oxford University Press, 2009), 375–90.

14. Robert Jay Lifton, "Protean Man," *Archives of General Psychiatry* 24, no. 4 (1971): 298–304.

15. Robert Shaw, *The Man in the Glass Booth* (London: Chatto & Windus, 1967).

16. Matthew Stover, *Star Wars: Revenge of the Sith* (New York: Ballantine, 2005).

17. Andrew Gordon, "Star Wars: A Myth for Our Time," in *Screening the Sacred: Religion, Myth and Ideology in Popular American Film*, ed. Joel W. Martin and Conrad E. Ostwalt (Boulder, CO: Westview, 1995).

18. Eugen Herrigel, *Zen in the Art of Archery* (New York: Pantheon, 1953); Daisetz Teitaro Suzuki, *Zen Buddhism* (Garden City, NY: Doubleday, 1956); Paul Reps and Nyogen Senzaki, *Zen Flesh, Zen Bones* (Rutland, VT: Charles E. Tuttle, 1957); Alan W. Watts, *The Way of Zen* (New York: Pantheon, 1957).

19. Veronica Whitney-Robinson and Haden Blackman, *Star Wars Galaxies: The Ruins of Dantooine* (New York: Ballantine, 2004).

20. The earlier system is presented in Chris McCubbin, David Ladyman, and Tuesday Frase, eds., *Star Wars Galaxies: The Total Experience* (Roseville, CA: Prima Games, 2005), and the newer version in Chris McCubbin, *Star Wars Galaxies: The Complete Guide* (Roseville, CA: Prima Games, 2005).

21. William Sims Bainbridge, *Dimensions of Science Fiction* (Cambridge, MA: Harvard University Press, 1986).

22. Alfred Bester, *The Demolished Man* (Chicago: Shasta, 1953); Bester, *The Stars My Destination* (New York: New American Library, 1956).

23. J. Gregory Keyes, *Dark Genesis: The Birth of the Psi Corps* (New York: Ballantine, 1998); Keyes, *Deadly Relations: Bester Ascendant* (New York: Ballantine, 1999); Keyes, *Final Reckoning: The Fate of Bester* (New York: Ballantine, 1999).

24. William Sims Bainbridge and Rodney Stark, "Scientology: To Be Perfectly Clear," *Sociological Analysis* 41 (1980): 128–36; William Sims Bainbridge, "Science and Religion: The Case of Scientology," in *The Future of New Religious Movements*, ed. David G. Bromley and Phillip E. Hammond (Macon, GA: Mercer University Press, 1987), 59–79; Bainbridge, "The Cultural Context of Scientology," in *Scientology*, ed. James R. Lewis (New York: Oxford University Press, 2009), 35–51.

25. William Sims Bainbridge, *The Sociology of Religious Movements* (New York: Routledge, 1997).

26. *AoCWiki*, "Necromancer," http://aoc.wikia.com/wiki/Necromancer.

27. *AoCWiki*, "Pets," http://aoc.wikia.com/wiki/Pets.

28. Lionel Wafer, *A New Voyage and Description of the Isthmus of America* (Cleveland: Burrows, 1903).

29. Catullus, "Letter to a Supernatural Being," in *Human Futures: Art in an Age of Uncertainty*, ed. Andy Miah (Liverpool, UK: Liverpool University Press, 2008), 247–55; Rumilisoun [William Sims Bainbridge], "Rebirth of Worlds," *Communications of the ACM* 53, no. 12 (2010): 128.

30. Louis Effingham De Forest, *Ancestry of William Seaman Bainbridge* (Oxford: Scrivener, 1950).

31. William Adee Whitehead, ed., *Documents Relating to the Colonial History of the State of New Jersey*, vol. 7 (Newark, NJ: Daily Advertiser Printing House, 1883), 458.

32. Francis Bazley Lee, ed., *Genealogical and Personal Memorial of Mercer County, New Jersey*, vol. 1 (New York: Lewis, 1907), 10.

33. Murray Rothbard, *Conceived in Liberty*, vol. 2, *"Salutary Neglect": The American Colonies in the First Half of the 18th Century* (Auburn, AL: Mises Institute, 1975), 49.

34. Paul Finkelman, ed., *Abolitionists in Northern Courts: The Pamphlet Literature* (Clark, NJ: Lawbook Exchange, 2007), 55.

35. William Seaman Bainbridge, *Report on Medical and Surgical Developments of the War* (Washington, DC: Government Printing Office, 1919).

36. William Seaman Bainbridge, *A Report on Present Conditions in the Ruhr and Rhineland* (New York: New York Commandery, Military Order of Foreign Wars, 1923).

37. Consuelo Andrew Seoane, *Beyond the Ranges* (New York: Robert Spellar, 1960).

38. Louis Livingston Seaman, *The Real Triumph of Japan: The Conquest of the Silent Foe* (New York: Appleton, 1906), 263.

39. Several of the espionage charts of Japanese coastal defenses have been published in a book compiled by Con's third wife: Rhoda Low Seoane, *Uttermost East and the Longest War* (New York: Vantage, 1968).

40. Meyer Fortes, "Pietas in Ancestor Worship," *Journal of the Royal Anthropological Institute of Great Britain and Ireland* 91, no. 2 (1961): 166–91.

41. Zaheer Hussain and Mark D. Griffiths, "Gender Swapping and Socializing in Cyberspace: An Exploratory Study," *CyberPsychology and Behavior* 11 (2008): 47–53; Nicolas Ducheneaut, Ming-Hui Wen, Nicholas Yee, and Greg Wadley, "Body and Mind: A Study of Avatar Personalization in Three Virtual Worlds," in *Proceedings of the 27th International Conference on Human Factors in Computing Systems* (New York: ACM, 2009), 1151–60; Searle Huh and Dmitri Williams, "Dude Looks Like a Lady: Gender Swapping in an Online Game," in *Online Worlds*, ed. William Sims Bainbridge (Guildford, UK: Springer, 2010), 161–74; Dmitri Williams, Tracy L. M. Kennedy, and Robert J. Moore, "Behind the Avatar: The Patterns, Practices and Functions of Role Playing in MMOs," *Games and Culture* 6, no. 2 (2011): 171–200.

CHAPTER 5

1. William Sims Bainbridge and Rodney Stark, "Cult Formation: Three Compatible Models," *Sociological Analysis* 40 (1979): 285–95.

2. Sigmund Freud, *The Future of an Illusion* (Garden City, NY: Doubleday, 1961); Freud, *Civilization and Its Discontents* (New York: Norton, 1962); George Devereux, ed., *Psychoanalysis and the Occult* (New York: International Universities Press, 1953); Geza Roheim, *Magic and Schizophrenia* (Bloomington: Indiana University Press, 1955); Weston La Barre, *They Shall Take Up Serpents* (New York: Schocken, 1969); La Barre, *The Ghost Dance* (New York: Dell, 1972).

3. William Sims Bainbridge, "The Psychoanalytic Movement," in *Leadership in Science and Technology*, ed. William Sims Bainbridge (Thousand Oaks, CA: SAGE, 2011), 520–28.

4. Julian Silverman, "Shamans and Acute Schizophrenia," *American Anthropologist* 69 (1967): 21–32.

5. Rodney Stark and William Sims Bainbridge, *A Theory of Religion* (New York: Lang, 1987).

6. E. E. Evans-Pritchard, *Witchcraft, Oracles and Magic among the Azande* (Oxford: Clarendon, 1937).

7. Herbert Spencer, *The Study of Sociology* (New York: Appleton, 1874).

8. Émile Durkheim, *The Division of Labor in Society* (New York: Free Press, 1964).

9. William Sims Bainbridge, "A Prophet's Reward: Dynamics of Religious Exchange," in *Sacred Markets, Sacred Canopies*, ed. Ted G. Jelen (Lanham, MD: Rowman & Littlefield, 2002), 63–89; Bainbridge, "Sacred Algorithms: Exchange Theory of Religious Claims," in *Defining Religion*, ed. David Bromley and Larry Greil (Amsterdam: JAI Elsevier, 2003), 21–37.

10. *WoWWiki*, "Priest Races," http://www.wowwiki.com/Priest_races.

11. Robert E. Howard, "The Hyborian Age," available online at http://gutenberg.net.au/ebooks06/0603571.txt.

12. L. Sprague De Camp, Catherine Crook de Camp, and Jane Whittington Griffin, *Dark Valley Destiny: The Life of Robert E. Howard* (New York: Bluejay, 1983).

13. In chapter 1 of Robert E. Howard, *The Hour of the Dragon*, available online at http://gutenberg.net.au/ebooks06/0600981.txt.

14. Robert E. Howard, "Black Colossus," 1933, available online at http://gutenberg.net.au/ebooks06/0600931.txt.

15. H. P. Lovecraft, quoted by Paul A. Carter, *The Creation of Tomorrow* (New York: Columbia University Press, 1977), 7.

16. Sigmund Freud, *Civilization and Its Discontents* (New York: J. Cape and H. Smith, 1930); Freud, *The Future of an Illusion* (Garden City, NY: Doubleday, 1961).

17. H. P. Lovecraft, "The Call of Cthulhu," 1926, available online at http://gutenberg.net.au/ebooks06/0600031.txt.

18. Edward Gibbon, *History of the Decline and Fall of the Roman Empire* (New York: Hurst, 1880).

19. Oswald Spengler, *The Decline of the West*, trans. Charles Francis Atkinson, 2 vols. (New York: A. A. Knopf, 1926–1928).

20. Pitirim A. Sorokin, *Social and Cultural Dynamics*, 4 vols. (New York: American Book Company, 1937–1941).

21. *FFXIclopedia*, "White Mage," http://wiki.ffxiclopedia.org/wiki/White_Mage.

22. http://theinstance.net/.

23. http://www.wowarmory.com/; note that the structure of the Armory has changed since I collected the date reported here.

24. http://www.warcraftrealms.com/census.php; retrieved November 14, 2008.

25. Shelley J. Correll, "Constraints into Preferences: Gender, Status, and Emerging Career Aspirations," *American Sociological Review* 69 (2004): 93–113.

26. Nicolas Ducheneaut, Nick Yee, Eric Nickell, and Robert J. Moore, "Building an MMO with Mass Appeal: A Look at Gameplay in World of Warcraft," *Games and Culture* 1 (2006): 281–317.

27. *WoWWiki*, "Class," http://www.wowwiki.com/Class.

28. Positive correlations between mining and the three crafting professions dependent upon it illustrate their consistent connections: blacksmithing (0.31 and 0.37), engineering (0.29 and 0.30), and jewelcrafting (0.24 and 0.24).

29. The correlations between enchanting and tailoring are 0.54 in the AIE dataset and 0.48 in the Two Realms dataset.

30. Robert Washington and David Karen, "Sport and Society," *Annual Review of Sociology* 27 (2001): 187–212; Mary R. Jackman, "Violence in Social Life," *Annual Review of Sociology* 28 (2002): 387–415.

31. Alan S. Miller and Rodney Stark, "Gender and Religiousness: Can Socialization Explanations Be Saved?" *American Journal of Sociology* 107 (2002): 1399–423.

32. Alice S. Rossi, "Gender and Parenthood," *American Sociological Review* 49 (1984): 1–19; Beth Anne Shelton and Daphne John, "The Division of Household Labor," *Annual Review of Sociology* 22 (1996): 299–322.

33. Heather A. Turner and R. Jay Turner, "Gender, Social Status, and Emotional Reliance," *Journal of Health and Social Behavior* 40 (1999): 360–73.

34. Lionel Tiger, *Men in Groups* (New York: Random House, 1969).

35. *WoWWiki*, "Priest Talents," http://www.wowwiki.com/Priest_talents.

36. *WoWWiki*, "Warrior Talents," http://www.wowwiki.com/Warrior_talents.

37. Bronislaw Malinowski, *Argonauts of the Western Pacific* (London: Routledge, 1922).

38. *A Wiki in the Desert*, "Path of the Pilgrim," http://www.atitd.org/wiki/tale4/Path_of_the_Pilgrim.

39. *A Wiki in the Desert*, "Test of Festivals," http://www.atitd.org/wiki/tale4/Test_of_Festivals.

40. *A Wiki in the Desert*, "Test of Beacons," http://www.atitd.org/wiki/tale4/Test_of_Beacons.

41. *A Wiki in the Desert*, "Test of Leavened Bread," http://www.atitd.org/wiki/tale4/Test_of_Leavened_Bread.

42. *A Wiki in the Desert*, "Remembrance Ceremonies," http://www.atitd.org/wiki/tale4/Remembrance_Ceremonies.

43. *A Wiki in the Desert*, "Test of the Humble Priests," http://www.atitd.org/wiki/tale4/Test_of_the_Humble_Priests.

CHAPTER 6

1. William Sims Bainbridge, ed., *Online Worlds: Convergence of the Real and the Virtual* (London: Springer, 2010); this book is the proceedings from the conference.

2. *WoWWiki*, "Shrine of the Fallen Warrior," http://www.wowwiki.com/Shrine_of_the_Fallen_Warrior.

3. Percy Bysshe Shelley, "Ozymandias," in *Poems by Wordsworth, Coleridge, Shelley, and Keats*, ed. James Weber Linn (New York: Holt, 1911), 105.

4. Jerry S. Wiggins, ed., *The Five-Factor Model of Personality: Theoretical Perspectives* (New York: Guilford, 1996).

5. Christopher McIntosh, *Gardens of the Gods: Myth, Magic and Meaning* (London: I. B. Tauris, 2005), 14.

6. Louis H. Sullivan, "The Tall Office Building Artistically Considered," *Lippincott's Magazine*, March 1896, 403–9; quotation from 408.

7. William Sims Bainbridge and Wilma Alice Bainbridge, "Electronic Game Research Methodologies: Studying Religious Implications," *Review of Religious Research* 49, no. 1 (2007): 35–53.

8. Erik Champion, *Playing with the Past* (London: Springer, 2011).

9. Chris is my first cousin.

10. James L. Garlow and Peter Jones, *Cracking Da Vinci's Code* (Colorado Springs, CO: Victor, 2004).

11. "The Da Vinci Code, the Catholic Church and Opus Dei: A Response to The Da Vinci Code from the Prelature of Opus Dei in the United States," statement on the Opus Dei website, http://www.opusdei.us/art.php?p=6437.

12. "Personal Prelature," Opus Dei website, http://www.opusdei.us/sec.php?s=1008.

13. Marco Polo, *The Travels of Marco Polo* (Edinburgh: Oliver & Boyd, 1845), 277.

14. Nate Ahearn, "The Da Vinci Code Review," TeamXBox, May 22, 2006; http://reviews. teamxbox.com/xbox/1174/The-Da-Vinci-Code/p.3/.

15. http://translate.google.com/#la|en|.

16. Dan Brown, *The Da Vinci Code: Special Illustrated Edition* (New York: Doubleday, 2004), 96.

17. Dan Brown, *The Da Vinci Code: Special Illustrated Edition* (New York: Doubleday, 2004), 110.

18. Lynn Picknett and Clive Prince, *The Templar Revelation: Secret Guardians of the True Identity of Christ* (New York: Simon & Schuster, 1997).

19. *Wikipedia*, "Saint-Sulpice, Paris," http://en.wikipedia.org/wiki/%C3%89glise_Saint-Sulpice,_Paris.

20. Pope John Paul II, "Meditation and Prayers for the Stations of the Cross at the Colosseum," available online at http://www.pcf.va/holy_father/john_paul_ii/speeches/documents/hf_jp-ii_spe_20000421_via-crucis_en.html.

21. Dan Brown, *The Da Vinci Code: Special Illustrated Edition* (New York: Doubleday, 2004), 344.

22. Temple Church History, Temple Church, London website, http://www.templechurch.com/history-2/.

23. Spheriscope: Temple Church, http://www.spheriscope.com/templetour/.

24. *TOR Wiki*, "Tython," http://swtor.wikia.com/wiki/Tython.

25. *FFXIclopedia*, "Bastok," http://wiki.ffxiclopedia.org/wiki/Bastok.

26. *FFXIclopedia*, "Windurst," http://wiki.ffxiclopedia.org/wiki/Windurst.

27. *FFXIclopedia*, "San d'Oria," http://wiki.ffxiclopedia.org/wiki/San_d'Oria; *FFXIclopedia*, "Cathedral," http://wiki.ffxiclopedia.org/wiki/Cathedral; *FFXIclopedia*, "Altana," http://wiki.ffxiclopedia.org/wiki/Altana.

28. *EQII Stratics*, "Cities and Factions: Qeynos," http://eq2.stratics.com/content/lore/lore_cities_qeynos.php.

29. Geoffrey Ashe, *The Glastonbury Tor Maze* (Glastonbury, UK: Gothic Image, 1979).

30. C. A. Raleigh Radford, *Glastonbury Abbey* (London: Pitkin, 1973).

31. Lionel Smithett Lewis, *St. Joseph of Arimathea at Glastonbury* (Cambridge, UK: Clarke, 1922); E. Raymond Capt, *The Traditions of Glastonbury* (Thousand Oaks, CA: Artisan, 1983); Glastonbury Advertising Association, *The Glastonbury Guide* (Glastonbury, UK: Glastonbury Advertising Association, n.d. [prior to 1985]).

32. William Blake, *The Portable Blake* (New York: Viking, 1946), 412.

33. Geoffrey Chaucer, *The Canterbury Tales*, ed. Robert Boenig and Andrew Taylor (Peterborough, ON: Broadview, 2008).

34. Geoffrey Ashe, ed., *The Quest for Arthur's Britain* (London: Paladin, 1968); Leslie Alcock, *Arthur's Britain* (Harmondsworth, UK: Penguin, 1971); Graham Ashton, *The Realm of King Arthur* (Newport, UK: Dixon, 1974).

35. J. R. R. Tolkien, *The Hobbit; or, There and Back Again* (New York: Ballantine, 1982), 41, 72.

36. J. R. R. Tolkien, *The Fellowship of the Ring* (New York: Ballantine, 1982), 173, 245; Elrond's house also appears in *The Hobbit*.

37. Alvin W. Gouldner, *Enter Plato* (New York: Basic Books, 1965); Gouldner, *The Hellenic World: A Sociological Analysis* (New York: Harper & Row, 1969).

38. Johan Huizinga, *Homo Ludens: A Study of the Play-Element in Culture* (London: Routledge & Kegan Paul, 1949).

CHAPTER 7

1. Rodney Stark and William Sims Bainbridge, *A Theory of Religion* (New York: Lang, 1987); William Sims Bainbridge, "Religion and Science," in *Leadership in Science and Technology*, ed. William Sims Bainbridge (Thousand Oaks, CA: SAGE, 2012), 307–15.

2. James George Frazer, *The Golden Bough: A Study in Magic and Religion* (London: Macmillan, 1900), 63.

3. Alfred Korzybski, *Science and Sanity: An Introduction to Non-Aristotelian Systems and General Semantics* (Lancaster, PA: International Non-Aristotelian Library, 1941).

4. *Wikipedia*, "Figures of Speech," http://en.wikipedia.org/wiki/Figures_of_speech.

5. Reo F. Fortune, *Sorcerers of Dobu* (London: Routledge, 1932).

6. William Sims Bainbridge, "Virtual Sustainability," *Sustainability* 2, no. 10 (2010): 3195–210.

7. William Sims Bainbridge, *The Sociology of Religious Movements* (New York: Routledge, 1997), 155.

8. *WoWWiki*, "Priest Abilities," http://www.wowwiki.com/Priest_abilities.

9. William Sims Bainbridge, *Dimensions of Science Fiction* (Cambridge, MA: Harvard University Press, 1986); Bainbridge, "Science Fiction," in *Leadership in Science and Technology*, ed. William Sims Bainbridge (Thousand Oaks, CA: SAGE, 2012), 537–45.

10. William Sims Bainbridge, "The Cultural Context of Scientology," in *Scientology*, ed. James R. Lewis (New York: Oxford University Press, 2009), 35–51.

11. L. Sprague de Camp and Fletcher Pratt, *The Incomplete Enchanter* (New York: Holt, 1941).

12. Fritz Leiber, *Gather, Darkness!* (New York: Pellegrini & Cudahy, 1950).

13. Geoffrey Chaucer, *The Canterbury Tales*, ed. Robert Boenig and Andrew Taylor (Peterborough, ON: Broadview, 2008).

14. Michael Searle, *The Lord of the Rings Online: Shadows of Angmar Prima Official Game Guide* (Roseville, CA: Prima, 2007), 111.

15. Chris McCubbin, *The Matrix Online: Prima Official Game Guide* (Roseville, CA: Prima Games, 2005).

16. Jean Baudrillard, *Simulacra and Simulation* (Ann Arbor: University of Michigan Press, 1994).

17. William Irwin, ed., *The Matrix and Philosophy: Welcome to the Desert of the Real* (Chicago: Open Court, 2002); Glenn Yeffeth, ed., *Taking the Red Pill: Science, Philosophy, and Religion in The Matrix* (Dallas: BenBella, 2003).

18. Peter Olafson, *The Elder Scrolls IV: Oblivion, Official Game Guide* (Rockville, MD: Bethesda Softworks, 2006).

19. *A Pocket Guide to the Empire and Its Environs* (Rockville, MD: Bethesda Softworks, 2006), ii.

20. Lionel Wafer, *A New Voyage and Description of the Isthmus of America* (Cleveland: Burrows, 1903).

21. *Pirates of the Caribbean Online Wiki*, "Allies," http://piratesonline.wikia.com/wiki/Allies.

22. *Pirates of the Caribbean Online Wiki*, "Voodoo Doll," http://piratesonline.wikia.com/wiki/Category:Voodoo_Doll.

23. Homer, *The Odyssey of Homer*, trans. William Cullen Bryant (Boston: Osgood, 1871), 1:123.

24. Rob Chestny, *The Journal of Master Gnost-Dural* (San Francisco: Chronicle, 2011), 10.

25. Alfred Bester, *The Demolished Man* (Chicago: Shasta, 1953); Bester, *The Stars My Destination* (New York: New American Library, 1956).

26. J. W. Rinzer, *The Making of Star Wars* (New York: Ballantine, 2007); Robert R. Barrett, "How John Carter Became Flash Gordon," *Burroughs Bulletin* 60 (2004): 19–26; Bill Hillman and Sue-On Hillman, "ERB's John Carter/Flash Gordon Connection I," *ERBZine*, http://www.erbzine.com/mag33/3393.html.

27. Edgar Rice Burroughs, *The Gods of Mars* (Chicago: A. C. McClurg, 1918).

28. Mircea Eliade, *The Forge and the Crucible: The Origins and Structure of Alchemy* (New York: Harper, 1962); Carl Gustav Jung, *Alchemical Studies* (Princeton, NJ: Princeton University Press, 1967).

29. Arnold van Gennep, *The Rites of Passage* (London: Routledge & Paul, 1960).

30. *WoWWiki*, "Alchemy," http://www.wowwiki.com/Alchemy.

31. William Sims Bainbridge, *The Warcraft Civilization: Social Science in a Virtual World* (Cambridge, MA: MIT Press, 2010), 79.

32. Aihe Wang, *Cosmology and Political Culture in Early China* (New York: Cambridge University Press, 2000).

33. *PWpedia*, "Genie Basics," http://pwi-wiki.perfectworld.com/index.php/Genie_Basics.

34. Alexander Roberts and James Donaldson, eds., *The Works of Lactantius*, Ante-Nicene Christian Library 21 (Edinburgh: Clark, 1871), 1:16.

CHAPTER 8

1. William Sims Bainbridge, "Values," in *The Encyclopedia of Language and Linguistics*, ed. R. E. Asher and J. M. Y. Simpson (Oxford: Pergamon, 1994), 4888–92.

2. Talcott Parsons and Edward A. Shils, eds., *Toward a General Theory of Action* (Cambridge, MA: Harvard University Press, 1951); Talcott Parsons, "Evolutionary Universals in Society," *American Sociological Review* 29 (1964): 339–57.

3. Leon Festinger, *A Theory of Cognitive Dissonance* (Evanston, IL: Row, Peterson, 1957); Leon Festinger, Henry W. Riecken, and Stanley Schachter, *When Prophecy Fails* (Minneapolis: University of Minnesota Press, 1956).

4. Allen Newell, *Unified Theories of Cognition* (Cambridge, MA: Harvard University Press, 1990); Herbert A. Simon, *The Sciences of the Artificial* (Cambridge, MA: MIT Press, 1996).

5. H. Richard Niebuhr, *The Social Sources of Denominationalism* (New York: Holt, 1929).

6. Travis Hirschi, *Causes of Delinquency* (Berkeley: University of California Press, 1969).

7. Neil J. Smelser, *Theory of Collective Behavior* (New York: Free Press of Glencoe, 1963).

8. Robert K. Merton, "Social Structure and Anomie," in *Social Theory and Social Structure*, rev. ed. (New York: Free Press, 1968), 185–214.

9. Nels Anderson, *The Hobo* (Chicago: University of Chicago Press, 1923); Frederic M. Thrasher, *The Gang* (Chicago: University of Chicago Press, 1927); Clifford Shaw and Henry D. McKay, *Delinquency Areas* (Chicago: University of Chicago Press, 1927).

10. Rodney Stark and William Sims Bainbridge, "Networks of Faith: Interpersonal Bonds and Recruitment to Cults and Sects," *American Journal of Sociology* 85 (1980): 1376–95.

11. Edwin H. Sutherland, *Principles of Criminology* (Chicago: J. B. Lippincott, 1947).

12. Edward Gibbon, *The History of the Decline and Fall of the Roman Empire* (London: Bohn, 1854), 36.

13. Franz Boas, "The Principles of Ethnological Classification," in *A Franz Boas Reader: The Shaping of American Anthropology, 1883–1911*, ed. George W. Stocking, Jr. (Chicago: University of Chicago Press, 1974), 61–67; Boas, *Race, Language, and Culture* (New York: Free Press, 1966); Robert H. Lowie, *Culture and Ethnology* (New York: D. C. McMurtrie, 1917).

14. Bronislaw Malinowski, *Argonauts of the Western Pacific* (London: Routledge, 1922); Malinowski, *Sex and Repression in Savage Society* (New York: Harcourt, Brace, 1927); Malinowski, *Magic, Science and Religion* (Boston: Beacon, 1948).

15. *New York City Mission Society Monthly*, April 1892, 79.

16. Kenneth D. Miller and Ethel Prince Miller, *The People Are the City* (New York: Macmillan, 1962), 73.

17. *Seventieth Annual Report of the Woman's Branch of the New York City Mission and Tract Society*, February 1893, 12.

18. *New York City Mission Society Monthly*, February 1896, 74.

19. http://www.faxiononline.com/about/faq.

20. http://www.faxiononline.com/about/classes.

21. Beau Hindman, "Massively's First Look at Faxion Online," *Massively*, January 21, 2011; http://massively.joystiq.com/2011/01/21/massivelys-first-look-at-faxion-online/.

22. http://www.faxiononline.com/content/10-commandments-pvp.

23. *Aion Wiki*, "Elyos," http://aion.wikia.com/wiki/Elyos.

24. *Aion Wiki*, "Asmodian," http://aion.wikia.com/wiki/Asmodian.

25. C. S. Lewis, *The Lion, the Witch and the Wardrobe* (London: G. Bles, 1950).

26. C. S. Lewis, *The Screwtape Letters* (London: G. Bles, 1942).

27. C. S. Lewis, *Out of the Silent Planet* (New York: Macmillan, 1965); Lewis, *Perelandra* (New York: Macmillan, 1965); Lewis, *That Hideous Strength* (New York: Macmillan, 1965).

28. Available online at http://www.gamersfirst.com/fallenearth/?q=the-fall.

29. Available online at http://www.gamersfirst.com/fallenearth/?q=factions.

30. Catherine Brown, *The Sims Medieval Prima Official Game Guide* (Roseville, CA: Prima Games, 2011).

31. *The Sims Medieval Wiki*, "Jacoban," http://thesimsmedieval.wikia.com/wiki/Jacoban.

32. *The Sims Medieval Wiki*, "Peteran," http://thesimsmedieval.wikia.com/wiki/Peteran.

33. Émile Durkheim, *Suicide* (New York: Free Press, 1951).

34. Adolph Wagner, *Die Gesetzmässigkeit in den Scheinbar Willkührlichen Menschlichen Handlungen vom Standpunkte der Statistik* (Hamburg, Germany: Boyes & Geisler, 1864); Henry Morselli, *Suicide: An Essay on Comparative Moral Statistics* (New York: Appleton, 1882).

35. Travis Hirschi and Rodney Stark, "Hellfire and Delinquency," *Social Problems* 17 (1969): 202–13.

36. Rodney Stark and William Sims Bainbridge, *Religion, Deviance, and Social Control* (New York: Routledge, 1996).

37. Whitney Pope, *Durkheim's Suicide: A Classic Analyzed* (Chicago: University of Chicago Press, 1976).

38. William Sims Bainbridge and Rodney Stark, "Suicide, Homicide, and Religion: Durkheim Reassessed," *Annual Review of the Social Sciences of Religion* 5 (1981): 33–56.

39. William Sims Bainbridge, "Explaining the Church Member Rate," *Social Forces* 68 (1990): 1287–96.

40. William Sims Bainbridge, "The Religious Ecology of Deviance," *American Sociological Review* 54 (1989): 288–95; Bainbridge, *Across the Secular Abyss* (Lanham, MD: Lexington, 2007).

41. Robert E. Howard, "The Hyborian Age," n.d.; http://gutenberg.net.au/ebooks06/0603571.txt.

42. Robert E. Howard, "Queen of the Black Coast," 1934; http://gutenberg.net.au/ebooks06/0600961.txt.

43. Robert E. Howard, "The Tower of the Elephant," 1933; http://gutenberg.net.au/ebooks06/0600831.txt.

44. Robert E. Howard, "The Scarlet Citadel," 1933; http://gutenberg.net.au/ebooks06/0600961.txt.

45. Robert E. Howard, "The Phoenix on the Sword," 1932; http://gutenberg.net.au/ebooks06/0600811.txt.

46. Thomas Hobbes, *Leviathan, or, The Matter, Forme, and Power of a Common-wealth Ecclesiasticall and Civill* (London: Crooke, 1651); Jean-Jacques Rousseau, *The Social Contract: or, Principles of Political Law* (New York: Eckler, 1893).

47. Edward C. Banfield, *The Moral Basis of a Backward Society* (Glencoe, IL: Free Press, 1958).

48. Chris Metzen, "Of Blood and Honor," in *Warcraft Archive* (New York: Pocket Books, 2002), 545–613.

CHAPTER 9

1. J. Gordon Melton, *Melton's Encyclopedia of American Religions* (Detroit: Gale, Cengage Learning, 2009).

2. Rodney Stark and William Sims Bainbridge, "Of Churches, Sects, and Cults: Preliminary Concepts for a Theory of Religious Movements," *Journal for the Scientific Study of Religion* 18 (1979): 117–31.

3. Karl Marx, "On the Jewish Question," in *Writings of the Young Marx on Philosophy and Society* (Garden City, NY: Doubleday, 1967), 216–48; cf. Dwight B. Billings, "Religion as Opposition: A Gramscian Analysis," *American Journal of Sociology* 96, no. 1 (1990): 1–31.

4. George Caspar Homans, *The Human Group* (New York: Harcourt, Brace, 1950).

5. William Sims Bainbridge, *Satan's Power: A Deviant Psychotherapy Cult* (Berkeley: University of California Press, 1978), 14.

6. George Grote, *Plato, and the Other Companions of Sokrates* (London: John Murray, 1867), 3:123; Plato, *The Republic* (New York: Oxford University Press, 2008); Thomas Hobbes, *Leviathan, or, The Matter, Forme, and Power of a Common-wealth Ecclesiasticall and Civill* (London: Crooke, 1651).

7. William Sims Bainbridge, *Satan's Power: A Deviant Psychotherapy Cult* (Berkeley: University of California Press, 1978).

8. William Sims Bainbridge, *The Endtime Family: Children of God* (Albany: State University of New York Press, 2002).

9. Charleton Thomas Lewis, *A Latin Dictionary for Schools* (New York: American Book Company, 1916), 251.

10. Rodney Stark and William Sims Bainbridge, *A Theory of Religion* (New York: Lang, 1987).

11. William H. Friedland, "For a Sociological Concept of Charisma," *Social Forces* 43 (1964): 18–26.

12. Eileen Barker, *The Making of a Moonie: Choice or Brainwashing?* (New York: Blackwell, 1984); William Sims Bainbridge, "The Decline of the Shakers: Evidence from the United States Census," *Communal Societies* 4 (1984): 19–34.

13. John Lofland and Rodney Stark, "Becoming a World-Saver: A Theory of Conversion to a Deviant Perspective," *American Sociological Review* 30, no. 6 (1965): 862–75; John Lofland, *Doomsday Cult* (Englewood Cliffs, NJ: Prentice-Hall, 1966).

14. Frederic M. Thrasher, *The Gang* (Chicago: University of Chicago Press, 1927).

15. *WoWWiki*, "Scarlet Crusade," http://www.wowwiki.com/Scarlet_Crusade.

16. William Sims Bainbridge, "When Virtual Worlds Expand," in *Online Worlds: Convergence of the Real and the Virtual*, ed. William Sims Bainbridge (London: Springer, 2010), 237–52.

17. William Sims Bainbridge, *The Warcraft Civilization: Social Science in a Virtual World* (Cambridge, MA: MIT Press, 2010), 120.

18. Mary Douglas, *Purity and Danger: An Analysis of Concepts of Pollution and Taboo* (New York: Praeger, 1966).

19. *WoWWiki*, "Twisting Nether," http://www.wowwiki.com/Twisting_Nether.

20. Chris Metzen, "Of Blood and Honor," in *Warcraft Archive* (New York: Pocket Books, 2002), 545–613.

21. William Sims Bainbridge and Rodney Stark, "Cult Formation: Three Compatible Models," *Sociological Analysis* 40 (1979): 285–95.

22. *Wikipedia*, "Sigmar," http://en.wikipedia.org/wiki/Sigmar.

23. William Sims Bainbridge, "Cultural Genetics," in *Religious Movements*, ed. Rodney Stark (New York: Paragon, 1985), 157–98.

24. William Sims Bainbridge, *Satan's Power: A Deviant Psychotherapy Cult* (Berkeley: University of California Press, 1978); Bainbridge, "Social Construction from Within," in *The Satanism Scare*, ed. James T. Richardson, Joel Best, and David Bromley (New York: Aldine de Gruyter, 1991), 297–310.

25. *Telarapedia*, "Dragon Cult," http://telarapedia.com/wiki/Dragon_Cult.

26. Herbert Blumer, "Social Movements," in *Studies in Social Movements*, ed. Barry McLaughlin (New York: Free Press, 1969), 8–29.

27. Talcott Parsons and Edward A. Shils, eds., *Toward a General Theory of Action* (Cambridge, MA: Harvard University Press, 1951).

28. Friedrich Nietzsche, *The Birth of Tragedy* (New York: Random House, 1967).

29. Max Weber, *The Protestant Ethic and the Spirit of Capitalism* (New York: Scribner, 1930).

30. *DDO Wiki*, "The Church and the Cult," http://ddowiki.com/page/The_Church_and_the_Cult.

31. *EQ2i*, "The Court of Truth (Faction)," http://eq2.wikia.com/wiki/Category:The_Court_of_Truth_(Faction).

32. *EQ2i*, "The Court of the Blades (Faction)," http://eq2.wikia.com/wiki/Category:The_Court_of_the_Blades_(Faction).

33. *EQ2i*, "The Court of the Coin (Faction)," http://eq2.wikia.com/wiki/Category:The_Court_of_the_Coin_(Faction).

34. *WoWWiki*, "Desolace," http://www.wowwiki.com/Desolace.

35. *EQ2i*, "The Pillars of Flame," http://eq2.wikia.com/wiki/The_Pillars_of_Flame.

36. *EQ2i*, "Ashen Order," http://eq2.wikia.com/wiki/Ashen_Order.

37. *EQ2i*, "Ashen Disciples," http://eq2.wikia.com/wiki/Ashen_Disciples.

38. William Sims Bainbridge, *The Endtime Family: Children of God* (Albany: State University of New York Press, 2002).

39. Bill Gates, *The Road Ahead* (New York: Viking, 1995).

40. D. W. Winnicott, *Playing and Reality* (New York: Basic Books, 1971).

41. Desmond Morris, *The Naked Ape: A Zoologist's Study of the Human Animal* (New York: McGraw-Hill, 1967).

42. Herber Blumer, *Symbolic Interactionism: Perspective and Method* (Englewood Cliffs, NJ: Prentice-Hall, 1969).

43. Erving Goffman, *The Presentation of Self in Everyday Life* (Edinburgh: University of Edinburgh, Social Sciences Research Centre, 1956).

44. Charles Horton Cooley, *Human Nature and the Social Order* (New York: Scribner's, 1922).

45. Arthur Schopenhauer, *The World as Will and Idea*, trans. R. B. Haldane and J. Kemp, 3 vols. (London: Trübner, 1883–1886).

46. Richard Wagner, "The Art-Work of the Future," in *Richard Wagner's Prose Works*, trans. William Ashton Ellis (London: K. Paul, Trench, Trübner, 1895), 69–213.

47. *WoWWiki*, "Lament of the Highborne," http://www.wowwiki.com/Lament_of_the_Highborne.

48. Transcription of lyrics from SongMeanings, http://www.songmeanings.net/songs/view/3530822107858776371/.

49. "World Of Warcraft: Dancing," YouTube, posted by animpinabox, May 18, 2007, http://www.youtube.com/watch?v=066_q4DIeqk.

50. William Sims Bainbridge, *Satan's Power* (Berkeley: University of California Press, 1978), 149.

51. Steven M. Tipton, *Getting Saved from the Sixties: Moral Meaning in Conversion and Cultural Change* (Berkeley: University of California Press, 1982).

52. Edward Castronova, *Exodus to the Virtual World: How Online Fun Is Changing Reality* (New York: Palgrave Macmillan, 2007).

CHAPTER 10

1. Lisbeth Klastrup, "Death Matters: Understanding Gameworld Experiences," in *Proceedings of the 2006 ACM SIGCHI International Conference on Advances in Computer Entertainment Technology* (New York: ACM, 2006); Klastrup, "What Makes *World of Warcraft* a World? A Note on Death and Dying," in *Digital Culture, Play and Identity: A World of Warcraft Reader*, ed. Hilde G. Corneliussen and Jill Walker Rettberg (Cambridge, MA: MIT Press, 2008), 143–66.

2. *WoWWiki*, "Death," http://www.wowwiki.com/Death.

3. Mike Mearls, Stephen Schubert, and James Wyatt, *Dungeons and Dragons Monster Manual* (Renton, WA: Wizards of the Coast, 2008), 224.

4. Mike Mearls, Stephen Schubert, and James Wyatt, *Dungeons & Dragons Monster Manual* (Renton, WA: Wizards of the Coast, 2008), 225.

5. http://www.everquest2.com/Antonia%20Bayle/Cleora/.

6. Tom Goldman, "Peaceful World of Warcraft Player Hits Max Level without Kills," *The Escapist*, April 10, 2011, http://www.escapistmagazine.com/news/view/109134-Peaceful-World-of-Warcraft-Player-Hits-Max-Level-Without-Kills; the *World of Warcraft* Armory database confirms these claims.

7. "Kindred," Forsaken World website, http://fw.perfectworld.com/gameinfo/race/kindred.

8. *DDO Wiki*, "The Bloody Crypt," http://ddowiki.com/page/The_Bloody_Crypt.

9. *DDO Wiki*, "The Shadow Crypt," http://ddowiki.com/page/The_Shadow_Crypt.

10. *WoWWiki*, "Caylee Dak," http://www.wowwiki.com/Caylee_Dak.

11. *Wikipedia*, "Do Not Stand at My Grave and Weep," http://en.wikipedia.org/wiki/Do_not_stand_at_my_grave_and_weep.

12. http://wiki.wwiionline.com/mediawiki/index.php/Memorial.

13. "World War II Online Funeral SDSHill," YouTube, uploaded by wwiiolvideo, August 11, 2007, http://www.youtube.com/watch?v=iuUEXxnUvJw.

14. Carsadon, "World War II Online Funeral SDSHill," *Carsadon's Blog*, June 15, 2008, http://carsadon.wordpress.com/2008/06/15/world-war-ii-online-funeral-sdshill/.

15. "Memorial to Fayedin," Illidrama, http://forums.illidrama.com/showthread.php?1826-Memorial-to-Fayejin.

16. *WoWWiki*, "Server:Illidan US," http://www.wowwiki.com/Server:Illidan_US.

17. "Serenity Now Bombs a World of Warcraft Funeral," YouTube, uploaded by jon01, March 19, 2008, http://www.youtube.com/watch?v=IHJVolaC8pw.

18. "That funeral video," Serenity Now, http://www.serenity-now.org/forums/index.php?topic=9102.0.

19. William Sims Bainbridge, "Science, Technology, and Reality in *The Matrix Online* and *Tabula Rasa*," in *Online Worlds: Convergence of the Real and the Virtual*, ed. William Sims Bainbridge (London: Springer, 2010), 57–70; Bainbridge, *The Virtual Future* (London: Springer, 2011).

20. "Tabula Rasa—Final Minutes before Closing," YouTube, uploaded by iRacerMatt, March 1, 2009, http://www.youtube.com/watch?v=fxAtDpxypSw.

21. "Tabula Rasa Centaurus server going down . . .," YouTube, uploaded by Plukh, February 28, 2009, http://www.youtube.com/watch?v=jVh1J9MxZL4; YouTube, uploaded by Thenesmaster, http://www.youtube.com/watch?v=DjezZqBgO3A.

22. "Tabula Rasa Server Shutdown Event HD," YouTube, uploaded by CommanderGrog, March 5, 2009, http://www.youtube.com/watch?v=j_4B22Y8z28.

23. "Tabula Rasa The Last Moments," YouTube, uploaded by KevSniper, March 2, 2009, http://www.youtube.com/watch?v=xz-3Sy0eaXE.

24. "MxO Shutdown. Last Few Minutes.," YouTube, uploaded by blokenamedbob, August 1, 2009, http://www.youtube.com/watch?v=iTYNLKcsjhA.

25. http://www.mmorpg.com/photo/5be89f35-534b-4797-a008-6cb032adc.

26. "MxO—The End of the Game—Last Bit of Fun," YouTube, uploaded by tsusai, August 1, 2009, http://www.youtube.com/watch?v=qNERcfNoPFM.

27. "mxo ending," YouTube, uploaded by M1ke212, August 1, 2009, http://www.youtube.com/watch?v=ZmKIU_6J0HY.

28. "Mxo END—In the Light," YouTube, uploaded by S0NICShadow, August 3, 2009, http://www.youtube.com/watch?v=I1hMKSSzajo.

29. "End of the Matrix Online Part 1," YouTube, uploaded by Thundr, August 1, 2009, http://www.youtube.com/watch?v=JjxXIn4V1as. Transcription of lyrics from Filmtracks, http://www.filmtracks.com/comments/titles/matrix_revolutions/index.cgi?read=321&expand=1.

CHAPTER 11

1. Richard Dawid, "Underdetermination and Theory Succession from the Perspective of String Theory," *Philosophy of Science* 76, no. 3 (2006): 298–322; cf. Mario Livio and Martin J. Rees, "Anthropic Reasoning," *Science* 309 (2005): 1022–23.

2. William Sims Bainbridge, "The Omicron Point: Sociological Application of the Anthropic Theory," in *Chaos and Complexity in Sociology: Myths, Models and Theory*, ed. R. A. Eve, S. Horsfall, and M. E. Lee (Thousand Oaks, CA: SAGE Publications, 1997), 91–101.

3. Pierre Teilhard de Chardin, *The Future of Man* (New York: Harper, 1964).

4. George Willis Botsford and Charles Alexander Robinson, *Hellenic History* (New York: Macmillan, 1956), 97–99.

5. Plato, *The Laws of Plato*, trans. A. E. Taylor (London: Dent, 1934), 275.

6. Plato, *The Laws of Plato*, trans. A. E. Taylor (London: Dent, 1934), 277; George Willis Botsford and Charles Alexander Robinson, *Hellenic History* (New York: Macmillan, 1956), 256–57; cf. Karl Marx, *Differenz der demokritischen und epikureischen Naturphilosophie* (Jena, Germany: Friedrich-Schiller Universität, 1841); Theodor Gomperz, *Greek Thinkers* (London: Murray, 1901); Norman Wentworth DeWitt, *St. Paul and Epicurus* (Minneapolis: University of Minnesota Press, 1954).

7. Lawrence J. Henderson, *The Fitness of the Environment* (New York: Macmillan, 1913); Henderson, *The Order of Nature* (Cambridge, MA: Harvard University Press, 1917).

8. http://exoplanet.eu/.

9. John D. Barrow and Frank J. Tipler, *The Anthropic Cosmological Principle* (New York: Oxford University Press, 1986), 253.

10. John D. Barrow and Frank J. Tipler, *The Anthropic Cosmological Principle* (New York: Oxford University Press, 1986), 336.

11. Bernard J. Carr and Martin J. Rees, "The Anthropic Principle and the Structure of the Physical World," *Nature* 278 (1979): 605–12; John Gribbin and Martin J. Rees, *Cosmic Coincidences: Dark Matter, Mankind, and Anthropic Cosmology* (New York: Bantam, 1989).

12. Alan H. Guth, "Inflationary Universe: A Possible Solution to the Horizon and Flatness Problems," *Physical Review D* 23 (1981): 347–56.

13. Andrei Linde, "The Self-Reproducing Inflationary Universe," *Scientific American*, November 1994, 48–55.

14. Bruce Western, "Bayesian Thinking about Macrosociology," *American Journal of Sociology* 107, no. 2 (2001): 353–78.

15. George C. Homans, *The Nature of Social Science* (New York: Harcourt, Brace & World, 1967); Homans, *Social Behavior: Its Elementary Forms* (New York: Harcourt, Brace, Jovanovich, 1974).

16. John Archibald Wheeler, "Beyond the Black Hole," in *Some Strangeness in the Proportion: A Centennial Symposium to Celebrate the Achievements of Albert Einstein* (Reading, MA: Addison-Wesley, 1980), 341–75.

17. Edward P. Tryon, "Is the Universe a Vacuum Fluctuation?" *Nature* 246 (1973): 396–97; J. Richard Gott, "Creation of Open Universes from de Sitter Space," *Nature* 295 (1982): 304–7.

18. John Leslie, "Anthropic Principle, World Ensemble, Design," *American Philosophical Quarterly* 19 (1982): 141–51.

19. Tracy Kidder, *The Soul of a New Machine* (Boston: Little, Brown, 1981).

20. Mike Searle and the Sindicate, *Pirates of the Burning Sea Official Game Guide* (Roseville, CA: Prima Games, 2008).

21. Colin Woodard, *The Republic of Pirates* (Orlando, FL: Harcourt, 2007).

22. Erich von Däniken, *Chariots of the Gods?* (London: Souvenir, 1969); William Sims Bainbridge, "Chariots of the Gullible," *Skeptical Inquirer* 3, no. 2 (1978): 33–48.

23. Arthur C. Clarke, *Profiles of the Future* (New York: Harper & Row, 1973), 21.

24. General British [Richard Garriott], *Welcome to the AFS: Allied Free Sentients Official Field Manual* (Austin, TX: Destination Games, 2007), 55.

25. Rumilisoun [William Sims Bainbridge], "Rebirth of Worlds," *Communications of the ACM* 53, no. 12 (2010): 128.

26. http://truly-free.lineage2.com/path.

27. Arnold van Gennep, *The Rites of Passage* (Chicago: University of Chicago Press, 1960); Mircea Eliade, *The Forge and the Crucible: The Origins and Structure of Alchemy* (Chicago: University of Chicago Press, 1978).

28. *Perfect World* online game guide: http://pwi.perfectworld.com/gameinfo/guide/vacuity.

29. Friedrich Wilhelm Nietzsche, *Beyond Good and Evil: Prelude to a Philosophy of the Future*, trans. Walter Kaufmann (New York: Vintage, 1966).

INDEX